A Biography of Story,
a Brief History of Humanity

A Biography
of Story,
A Brief History
of Humanity

TRISH NICHOLSON

Matador
9 Priory Business Park,
Wistow Road, Kibworth Beauchamp,
Leicestershire. LE8 0RX
Tel: (+44) 116 279 2299
Fax: (+44) 116 279 2277
Email: books@troubador.co.uk
Web: www.troubador.co.uk/matador

ISBN PB 978 1785899 492
ISBN HB 978 1785899 508

Artwork by Graeme Neil Reid

British Library Cataloguing in Publication Data.
A catalogue record for this book is available from the British Library.

Printed and bound in the UK by TJ International, Padstow, Cornwall
Typeset in 12pt Aldine by Troubador Publishing Ltd, Leicester, UK

Matador is an imprint of Troubador Publishing Ltd

To all who love Story,
wherever you are.

A note on text layout: for ease of reference, all individual stories related here are indented. Extracts from original sources are contained in quotation marks; passages that I have summarised or paraphrased are not. In both cases, endnotes cite bibliographic sources unless these are already made clear in the text.

First thoughts

There are so many stories to tell, too many, such an excess of intertwined lives events miracles places rumours, so dense a commingling of the improbable and the mundane!
Salman Rushdie
Midnight's Children

'I am ruminating,' said Mr Pickwick, 'on the strange mutability of human affairs.'
Charles Dickens
Pickwick Papers

All who crave to know what their ancestors were like, will find an inexhaustible fount of joy and instruction in literature.
G. M. Trevelyan
English Social History

Table of Contents

Before we meet Story: facts with imagination

This is a true story. It is our own story told through the tales of storytellers from many parts of the world. Some of the tales you may know, others, perhaps not.

As a storywriter and a social anthropologist, I have drawn on both of these passions to create a 'biography' of Story that is factually accurate yet presented with imagination. Starting from the emergence of language and going through to the digital revolution, each chapter is constructed around a significant era of human history and considers the questions: Who were the storytellers? What events did they live through and respond to? How did these events affect the nature of Story? And how did Story influence events?

To achieve this interweaving of history and literature I found some remarkable storytellers to be our escorts. They include peasants and poets, playwrights and novelists and the creators of short stories: the daughters, sons, lovers and protégés of Story. Framed by an outline of history, the storytellers reveal a more personal experience of the age in which they lived with extracts from their epics, verses, tales, fables, or sagas and with anecdotes from their lives. Through their eyes we see the development and purpose of stories and better understand Story's mission.

Stories are universal and there is a good reason for that: narrative is the mode in which our species thinks. It seems that our brains have evolved to sense the world in stories. As research uncovers more complex language skills and tool use among non-human primates and other animals, these are no longer the defining features of being human – but the storytelling brain is. As far as we know, no other creature tells stories.

The development of words would have been a long process. Stories had to wait even longer, for syntax and sentences, before they could explain past and present experience, pass on ideas, help to plan the future and, eventually, draw on symbolic thought to talk about non-physical things. We cannot know exactly when any of these events happened. But storytelling probably developed at least 300,000 years ago, when there is evidence of controlled fire used by fairly large groups of cave-dwellers, indicating an increasingly complex social organisation. These earliest findings at Qesem Cave, near the present settlement of Rosh Ha'ayin near the Israel–Palestine border, were first reported in April 2014 in the *Journal of Archaeological Science* and will doubtless generate much discussion; in particular, the conclusion that evidence of controlled fire use could push current estimates of human cultural activity back to much earlier dates. In this continuous and accumulative thread of humanity, it is conceivable that elements of these early experiences and the stories they generated linger as archetypes in the depths of our psyche.

Because Story emanates from our nature, it is necessary to set her biography in the context of human development, but I want to avoid any suggestion of linear progression in storytelling. This is not an evolution of literature; not an attempt to characterise early or indigenous stories as in any sense 'less' than later ones. Once we had cognitive and vocal capacity sufficient for storytelling, these skills set in motion change, diversity, mixing and sharing across cultures, times and places and, above all, accumulation: it is a continuing process. We know that by 5000 BC fables, myths, epics, and domestic tales already co-habited orally. These were among the first to be given permanence by early writing systems, but they were already an inheritance from many thousands of years of storytelling.

The simplicity of the most meagre tale can be deceptive and is of no less value than any other. Every narrative detail and structure is a product of its time, place and culture, but all perform Story's roles within their context. Seeing through the eyes of storytellers as far as possible will, I hope, achieve this sense of complex interweaving and diversity over time rather than any concept of progress towards a notional literary Valhalla. Oral traditions are not only something from the past; story performance is still with us, fulfilling our insatiable desire for revelation, insight, meaning, identity, connection, wisdom and entertainment – all the gifts of Story. With this caution about Story's timelessness, her agelessness, this book is an attempt at her 'biography'.

The necessity, at times, to make reasoned use of conjecture is a familiar feature of biography where data may be missing for certain periods, and when biographers attempt to access a subject's inner world by imaginative but judicious inference. Obviously, there is no documentary evidence of oral storytelling before the invention of writing, although some of the earliest written stories so far found – incised on clay tablets around 2700 BC – were certainly derived from oral tales which were much older. Nonetheless, it seemed worth including some idea of the very beginnings of storytelling, and I have approached this through traditional stories of indigenous foraging and hunting peoples who developed their cultures and tales in a similar physical environment and faced the same issues as our early ancestors.

For later periods, documentary evidence of all kinds is so abundant as to be almost overwhelming. Not only in terms of stories themselves, but also for the social and historical detail on which biographers must rely to grasp the essence of both their subjects and the ages in which they lived. That is challenge enough for a single life. To venture a biography of 'Story' as a conceptualised 'character', an omniscient presence with multiple personalities, whose life extends almost the entire length of human history, may be regarded by many as foolhardy.

Because of Story's longevity, the tough question arose as to how to select events, stories and storytellers to convey the quality of each age, the role that Story played, and the ways in which she was affected. For this I established a few criteria. I chose as

Chapter One

In the beginning were the words

Story is born and keeps us company on our foraging, by our firesides and on our long migrations across the world. She shares the wisdom for us to live together and survive in our natural environment. And She spins creation stories in which still waters yield life and we hold parties with the animals.

They had story-power.

1

You know me. You have always known me, for I am Story. Sit with me awhile as I weave these yarns and I will tell you my tale.

Resting under the arms of an acacia tree, grateful for its shade, the old woman looked deep in thought while her kinsfolk, sitting on the ground around her, waited. Slowly, she leaned forward and began to draw in the sand with her digging stick as she told them the story of the *buumbuul*.

Long ago, Baiame, the provider of all things, kept for himself the *buumbuul,* the sweet resinous globs that hung from the branches of certain gum trees like little bags of honey. He forbade the men and women of that time to touch them. Some people resented this harsh restriction because the sacred food was thought a great delicacy, but the elders were firm and made sure no one even went near the trees.

As time passed, Baiame recognised the strength and respect shown by the people in obeying his instructions, and rewarded them by giving them the *buumbuul* for their own food. "Look on the *coolabah* and *bibbil* trees," he said, "and you will find that the food reserved for the gods has been given to men."

After that, the *buumbuul* was collected every year and became a favourite food, eaten raw from the tree or dissolved in water as a delicious drink. Sometime later, during one season, the trees produced so much sweetness it ran down their trunks, forming big hard lumps that could be carried home. And this was another sign of Baiame's generosity because, the following year, a great drought afflicted the land, and those early humans might not have survived without the *buumbuul*. So we know that when the *buumbuul* is prolific, a drought will surely follow.[1]

Although we cannot know what the stories were when our ancestors foraged among the scrublands and trees of the African savannah, this Australian Aboriginal story, and the traditional tales of other modern hunting and gathering societies, provide insights into what Story's nature might have been, because these peoples inherited ancient cultures which survived similar experiences to those of our early ancestors and, until recently, still depended entirely on the natural resources around them to cope with the vagaries of a changing and challenging environment.

For our ancestors, too, great droughts were likely followed by devastating floods, earthquakes shifted the ground beneath their feet, and deadly predators stalked the unwary forager. Only care and cunning rewarded the endless search for edible berries and flowers, nuts and seeds, wild honey, insects and the small fish and animals that made up their diet. Finding a fresh spring or digging successfully to discover a source of clear water along their path would be a matter for rejoicing. But sun burned during the day, and cold dampness marked long nights endured in menacing darkness when the moon waned or was hidden by cloud.

The first storytellers were those with perception and memory to detect the patterns in their surroundings, to predict the causes and results that led them to dig in the right place for water, and to find which shrubs were in fruit. Special rocks, stone cairns and probably scored tree-trunks too, were important markers for paths, springs, and territory; each would have been explained, remembered and passed on through stories. Above all, these storytellers possessed the skills to impart their knowledge by enthralling others with narrative that made sense of their world and provided the means of thriving within it. They had story-power.

For early humans, dependency on the environment was not passive, not a simple determinism. Rather, nature provided the clues and resources for those with imagination and ingenuity to learn ways of applying her bounty to overcome her discomforts; wrapping themselves in strips of tree bark or leafy branches to warm their nights; tracking bees to find their honey stores; noting the seasons when grubs and insects were abundant and one fruiting plant succeeded another; discovering the habits of small prey that they could trap with simple but clever devices, and finding out which foods they could store against periods of hunger. Their efforts were multiplied by the cooperation of their kin as they foraged and hunted in small groups or bands, camping near water sources or sheltering in caves to follow seasonal patterns of abundance and scarcity, surviving constant cycles of joy and dread.

Indications of such inventive inspiration and the value of sharing knowledge with companions are found in another Aboriginal story:

> Two brothers, bearded giants who walked the land long ago, saw one day, for the first time, bees gathering nectar from the flowers of a bloodwood tree and flying off with it. The younger brother wondered where the bees took their treasure, but the older brother knew how to find out. He told the younger boy to cut a long forked stick, while he found a spider's cocoon on the underside of a leaf and carefully unwound its wispy web. When his young brother returned with the stick, he used it to climb into the bloodwood tree and put tiny pieces of web on the bees' fur, so they could track the bees back to their nest. Which they did, finding it in a hollow tree, and breaking through the bark with their clubs to reach the bees' honey store.[2]

In addition to wooden clubs, spears, digging sticks and, no doubt, traps, nooses and carrying slings woven from plant fibres, these early ancestors of ours had already been fashioning stone tools for millennia: flints for cutting, stone scrapers and axes, and heavier stones for chipping, grinding and pounding. The successful ones followed the best food supplies, found clean water, and moved out of danger. There had already been a gradual dispersal. Curiosity, and the search for sustenance as climatic conditions changed, led them over the next ridge into the valley beyond, and the land beyond that. When a group became too large to manage, the food within their gathering area too meagre to distribute, some would move off in another direction. So, by gradual steps, extending seasonal routes, accumulating new knowledge, they spread out from Africa on the first prolonged migration to roam eventually as far as Europe and Asia, where they adjusted to different climates, strange environments and previously unknown flora and fauna.

These early migrants, the people whom we named *Homo erectus* and whose brains were almost as large as ours, had wrested a living from nature and successfully raised their children for over two million years. Somewhere at the beginning of that period – or more likely, long before – they had developed what we call 'conscious awareness': recognition of 'me' as separate from 'you' and the capacity of both of us for independent, unpredictable actions that affect each other.

The idea of conscious awareness troubles everyone from scientists to philosophers. We know it is there but not what it is exactly. It is not a 'thing', an organ in the brain, because it is both inside and outside – more a process taking place between our inner selves and everything we sense beyond. In a similar way, we cannot see or hear 'delicious', but we know it exists when we experience it as the interaction between a certain food and the myriad sensing cells in our mouths. 'Delicious' is more than the food or its separate ingredients, and more than our taste buds or even the anticipation of a familiar delicacy: it is the sum performance of all of these.

Becoming aware of ourselves as distinct personal entities with volition to act upon the environment – even in limited ways – was a turning point for our earliest ancestors. The realisation that other humans also had their own image of themselves with their intentions and powers to act, meant that better means of communication – language – was not only desirable, but essential. Survival depends on knowledge of the social as well as the physical environment, although our understanding is always incomplete. Even now, with our sophisticated language systems, we often misunderstand each other, sometimes with fatal results.

Early humans would have communicated with the gestures and sounds commanded by all primates, which they no doubt refined and developed, but at some point, perhaps during the latter part of Erectus' hundreds of thousands of generations, their gestures and sounds developed into spoken words with meanings which could be recognised, remembered and passed from one person to another and from one generation to the next; not as a static code, but as a constellation of possibilities ever transforming and expanding to express new ideas and experiences.

It began with the naming of things. To confer a name on a particular plant, for example, pays it special attention, creates a relationship and forges a link of empathy between our inner world and the outer world of nature. We give it meaning. In a sense, by speaking its name we breathe life into each element of the natural environment as part of our own lives. Soon, there were names for each part of the plant good for different purposes in each season – the bud, young leaf, old leaf, stem, smell, fibre, juice, fruit, and root. Each word exposed new ways of knowing. The qualities of earth, sky and water in their various times and places, once named, could be compared, discussed, their meanings and understandings passed on. In the same way, naming each other recognises and gives voice to relationships, whether intimate with secret names or distant with words denoting the status of a stranger. Naming minted the coinage of personal and social communication.

In these fertile conditions, Language and Thought first conceived Story. Generous parents who offered a rich inheritance and continue to nurture Story to this day. For these three are the immortal spirits of humanity.

Thought provided the basic concepts of space, time and matter: the distance and locations of things and their relationship to each other, the recognition of past and future as well as present, and the identification and differing nature of what was visible. Significantly, Thought also gave the idea of causation: if this is done then that will follow, and the question Story has always loved best – what if?

Language's gifts were many and varied: marvellous words to describe sounds, movements, actions, and to impart feelings. Chief among these gifts, Story valued metaphor because it enabled her to enrich and expand the meaning of one thing by attaching to it the identity of another and, she soon discovered, allowed her to talk of things felt and wondered at, though unseen. At some later date – perhaps at Story's coming of age – Thought had gifted her symbols, opening the way not only to talk about invisible phenomena, the spiritual mysteries of life and death of all things, but also to empower words with actions – the gestures, images, music and dance of rituals – as a way to communicate with these elemental forces. Symbols created deeper, richer understanding of the nature of things; now names could reveal hidden mysteries, or conceal them as esoteric knowledge wielding its own special potency.

Over thousands of years – for this wondrous unfolding took time – the magic of the whole inheritance to Story became the lithesome, vibrant nature of this treasure of words: each item was complete yet unfinished; together they could multiply, rearrange, combine, divide, and assemble new forms in a perpetual flow of creativity which at times came in a gentle trickle, and at others, in a surge of immense power.

And in her gratitude, Story richly re-endowed Thought and Language in gradually changing the way we think, even our cognitive patterns and formations, so that it is human nature to perceive and understand the world as narrative. It is the way our minds function.

From such beginnings, Story launched her mission for humanity – to preserve and enhance the wisdom of the most skilful and inventive – by making memorable the ideas and experience of those who had gone before as well as those in the present. In this way,

Story enabled the intricate knowledge of place, weather, resources, and methods of either benefitting from them or ameliorating their effects, to accumulate and develop into lore for survival of future generations. Those who knew the lore, remembered the stories and told them most effectively – those with story-power – led their groups to flourish while others failed.

A significant part of early humans' flair for survival was their understanding of their role in the natural order, their interdependence on animal and plant life which both sustained and threatened them. Many indigenous stories hint at this by describing humans and animals in various ways and circumstances as interchangeable; not through some magical transmogrification, but in a more natural way as associated ideas, elements of conceptual equivalence that often contain seeds of the nature of this relationship. In such stories, animals often speak and may be helpful to humans – revealing important secrets for example – or they may be harmful, depending on their own characters and on the appropriate behaviour of humans towards the animals and each other. In tales of the Tse-shaht Indians of the Canadian West Coast, all creatures are 'people'; some are 'human people', others, 'wolf people' or 'deer people' and so on.

> *Paw-qwin-mit*, Son of Skate, was the champion spear thrower for his entire region, reputed to be so agile and deceptive in his movements that it was impossible to hit him with a tournament spear. With broad shoulders and long slim legs, this fit, brave and kind-hearted young man was a popular hero to everyone in his village, except to *Ko-ishin-mit* – noisy, boastful, foolish Son of Raven. All through winter, *Ko-ishin-mit* went around the village taunting *Paw-qwin-mit* that his shoulders were so broad he would be easy to hit with a spear, and that he, Son of Raven, could certainly do it. But *Paw-qwin-mit* indulgently took no notice of this silly behaviour.
>
> With spring, came the event everyone awaited with great excitement – the Grand Spear Throwing Tournament. As

reigning champion, *Paw-qwin-mit* defended his title by standing as the target, demonstrating his skill in eluding the spears. The rules were strict and closely observed by the Elder: spear throwers competed in pairs, each in turn making two throws of a spear from a stated distance. The air grew tense as round after round of the finest and strongest young men of the region aimed their spears at *Paw-qwin-mit's* chest, hurling them with all their might. A fearful silence followed each command: "On your marks. Ready. Throw." But each time a spear sped through the air, cool-headed *Paw-qwin-mit* feinted and swerved, letting the spears thud harmlessly into the ground beside him. This continued until the final round between the two most experienced and skilful throwers.

On the fourth launch, expertly dispatched, the crowd gasped as the spear pierced a bank a finger's width from their young hero. It was the final throw, but since both contestants had performed equally well and the outcome was indecisive, *Paw-qwin-mit* offered them one additional throw each as a tie-breaker. Each spear thrower took his time to draw carefully on his reserves of strength, but neither spear landed so close again.

The verdict of a tie between the two finalists, leaving *Paw-qwin-mit* the unbeaten champion, raised jubilant cheers from the crowd. But only minutes before the Elder was due to declare the tournament at an end, *Ko-ishin-mit* came swaggering into the arena, dressed in extravagant finery, declaring at the top of his loud, croaky voice, that he would challenge *Paw-qwin-mit* to a dual to the finish, and that he, *Ko-ishin-mit,* would throw first. An individual challenge to the final winner was within the rules, but everyone was aghast. All knew he would stand no chance against the champion and hoped it was merely a joke. *Ko-ishin-mit* enjoyed their consternation, misinterpreting its cause, and repeated his challenge, declaring his opponent a coward if he did not accept it. *Paw-qwin-mit* hesitated, but both he and the Elder knew that he had to defend his honour and his title. With a heavy heart, *Paw-qwin-mit* went to collect, not his best spear, but a two-pronged practice shaft, and returned to take up his position in the arena.

With a showy and unnecessary flourish (which gave his opponent a clear idea of the spear's trajectory) *Ko-ishin-mit* made his first throw, which *Paw-qwin-mit* easily evaded. Apart from the foolishness of boasting, *Ko-ishin-mit* had not the wisdom to realise that when broad-shouldered Son of Skate turned sideways, his profile was almost too slim for a spear to snag.

Now *Paw-qwin-mit* prepared for his turn. *Ko-ishin-mit,* foolish Son of Raven, attempted a diversion with his noisy croaking and jumping up and down, while the champion calmly watched his every movement before taking careful aim. With incredible speed, his spear reached *Ko-ishin-mit* who, in an instant, was pinned, helpless, to the ground – his legs neatly clasped between the two prongs of *Paw-qwim-mit's* practice shaft.[3]

Despite the distance of time and culture, we can recognise in this old folk-tale the value placed on human qualities of honour, fairness and compassion, and the foolishness of bragging and self-aggrandisement that leads to misreading people's reactions. But even in the original, much longer version, we cannot share the full meaning of such indigenous stories: the humour, nuances and implications that are apparent to someone who has grown up in the culture, one who is intimately familiar with the natural environment and to whom the qualities of 'raven-ness' and 'skate-ness' have deeper, broader interpretations, not to mention knowledge of the finer points of spear throwing.

Such stories apply a number of ways to overcome the inherent limitations of words and syntax: the fact that they must follow a linear progression and be grasped a word or brief phrase at a time and on a single plane. Word choices – especially in their sounds and imagery – provide added dimensions of meaning, as does the performance of the storyteller in gesture, voice and manner, even in the location and timing of the telling, revealing a gestalt whose full nature is realised only through hearing a tale numerous times in varying forms and situations. The way oral stories would originally have been enjoyed and understood.

Stories triggered mental pictures, tapped earlier knowledge, stimulated intuition and released emotions in the process. In this sense, the performance of a story became a lived experience on many levels. As each slight turn of a child's kaleidoscope reassembles the same shapes and colours into an infinite variety of motifs, each a fresh revelation to the eye and the imagination, so the retelling of favourite stories and myths inspires their hearers anew. And one of the challenges that Story had to address was the balance between the desires of an individual and the needs of the group.

Each person develops their own inner story through which outside events and others' stories are understood and, once we are aware that others do the same, there exists a capacity for empathy, though it is always imperfect. The intentions of the 'other' can never be fully known. Trust must be weighed, for a miscalculation could be hazardous, even fatal. Although dealing with strangers may often have resulted in conflict – even deadly clashes – the more constant sources of tension were likely the unavoidably competitive relationships within close groups, between siblings, and between one generation and the next, for example. Living alongside others has been a mixed blessing for the length of human history.

Many indigenous stories relate how groups of descendants became subdivided according to their lineages or other criteria, each associated with a different animal, bird or reptile which indicates some characteristic of the subgroup, and may carry an embargo on killing that species. Such rules would regulate hunting in an area of scarce resources. But this is only one level of meaning. These animal associations could also provide individual and group identity; define who are kin and non-kin (regardless of actual blood lines); confer differential status; indicate who owes greater obligation or loyalty to one person rather than another, and account for who can mate with whom. For Story is no simple gossip: she has a deep character of many attributes accorded by the storyteller and the listeners in any particular circumstance, one of which is the necessity to cooperate and live in harmony with those around us.

From the outset, Story was – and still is – deeply engaged in understanding, explaining and resolving this conflict of wills and needs between individuals, and between each person and the group on which they depended for existence. For our forebears, exclusion was a death sentence. Inclusion exacted compliance. What this consisted of varied between groups and peoples, but would have included not only subjugating personal desire for the wider good, either now or in the future, but also carrying the accumulated knowledge of the group. And for some, it would involve the fulfilment of special responsibilities to maintain the group's sources of sustenance for each member's physical, social and inner wellbeing.

Such is the role, in central Australia, of the Aboriginal 'Dreaming' – though this translation is a western misinterpretation: elements of the rituals may occasionally arise from dreams, but it is not about dreaming. *Jukurrpa* is about balancing and incorporating the environment and the people it sustains with the distant past, the infinite future and with the present. The stories, songs, rites and dances carried out at sacred sites in each 'dreaming ground' acknowledge the wisdom and actions of ancestors, those whose spiritual presence is recognised in various animals and features of the landscape. Rituals ensure the renewal of natural forces by prescribing action to safeguard and maintain them, and they confer identity on individuals and groups in relation to the land and the past. That is a powerful purpose. A unified body of lore which is 'women's business', carried out as part of the nurturing role of women in each tribal group for their 'dreaming grounds'; women who inherit the ritual knowledge and responsibility for the benefit of all. Aboriginal women have also their own rites and esoteric secrets in relation to themselves, and so have the men, but the *jukurrpa* is an all-encompassing 'Law' for continuance of the social and natural order.[4]

Visual storytelling, an ancient art of Aboriginal Australia.

In earth's history since the evolution of humanity there have been many environmental upheavals. Not only gradual changes in climate, tilting land and rising sea levels, but sudden traumas such as volcanic eruptions, eclipses of the sun and the spread of vast flood waters. Story is equally involved in the relationship between humans and nature, as between individuals and groups. Inundation myths and stories of great deluges are known so widely around the world that they likely originated from such prehistoric events immortalised in oral tales passed down as survival wisdom even to present generations.

The Moken tribe, nomadic sea people and boat dwellers around the coasts and archipelagos of Burma and southern Thailand, practically have the ocean flowing in their veins – many were born at sea in their parents' boats. The name 'Moken' means 'immersed in water'. Their elders tell many tales of *laboon*, the 'seventh wave', sent to clear the world of evil and to enable a new start. In one of these stories, a wave was so huge that it inundated all the land except the tops of the highest mountains. Those who survived, a few people from every race, gathered together and were sent a prophet to urge them to repopulate the world. It was such a special time that even men were able to give birth.[5]

On Christmas Day 2004, while gathering wild honey near the beach, a young Moken tribesman noticed the sea being sucked back in an extraordinary way, leaving boats stranded in wet sand blemished with heaps of glistening seaweed. When young Ngoei saw this, he rushed home to consult the elders. Salama, the tribal chief, said it was the coming of *laboon* that had swallowed whole islands in ancient times, and warned everyone to run towards the mountains. Young men already out fishing in their *kabang*, their traditional long wooden canoes, were tossed about by a thirty-metre wave and their boats drawn out into deep water.

Few will have forgotten that tsunami: it devastated coastal communities of South East Asia, killing almost a quarter of a million people. But with the strength of cultural knowledge that Story had preserved, every person of the Moken tribe survived; their fishermen, too, came safely back from far out at sea and saved many people left stranded on protruding rocks and floating debris.

In manifold ways, Story interacted with each vital event in humanity's hazardous journey through many thousands of years and across vast horizons. And these ancestors of ours were about to make a spectacular discovery. An ingenious invention that had a huge and far reaching impact on their lives; one which remains to this day imprinted on our psyche as a symbol with a multitude of meanings, significant on many levels.

It might often have occurred that a tree was struck by lightning, and that people came upon the burning mass with the wit to remove a piece of smouldering wood, urge it into flame and light a fire. But once it went out, it was lost. This, though, was something quite different: someone had worked out how to make fire at will and in any place of their choosing.

For millennia they would have witnessed from time to time this monstrous force with the energy to ravage an entire landscape and destroy, in seconds, all in its path, including their kinsfolk. But those who survived would also have seen, afterwards, after the rains, vibrant new growth and renewal of life. A truly terrifying mystery: this raging, engulfing inferno of heat and light that brought instant death and resulted, with the help of water, in gradual rebirth. Because of its intermittent, unpredictable appearance, many had never seen it themselves, but had heard about it only through the stories of elders who had.

Imagine the awe and excitement of creating that first flame with just the correct amount of friction in the presence of some tindery material under the right conditions – not to mention the accidents, injuries and burnt dinners that likely resulted from trial and error by inexpert hands. For, like many natural forces humanity has got its hands on since, they could create fire, but learning to control it was another matter.

As long ago as 300,000 years, a large group of people sat around a fire in Qesem Cave (in present day Palestine). They were cooking meat, perhaps the rewards of a successful communal hunting expedition. Flints used for cutting it up lay handy beside the hearth. Such gatherings had been a regular event for them for many years; the hearth big enough for everyone to feel the warmth of the fire, several smaller groups coming together, occupying their own part of the cave. These are the facts we know, and for sure, thousands of years before this, other peoples elsewhere had also tamed fire for their own use.[6]

Fire changed their lives significantly, producing previously unknown possibilities. Fire kept them warm and dry during cold, wet seasons. They could now cook their food. Previously indigestible but easily available tubers and other mature vegetation could be eaten when cooked, and the spoils of their hunting roasted, increasing variety and protein in their diet. Fires kept at bay the wild beasts that preyed on them at night, and even deterred pesky insects whose buzzing and biting drove people crazy on warm damp evenings and sometimes made them sick. In time, they learned to use fire to flush out game when hunting; burn off dead grasses to encourage new growth; subdue the bees to raid their honey and to fell a tree by burning around its base. They even discovered how to carry smouldering embers with them to new campsites to save the arduous task of making new fire. And long into the future, they would learn that fire hardens clay to make stronger pots and smelts metal ores to fashion tools and weapons from copper, bronze and iron. Perhaps most important for Story, they had warmth and light at their command and a safe focal point for social gatherings. Light during the long evenings extended their active hours, enabled them to mend their traps and nets, weave new carrying slings, perhaps turn a hollow reed into a flute – and share stories and songs around the fire. A landmark in human culture, fire has ever since been to us a symbol of life, renewal and conviviality.

Precisely how and when this momentous discovery was first made is unlikely ever to be known, and it would have happened in more than one place at different times. The man or woman in each band who produced fire doubtless became a local hero, perhaps even a great leader or revered storyteller. How often they must have told their tale of when that initial flame flickered. Perhaps it began with a chance spark when chipping at flints with a stone, or smouldering heat produced while drilling a hole in wood for some other purpose. They would have recounted the determination needed to kindle the flame, the patience required in attempting to reproduce that first success, and persistence to refine the art. A tale no doubt elaborated with each telling, passed on through the mouths of their descendants. Sadly, their personal accounts are lost, eroded to dust blown through the chasms of time that separate us. But Story has been prodigious in recalling the originality, tenacity and courage necessary to perform this feat and, as is her wont, blending into each tale other cultural values and memories according to each people's tradition.

In ancient Greece, long before city states and a complex pantheon of gods, the fire in the domestic hearth was a symbol of that particular lineage; it defined family membership. Sons kept it lit constantly as an altar to honour the ancestors and ensure continuity of life and wellbeing. When a daughter married, she gave up her membership, and was ritually enrolled before the hearth of her husband, honouring his household gods. In a later Greek myth, a hero-god, Prometheus, one of the Titans, stole fire from the god Vulcan to benefit humanity. But in traditional indigenous stories it is frequently one of the animals or an adventurous youth who captures fire, and the tale includes some reference to trees which make good kindling. Humans' discomfort without fire is always a feature; without it they are often seen as incomplete and no better than the other animals. Fire is usually stolen from some terrible source after prolonged and arduous attempts involving clever tricks and great bravery – emotionally closer to what must have been the original wonder at this new prize.

'Long, long ago, Iwarame, the caiman, was a person like all the other animals. All the animals could speak. There were Sanema-Yanomami Indians as well back then but the people ate their food raw because they did not have the secret of fire.'

In these tropical forests of Venezuela, Caiman was the most powerful animal because he roasted his meat, wafting tantalising aromas to all the other animals and people. He kept the fire in his mouth, which was closed when he slept, so it was impossible to reach. But the humans thought of an idea. They decided to hold a big party for all the Sanema and all the animals. *Iwarame* was invited, and left his cave to attend the event. All the animals and birds performed tricks and jokes to make everyone laugh; guests were falling about with hilarity – all except *Iwarame* who kept his mouth shut. He didn't even smile when *Jashimo*, the purple gallinule with its glowing red beak, and *Hima* the dog played ridiculous antics like throwing dung about, which had all the other animals in hysterics. Finally, *Jiomonikoshwan*, the clever green-tailed jacamar – its belly as red as fire – performed an exotic dance and, while passing *Iwarame*, lifted its tail and shot a stream of excrement at him. This made *Iwarame* laugh so loud that flames escaped from his mouth. Instantly, *Maipomue*, the humming bird, darted into his mouth and flew out with a ball of fire in his beak, which he placed in the heart of the sacred *Puloi* tree. And this is where Sanema and Yanomami go to find fire.[7]

Extraordinary feats are often made memorable in indigenous stories by relating dangerous or forbidden actions that reverse the normal order, such as playing with excrement: a coarse jest that still makes us giggle even if we do not admit it. This tale, too, celebrates cooperation between humans and animals, the latter described with colour symbols of fire.

In a story of the Tse-Shaht people, *Ah-tush-mit*, Son of Deer, was the one who finally succeeded in stealing fire from the fierce and terrible Wolf People – the only ones to have fire and they guarded it jealously.

> Young *Ah-tush-mit*, who loved to dance and sing, was not taken seriously by his people, but the Chief supported his request to attempt to steal the fire because the strongest, bravest and wisest men of the tribe had already tried and failed. But *Ah-tush-mit* kept a secret which he told no one. With help from his village, he dressed up in a colourful costume with painted cedar-bark knee and head-bands, and went off to attempt his dangerous mission among the Wolf People. When he arrived, he sang and danced so loudly outside the grand house of the Wolf People that they eventually let him in to entertain them. So enchanted were they by his performance that, despite his fear of their huge jaws and sharp teeth, *Ah-tush-mit* was able to dance closer and closer to their great hearth, finally summoning the courage to leap right over the flames. The Wolf People were amazed, and laughed to see poor little *Ah-tush-mit's* legs smouldering, but he leapt straight out of the door and sped home as fast as he could. His knees were burned, but he had succeeded in stealing fire because of his clever secret. He had tucked into his decorative knee bands some very dry, resinous sticks of the spruce tree. When these caught fire, his cedar-bark knee bands had smouldered until he reached home where the jubilant villagers fanned them into flames.[8]

Ah-tush-mit leaps right over the flames.

The quest and its struggles have ever been at the heart of story-making. Throughout our human history, bands of people continued to move across the landscape, but around 100,000 years ago a new wave of migration began from Africa. We have named these people *Homo sapiens* – we do not, of course, know what they called themselves. Scattered in many separate groups over the eastern and southern parts of the continent, they were likely prompted to move further and further out by climatic changes and the formation of larger groups that needed to be fed. Armed with better tools, hunting techniques and fire-making, their passage began into the Middle East, extending into Europe as the last great ice-age receded, and spreading in time to Asia. In many of these places they came upon strangers, descendants of the first major migration. With some they traded and exchanged stories, living peaceably and creating new offspring together; with others they fought and prevailed or died. Whenever conditions changed for the worse and resources were scarce, they all competed with each other; inevitably many groups perished from disease, conflict, natural disasters or lack of food. But migration extended eventually to the Pacific and to the Americas, following ancient land-bridges now permanently inundated, or crossing water on boats and rafts. Some continued a nomadic life, or moved seasonally with the game, others formed small villages among the hills, valleys and forests, and along the coasts.

And Story went with them, spurred them on, spread ideas and enriched their cultures. She was entirely free – she was everywhere, moving among all the peoples, providing each the tales they needed to remember their past, guide their present and consider their future. Everyone heard the stories and made them their own in infinite variety. But our ancestors had been asking bigger questions gathered around their hearths. Where did we and all the animals and birds come from? Why do the moon and the sun go away each day and never meet? Where do we go when we die?

People had watched, since long ago, the work of sun, moon and stars, their comings and goings. On clear nights, they became familiar with the passages of certain stars they named and followed as beacons on their journeys. They recognised the seasonal effects of the sun on their food supplies, welcomed its warmth and regretted its departures. The moon was more mysterious, its influence less apparent, but they could mark time by its fattening and thinning and they mourned the nights when it did not appear, especially before the days of fire. Story had been too busy with more immediate needs to dwell too much on these distant celestial bodies whose daily presence and absence, while intriguing, at least followed a regular rhythm. But now she gave birth to an exuberance of creation myths where ancestors, beasts and spirits stalked heaven and earth. A multiplicity of stories grew because not all the storytellers imagined the same answers and not everyone admired the same stories: that has ever been the case.

Ancestral knowledge of sea and sky had led Māori to migrate beyond South-East Asian coasts. Over centuries, they spread through Melanesia and Polynesia, developing their double-hulled canoes for the longer journeys to New Zealand. Successions of stars rising and fading from the horizon guided their night voyages – the longest distance perhaps taking up the passage of twelve such stars before dawn. Sea swells, wind direction, bird flight and landforms all played a role in navigation; it is no wonder that variations of Māori creation myths all weave in and out of natural elements. The genealogy or *whakapapa* of creation names some twenty 'generations' of the universe proceeding through three main phases.

> Before the beginning was *Te Kore*, a void of potential energy, then *Te Po*, the great restless darkness, followed by the emergence of light and life, the *Te Ao-marama*. During this final phase arose Ranginui the sky father, and Papatuanuku the earth mother.
>
> Ranginui and Papatuanuku bore many children, clasping their offspring between them in such a close embrace that it cut out the light of the sun. So the children plotted to separate their parents to let in light and give themselves freedom of movement. One of the sons, Tane, gradually separated his parents by resting his shoulders on Papatuanuku and, placing his feet upon Ranginui, pushed him out into the sky. The earth was stained red by the blood spilled during their tearing apart, and the land flooded with Ranginui's tears of grief for the loss of his partner. To save the land from drowning, the children turned the earth around so that Ranginui did not have to gaze upon his loss all the time. Thereafter, the floods receded; his tears now form only morning dew. Tane became *atua* – 'divine spirit' – of the mighty forest trees which stand between heaven and earth. And he and his brothers, all deities of different elements, worked together to fashion women with advice from Papatuanuku.[9]

The genealogy continues from this creation, through the first ancestors and later generations, to the present day where every child reared in Māori tradition learns to recite their own *whakapapa* or genealogy.

That life began in some association with flood waters – a concept supported in primeval geologies – is so common among creation myths, it is tempting to think of this idea as an archaic memory embedded in our psyche and perpetuated by Story since the origins of language. The power of words to create life is clear in the ancient oral traditions of the Central American Mayan culture, preserved in a transcription written down in 1701 by a Dominican monk, Francisco Ximénez. This document, known as the *Popol Vuh,* Book of the People, i.e. of the K'iche' (Quiché) nation of Guatemala, includes a myth of five successive creations that bear uncanny glimpses of what we currently understand of human evolution.

> Before life, there was merely featureless sky and still waters, a tranquil nothingness lingering in darkness. The only light was that surrounding Tepeu, the Maker, the Heart of Heaven and Heart of Earth, and Gucumatz, the 'forefathers', creative powers who came together to express their intention for the creation of light and life. These were the first words. As the waters receded, earth emerged into the void, high mountains were revealed and the water divided into rivers. Thus the earth was the first creation. In the second creation, animals inhabited the earth. Men fashioned from clay were the third creation. But these men of mud were dissolved by water from a deluge. In a fourth attempt, men of wood were made who were far stronger. But neither clay nor wood produced beings with souls, thought and language. When the gods realised their wooden creatures lacked the ability to honour their Makers, they grew angry and destroyed them.
>
> All this had taken place in the darkness, as sun, moon and stars had not yet appeared. Two of the creative powers,

The Former or Xpiyacoc, a male deity, and The Shaper or Xmucane, a female deity, saw that creation was incomplete; it lacked humanity to populate the land. They joined their thoughts together and 'spoke the creation' of people, but it was Xmucane who took white and yellow ears of maize, ground them nine times to the finest powder and mixed it with water to form maize dough. From this she fashioned the first four men of human flesh, and made wives for them while they slept. Four animals – fox, coyote, parakeet and raven – had revealed the path to the white and yellow ears of corn, still in darkness where maize seeds germinate.

These new people, the founders of the K'iche', could think, speak, listen to each other and move about freely; they gave thanks to their creators for their identity and self-awareness. But The Former and The Shaper saw that these humans knew too much: they had almost complete knowledge of everything in the sky and on the earth; it was not good that they should become like gods instead of peopling the land and planting corn. So they veiled the vision of humanity until only their immediate surroundings were clear and known to them. In this way, they remade the essence of their creation, and the wisdom of the first four people was lost.[10]

It is conceivable that since the inception of the universe – or of multiple universes as we now believe – some invisible energy force, a universal consciousness, has been at play. Perhaps the human project, the perpetual restlessness of our species, is a search to regain that lost wisdom. Heaven knows we are in need of it. However this may be, once humans achieved conscious awareness and symbolic thought, each culture related in its own way to the physical and spiritual worlds it experienced; they formed answers to unceasing questions from the human mind and began the quest to understand the 'why' of all things. Intriguing is the fact that, amidst all this variety, Story wove so many common threads.

Some great spirits were remote, unnamed and uninterested in the puny activities of humans, although godly squabbles might have dire effects on humbler beings. Lesser deities with sometimes dubious intentions inhabited mountains, trees and stones, or flowed through streams and plants, benign, even generous, but moody. Some had little influence on humans unless disturbed, then requiring appeasement. More often, deities were only too present and demanding; mischievous, powerful yet rarely beyond a little bribery, bullying or trickery to achieve people's desires, for Story patterned these spirits in the likeness of humans even though, much later, some humans thought themselves fashioned after the gods.

Storytellers calmed fears of the unknown and unknowable while shamans and healers dipped into the same well to cool ailments of the human body and spirit, ameliorating opposing forces and wills, stilling the quavering of life's delicate balance. Change and opportunity accelerated, posing new challenges as time, skill and inspiration blossomed into novel enterprises everywhere. In the space of a score of thousand years rather than hundreds, houses with clay roofs were built in central Europe; in Asia they made sculptures, in Japan, ceramics; massive stone temples were constructed in Turkey and megalithic tombs in western Europe, and in favoured valleys of China, the Middle East and the Mediterranean, people began to grow their food, domesticate animals, create pottery to store their goods, and invent metal tools. The same inventiveness also produced more effective weapons, because some peoples had begun to settle in towns. Houses, farms and grain stores had to be defended; land wrested from surrounding nomadic tribes; authority established and slaves procured to work the land. Accumulation of possessions led to the concentration of power which had to be grasped and held, or lost to another.

For these people, there was no more hiving off to fresh horizons when resources grew scarce. When the gods withheld the rains, devastated the crops with hail, or laid waste the cattle or the people with disease, they were appeased with desperate measures.

Story spoke of all this, aware that here, the animals no longer held parties or passed their wisdom to humans; that deities multiplied, the means of influencing them more elaborate and drastic, and that human heroes emerged calling themselves kings and sometimes, gods. But Story herself was about to be caught up in a new-fangled invention that would set the pattern for her own future struggles and change her life forever.

Chapter Two

And the words were inscribed into stone

While we plant crops, build towns, trade with friends and fend off enemies, the scribes develop writing. Story wears her new lines, dots and curlicues with caution, but delights in the recording of Gilgamesh and the ancient epics of Homer and Valmiki.

Thoth in his role as scribe to the gods.

2

"Look," said Thoth, "I have made writing, and I will give it to all mankind that they may become wise." King Thamus looked. "Nothing good will come from that." And he returned to instructing the builders on making bricks for the great pyramid at Saqqara.

[Overheard in Egypt around 3000 BC]

In ancient Egypt, the god Thoth created writing, along with art and science, in his role as scribe to the gods and keeper of the sacred calendar – in the Book of Thoth he wrote all wisdom. In Mesopotamia, the art of writing was gifted by the Sumerian god Enlil. Among the Maya of Mesoamerica, Itzamna, sorcerer and creator of the world, performed the deed. In China, not a god, but Ts'ang Chieh, a venerable sage in the service of the Yellow Emperor, invented writing to communicate with the gods and ancestors. In each case, writing was said to be divinely inspired, the tool of deities, priests and rulers, its secrets protected from the curiosity of lesser mortals with spells and curses.

One of the earliest stories we have found written down – on a papyrus scroll – was recorded in Egypt around 1400 BC (almost 2,000 years after hieroglyphs first appeared) and was by that well-known author, Anonymous. The tale, of how Setna, son of Pharaoh User-maatra, tried to steal the Book of Thoth, probably originated as an older oral story. And it allows us to feel some of the wonder surrounding written words, the desire for the wisdom they contained, and the hope that their magic would reveal the ultimate prize – access to the all-knowing immortality of the gods.

When Setna, renowned as a gifted scribe and scholar of distinction, discovered that the Magic Book of Thoth was concealed in a tomb in the cemetery of Memphis, it is not surprising that he should seek it out. For he was a magician without equal himself, and knew the Book contained spells that would empower him to enchant heaven and earth, to understand the languages of all creatures, and to renew his life forever.

So Setna went to Memphis and succeeded in tracing the tomb. He pushed his way inside, and found himself facing the seated body of Neferkaptah, son of King Mernebptah. Beside him sat the Ka (the spirit) of his wife Ahura, who was also his sister. Although her body was entombed in faraway Koptos with that of their child, her Ka stayed with the man she loved. Between them lay the Book of Thoth.

The Ka of Neferkaptah challenged the intruder and, on hearing his intentions, forbade him to touch the Book. When Setna threatened to take it by force, Ahura said to him: "Do not take this book, for it will bring trouble on you, as it has upon us. Listen to what we have suffered for it."

Ahura told how Neferkaptah had also been a purveyor of magic and a dedicated scholar, spending all his days studying the temple inscriptions, until one day, a priest told him that the only wisdom worth reading was in the book written by Thoth himself. For it contained the power to enchant heaven and earth, to understand the languages of all creatures, and to confer eternal life among the gods. And he knew where it was. Duly rewarded with silver, the priest revealed that the Book was held in the middle of a river at a distant place called Koptos, and described the fearful means by which it was closely guarded.

In the river was an iron box; inside that was a bronze

box containing a sycamore box, in which was a box of ivory enclosing an ebony box, which held a silver box; inside the silver box was a box of gold in which the Book of Thoth lay. But they were surrounded by snakes and scorpions, and guarded by a deathless serpent.

On being told all of this by Neferkaptah, Ahura tried to dissuade him from his mission, but to no avail. She, and their young son Merab, joined him on the royal boat to sail immediately for Koptos, where they first made offerings in the temple of Isis, the great protectress and goddess of magic and medicine.

After labouring three days and nights in the river, Neferkaptah overcame the snakes and scorpions, and opened each of the seven boxes, finding in the last, the Book of Thoth guarded by the deathless serpent. He fought with the serpent. Twice he killed it and the beast rose up again, but the third time he cut it in two, separating the parts with sand and it was truly dead.

Neferkaptah chanted spells from the Book which enabled him to return himself to the river bank where Ahura and Merab waited, wondering if they would ever see him again. Jubilant, the family set sail for home. But Thoth had learned of their deed, and in his anger, caused the child Merab to fall into the river and drown. His parents returned to Koptos to bury the boy in a noble tomb before continuing their journey. Not far on the way, Aruha also fell into the river and drowned. Neferkaptah sailed back to Koptos to entomb her with their son, and once again steered the royal boat towards home.

Alone with his grief, Neferkaptah decided it was better to join his wife and son than to continue life without them. After binding the Book tightly to his body, he threw himself into the river. But when his father, the king, heard what had happened, he had his son's body brought to Memphis for a royal burial.

After relating all that she and Neferkaptah had endured, the Ka of Ahura told Setna again, not to take the Book. "I have told you the sorrow it has brought us. For the sake of it, we have given up our life on earth."

Undeterred, Setna took the Book of Thoth, impelled by his desire for the wisdom it contained. In his turn, he, too, was visited by trials and temptations. During one of these, he allowed all his children to be slain before his eyes.

Soon afterwards, great was Setna's relief when he realised that this disaster had been a warning hallucination sent by Neferkaptah, and Setna returned the Book to the tomb. Then Neferkaptah asked him to accomplish one final deed for him: he was to seek out the burial place in Koptos where lay the bodies of Ahura and Merab, and bring them back to join him in Memphis.

This, Setna did, after many labours because the tomb at Koptos had become buried under the town and its whereabouts unknown. And so, the bodies of Ahura and Mareb were reunited with Neferkaptah, the Book of Thoth placed between them as before, and the tomb covered over with earth, never to be discovered again.[11]

The perils of seeking immortality, of overreaching our human limitations to emulate the gods at any price, is a lesson Story has been teaching us ever since. And the serpent is one of her busiest agents in this endeavour, thwarting the efforts of the Mesopotamian tyrant Gilgamesh, as we shall see shortly and, 2,000 years later, diverting Adam and Eve from the eternal paradise of innocence. But always, there is the possibility of redemption.

Although it may seem so from this distance, the advent of writing was not a Eureka moment: writing was not 'invented', it had emerged gradually in a variety of forms and places, meeting the imperative to communicate in a lasting medium, to aid memory and overcome the transience of speech.

Thousands of drawings and paintings in prehistoric caves all over the world attest to this human desire to implant a permanent message. Their various purposes likely included claims to certain sites; records of hunting expeditions and division of the spoils; personal and group identities in hand imprints; aids to memory of past events – perhaps challenged even then by opposing graffiti – and, of course, stories. But these were visual aids, not writing. In the same way, small clay tokens and wooden tallies bearing scores and signs dating from 8000 BC, found in many places but especially in Mesopotamia, were merely counters and identifiers to register quantities and ownership.

Much later, knotted cord systems, such as the Inca *quipu* in Peru, could record a great deal of numerical information on trade and tribute, and may also have been *aides-mémoire* for ideas, like the Roman Catholic rosary – a beaded, rather than a knotted, 'cord'. But one of the major disadvantages of communication based on objects as symbols is that their meaning is understood only by members of the group or culture that know them. They could recall familiar stories, but to outsiders they could be ambiguous, sometimes with dire results.

The Greek traveller, Herodotus – as much storyteller as historian – tells the story of the Persian King Darius who was at war with the Scythians, and upon receiving a pictographic message from them in the form of a gift comprising a bird, a mouse, a frog, and five arrows, Darius understands it as a sign for surrender. To him, the bird is like the speedy horses on which the Scythians wage war, the mouse signifies earth in which it lives, the frog, similarly, indicates water, and the arrows represent strength: they meant that the Scythians were willing to give up all of these for peace. But one of his sages, Gobryas, disagrees, giving this alternative rendering: 'Unless O Persians, ye become birds and fly into the air, or become mice and hide yourselves beneath the earth, or become frogs and leap into the lakes, ye shall never return home again, but be stricken by these arrows.' As it turned out, Gobryas was right.[12]

These pictures, tallies, cords – and gifts from strangers – all lack two essential features for a 'complete' writing system: the capacity to impart 'all and every thought that can be expressed in a language', and a standardised set of signs that represent the spoken sounds of a language, i.e. signs that are phonetic.

From around 4000 BC, the Sumerians of Mesopotamia felt a pressing need for such a system. The residents of their walled towns brought in agricultural produce from surrounding areas – hides, fleeces, grain and wine – their craftsmen fashioned metals, wood and stone, and merchants traded further afield for cloth, oils, timber and spices. Contracts were necessary, accounts had to be kept, taxes collected, laws decreed, and administrators itched to issue forms and regulations.

Using materials readily at hand – the soft clay of the region and its ubiquitous reeds – Sumerian scribes gradually developed a system of markings that represented the sound of spoken words rather than the image of visual objects. Marks were made by pecking the cut end of a reed into tablets of damp clay; the reeds' impressions being wedge-shaped – cuneiform – that became the name for this form of writing. It took some time: the farmers and merchants demanding progress, a growing body of scribes honing their skills, but by 2500 BC cuneiform signs represented spoken words – and government administrators proliferated.

Cuneiform writing.

Spread along trading routes by merchants and travellers, phonetic writing had a wide influence on the writing systems of other peoples throughout the Middle East, Central Asia and as far as northern

India and possibly China. In each case, the marks, the signs, were adjusted or new ones created according to the way words were spoken in each language, and were influenced by local culture and the materials they used. In Egypt, for example, many existing hieroglyphs were adapted to become phonetic in ways that suited a paint brush and the smooth surface of papyrus.

In some places, writing was confined to priestly scribes as part of esoteric knowledge – the religious mysteries that bolstered their power – and almost everywhere, early inscriptions glorified the state, declared the divine status of their kings, and celebrated the epic deeds of heroes in crushing their enemies. As might be expected in these patriarchal societies, scribes were predominantly male, but we know of one exception around 2300 BC. Princess Enheduanna, a daughter of King Sargon I of Akkad, and the high priestess of the moon goddess, Inanna, signed her name on the clay tablet on which she had written songs in praise of Inanna.[13] But scribes also elaborated their accounts of kings, gods and victories with traditional tales containing older, deeper meanings, and so some of these ancient oral stories were written down for the first time.

One of them, the earliest known, inscribed onto clay tablets possibly around 2700 BC, is the Epic of Gilgamesh, ruler of Erech (Uruk) in the South of Babylonia (present day Iraq). The original oral tale had its roots in Sumerian culture hundreds of years earlier, when it might already have comprised several stories woven together, because the legend recounts events perhaps as long ago as 5000 BC, when each small city was ruled by a king on whose character the fortunes of its residents wholly depended. In those days, the identities of gods and kings were intimately linked. In the inscription giving the list of kings, Gilgamesh's reign follows that of Tammuz, a god of vegetation and one of the husbands of Ishtar, the goddess of love. Gilgamesh himself is part god, his mother, Ninsun being a goddess. But in this legend, it is his humanity that gives him concern and becomes his downfall.

Within the high walls of Erech, Gilgamesh ruled with such brutal tyranny, claiming the labours of all for his own purposes, even men's wives and daughters, that his citizens implored the gods to send a rival to replace him. The goddess Aruru, maker of all mankind, fashioned from clay the wild man, Enkidu, a creature of immense strength who lived in the desert knowing no man, foraging for his food alongside the cattle and suckling their milk.

Local hunters feared him and described his enormous powers to Gilgamesh, asking for his protection. Gilgamesh sent a temple courtesan to seduce Enkidu, acquaint him with the food and wine of Erech, clothe him and lure him into the town. Over six days and seven nights, Enkidu sated his passion for the temptress. Enraptured with her, he followed her to Erech, where people thronged in the streets to marvel at him, a true rival to their despot.

When Gilgamesh tries to claim his kingly rights over Enkidu's lover, the violent combat between these two men, built like aurochs, grappling and snorting like bulls, makes the very walls quiver. But the outcome is not what the citizens had longed for. Mutual respect leads to deep friendship; they become as brothers.

Gilgamesh enlists his friend to go with him to challenge Humbaba, the terrifying mountain guardian of the Forest of cedars, whose breath is fire and instant death. For Gilgamesh is determined to fell the cedars, "'the rich yield of its mountains,'" to enhance his city "'that I may gain fame everlasting.'"

Gilgamesh orders his artisans to make the finest weapons. After making offerings to the gods, and against all advice and entreaties, the two set out on their mission, Enkidu ahead because he knows the land and will protect his friend. After many days, enduring sickness and many trials on the way, they overcome Humbaba with help from the Sun God who sends chill winds from all directions, and finally Humbaba is beheaded. Gilgamesh fells the cedar forest.

Seeing Gilgamesh resplendent after his heroic deed, Ishtar, Goddess of Love, desires him to be her husband. He refuses her, recounting with insults all the husbands Ishtar has had and ruined in the past: "'Thou'rt but a sandal which causeth its owner to trip by the wayside.'" In her fury at being scorned, Ishtar asks her father, the Sky God, to inflict a Heavenly Bull upon Erech to destroy the two heroes.

The beast defeats three hundred men before Enkidu, grasping its horns, flings it to the ground and kills it.

But Gilgamesh's exultation is short-lived. Angered by this challenge to divine power, the gods meet and decide

Gilgamesh: The defeat of the divine bull.

that the direst punishment for Gilgamesh is the death of Enkidu.

Gilgamesh is distraught at the loss of his companion; even more, brought so close to death, he fears his own. He undertakes a long and desperate journey towards the Mountains of Musha, where the wardens of Shamash, the Sun, watch its traverse from the Zenith of Heaven, to the dark Depths of Hell. Gilgamesh travels through darkness where no man has been before, until he reaches the full radiance of the Sun and sees there the Tree of the Gods laden with fruit. He asks Shamash if he will be banished to darkness for ever when he dies. "'When will the man who is dead look on the light of the Sunshine?'" But Shamash tells him he will not find the light he seeks.

Emaciated and in rags, Gilgamesh continues his journey and meets Siduru, the Wine-Maker, who encourages him to enjoy the life he has and abandon his useless quest. Unconvinced, Gilgamesh asks her how to cross the Waters of Death. She replies: "'There hath never been a crossing, O Gilgamesh: never aforetime anyone, coming thus far, hath been able to traverse the Ocean.'" But seeing his determination, she tells him the name of the boatman.

Gilgamesh finally reaches the boatman, Uta-Napishtim, who agrees to help him, but first relates how he himself achieved eternal life. He tells how Anu and Enril, the Great Gods, planned to drown Shurippak, the old city on the banks of the Euphrates, with a mighty flood. Enril warned only Uta-Napishtim, instructing him to build a boat and save every creature. Uta-Napishtim provisioned the vessel and loaded it with his kinsfolk, his craftsmen, cattle, and all his possessions. On the appointed day, they fastened the hatches, and waited.

For six days the tempest raged. The lesser gods cowered in terror, Ishtar blaming herself for speaking evil in the Assemblage of the Gods.

On the seventh day, all was calm, but the deluge covered the land and all humanity had returned to clay. Uta-Napishtim's boat, alone, rested on a mountain top. Once the waters had abated, he released all the beasts. Seeing what had taken place, Enril blessed Uta-Napishtim and his wife, deeming them equal to the gods.

Then Uta-Napishtim tells Gilgamesh that if he would ask the Assemblage of the Gods for eternal life, he must stay awake for six days and seven nights.

But Gilgamesh, overcome by his human weakness, sleeps.

Uta-Napishtim wakes him and bids him return home, giving him as a parting gift, the knowledge that if he gathers a certain thorny plant from the bottom of the sea, it will restore his youth. Gilgamesh gathers the plant, and in high spirits bids the boatman steer them towards Erech. During the journey, they rest, and while Gilgamesh bathes in a pool, a serpent smells the fragrance of the plant and snatches it from him.

Returned, wretched, to Erech, Gilgamesh tries every means to summon the ghost of Enkidu to learn from him what death is like. When the earth finally releases his spirit, they embrace, but Enkidu is reluctant to answer his question. "'Were I to tell thee what I have seen of the laws of the Underworld – sit thee down weeping.'"

Gilgamesh insists, and listens to the fate that one day awaits him.[14]

He need not have worried quite so soon: according to the list of kings, his reign lasted 126 years.

It is not only the 'magic' of writing that allows us to know Gilgamesh and Enkidu: the elements also played a role. Destructive fires were a common hazard, destroying all in their path, yet those same flames baked the soft clay tablets, transforming them into more resilient pottery which has survived, albeit in damaged fragments. But fate dealt a tragic early death to the man who rediscovered and translated them.

George Smith, the son of a Chelsea carpenter, left school in 1854 at the age of fourteen. In an unexceptional way, he and his wife raised six children, but he became obsessed by Assyrian and biblical archaeology and spent every spare moment in the British Museum. Eventually, the museum paid him a small stipend to assist with cataloguing. It was while delving into a box of old broken pottery shards that he found a fragment of cuneiform script describing a great flood, an account which had been written down over a thousand years before the biblical Noah story. The clay tablet had languished in museum dust for more than twenty years because no one had known how to decipher it. It wasn't simply that the language was archaic: the script used neither vowels nor punctuation, and the words all ran into each other. (A reminder to us all that lack of punctuation and syntax may consign our own scribblings to oblivion.)

This 'Deluge Tablet', as it became known, stirred such a hornet's nest of public interest, challenging as it did the received wisdom on biblical history and literature, that *The Daily Telegraph* funded an archaeological dig in Nineveh, enabling George to pursue his quest to find the rest of the fragments and complete the epic.

George had never before been out of England. After suffering horribly during the long sea voyage, he was held up for months by local bureaucratic tangles. His excavations were successful, however, producing also fragments of other lost legends, including the Tower of Babel. A second expedition followed.

On his third trip, in 1875, he was delayed so long by officialdom that by the time he arrived at Nineveh, temperatures had soared to 40+ degrees centigrade and he became ill. The last jottings in his notebooks reveal his despair and delirium. This young hero with a natural genius for his subject died on his journey back to England.[15]

Although unable to complete his final excavation, George Smith's efforts opened the way for further scholarship that enriched linguistics, history, literature and even the science of the earth's origins – and allowed Story to bring us Gilgamesh.

Over the years, many renderings have been offered as to the deeper meanings of this epic, including the idea that Enkidu represents the darker side of the human psyche. Others have seen it as a heroic impersonation of celestial bodies, a representation of ancient creation mythology describing the separation of sun and moon, and the sun's diurnal journey through darkness. But interpretation is a hazardous enterprise at this distance, because we don't know the motives of whoever ordered its original inscription or the nature of its intended readers, and in any case, it is a medley of several ancient tales translated from a long-lost language and culture. As with all stories, we are free to make of it what we will, responding to what resonates with us or challenges our own inner narrative. There can be no definitive judgement: 'this is what this story means' – even from its author. It is the reader who captures and realises a story projected into the world by its original creator. And Gilgamesh has been edited and rewritten many times since, each scribe adding his own constructions – and 'typos' – according to the age in which he lived. It was especially popular in the seventh and eighth centuries AD and many 'modern' versions stem from that period.

To avoid this problem of multi-layered storytelling, the summary above is based on R. Campbell Thompson's literal translation from the original Assyrian and Babylonian fragments, in which he states clearly which words are unclear or missing and likely reconstructions are added. Reading it, certain themes arising from human activities 5,000 years ago are evocatively contemporary. In particular, the competition for resources between the citizens of burgeoning urban centres and nomadic herders sustained by the environment outside the city walls – such creatures were seen as wild uncivilised beings by sophisticated city dwellers. A deep conflict of interests represented for millennia by the pressure of barbarians forever at the gate. And one wonders, with hindsight, whether the flood had anything to do with felling cedar forests.

Gilgamesh tests the limits of humanity by challenging the gods of natural forces, and loses that power struggle, grimly embracing his mortality. With the realisation that humans – even despots – are not gods, arise the problems with which we still struggle: the balance between the ruler and the ruled; the boundaries between society and the person, and the paradox that freedom for each of us requires control of all of us.

As with Neferkaptah and Setna, Story leads Gilgamesh on arduous journeys, an essentially human motif in which we can see curiosity, inner struggle and transformation, as well as the outward exploration of the forager, the migrant and, from at least the time of Erech, the trader scouting in far-off lands. Whether we view the journey primarily as a spiritual or as a physical phenomenon, our species is forever 'becoming', yearning, seeking beyond its reach.

The hard-earned wisdom of Gilgamesh seems already lost by

350 BC, when Appius Claudius Caecus, chief executive and highest authority in the Roman Republic, coined the phrase *Homo faber:* man the creator, the fabricator with the artefacts and abilities to control his surroundings. He used it in his now famous statement: 'Every man is the maker of his destiny.' The harsh truth which Gilgamesh recognised, and which we seem unable to grasp, is that humanity does indeed forge its own destiny, but since we do so under an illusion of control we do not possess, it promises the ultimate destruction of our environment and ourselves.

Although it appears as though the first stories put into writing were only about rulers and heroes – those with power, as might be expected – our knowledge depends on what has been found, what fate has left for us. And she has granted us a glimpse of another kind of story of unknown authorship, recorded in Egypt around 1400 BC by the scribe Anena, who operated a script-writing service during the reign of Rameses ll. The story of Anpu and his younger brother, Bata, is initially one of domestic strife with a plot used repeatedly since, and which might easily be the theme of a modern soap opera. The brothers run a successful family business until the wife of Anpu attempts, unsuccessfully, to seduce Bata. Afraid of the consequences of his robust rejection, she tells Anpu that his brother assaulted her. Bata denies it, but to escape his brother's wrath, he leaves the country. When Anpu realises the truth, and further angered by the needless loss of his brother, he kills his wife. The story embeds what may be much older tales, because the mid-section concerns events during Bata's long exile – his transformation into a magical oxen and a tree, his marriage to a princess – and eventually Bata becomes a pharaoh and reigns over Egypt, returning us to the theme of kings and rulers.

Of particular interest is that the papyrus scroll is signed off by Anena as owner of the roll, and he adds: 'He who speaks against this roll, may Tahuti smite him.'[16] (Tahuti is an alias for the god Thoth). This curse must surely be one of the earliest attempts to deter the critics. Scribes were jealous of their reputation. In Egypt, scribing was an honoured profession; eminent scribes were among the elite who could own slaves, a status not granted to them elsewhere in the ancient world.

But we must continue our tale, for writing's own epic has another important episode which greatly increased Story's travels throughout the world. Useful though these early writing systems were – and they were applied for thousands of years – they required many symbols and characters to express 'all and every thought' and the huge number of words and syllables the human tongue may utter. Writing hundreds, even thousands, of signs was slow and cumbersome, and for merchants and traders, and those busy bureaucrats, too much depended on the work of scribes: they needed a simpler, quicker way.

Credit for the initial idea of this new system, which we know as an alphabet, should probably go to the Phoenicians: a loose federation of rival city states that flourished around 1500 BC along the eastern Mediterranean and the Levant (present day Lebanon, Israel, Palestine and their hinterlands). Aggressive maritime traders, the Phoenicians were famous in the ancient world for their trade in purple dye – much in demand for the raiment of kings, and now for that of elderly ladies – and for the cedar wood, which built their galleys and was also exported.

The first alphabet required little more than thirty simple signs, each representing a vocal sound or a group of sounds. Instead of having to know symbols for every word or syllable, anyone could learn the alphabet and so easily write or decipher any word that was written with its signs – anyone, that is, permitted by their society to do so. The idea spread rapidly and was adapted by other language speakers. The Phoenician alphabet included no vowels – Arabic and Hebrew scripts still do not – they were less important in their language, and people were expected to know where to insert them when reading aloud. It was the Greeks who added vowels, by converting signs for those consonants which were not necessary in their language.

Surprisingly, although the Greeks had already acquired the earlier systems of writing, also from the Phoenicians, people of influence had little use for writing and the art was almost lost. Theirs was a culture based on oratory, on the discourse of philosophers, scholars and statesmen who made up the higher echelons of society. To write down your argument was, in a sense, cheating: it was incomplete without the challenge of debate, without dialogue. Socrates is quoted as saying: "every serious man in dealing with really serious subjects carefully avoids writing" and it appears that he followed this dictum himself and never wrote. No doubt this stonemason and philosopher had learned to both read and write, though it would have made no difference to the quality of Socrates' intellect had he been illiterate.

Plato tells us that Socrates related an Egyptian legend about the god Theuth (Thoth) gifting the art of writing as an aid to memory, and the response of King Thamus that the effects were likely to be the opposite: not true memory from understanding, merely partial reminders. People would appear to be knowledgeable without possessing real wisdom.[17] A sentiment echoed in Alexander Pope's observation: 'a little learning is a dangerous thing'. Google does not think.

Clearly, an element of secrecy, of protectionism, also entered into the reluctance of early Greek scholars to commit their thoughts to writing, not 'to expose them to unseemly and degrading treatment' by *hoi polloi*. For literacy had already spread in Greece as elsewhere among merchants, artisans and administrators, though not to the lower levels of society who still revelled in their oral tales. Despite this early aversion, Greek culture had made a significant contribution to the spread of writing by adding vowels to the alphabet, and when the Romans in due course had their turn at supremacy, they produced, in their Latin script, the alphabet which has since been adopted by much of the literate world.

Of the other main writing systems that remain, Chinese and Japanese do not use an alphabet, which hasn't prevented them from producing more books than almost anyone else. The Arabic scripts do not use vowels, yet some of the world's greatest literature has been written with them. All these systems, though very different, are equally effective in expressing their respective language groups and culture.

It would be a mistake to imagine that the early spread of writing systems happened in an atmosphere of collegial cooperation, of scribes' weekend conferences and peaceful trading exchanges. Story tells a different tale. The whole era was extremely bloody. At the beginning of the period, Egypt held sway over most of the Mediterranean, a command later challenged by the mysterious but belligerent 'Sea People' – barbarians in boats about whom we know only that they included the Philistines. Kings and cities rose and fell like so many toy soldiers in vicious spirals of greed and glory: Persians fought the Phoenicians, Phoenicians battled with the Greeks, Greeks invaded the Turks, and the Scythian horsemen of Central Asia attacked everyone. Later, Greeks and Romans extended their empires with more rape and rampage: 'cultural borrowing' was, as often as not, a case of 'cultural bludgeoning'. But trade continued: armies require supplies, merchants need profits, and Story followed their trails also, dodging hooves and spears as best she could.

Written words confer authority. Victors rewrote history in their own favour. In stone, an expression becomes an edict, an edict becomes 'the truth'; those without the means to erect their own monuments have recourse only to graffiti or defacement as an alternative statement. Socrates' complaint about the written word escaping the challenges of debate, its seeming completeness about which no more need be said, is valid even now when access to both the principal debate, and to literacy, are denied to so many. Illiteracy does not prevent people from thinking, from possessing wisdom, but it greatly restrains their power to act in a society based on the written word.

But to return to our tale. During these turbulent times, Story became something of a war correspondent, weaving details of deadly battles at sea and on land into older traditions of fate and survival – creating what we recognise as the classic 'epic'. Epics – grand narrative poems – characteristically involve arduous journeys or sustained quests and struggles which have far-reaching and significant implications for all humanity. They may centre on powerful kings, meddling gods, honour, or heroic deeds, but especially on the latter and on appropriate manly demeanour. Women are rarely more than courtesans, war prizes, or slaves; at best, they are wives waiting for their hero's return – unless they are goddesses, and even then, subject to the whims of male gods. If these were the principal stories of the time, rather than those of fertility goddesses and nurturing female deities, it is because they were selected to be written down in keeping with prevailing patriarchal values. In this sense, writing became a form of censorship, either rejecting or grasping and refashioning what had gone before; and this also affects what will come after.

The epic poems of Homer – recorded shortly after the Greeks established their alphabet, around 700 BC – have had a huge influence on both social attitudes and literature in Europe, partly because of their almost continuous use in the education of poets and schoolboys since the time they were written. Aristotle referred to them in his teaching and Alexander the Great is reputed to have carried a copy of *The Iliad* on his campaigns. They were very nearly lost, though, and survived only through fate of impending war: knowledge of Greek literature in the western parts of the Roman Empire dwindled with its collapse and only in the east, around Constantinople, was there a concentration of Greek speakers. When invasion by Ottoman Turks seemed imminent, these scholars fled with their manuscripts, incidentally bringing Homer to Western Europe.

No one knows who Homer was, what city raised him, or even whether he existed at all: the name may represent more than one author. And the tradition that he was blind may simply be a way of saying that he was a performing oral poet-storyteller with no need to read or write, or it may symbolise the inner wisdom of the visionary, the aged sage. Whoever he was, debate continues as to whether Homer wrote both *The Iliad* and *The Odyssey* – experts identify certain stylistic features indicating a different authorship for the latter – but there is no doubt that they both follow a centuries-old tradition of oral stories. This can be seen both in their structure of familiar sequences and repetitions as a performer's aid to memory, and in their themes of journeys and battles, events gleaned from earlier legends of ancient Greek heroes who are sometimes semi-divine. The language Homer used, too, was already archaic in his own time – a common feature of traditional oral poetry as a formal performance art – and although *The Iliad* probably owes more to imagination and story craft than to historical fact, the echoes of a conceivable past reverberate through the epic.

The story of *The Iliad* focuses on a small number of aristocratic warriors – notably Achilles, a flawed hero and his own worst enemy – and numerous battle scenes between the Greeks and Trojans, whose historic enmities are heightened by the abduction of Helen of Troy. The plot thickens with constant interference by the gods following their own agendas from the heights of Mount Olympus.

In a sense, *The Odyssey* is a sequel in that the action opens immediately after the Trojan War in which the hero, Odysseus, took part, but his sea voyage from Troy back to Ithaca lasts ten years as a result of ineptitude, adventure and catastrophe, including the inevitable shenanigans of sundry deities. Odysseus is challenged by giants, seduced by sirens, and ship-wrecked, but finally overcomes all, returning to his faithful and long-suffering wife, Penelope.

During his long absence, Penelope has been pestered by gold-digging suitors, from which her adolescent son could not protect her, and they pose a threat to Odysseus should he return. When he does, in disguise, and is recognised only by Penelope, she is inspired by the gods to set up an archery competition as part of a plot to kill the suitors:

> 'Bright-eyed Athena then placed inside the heart
> of wise Penelope, Icarius' daughter,
> the thought that she should set up in Odysseus' halls
> the bow and the gray iron axes for the suitors,
> as a competition and the prelude to their deaths.'

Penelope vows to marry whoever wins:

> 'So come now, suitors, since I seem to be
> the prize you seek, I'll place this great bow here
> belonging to godlike Odysseus. And then,
> whichever one of you can grip this bow
> and string it with the greatest ease, then shoot
> an arrow through twelve axes, all of them,
> I'll go with him, leaving my married home.'[18]

Penelope engineers the presence of Odysseus, still incognito. But the bow is a divine heirloom which only Odysseus has the strength to string and bend. When he does so successfully, his identity is revealed and, as previously planned, he and his son attack the suitors.

In contrast to *The Iliad*, *The Odyssey* depicts also the lives of lesser folk, heroes only in their capacity to survive the hardships of menial life and to serve their illustrious masters. Chief among these is the swine-herd, Eumaeus. Near the end of his journey, and having finally arrived in Ithaca, Odysseus, passing himself off as no more than an old tramp, earns his supper and a night's lodging in Eumaeus' humble quarters by telling a story. (It seems that itinerate storytellers were already an old tradition.) The next day, granted further hospitality, he asks Eumaeus how he came to be in Ithaca, for he was not a local man.

> Eumaeus describes a small, fertile island, which favoured the inhabitants with good health. '"When men grow old there, Apollo of the Silver Bow, in company with Artemis, comes to them and kills them gently with his shafts."' The island bore two cities, so prosperous they attracted Phoenician traders, and Eumaeus' father, Ctesius was king over all.
>
> One of the family's slaves was Phoenician, a skilled and beautiful woman. And once, while she was washing clothes by the shore, one of these trade ships pulled in nearby. The cunning sailors saw her and sought to charm

her, asking her who she was. She told them she was from the city of Sidon, the daughter of a wealthy household, but on her way back to the family palace one day, she had been seized by pirates and sold for a great price to her present master. The sailors convinced her that her parents still lived and flourished, and offered to take her back with them when they returned.

On the assurance that the sailors would take her safely home, it was agreed that they would give her a secret sign when their ship was ready to sail. To pay her passage, she would bring with her all the gold she could lay her hands upon, and also her master's young son whom she nursed. She assured them: "'He should bring a high price, if you sell him among men of other lands and other speech.'"

A year passed during which this pact was kept secret. And when the ship was fully laden with goods and ready to sail, the silent sign was given by a messenger. Seeing her master was away in the town, the woman snatched up gold goblets from the table, took the innocent child of the house by the hand, and rushed to the harbour to board the ship.

Zeus gave them fair winds and they sailed for six days and nights. But on the seventh day, the goddess Artemis struck the woman dead, and her body was thrown overboard, causing Eumaeus great sorrow. "'With the help of wind and wave they came to Ithaca, where Laertes bought me. It was thus that I first beheld this place.'"[19]

In the completeness of this story and its ring of truth – considering the nature of the times – it could well have been an older oral tale, even a true story that the poet adopted and wove into the greater epic in revealing the characters of both Odysseus and Eumaeus.

For the next several hundred years, written versions of these epics were prompts and exemplars for aspiring performers and poets. It mattered little to the general public who could not read; they watched and heard them, enthralled, and no doubt fed those episodes they remembered into oral tales of their own, told to their children, neighbours and friends. Even during the period when Homer was no longer known or read, parts of the tradition he gathered and developed into epic proportions would have continued as informal folk-tales around many hearths.

And if we ever need reminding that Story works from within each culture – each constellation of minds sharing values – and that an understanding of why and how stories originate is the only sound basis for 'literary criticism', we should read the equally great Indian epic poem *The Ramayana*. Though from roughly the same period as Homer's epics, it was not written down until later (around 400 BC) by the Sanskrit scholar, Maharshi Valmiki.

Like Homer, Valmiki has become a legendary figure about whom no certain facts are known. The Sanskrit word 'valmiki' implies emergence from an ant-hill: by tradition, Valmiki's original name was Ratnakara; he was a peasant boy raised by foster parents whose poverty led him to highway robbery as a means of sustenance. While pursuing this livelihood, he intercepted on the road, Brahmarshi Narada, a divine sage, and came under his influence, eventually establishing his own ashram and himself becoming a Hindu scholar and teacher – a Maharshi. In the introduction to this vast poem of twenty-four-thousand stanzas, Valmiki credits Narada with its inspiration – Valmiki's own redemption forming an outer arc foreshadowing the story of virtue's victory over corruption.

> In the splendid city of Ayodhya – the capital of Kosala – the wise and much-loved King Dasaratha is in despair at remaining childless despite retaining three wives. Following a sage's advice to conduct a year of special sacrifices, the king is eventually rewarded with a son from each of two wives, and twin boys from the third. Kausalya gives birth to the first-born, Rama, who grows into an exemplary youth in intelligence, beauty and obedience. When Viswamithra, a renowned teacher and holy man, asks for Rama to come as his protector on a long, hazardous

pilgrimage, it is little wonder that Dasaratha is extremely reluctant to part with his beloved son. But Viswamithra convinces him that it is for Rama's own benefit to leave the comforts of home and develop his character.

During their journey across vast deserts, mountains and forests, Viswamithra explains, with a story, each of the many threats and demons they encounter who are intent on disrupting their mission, and Rama defeats them each in turn. When they reach the city of Mithila, Rama sees Sita on a balcony and falls as deeply in love with her as she does with him. Sita's father, King of Janaka, has set an impossible task for the girl's suitors in the hopes of never parting with her. But the ancient bow which others cannot even lift, let alone string, is not only bent but broken in two in Rama's hands and, in due course, he marries his beloved Sita and they return to Ayodhya.

The aging Dasaratha prepares to retire and crown his eldest son, Rama, in his place, but on the eve of the coronation, his second wife, Kaikeyi, insists that Dasaratha honours an old promise to grant her any wish. She demands that her own son, Bharatha, be made king, and that Rama be banished to the wilderness for fourteen years. Though distraught, Dasaratha is bound by his promise. Rama willingly obeys, and both Sita and Lakshmana, one of Rama's younger brothers, join him in exile.

They experience many adventures, ridding the earth of hideous creatures which disrupt the meditations of holy men, and befriending, in the process, Hanuman the king of monkeys. All is well, until Ravana, the infamous ten-headed demon-king of Lanka (Sri Lanka) abducts Sita by trickery and force, carrying her off to his kingdom. With the help of Hanuman's army of monkeys, Rama and Lakshmana build a causeway to Lanka and eventually kill the evil Ravana, returning to Ayodhya amid great jubilation.

Although Sita had resisted Ravana and remained faithful, Rama – uncharitably, but in keeping with cultural expectations – insists she undergo an ordeal by fire to prove her purity. Sita's virtue compels the flames to lift her out of danger, but chagrined by Rama's lack of trust, she disappears underground.

As Rama mourns her loss, it is revealed to him that he is a reincarnation of the Supreme God Vishnu, and that Sita is the reincarnation of Lakshmi, the Goddess of beauty and fortune. They are reunited and, having accomplished their mission on earth, Rama and Sita return to the heavens as Vishnu and Lakshmi.[20]

Similarities of theme in both the Homeric poems and in *The Ramayana* – heroic feats of strength; battles during long journeys; gods who are mortals and vice versa; the abduction of an esteemed woman, and even the ancient, archer's bow as a test of virility – need not surprise us. They arise from the accumulated experience of humanity: bows were among the oldest artefacts for survival in both hunting and fighting long before agriculture; abduction and rape of women are as much a part of modern armed struggles as they always were, and as for conflict – it is the essential human trait expressed in some form or another in every story. Taken together, these are common elements of what we call an 'epic', whether written on clay, papyrus, vellum, bamboo in China, or processed palm leaves in India.

Both sets of epics can be appreciated on various levels, but among the major differences are that the gods in Valmiki's work are not the capricious beings of Mount Olympus whom mortals can, on occasion, manipulate to achieve their own earthly and earthy desires, and the plot is not derived from historical and political events, but in a more direct way from the struggle between good and evil – the lines between them drawn more consistently and clearly. As an epic rooted in a specific religious tradition, *The Ramayana* draws upon its Hindu mythology: boons from the gods are achieved through prayer, sacrifice and moral means. Deities do misbehave in *The Ramayana,* and some have been transformed by circumstances into forces of darkness, but in the story they are punished by the high gods. Evil is overcome by Rama in a dramatisation of human frailty seeking moral direction; an inner journey so universal that its significance transcends time and place.

Perhaps this is why *The Ramayana* had, and continues to have, such an impact on the lives not only of Indians, but also peoples all over southern Asia, regardless of caste, education or financial standing; an influence far wider and deeper than that of the Homeric epics in Europe where today they rarely touch the lives of ordinary people beyond a proverbial reference to a Trojan Horse or a comic-strip image of Cyclops. Engage anyone on a bus in Delhi in conversation about Rama and Sita and you could end up missing your stop; ask a commuter on a London double-decker about Odysseus and Penelope and, at best, you are likely to receive a bemused stare.

Translated over the centuries into almost every dialect and language of the Indian sub-continent, and the languages of most southern Asian countries, *The Ramayana* is still sung or recited from memory by storytellers, illustrating its commonplace wisdom – as they always have – with snippets of current news and local scandals, and with metaphors from modern life. In Delhi, during the fourteen-day festival of Dussehra (Dasara), and the following commemoration of Divali, bejewelled heroes and gods mingle with the populace through the performances of singers, dancers, storytellers, puppeteers and processing elephants. In a cacophony of horns, drums and crashing cymbals, interrupted at intervals by bellowing bullocks caught up in a snarl of cart wheels, blue smoke swirls from ten-metre high images of the demon-king Ravana as he burns to cinders. Finally, the light of fires and flares defeats darkness and celebrates the triumphal end of the story. In air thick with the smell of hot cooking oil bubbling around *jelabies,* and the seductive cries of *paan* sellers – both delicacies consumed in great quantities as epics are vigorous stimulants to appetite – everyone becomes a performer in some sense, vanquishing evil and redeeming humanity. From deeper memory, the sun triumphs with the dawn and Story celebrates another day of life.

And always, like all stories enjoyed as oral encounters, they alter in subtle ways with time and place, accentuating what meets the needs of their audience.

Language and, more tardily, writing, adapt and change, moulded by each age and each culture. They are ongoing and can never be considered 'finished' or truly complete. Oral traditions, too, are continuous, their role as a medium of stories was shared over millennia with cave paintings, dance, music and ritual, but oral stories are different from systems of writing. They are more organic in their nature; they presuppose the presence of others to hear the voice and see the gestures as a shared experience. Story was ambivalent about the advent of writing, the fixing of a story onto a permanent medium where her words – if not her spirit – could be gleaned without the presence of any other person.

In fact, this is not what happened at first. Stories that were written down were read aloud; private, silent reading was not common for several thousand years. All the same, written stories tended to become 'official' and represent the interests and values of those with the skills and power to execute the writing: there was no direct interaction between the story writer and their audience. Socrates was not thinking of people's stories in his discourse, quite the reverse, but his point is relevant to them also: written narratives became set, without spontaneous discussion they could not be challenged. Through oral transmission, alternative views and different stories continued to be spoken among other classes of people; in the West, we are able to hear only faint echoes of these in the remnants of folk-tales gathered and written down many hundreds of years later – we will come to those.

But Story recognised, too, the benefit writing had brought in preserving legends that might otherwise have been lost completely, or been handed down verbally into finally unrecognisable forms. And in time, many more people were able to read them, and write their own.

We leave writing's own tale here while Story continues our journey, for which we must first return briefly to the Mediterranean. From 460 BC, Athens entered a golden age of art, literature, architecture and democracy, led by the lawyer and military commander Pericles – whose name means 'surrounded in glory' – who had the wisdom to consolidate Greek domains rather than seek further conquests. One can only marvel at the prescience of parents in naming their children. During the twenty years of his power, the Parthenon and Acropolis were restored, but Pericles knew that grand projects and laudatory inscriptions were not enough. Among his new laws were those permitting marriage between plebeians and patricians, and free access for the poor to theatrical performances – encouraging the common people to enjoy the plays, poetry and stories that formed their heritage. He is quoted as saying: "What you leave behind is not what is engraved on stone monuments, but what is woven into the lives of others."

And shortly after Pericles dies of plague in 429 BC, Plato is born, later to become Socrates' most ardent disciple, and the ebb and flow of wars, politics and philosophies continues. In 388 BC, Socrates is executed for heretical teaching, and then Aristotle is born and becomes a student of Plato. We meet Aristotle again because he had a huge influence on Story, but he was also tutor to the teenager who became Alexander the Great – in whose name the equally great library was completed forty years after his death in the city of Alexandria, the city he founded after his conquest of Egypt and which became, for a while, the centre of culture for the entire Mediterranean region.

Alexander was from Macedonia, a kingdom on the northern margins of the Greek Empire. He inherited the kingship after the assassination of his father, and whether or not he gleaned any military strategy from Aristotle's interest in human psychology, he went on to defeat both the Persian and Egyptian Empires and to invade the Indus Valley of India, leaving satraps – governors – to control the areas he subdued. However, as happens so often with conquering heroes, it all fell apart when he died. (Be patient, there is a reason for telling you all of this.) His ambitious generals warred against each other to take over his vast Empire. One of them, Seleucus Nicator, took over Babylon and sought to extend into Alexander's Indian dominions. His advance was stalled by a local belligerent expansionist, Chandragupta, who was intent on establishing the first empire in India, his own Maurya Dynasty.

In the event, Seleucus realised he was overextended and would be better off focusing his attention on Babylon. He transferred his Indus territories to Chandragupta; a treaty reinforced by Seleucus agreeing to give his daughter in marriage, for which, to his great delight, he received from Chandragupta a dowry of 500 war elephants to pursue

Seleucus' war elephants

his campaigns elsewhere. What the young bride thought of this arrangement is not recorded.

At this point, we leave Seleucus to create his Empire – for as long as it lasts – and follow the trail of those elephants back through India, for the wise, talking animals have returned. Though in truth, they had never left.

Chapter Three

The hawk, the owl and the elephant

Story reminds us of the wisdom of the animals. Bed bugs, owls, hawks and foxes track back and forth across the world, mingling in Aesop's fables and ancient Indian tales, all following the trails of travellers and conquerors along the Silk Route and over the seas.

Aesop was framed for the theft of a gold cup.

3

*Only the wisdom of animals can save us
from the folly of gods and kings.*

[Deserving to be an ancient proverb]

Even if we no longer held parties with the animals, they remained with us on our human journey to pass on their wisdom in fables, and they nestled in stories framed as tales within tales within tales.

There once lived a bed-bug called Mandavisarpini who made a nest in the folds of the milk-white linen that lined the king's ornamental bed. One day he saw a flea enter the bedroom and told him to leave as he'd come to the wrong place.

The flea, one Agnimukha, replied: "Sir, that is not the way to treat a guest, you should be more hospitable. I have tasted the blood of ordinary men and animals but never that of a king. It must be rich indeed. Please allow me to relish such a delicacy."

Receiving no reply, he continued: "Everything we do in life is to overcome hunger. I come to you for food. It is not right for you to drink the king's blood on your own; you should share it with me."

The bug told the flea that he was being impatient. "I suck the king's blood only when he is fast asleep. Wait until I have finished, then you can have your fill." The flea agreed to this arrangement.

Shortly afterwards, the king entered the room and lay down in the bed. But the impetuous flea began feasting on him before he was asleep. Stung by the bite, the king jumped out of bed and asked his servants to find what bit him. The king's men pulled back the linen and examined it carefully, but the flea had hidden in a crevice of the bed. The servants found the bed-bug and killed him instantly.[21]

Did the beast-fable originate in India, or in ancient Greece? Unless the Eastern names gave it away, it may come as a surprise that this is not one of Aesop's fables. There must have been ancient Greek bed-bugs; it's simply that they did not inspire the muse in the same way as foxes, lions, asses, wolves and hawks. Centuries later, the bugs and the fleas occasionally hop among Aesop's animals because, while he was gathering his fables in Greece, others were doing the same in distant lands and eventually some of the tales became mixed up.

But we must deal first with the itch of the bed-bug. This brief tale is inside another story in which a jackal, Dimnah, is trying to persuade his boss – Lion, king of all the animals – that a stray bullock newly arrived in the area is a danger to him, and that Lion should kill him before he himself is killed. Incitement to war within the animal kingdom is a serious step and must have pressing cause, but the truth of the matter is that the bullock has been so friendly that Lion has become quite attached to him, making Dimnah jealous.

We know that, because this is a story inside yet another story in which Dimnah's brother, Kalilah, listens to his accounts of life as an advisor at court, and tries to dissuade him from the folly of manipulating Lion in such a dishonourable and dangerous game, telling him other stories to emphasise his point when Dimnah responds defiantly.

But the story of Kalilah and Dimnah is inside a wider tale: that of the aged physician, philosopher and teacher, Dr Bidpai, who, at great risk to his life and for the benefit of his terrified fellow citizens attempts to instruct the tyrant king of India, Dabschelim, to more appropriate behaviour.

The first time Dr Bidpai had the temerity to seek an audience with the king and tell him as diplomatically as he could that he was behaving badly, Dr Bidpai was beaten up and thrown into the foulest dungeon available – which, by his own account, was extremely foul. And the king promptly forgot about the wretched fellow because that was the night he saw a shooting star.

Dabschelim, the king, suffered from insomnia. Studying the heavens was how he whiled away long nights in the magnificent observatory which housed his jewel-encrusted astrolabe. After experiencing the amazing sight of the meteor, the king slept as never before, and had a vivid dream in which he was directed to go to the mountain of Zindawar, two days' ride to the northeast, where he would find unimaginable wealth. He set out with his entourage the next day and duly found the cave with the help of an obliging hermit. Inside the cave were dozens of old chests each full of priceless gemstones. While thrusting avaricious hands into pearls and rubies, letting them dribble from between his fingers, Dabschelim came upon an ancient silk scroll covered in writing he could not decipher.

A translator was summoned and on carefully examining the document, declared it to be an archaic Syriac script, the Last Will and Testimony of King Houschenck who signed himself 'King of the Past'. The preamble to the Will stated that the intended beneficiary was none other than King Dabschelim himself. The treasures contained in the scroll were thirteen precepts of good governance that led to true greatness and happiness, with the admonition that they could be understood only through the counsel of a certain aged physician, philosopher and teacher of the name Bidpai – if such a one could be found.

This learned man alone held the secret to greatness? Bidpai … the name sounded familiar to Dabschelim for some reason…[22]

But who was this King Dabschelim and why was the whole cycle of stories compiled in the first place? As it happens, there is some historical foundation. Remember the war elephants at the end of the last chapter?

When Alexander the Great conquered that part of India, he left the inhabitants governed by a satrap they hated for his greed and cruelty. When the territory was later relinquished by Seleucus to Chandragupta Maurya, the people were able to elect their own king. But their choice, King Dabschelim, became a worse despot than the satrap. Good governance – for which, read 'unassailable autocracy' – was an important issue to the new Mauryan Empire. King Chandragupta's chief advisor, Chanakya (aka Kautilya, and Visnugupta) had written a treatise on the economic, social and political policies, and military strategies required to sustain an empire. The *Arthashastra*, as it was called, is a practical manual including management to-do lists; scientific and technical data; a whole chapter on maintaining forests for war elephants, and advice as to how spying on one's own citizens, assassination, torture, purges and other routine tasks of statecraft might be employed to best effect. The document remained a seminal text for educating princes for over a thousand years and, one suspects, is still being read by closet autocrats in modern 'democracies'.

However, to return to our story: there was a chance that the lives of Dabschelim's hapless subjects might improve because, surrounded in the cave by promises of greatness, he suddenly remembered who Bidpai was … and *where* he was, and sent messengers racing ahead of his entourage with instructions to rescue Bidpai from that foulest of dungeons – if it was not already too late.

Fortunately, the physician was a tough old nut and had managed to survive his ordeal, although he was in a parlous state. Over subsequent months of nursing him back to health, King Dabschelim invited Dr Bidpai to his lavish quarters in the palace, and listened attentively to the story of Kalilah and Dimnah. And it would be pleasant to think that he became a model ruler as a result.

At least, that is the legend based on facts that frame the Indian version of the *Fables of Bidpai* (or *Pilpay*), also known as *The Book of Kalilah and Dimnah.*

But the numerous fables embedded within this story are much older, having been passed down over many centuries as *niti shastra* – worldly wisdom for a decent life – their origins so ancient they can no longer be traced with certainty. Their earliest appearance for which we have documentary evidence is in the Sanskrit *Panchatantra*; the exact date of the oldest extant edition is not certain, but could be from around 300 BC. '*Pancha*', meaning 'five', and *tantra* meaning techniques or principles, the collection consists of five groups of tales around different related themes. The first theme, and by far the largest group accounting for almost half the work, is the *Mitrabheda* concerning the separation of friends, told through tales of creatures such as the bed-bug. The other four sections cover: making friends; conflict and peace; losing what was gained, and rash deeds. By tradition, the *Panchatantra* was written by a Sanskrit scholar, Vishnu Sharma, but it is unclear whether he was the author or a fictional character framing the collection. The prologue describes a powerful and scholarly king, Sudarshan, who was disappointed by the poor performance of his three sons in their studies; formal texts of science, philosophy and politics were clearly beyond them. Vishnu Sharma, who had been identified as an exceptional teacher, suggested a less conventional method by which he vowed to instruct them in the essentials within six months. Refusing the financial rewards offered, he set to work teaching the young princes through the medium of a series of animal stories that had already been told for centuries.

There is a ring of truth in this. Although a few of the fables have been identified with narratives in the ancient Hindu *Vedas* and *Upanishads* dating from around 1500 BC, the whole tenor of the *Panchatantra* is towards secular leadership, diplomacy and relationships, not religion. Morals drawn from the tales are more often to do with shrewdness and expediency than 'good behaviour' for its own sake and, for dim-witted princes, could have provided an effective alternative to studying more challenging sources such as the *Arthashastra* – mentioned by Vishnu Sharma as an authority on kingly wisdom. Another collection, *Hitopadesha*, also apparently authored by Vishnu Sharma, has the same prologue, but consists of only four sections, and includes tales from elsewhere as well as from the *Panchatantra*; it represents the continuous narrative of the author in tutoring his charges, and includes their delighted response.

Later translators created different introductory frames to the tales of Kalilah and Dimnah according to their own legends and cultures, adding or omitting certain of the fables as they saw fit. One of the first translations was into Pehlevi (a Middle Persian writing system), and states that the Persian King of Kings, Khusro (Chosroe I) Nausherawan (531-579 AD), sent his physician, Dr Barzoye, to India to acquire and translate the text. The translation took him over a year and a great deal of labour to complete, and he incorporated many flourishes related to Persian culture. The king and court were delighted, but the only reward Barzoye requested was that his biography should be added as a preliminary to the book. It appears to have been more of an autobiography and a long one at that, though perhaps an excusable vanity after such arduous scholarship. By 750 AD, Barzoye's text was translated into Arabic from which it passed into Syriac and into several European languages including Spanish, Hebrew and Greek. This latter translation (around 1000 AD) was made by Symeon son of Seth who could not resist slipping into the tales some snippets of *The Iliad* and *The Odyssey,* an edition which led to an Italian version published in 1583 and left strands woven into Italian folk-tales.[23]

Simultaneously, Kalilah and Dimnah tales spread via trading caravans, military expeditions, scholars, and other travellers to China, Tibet and Mongolia – the predations of successive Mongol hordes forging another route for cultural influence into Europe.

Into the mix at some unknown but early juncture, Buddhist tales – the Jataka stories – became entangled with *Panchatantra* fables. Buddha, Prince Siddartha Gautama born in 527 BC, would have taught through storytelling as he was no doubt taught – the professional oral storyteller was already an old tradition in his time – and in some of the later re-telling by his followers, Buddha himself is represented in a number of the fables as an animal, an Enlightened One usually unrecognised until the denouement of the story when the moral is clear. But in Buddhist versions, Lion gives up eating meat and lives only on fruit, and in another story Brahmans (highest caste Hindus) are depicted as tricksters and villains and given a hard time. The morals drawn and stated in these versions are based on the religious principles of Buddhism.

For this is the way with fables (short narratives, often involving animals and highlighting moral precepts) they are re-interpreted with each oral telling and, once written down, each translation is suited to a particular culture: species of animals and trees may change because, as we saw in the earlier story of Skate the champion spear thrower and foolish Son of Raven, the animals and plants among which peoples have developed contain deep symbolic meanings for their culture. Morals drawn from the stories likewise depend on local mores: the story of the bed-bug and the flea in our modern era of individualism is more likely to be interpreted as 'the survival of the smartest' rather than advice on trust and friendship. One of the reasons for these adaptations is that part of the power of a fable is its base in facts, and such facts vary from one locality to another. But all focus on the same broad intent: providing common sense wisdom on how to live amongst others while remaining true to ourselves, and the consequences of failing to do so.

It is not clear at what point the products of this translating, selecting from, and adding to, the *Panchatantra*, took on a distinct identity as *The Story of Kalilah and Dimnah*. These texts share a long, convoluted and contested history, but what we have inherited under that title are varying editions of an inspiring combination of Indian (Hindu and Buddhist), Persian, and Arabic storytelling. Elements of these originally secular stories, and even whole tales, have been recruited by the world's principal religions, appearing in the Qu'ran, the Talmud, and the Bible, as well as in major Hindu and Buddhist sacred texts.

The characteristic structure of the Kalilah and Dimnah stories – of frames within frames, forming a cycle of linked stories – creates a wholeness that is emotionally and intellectually satisfying, reminiscent of the old hand-knotted Persian carpets. In particular, the fine silk animal rugs woven in the royal workshops of the sixteenth-century Safavid Dynasty: the outer border of slightly different colour tones surrounds a narrower band, which in turn frames a large central medallion containing realistic animal figures embedded in a field of tiny, floral motifs; a common background shade holds them all together in a visually compelling way, yet each animal is unique and exquisite in its own character.

The framing structure was adopted into literature, along with some of the stories, to reappear in *A Thousand and One Nights* (though known also as *The Arabian Nights*, the stories originated among the Persians, who elaborated their tales much as they did their carpets). Later, the form appears in fourteenth-century Europe in Boccaccio's *Decameron* and Chaucer's *Canterbury Tales*; even Shakespeare lifted a few plot ideas, though by this time, the plots and characters served each author's own purposes and much of the original pedantry had become buried within new narratives.

The definitive features of early fables – sparse, plain language with the briefest of plots, sufficient only to impart a principle of instruction – have given way to more embellished stories filled out with descriptive and character detail intended primarily for entertainment. The misfortune of the bed-bug, related at the start of this chapter, is the story in its entirety from an English translation of an early Syriac edition: it takes little more than 200 words to tell. Ramsay Wood, in his enchanting 1980 re-telling, *Kalila and Dimna*, creates a 1,000-word story in which it is the blood of the king's beautiful young wife, 'the sleeping angel', on which the bed-bug feasts, describing it in anticipation to his friend the flea as: "'…rather special. It's a tender blood: sweet, yet with the invigorating whiff of an avenging demiurge about it – if you know what I mean."' He meets his end equally graphically: 'and very soon the maid's sharp fingernails begin to press steadily into both sides of his plump little body until he splits apart in such a way that it would be disgusting to describe it any further.'[24]

Though a deep treasure chest, India is neither the only, nor the earliest, source of the beast-fables; such stories and proverbs have been identified from as early as 3000 BC in the Mesopotamian cultures of Akkad and Sumer (the land of Gilgamesh) and if we slip back to Greece and listen to Aesop – whose life-time slightly overlapped with that of Buddha, though neither knew it – we discover that he is creating new animal fables, but also putting his own twist on the morals as he re-tells much older ones. The following fable is a brief aside in a long poem on such prosaic matters as agricultural productivity, written by the poet Hesiod who lived in Boeotia in central Greece in the seventh century BC – the same general period in which Homer's epics were written down, and three-hundred years or so before Aesop.

> 'And now I will tell a fable for princes who themselves understand. Thus said the hawk to the nightingale with speckled neck, while he carried her high up among the clouds, gripped fast in his talons, and she, pierced by his crooked talons, cried pitifully. To her he spoke disdainfully: "Miserable thing, why do you cry out? One far stronger than you now holds you fast, and you must go wherever I take you, songstress as you are. And if I please I will make my meal of you, or let you go. He is a fool who tries to withstand the stronger, for he does not get the mastery and suffers pain besides his shame." So said the swiftly flying hawk, the long-winged bird.'[25]

It might, of course, be sheer coincidence – there were hawks and nightingales aplenty in ancient Greece – but Aesop also dramatised their relationship in one of his tales:

> 'A nightingale was perched on a tall oak tree, singing as they always do. A hawk saw her, and as he had nothing

to eat, swooped down and snatched her up. She tried to escape from the jaws of death by begging him to let her go. She was too small, she said, to make a meal for a hawk; if he was hungry, he had better chase some bigger bird. But the hawk's answer was: "I should be crazy if I let slip the food I have in my claws to go after something which is not yet in sight."[26]

But Aesop draws a moral different from the ineffable power of the strong over the weak, perhaps one more meaningful to the common lot: 'It is the same with human beings. It is senseless to let the hope of a bigger prize tempt you to give up what you have in your grasp.'

As with the original author of the *Panchatantra*, and with Homer, there is doubt over the identity of Aesop; for Story immortalises her heroes by braiding them into our own imaginings. Our best source is Herodotus, writing a hundred years after Aesop's time. Although some of the geographical details of Herodotus' *Histories* may seem a little whimsical, Aesop's work was so well known in all levels of society – apparently Socrates passed the time in prison by thinking up verse versions of the fables he remembered – that there seems no reason to doubt the brief biographical details Herodotus mentions. They are given incidentally while he refutes some earlier account of a courtesan who became famous in Egypt during the reign of the Pharaoh Amasis, around 550 BC – our clue to the period in which Aesop lived:

> 'By descent she was of Thrace, and she was a slave of Iadmon the son of Hephaistopolis, a Samian [from the island of Samos] and a fellow-slave of Esop the maker of fables; for he too was the slave of Iadmon, as was proved especially in this fact, namely that when the people of Delphi repeatedly made proclamation in accordance with an oracle to find some one who would take up the blood-money for the death of Esop, no one else appeared, but at length the grandson of Iadmon, called Iadmon also,

took it up; thus it is shown that Esop too was a slave of Iadmon.'[27]

This is not conclusive evidence of his slave status, but these snippets of information produce yet more intrigue. The 'blood-money' is compensation that the oracle demanded from the people of Delphi after they had put Aesop to death. But why did they kill him? Herodotus clearly assumed his readers would know. Unverifiable later accounts suggest he was framed for the theft of a gold cup from a temple and hurled to his death by incensed locals, but we may never know the truth. Fancies soon fill gaps in history, and artistic licence of film and theatre has since bequeathed Aesop such distinguishing features as a hunchback, an ugly face, a dark complexion, and stammering speech – all suitably dramatic counterfoils for his wit and literary skill. Teasing out strands of the old storytellers' lives is like following a thread through the Cretan labyrinth; the 'Minotaur' we discover at the other end may turn out to be a goat rather than a bull.

Aesop's reputation has come down to us as an oral storyteller; we do not know when his fables were first put into writing, but if he wrote them down himself, it is possible that he was a scribe, which is not incompatible with being a slave. The status of 'slave' in Athens was defined by law and was hereditary; even being freed did not entitle one to citizenship. Although most slaves carried out physical and domestic labour, or ended their lives in fighting-pits, others performed skilled tasks. A great many scribes were needed in all the classical empires to copy not only literary works, but also volumes on law and administration, and to record legal proceedings, military campaigns and commercial transactions. Smart slaves were an efficient way to meet the demand, and training intelligent youths born into slavery was not the only method; the frequency of conquests over equally 'civilised' cities and states would have provided a ready supply of educated captives from among the vanquished.

Illustration for the fable 'The Tiger and the Fox'

Although many of Aesop's tales reveal insight into simple rural life, they strike at the core of human dilemmas, addressing deep philosophical questions with disarming simplicity. His fables were not merely for country folk, they appealed to intellectuals and plebeians alike; translations and varying editions in prose and verse have proliferated over the centuries, travelling even further than the *Panchatantra* stories. Whether entirely Aesop's tales or others that had been added and attributed to him, scores of collections containing at least some of his fables have appeared in most European languages (including fourteenth-century Welsh, in *Chwedlau Odo*), and in Central Asia (an edition in Uighur); other translations were made in India, Russia, Japan, and China, each with the flavour of its own period and culture. In sixteenth-century Mexico, forty-seven of Aesop's fables were translated into Nahuatl by a local scholar who enmeshed Aztec religious principles and rituals – the mind boggles to imagine how human sacrifice might have been incorporated.

And whether it has anything to do with Aesop, was introduced by missionaries, or is entirely indigenous, the Zulu oral tale of *Jabu and the Lion* forms a classic beast-fable:

Once upon a time, an honest and hard-working young herd boy released a lion from a trap on the lion's promise that he would not eat Jabu once he was freed. Instead of going on his way, the hungry lion decided to break his promise, but before he could harm Jabu, he was tricked by the jackal and trapped once again.

The moral: broken promises come back to bite you.

From time to time the question recurs of who originated the beast-fable: whether India copied Greek fables, or vice versa. If Aesop was a slave, either by birth or abduction, it is conceivable he was Indian, or even Persian, and knew fables from that source. Then, too, Greek sailors and traders almost certainly ventured during that time to the western parts of India accessible from the Persian Gulf and could have taken, and brought back, stories. But chauvinistic claims to primacy are unnecessary. The fable's ubiquitous appeal and almost limitless application suggest much wider origins. Far more likely is that, not only in ancient Greece and India but in 'ancient everywhere', animal stories arose as a medium of wisdom from the days when humans subsisted within the rules of nature, and questioned how they should live peaceably among themselves. It is as if these fables, like the animals and birds within them, came out of the trees, caves and bushes as we walked with Story over the earth during those early migrations, and we are reminded of such indigenous tales as the one in the first chapter about young *Ah-tush-mit*, Son of Deer, capturing fire, and the inherent moral that bravery, persistence and ingenuity, by even the youngest or humblest member of society, can overcome difficulties to win great prizes for his community.

The phrase 'orature' has been coined for the rich, literary heritage of Africa which was largely oral until the early nineteenth century, when several local scripts were established; for example, the Mende script of Sierra Leone, reputedly invented by a Muslim tailor. Centuries before, a script had been established in Ethiopia, derived from that of southern Arabia, and writing might have been used intermittently in parts of the northern African coast influenced by trade and conquest from the Mediterranean and by the Egyptian Empire. However, our access to original African stories – those untainted by colonisation – is limited, but they include transcriptions by early anthropologists who had spent years learning local languages. One such scholar, Gunter Wagner, working in the early 1940s among Bantu tribes of North Kavirondo, in Kenya, quotes the story of the chameleon's curse, confirming his conviction that it is not the result of missionary influence. The story is told by the Vugusu people, who explained to Wagner that evil, illness and death are not part of the 'normal order of things' which God established, but are due to forces acting against the natural order of life. Man became mortal as a result of being cursed by the chameleon:

'The chameleon came one day to the homestead of one of the sons of Maina, the eldest son of the tribal ancestor. He was sitting in front of his hut eating his evening meal. The chameleon begged him for food, but Maina's son refused. It kept on begging until he became impatient and drove the chameleon away. Before leaving, the chameleon uttered the following curse: "I am leaving now, but you all will die." Then the people began to breathe the air, get ill and die. Later, the chameleon visited the snake and begged it for food as well. The snake willingly gave the chameleon what it had asked for, and as a reward the chameleon uttered a blessing, saying that the snake should live on for ever. So, when it gets old, it merely casts its skin but does not die unless it is killed by force. Antelope, too, if not killed, will live for ever.'[28]

As Aesop might have said: A wise man shares what he has with others, so that when he is in need, others will share what they have with him – a vital principle in a place of seasonal hunger.

Wagner refers to this animal fable as a 'myth' because it is a fictional story supporting a system of belief and explains certain natural phenomena – the snake shedding its skin, and human mortality – as well as offering a rationale for the moral obligation to share food: all features frequently cited in defining 'myth' as opposed to other literary forms. And in passing, we can note the Vugusu's reference to an earlier age when humans were immortal; to a state of grace since lost, as in the Mayan creation myth described in the *Popol Vuh* where the gods veiled human knowledge. But Story is not bound by labels; she threads her wisdom through all narratives, mixing colours and textures according to the materials at hand and the minds she accompanies.

In the West, almost any beast-fable becomes attributed to Aesop, and the two major sets of fables – from Aesop and from the *Panchatantra* – are often mixed up in later collections and re-writes, but there is a subtle difference between them. Aesop's animals behave in the natural way that animals do, even though they can speak; in Indian fables, animals more often act like people, and this may be due to the cultural difference that in Eastern philosophy all

Illustration for an Aesop fable.

creatures are of the one essence, and some believe that humans can be reincarnated as animals, which allows the conflation of human and animal characters to be convincing.

Many of the later editions of 'Aesop's fables' would have derived from Latin rather than original Greek texts because, although there was a collection of fables known in Aesop's time written in Greek around 300 BC, it has been lost; as a result, we can no longer be sure exactly what Aesop wrote. The earliest extant anthology of almost everything attributed to him – correctly or not – is that translated in Rome, where fables were often used to illustrate points of rhetoric and to train orators in grammar and philosophy, as well as being a source of inspiration to poets. Phaedrus the fabulist (not to be confused with Phaedrus of Athens, one of Socrates' circle) wrote fables himself and undertook the first major translation of Aesop's work into Latin, using a common verse form of that time (iambic metre) that is not made to rhyme but to express ideas in a form similar to that of the dialogues in traditional drama.

Ironically, Phaedrus had been a slave, like Aesop. He was born around 15 BC in Thrace (coinciding roughly with modern Bulgaria and Romania) which was by then a northern client state of the Roman Empire, and he was taken as a child to Italy. Sadly, we know little more of him than that he was among the entourage of Emperor Augustus and there received a literary education – becoming, at some point, a freed man. And it is possible that he, too, was a scribe.

Perhaps a glowing intelligence and irrepressible talent won Phaedrus his freedom. He is reputed to have said that writing fables was the only effective form of expression open to a slave: a sentiment echoed by many a writer who finds the pen the only key to freedom from the many forms of modern 'enslavement'.

Unlike many other poets of his time, Phaedrus created original fables as well as reinterpreting the texts of others. But the liberties he sometimes took while transcribing and translating have caused some confusion as to what was his own work and what was probably Aesop's. However, examination of some of his manuscripts discovered at Parma in the eighteenth century, revealed that thirty of the sixty-four fables they contained were his own, i.e. new creations at the time they were written, and they were usually extremely short – what we might call 'flash fables'. The story of the sour grapes is credited to him. A hungry fox is unsuccessful in its attempts to reach some grapes growing high up on a vine. It walks away saying they were not ripe anyway and he has no wish to eat sour fruit. The moral: men, too, denigrate what they have failed to achieve themselves. Or, in another version: men blame circumstances for their own lack of achievement.

Phaedrus sometimes added his own morals at the end of Aesop's tales, as in the cynical note to the fable of the lion and the robber:

> A lion has just killed a cow when a robber appears, demanding a share of the meat. The lion tells him that being a thief he does not deserve it, and chases him off. A harmless traveller comes by, frightened at seeing a wild beast. The lion calms him and offers him a share of the carcass, stepping away so he will not be afraid to take it.

Phaedrus adds the moral that, though this is a laudable example, in reality the avaricious flourish while the forbearing remain poor. (An observation of particular relevance in our own times.)

Others added their own touch to Phaedrus' stories. In this fable, which is probably his and appears in several subsequent collections of 'Aesop's Tales', a Christian scribe has added a quote from the *Epistle of James*:

> 'A cock which had got the worst of a fight with its rival for the favours of the hens went and hid in a dark corner, while the victor climbed onto a high wall and crowed at the top of its voice. Immediately an eagle swooped down and snatched it up. The other was safe in the dark hiding-place, and was now able to woo the hens without fear of interruption.
>
> This story shows that God resists the proud but gives grace to the humble.'[29]

To add to the intrigue, some authorities attribute to Phaedrus the major collection of over a hundred Aesop-derived fables, later translated and published under the title of *Romulus* (with several variants in both prose and verse) which was especially popular in Medieval Europe; others claim that Romulus was yet another elusive legendary author of the fifth century AD who based his text on Phaedrus. Nonetheless, it appears that Phaedrus accomplished the major translation of Aesop's work as well as writing original fables, so we will give him the credit. We can simply enjoy the fables in their many manifestations and leave the critics to fight over the rest. A large part of that enjoyment is Aesop's and Phaedrus' penetrating wit. In a tale about Socrates, Phaedrus comments that 'friend' is a word freely banded about, but genuine friends are rare and he relates that Socrates, though a famous scholar, built himself a tiny house. When a neighbour asks why someone like him made himself such a modest dwelling, Socrates replies: "Ah, if only I could fill it with true friends."[30]

Aesop himself appears in a few of Phaedrus' little anecdotes. On one occasion, a rather tiresome fellow insists on reading to Aesop selections from a badly written book he has produced and in which he boasts of his own talent. Seeking Aesop's opinion he asks: "Surely I have not overestimated my genius?" Old Aesop, thoroughly tired of the whole thing assures him: "Certainly you are right to praise your own work, for no one else ever will."

Phaedrus survived his patron, Emperor Augustus, and lived through the reigns of Tiberius and Caligula, dying around 50 AD during the time of Claudius. Through his lifetime he would have been aware of the deaths of two of Rome's greatest writers – Livy and Ovid – and no doubt heard about the trial and crucifixion of Jesus of Nazareth in Judea which was under Roman rule. As this new religious cult gained momentum – by 41 AD adherents were already called 'Christians' and were evangelising in Rome's African dominions, establishing themselves in Alexandria – Phaedrus may even have been aware that their leaders drew upon Aesop's fables in their teaching and proselytising.

Not being a wealthy citizen, Phaedrus is unlikely to have been much affected by the massive financial crisis that erupted in Rome around this time, ruining many aristocratic families, and it is impossible to gauge whether he knew about Claudius' invasion in 43 AD of an island to the west called Briton, or the founding of his colonial capital at Londinium. It was the third invasion; Julius Caesar's last expedition in 54 BC had obtained promises of tribute from Cassivellaunus, one of the more powerful kings on the island, but the situation had changed. Claudius found resistance to Roman rule, and captured one of the ring-leaders, Caractacus, shipping him back to Rome.

These Britons were, of course, 'barbarians' to the Romans. And if barbarians have not been mentioned lately, it is not because they had gone away; they were constantly being repulsed from the margins of one empire or another, and occasionally they penetrated to the centre and caused havoc. Originally, the Greek *'barbaroi'* referred simply to someone who was not Greek, especially anyone who did not speak their language and was therefore foreign, strange and ignorant, which initially included the Romans. Not to be outdone, in their turn the Romans adopted the term for anyone who spoke neither Greek nor Latin. After the Greeks suffered a number of defeats at the swords of 'ignorant foreigners', the term began to imply savage, wild and uncivilised, and was even applied to the Persians who had an ancient civilisation to rival their own; but they sometimes beat the Greeks and that was frowned upon.

Among troublesome barbarians were a group of tribes the Greeks called Gauls, or Keltoi (known to us as Celts), who had already caused problems in the early days of the Roman Empire way back in 400 BC, when they had been encountered for the first time, appearing suddenly out of the Alps to overrun the Po Valley, scattering the Etruscans and eventually holding Rome to a ransom of gold that left the city almost broke. This and similar incidents had built the Celts a reputation:

> 'The Gauls are terrifying in aspect [...] tall of body, with rippling muscles, and white of skin. Their hair is blond, and not only naturally so, but they also make it their practice by artificial means to increase the colour which nature has given it, for they are always washing their hair in lime-water [...] the clothing they wear is striking – shirts

which have been dyed and embroidered in varied colours, and breeches, which in their tongue they call bracae. They wear striped coats, fastened by a buckle on their shoulder […] in which are set checks, close together and of varied hues…'

In battle, they intimidate the enemy by chanting to the din of horns and rhythmic beating of their swords upon their shields. And in a later passage:

'When their enemies fall they cut off their heads and fasten them about the necks of their horses […] these first fruits of battle they fasten by nails in their houses, just as men do in certain kinds of hunting with the heads of wild beasts they have killed. The heads of their most distinguished enemies they embalm in cedar oil and carefully preserve in a chest.' [31]

Invading Gauls 'negotiate' in Rome.

But the Greek historian who wrote this account went on to describe their lyric poets – *bards* – their music played on the lyre, and the learned philosophers they called Druids. Not only were Celtic artisans highly skilled in metal work and the arts, they had rich oral traditions.

Peoples sharing this culture had started migrating across Western Europe and crossing over to Briton and beyond perhaps as early as 2400 BC. And 2,000 years later, as one group of Celtic tribes was descending into the Po Valley, harassing the Etruscans and the Romans, others continued the move westward to Spain, Briton, and Ireland – Atlantic seaboard realms had long been a trading zone as well as a frequent battleground. Their descendants in Briton – among them Queen Boudicca – were those struggling against Roman oppression at the end of Claudius' reign.

Story is spending the cold windy nights and misty mornings in north-west Europe, threading wondrous interlaced patterns with bardic tales. If you're not afraid of ending up with your head preserved in cedar oil, let's wrap up warm in one of those colourful cloaks and join her.

Chapter Four

Saints and heroes

Celtic ancestors migrate across Europe taking with them their traditions and their storytellers and their gods of woodland groves that flourish in the new lands. And when Christian missionaries arrive and reweave the old tales of warriors and spirits, Story holds on to the threads of ancient Celtic mythology.

Poets were accorded high honours.

4

Oh Donnchad, great is the shame to thee to be seeking writing from myself on the feast of Finnian.

[A note scribbled by a grumpy Irish scribe in the margin of a thirteenth-century manuscript.[32]]

His name was Fland, a monk squinting in the paltry light of a tallow candle, breathing its acrid smoke in chill clammy air trapped, like Fland, within the stone walls of his monastery. With his colleagues enjoying the feast day and probably a celebratory sup of mead, his lot would be a slab of stale bread soaked in sour beer.

Let us leave poor Fland to his labours, walk out into the sallow winter sun, and sit with our kinsfolk on lush turf beneath the monastery enclosure where Brother Sean is telling the story of Saint Finnian's life, of how he came to lay the first stones of his abbey in Clonard, and counted Saint Ciaran among his pupils there. We have heard the tales so many times we know them without paying much heed, and soon, enchanted by the echo of the sea purring amongst rocks below, we drift in our imagination to ancient times.

No monastery of course, no saints. We listen as Story tells of Dagdha, the great provider and father of all the gods, whose voracious appetite for porridge is satisfied by his magic cauldron that remains full however many thousands are fed from it; of Anu, mother of all the world who drops stones from her apron to form the hills around us, and in her guise as Morrigan, goddess of love, war and sovereignty, conjoins with Dagdha to give birth to Brigid, a sun goddess and guardian of healers, artisans, fertility and poetry; and of the giant, Balor, he of the baneful eye which slaughters hundreds of the enemy with but a sweeping glance. Best of all, we hear tales of our heroes: wise Cormac mac Art, High King of Ireland, patron of the Fianna, his elite corps of warriors; and of valiant Cúchulainn, wrapped around with a crimson cloak in his gleaming chariot pulled by two miraculous horses. At the age of eight, he becomes a warrior whose body swells and warps to incredible strength when battle-rage is upon him. In his teens, Cúchulainn single-handedly defends Ulster, and faces the ultimate challenge of a fight to the death with his foster-brother, Ferdia.

The storytellers were the *fili (or filidh),* the Celtic poets and story-makers, trained in Druidic arts for twelve years until they could preserve the past by memorising hundreds of poems and stories, and continue the art with new praise songs, riddles, and satires. Often in verse and accompanied by a harpist, the rhythms, repetitions and alliteration made it easier for the bards and their audience to remember the words. Stories held power: they could confer benefits on performers and listeners, and were protected by a curse on anyone who repeated them in bad faith or without proper training.

Poems and stories, accompanied by ritual and music, were the means of maintaining relationships with the Otherworld: a supernatural realm, a sort of parallel universe of timelessness and perfection inhabited by spirits of nature and mythical figures such as the Tuatha Dé Danaan, who once brought to Ireland much of its culture. In myths, heroes and poets sometimes visit the Otherworld, returning with esoteric knowledge, but it was distinct from human existence and had nothing to do with rewards or punishments, nor any concept of heaven or hell.

Although Druids wrote in the Ogham runic script for occult purposes, storytelling was a strictly oral tradition where words were divinely inspired, spoken only by those qualified to utter them. To attain such inspiration, they are said to have reduced sensory distractions by lying on the ground for long periods, placing heavy boulders on their stomachs to keep themselves awake – a form of meditation perhaps modern writers should try in our age of frenetic sensory overload.

Not surprisingly, poets were accorded high honours. Achieving the ultimate level of master poet, or *Ollamh*, entitled them to wear six colours in the weave of their cloaks – only kings and queens wore more. But they were feared for the shame of their satirical curses that caused facial ulcers and even death: a fascinating allusion to the outer image of our persona, the 'loss of face', and the dire consequences of social exclusion. As a counterbalance to such poetic licence, if a person was satirised without true cause, ulcers and a swift death fell upon the poet.

A further eight years of arduous study would qualify *fili* for other Druidic roles as diviners, philosophers, physicians, judges, ritual celebrants, and counsellors to kings – a privileged combination of functions. Although we know less about Druid organisation in Ireland than elsewhere, there is no reason to think it was radically different. In continental Europe, Druids' conclaves and mobile networks reinforced their influence as a class beyond tribal boundaries; they had the capacity to unify political purpose among the disparate groups sharing a common Celtic language. Early Greeks had admired their scholarship and their philosophy of the immortality of the soul, and shared their preference for the spoken rather than the written word. But later, the Romans saw them as a potential threat to their expansion and sought to discredit them, laying heavy emphasis on the need to abolish their rituals of human sacrifice.

In Ireland, the slow encroachment of Christianity and the policies of the Roman church eroded the earlier power of Druids. Only the poets, the bards, continued oral traditions of poetry and storytelling, doing so well into the sixteenth century. But without the rigour and spiritual discipline of Druidic lore, some became itinerate pedlars of their own inventions, even threatening satire for personal gain, while others were co-opted by the new religion. Colum Cille, ex-Druid and sixth-century priest more familiar to us as Saint Columba, is said to have been called from his mission in Scotland (where, incidentally, he reported seeing a monster in Loch Ness) to attend the *Druim Cetta* – the Great Assembly. Among issues to be settled was the future of bards in Ireland. Estimated to number 1,200, each with a retinue of up to 30 followers and students, their maintenance was a burden to the community, and it was claimed that poets no longer told traditional stories but foisted 'lying fables' onto the people. King Aed mac Ainmerech of Connaught had banned them, including Dallan mac Forgaill, a doctor of wisdom and poetry in the province. It is likely that the 'lying fables' were Christianised versions of the old myths to which pagan kings took exception, because Dallan mac Forgaill asked Colum Cille for the protection of the Christian church. Colum Cille ruled in the poet's favour and named Dallan as *Ollamh* of all Ireland – a position which passed, after his death, to Senchan Torpeist.[33]

However, as none of the original tales was written down, Story depends on cultural memory – perhaps a thousand years of oral telling – and the work of Christian scribes hundreds of years later to bring us what remains of ancient Irish myths. It was ironic that pagan oral culture should survive through Christian writing, but as few could read, the power of Story was still controlled through oral transmission. Monks and missionaries became the new storytellers – and they had their own agendas.

Their scribes contended with greater frustrations than working on a public holiday: inking-over faded letters barely legible after centuries; poring over old glossaries to interpret words long obsolete; collating jumbled pages with missing folios, and handling fragile documents that crumbled in clumsy fingers. Not to mention running out of ink which caused them days of work grinding oak galls, soaking and mixing, to refill their ink horns. Often, they did not understand what they copied. No wonder they made mistakes and wrote their discontent in the margins.

Story's greatest debt, however, is to the compilers – erudite scholars who retrieved fragments of ancient texts and oral memories, marshalling them into reconstructions of older accounts. Others translated manuscripts, or assembled glossaries of the old Celtic languages long out of use. One such redeemer of Irish heritage was Cormac son of Cuilennán, born in 831 AD in the Munster province of Cashel (about 60 kilometres east of Limmerick). Cormac was bishop of Cashel and a distinguished scholar of languages and law. Through his work we find the first story of Senchan Torpeist, the sixth-century bard of Connaught holding the rank of *Ollamh* yet unable to meet the literary challenge of a female poet and healer.

As was customary among great poets, Senchan Torpeist decides to travel on a circuit, choosing the Isle of Man, which shared close historical and cultural ties with Ireland. Dressed in the grandest manner rivalling a prince, he gathers a retinue of fifty poets and apprentices, and prepares to set sail. As they are about to leave, a scruffy, acned youth appears on the shore, begging to be taken with them. Senchan's companions ridicule the boy's appearance, suggesting that the rags he wears are so verminous they could set off on their own. The boy calls out to Senchan that he would be of more use to him than his arrogant followers. Senchan, perhaps foreseeing some amusement on the voyage, lets the lad join them.

At the end of their sea journey, as they draw their vessel up onto the shore, they notice a grey-haired woman gathering seaweed among the rocks, and puzzle over the fact that, though her hands and feet are refined, her body is emaciated and dressed in tatters.

In reality, she is an Irish poet, one of the *aes dana* – a learned and noble class – and the daughter of Ua Dulsaine, a poet-physician. She had been travelling her own circuit around Britain when disaster struck her expedition, herself the sole survivor. Having suffered rape and starvation, the only hope to nullify her shame and regain her identity, is to find another poet to whom she can demonstrate her true status by asking him an erudite riddle.

She approaches the men. "Who are you who arrive here?"

"You must be a foreigner not to know that this is Senchan Torpeist, poet of all Ireland."

In the 'deep language' of poets, she speaks two lines of a metaphorical quatrain alluding to her situation, and asks Senchan to show his understanding by adding the next two lines.

After a long silence, the strange youth steps forward. "Old woman, it is not appropriate that you address Senchan, and the others will not talk to you."

"What do *you* say, then?" she asks.

He answers her well, and she speaks the first part of a second riddle, again asking Senchan for his response.

But the boy has quickly perceived her dilemma, and replies that she is the child of Ua Dulsaine, from Lia Toll Toursaige.

"In truth," declares Senchan, "are you the daughter of Ua Dulsaine, the woman poet being searched for throughout Ireland?"

"I am indeed."

Senchan provides fine clothes for her and brings her back to Ireland. The ugly youth, too, now appears with golden hair and splendid garments. He steps right-hand wise (i.e. in the direction of the sun as a good omen) around Senchan and his retinue and is never seen again. The story ends with the observation that he was truly the Spirit of Poetry.[34]

Apart from confirming that women practised Druidic arts, on the surface it appears that a woman and a spotty youth get the better of an eminent poet. As neither is honoured with a personal name, it seems more likely a satire on the arrogance of poets, but the story is rich in symbolism. Pustules on the boy's face – described with gleeful exaggeration in the original – are a sign of shame, perhaps for his poverty and ugliness, and the cause for the woman's shame is clearly stated: both are redeemed by the power of poetry. The message seems to be that true learning transcends social and natural disadvantage. Cormac recorded this story probably around 870 AD, but its origin is obviously earlier because he applied it in his glossary to illustrate the meaning of an archaic Irish word, and Senchan Torpeist is mentioned in other accounts as the *Ollamh* of Connaught in 598 AD.

Later in his career, Cormac succeeded his father, becoming King Cormac of Munster (not to be confused with Cormac mac Art, High King of Ireland in the third century). In that position he was expected to lead his warriors on campaigns to defend his province and to plunder others in revenge. To us, this might appear incongruous for a bishop, but as to his other learning, it was traditional in Ireland for princes and elite warriors to be educated or fostered with Druids as youths, and be taught the arts of poetry and music along with martial skills. In any case, as Christianity strengthened, monasteries proliferated and became linked to provincial kingships: the monastery legitimised the ruling dynasty, while the king's army protected the monastery. A reflection, perhaps, of each king in ancient Ireland maintaining his own Druid.

It was Cormac's glossary (aka *Sanas Cormaic*[35]) that Fland was copying unhappily on the feast of Finnian some three centuries later. That glossary, extracts of which appear in numerous later manuscripts[36], includes not only Cormac's original glosses, but also details gleaned from other sources that describe Cormac's dramatic death in the battle of Bealach Mughna in 903 AD, when he was in his seventies. It reads like part of an old Irish legend, but minus war gods and giants because, although Ireland was spared Roman occupation, Roman Christianity was increasing its hold on the country.

The previous year, Cormac had led a successful 'hosting' – a gathering of allied chiefs and their warriors – against the O'Neills and the Connaughtmen, defeating them and taking hostages. This time, Cerbhall, son of King Muirigen of Leinster, and Cathal, son of Conchobar king of Connaught, gather supporters to take their revenge on Munster. Cormac's men are routed, but as he escapes with the first battalion, his horse leaps into a trench and throws him. Members of his retreating force see him and help him up; one of them is a foster-son of his, Aedh, a scholar and nobleman. Cormac warns him: "O dear son, do not follow me, but escape as well as thou canst. I told thee before, that I should be slain in this battle." A few followers remain with Cormac, making their retreat along a road strewn with the bloody gore of dead men and horses. In this morass, the hind feet of Cormac's horse slip and it is pitched backwards, breaking Cormac's neck and back in the fall. Scarcely does he utter his dying words, *In manus tuas, Domine, commendo spiritum meum,*" than the advancing enemy descend on him, thrusting spears into his body while a low-ranking fighter, Fiach O'Ugfadhan of Denlis, cuts off his head.[37]

Although decapitating defeated enemies on the battlefield and riding off with their heads attached to the saddle – 'under the thigh' – was traditional practice recounted in numerous legends, it is described on this occasion as 'sad', probably because the head of a king was cut off by an ordinary ranker rather than a noble, but then, to flee from the battlefield lowered his 'honour price' and status. Cormac's role as a leader of the Church, a 'holy man', emphasised in his last words commending his soul to God, was likely an additional factor in reproaching the deed. Pagan acts of war were being replaced by Christian values, shown later in the account when one of the victorious chieftains takes up Cormac's head and kisses it and, instead of keeping it as a trophy, gives Cormac's complete body a Christian burial. But in the old pagan stories, an eloquent bard would have sung a praise poem for a fallen king of his province, and such a piece of typically extravagant praise is quoted for Cormac:

'Why should not the heart repine and the mind sicken at this enormous deed, the killing and the mangling with horrid arms, of the holy man, the most learned of all who came or will come of the men of Erin for ever? The complete master of Gaelic and Latin, the archbishop most pious, most pure, miraculous in chastity and prayer, a proficient in law, in every wisdom, knowledge and science; a paragon in poetry and learning, head of charity and every virtue and sage of education, supreme king of the two provinces of Munster in his time.'[38]

The mingling of pagan and Christian should not surprise us. Christianisation was a gradual process; well into the ninth century much of rural Ireland remained pagan; indeed, Leprechauns and other 'little people' are much in evidence today. Conversions had begun before Saint Patrick's time, when the early monastic movement spread from the shores of the Mediterranean and North Africa, and hermits established themselves in small oratories in Ireland. Over time, they gathered followers, eventually developing into monastic communities.

Many of these early Celtic Christians had been members of the Druidic class, and followed a mystic, nature-focused form of worship more akin to that of the Druids, whose characteristic tonsure they retained, along with the lunar calendar for establishing cyclical dates for Easter, and the inclusion of women priests. On the participation of women among the Celtic Christians, a contemporary churchman in Rome commented wryly, "Perhaps they don't have the same temptations as we have." – Perhaps not, because early monks in Ireland followed no rule of celibacy. As monasteries grew in size, and new ones were established in important central locations, they became almost 'townships' incorporating the extended families of abbots, monks, scribes, teachers and everyone else associated with the monastery's maintenance. Celtic Christianity continued to be influential in Ireland into the seventh century before finally being brought to heel by that stickler for conformity, Pope Gregory: both tonsure and calendar were changed, and out went the women.

But the rejection of women in the church was not only a religious ruling; it was part of the dominant patriarchal culture of Rome. Greek and Roman writers had already noted the freedoms that women enjoyed in Gaul, especially the inheritance and ownership of property, considering it a barbaric practice. Ammianus Marcellinus makes it clear that Celtic women were formidable opponents: 'A whole troop of foreigners would not be able to withstand a single Gaul if he called his wife to his assistance, who is usually very strong, and with blue eyes; especially when, swelling her neck, gnashing her teeth, and brandishing her sallow arms of enormous size, she begins to strike blows mingled with kicks, as if they were so many missiles sent from the string of a catapult.'[39] (Interestingly, the neck-swelling and teeth-gnashing are reminiscent of Cúchulainn's physical 'distortions' when battle-rage overtook him.) As Ammianus was a professional soldier, a member of the imperial guard who joined campaigns in Gaul, perhaps he wrote from personal experience, his shins bearing the scars to prove it.

It is possible that ancient records of old Irish lore, sourced by later scribes to make their compilations, were written by monks of the early Celtic Christian church, though none of their original manuscripts has survived.

Later compiling and copying of books was carried out by monks working together in monastery scriptoria. Many copies of the Bible and other religious texts were required for teaching. The most skilful scribes compiled books that would be treasured, considered sacred, perhaps gracing the altar with their richly decorated covers – the antithesis of Druidic reverence for the Word as divine inspiration too hallowed to be written. Such a book was the *Lebor na hUidre* (commonly known as the Book of the Dun Cow) containing, among other pre-Christian stories, the famous *Táin Bó Cuailnge* (The Cattle-Raid of Cooley) believed to have been recorded by Saint Ciaran around 540 AD, though clearly drawn from much older oral traditions.

As with so many events in the prolific blarney of Irish history, another story relates how Senchan Torpeist retrieved the legend from obscurity by addressing the hilltop memorial stone of Fergus mac Roig, one of the main characters. A mist descends, enshrouding Senchan who sleeps for three days and nights, during which time Fergus relates the entire story of the raid which Senchan writes down upon waking.

More generally, the book is attributed to Saint Ciaran, born Ciaran mac an tSaeir around 516 AD; according to legend, he was a local lad whose father was a joiner and chariot-maker in Connaught. He became a religious, was ordained a priest on the Isle of Aran, and later, gathered ten followers to found the Monastery of Clonmacnoise, in Donegal. Plague took him in his early thirties shortly afterwards. Ciaran would have heard old oral tales during his childhood, and legend has it that he inscribed them on vellum from the skin of his favourite brown cow, giving the document its name. The earliest version we have was compiled some 600 years later from various sources now lost to us. The principal compiler, Máel Muire, was a scholarly monk and chief scribe, also at Clonmacnoise. Máel Muire's memory was revered, not least because he traced his descent through bishops, anchorites and pilgrims in a direct line back 500 years, but also because *Lebor na hUidre* was the last manuscript he worked on before he was murdered in a bloody raid against Clonmacnoise in 1106. Some 200 years later, this book had its own 'war story' to tell, caught up in the rivalry and mutual ravaging that took place between powerful monasteries.

Lebor na hUidre was plundered from Clonmacnoise by Connaught men, taken as ransom for one of their fighters, the son of an *Ollamh* of history, who had been captured and held in Donegal after a previous raid some years before. The taking of such a treasured relic of their founder would have been a massive insult, but that the book should be deemed sufficient ransom indicates its value, and it was well looked after. During the 130 years it remained in Connaught, faded lettering was re-inked by Sigraid O'Cuirrndin, a poet and *Ollamh* of Breifne. The eventual rescue of *Lebor na hUidre* is recorded in an introduction to the manuscript: 'A prayer for Aed Ruad son of Niall Garb O'Donnell who carried off this book by force from the Connachtmen, and the Leabor Gearr along with it, after they had been absent from us from the time of Cathal Og O'Conor to that of Ruaidri son of Brian ...'[40]

Lebor na hUidre (Book of the Dun Cow) stayed in Donegal until the sixteenth century, but nothing further is known until it appears in the custody of Messrs Hedges and Smith of Dublin in 1837, and was subsequently bought by The Royal Irish Academy as part of a much larger collection for the knock-down price of 1,200 guineas. During its long history, some words became stained and illegible, leaves were lost, numerous scribes added material, erased whole sections and rearranged pages; in the introduction to his translation, Thomas Kinsella describes it as 'the mangled remains of miscellaneous scribal activities'. It can now be accessed on the internet. Such is the tenacity of Story to withstand the predations of rampage, rape, and time's own corrosion.

Ridiculously easy as it is now to download a translation of the *Táin,* or to pick from a bookshelf any number of stories rooted in the myth, it is sobering to recall the vision, labour, and risk to life entailed in its preservation that we may enjoy the story today.

Power struggles over land and resources, resulting in wars, treachery and acts of revenge within and between provinces were a way of life in ancient Ireland as they were over much of Europe; there are other stories of raids for cattle and hostages, but the *Táin* is the most extensive and elaborate, the best known, and the oldest such epic in western European literature. Considering the manuscript's turbulent history, we should be cautious in interpreting its meaning. Kinsella based his translation principally upon the Book of the Dun Cow – the oldest source – filling gaps or resolving confusion over words from the Book of Leinster and other later documents, but he adds nothing as a storyteller himself, which makes his translation an ideal source for us to delve into.[41]

In addition to the main story of the *Táin,* describing a major attack by the province of Connaught and its allies upon Ulster, the Book of the Dun Cow contains a collection of shorter accounts – *remscél*a – which give the back-stories of significant characters and events in the tale. They explain the mysterious triple birth of the culture hero, Cúchulainn of Ulster; the reason why exiles from Ulster supported the Connaught troops; the grudge that their leader, Fergus mac Roig held against King Conchobar of Ulster, and the illness – the 'pangs' – suffered by Ulstermen that prevented them from fighting until the final decisive battle. In the old oral traditions, all of these stories would have been familiar to their listeners, retold many times with personal flourishes over days or even weeks of storytelling.

An epic of heroic deeds and supernatural intervention amid multi-level conflicts, the *Táin* is a rattling good tale, but it also goes to some lengths to transmit a wealth of cultural knowledge, especially the customs of war and warriors. Each shield and weapon wielded in different combats is described in detail, as is the rich, many-layered battle dress of principal warriors, along with the regalia of each company in Connaught's advancing army and, later, in Ulster's. Each division wears distinctive colours in tunics and cloaks of different lengths; some wear brooches of silver, some of gold – all denote status and fealty. Rules of 'fair play' in war are noted for their breach. Many features hark back to Druidic mythology: the importance of prophesy (each army is accompanied by its seer-physician); the use of Ogham inscriptions as challenges and curses; supernatural intervention, and shape-shifting by figures from out of the *sidhe* – the mounds giving access to the Otherworld of spirits, magic and dead heroes.

The social custom of fostering sons with notable families, with Druids or even with kings for them to be educated in the arts and war-craft in 'boy camps', sometimes in distant locations, is significant to the plot of the *Táin*. The bonds of fostering create enduring kinship which, as the balance of power among chiefs and kings changes, may conflict in later life with political allegiance and loyalty to place. Fergus, an Ulster exile fighting on the side of Connaught, betrays them on several occasions because he is Cúchulainn's foster-father and an Ulsterman at heart. Their mutual promise to retreat from each other when faced in battle is the decisive factor in the final defeat of Connaught. In another example, Ferdia, renowned warrior of Connaught, trained with Cúchulainn in his youth; they are as brothers. When the war becomes desperate, Medb, Queen of Connaught, urges Ferdia to be loyal to his own people by challenging Cúchulainn in single combat, pointing out that, if it is right for Cúchulainn to defend Ulster because it is his mother's province, it is equally right for Ferdia to defend Connaught as the son of a Connaught king. Unconvinced, Ferdia has to be softened with drink and bribed with gold jewellery and Medb's daughter before he agrees. Even then, he is distraught before the combat, and he and Cúchulainn formally dissolve their friendship before their fight begins. During a prolonged battle they are evenly matched, until Cúchulainn finally kills Ferdia with the *gae bolga*, the vicious and deadly weapon unique to him, but he is left severely wounded, exhausted, and weakened by his mourning for Ferdia.

Having suffered heavy losses, both armies are augmented by men recruited from remote areas. Their descriptions echo old myths of earlier races and migrations such as the Firbolgs and the Fomorians whose descendants, usually depicted as strong but brutish fighters clad in rough, unadorned cloth, support one province or another according to their relative advantage. Apart from these, nothing is said of the peasantry and fighters in the ranks; figures for battle casualties are specified only for nobles and warriors, the rest are simply 'countless men'. Like most epics, the *Táin* is a 'celebrity' tale, reflecting a type of feudal hierarchical society where the status and 'honour value' (compensation due for death, injury or offence) of everyone from slave to king is laid down in the Brehon Laws, where warriors and poets are among the elite.

Although there is a separate category of Irish stories – the *dinsenchas* – relating the origin of place-names, many such stories are included also in the *Táin*. Throughout the long march of the Connaught army and the manoeuvres of Ulster's forces towards the final great battle, almost every event gives rise to a place-name in the landscape; some actions seem included purely as a record and *aide-mémoire* to topography. Fords across streams and rivers are favoured places for combat. Water is significant in Irish mythology as a natural element of spirits: the goddess of sovereignty, Morrigan, couples with Dagdha, father of the gods, astride a ford, and Cúchulainn's special weapon, the *gae bolga*, is dipped into the ford to prepare it for use. Launched from the foot, the *gae bolga* is thrust upwards between an opponent's legs from where thirty barbs expand into every limb. On a more prosaic level, fords as a location for combat no doubt reflect also their importance as territorial boundaries.

But the *Táin* is not only about traditional conflicts. In the 'mangled remains' left to us by monastery scribes, the role of Queen Medb appears to demonstrate, and was perhaps intended to encourage, a changing attitude towards the power of women in Ireland since the Church of Rome became powerful.

Although there appears to be no tradition in Ireland of women rulers, of 'queens' as such (Kinsella suggests that scribal misunderstanding of this may account for the depiction of Medb as 'queen' in the *Táin*), strong females abound in the old Irish myths. Scáthac nUanaind, one of two famous warrior sisters, directed a martial arts school on a Scottish island (possibly Skye) and taught many of Ireland's heroes, including Ferdia and Cúchulainn. It was she who gave the *gae bolga* exclusively to Cúchulainn and it won him every crucial victory. The curse under which Ulstermen suffer and are unable to fight until it has run its course was imposed by Macha, the mythical wife of Crunniuc mac Agnomain of Ulster, who boasted that his wife could outrun any of the king's horses. Challenged to prove it on pain of death, he insists Macha races even though pregnant. As a result, she dies giving birth to twins, uttering the curse in her last breath. Only women, boys, (and Cúchulainn, who became a warrior as a child) are immune. Another Macha, Macha Mong Ruadh daughter of Aedh Ruadh of Ulster, listed in the *Annals of the Four Masters* in 377 BC, is credited with raising Emain Macha, a site of great ritual and political significance, and of setting up Bron-Bherg, the first hospital in Ireland. (That early Irish medical practice was in advance of the times in the rest of Europe is well established.[42]) And Medb Lethderg, a goddess of

Leinster, appears as a deity of sovereignty to whom kings must be ritually married in order to legitimise their reign. She 'married' nine High Kings, including the great King Cormac mac Art. Perhaps in some confusion with her, Medb, Queen of Connaught, is depicted as having had several husbands, always replacing one man swiftly with another, but in the *Táin* she is referred to as a 'whore', not a goddess.

Macha puts a curse on the men of Ulster

Queen Medb herself is shown to be 'a forceful woman': she assesses and deploys her troops; leads three battles in her chariot destroying all before her, and is the first to inflict major injury on Cethern, a notable Ulster warrior. As Cethern describes her, 'She had a head of yellow hair and two gold birds on her shoulders. She had a purple cloak folded about her, with five hands breadth of gold on her back. She carried a light, stinging sharp-edged lance in her hand, and she held an iron sword with a woman's grip over her head – a massive figure.' But actions that would be laudable for a male warrior are turned to her discredit. Cethern asks the healer, Fingin, "This great wound here looks grave. What made it?" Fingin replies: "A vain, arrogant woman gave you that wound."[43]

Gender tensions and outright misogyny occur at numerous places in the *Táin*, most of which appear to be later insertions.

The oldest version of the *Táin* opens with Queen Medb and King

Ailill hosting a great army to attack Ulster, enlisting mercenaries and Ulster exiles to boost their own troops and those of their seven sons. No reason is given for the foray, nor would any have been necessary to the audience, there being no shortage of past acts requiring vengeance – including the exiles' grudge against Ulster – and opportunities for manly deeds warranting a share in the spoils of war were always welcome to warriors. However, the later Book of Leinster begins with an account of domestic friction between Medb and Ailill, which implies that the attack stems from Medb's feminine jealousy and avarice. Yet the pillaging of cattle, especially a famously potent bull, would have been sufficient reason for anyone to launch a raid.

> Medb's queenship of Connacht (Connaught) was granted by her father, Eocho Fedlech High King of Erin through eleven generations. But in the undercurrents of conjugal rivalry, King Ailill, the husband she chose from among the royal sons of Leinster, claims an additional right to kingship from his mother, Mata of Muresc, daughter of Magach of Connacht. While not denying this connection, Medb is emphatic about the reasons she chose Ailill as husband-king: because he is her equal in generosity of gift-giving, is as courageous as she on the battle field, and is not jealous of the many lovers she deems her right as a free woman. Such points are scored after Ailill provokes his wife with the comment: "You are better off now than the day I took you." Medb scoffs at this, enumerating the strength of her forces. Ailill retorts that no one is wealthier than he – a claim to superiority she staunchly denies, reminding him that it was she who chose him, and citing the bounteous bride-price she brought to their union. "You are a man dependent upon a woman's maintenance."
>
> To resolve the issue, Medb and Ailill assemble and compare each of their possessions: household utensils, jewellery, clothes, their horses, sheep, pigs and cattle.

Each is equal – with one exception. Ailill's magnificent bull, Finnbennach, the White Horned, is unmatched by one of hers. Worse, the bull was born to one of her own cows, but deeming it no honour to be owned by a woman, had joined Ailill's herd. Medb asks her messenger: "Is there a bull in all Ireland to match Ailill's?" Told of the Brown Bull of Cuailnge owned by Dáire mac Fiachna, a henchman of King Conchobar of Ulster, she sends nine couriers to negotiate the loan of his bull at stud for a year in return for fifty heifers. Perhaps foreseeing resistance among Ulstermen to the loan of their icon, she adds that if Dáire brings the bull to Connacht himself, she will reward him with chariots, choice land to match his own in Ulster, and the enjoyment of her own friendly thighs.

Dáire is liberal in his hospitality and delighted with the offer. Until, later that night, loose-tongued with ale, a courier boasts: "Had Dáire not yielded the bull so readily, it would have been seized by the force of Medb and Ailill and the cunning of Fergus mac Roig." Stung by the insinuation of weakness, Dáire retracts his agreement.

On hearing what happened, Medb responds: "He knew the bull would be taken if not given willingly, and taken it shall be!"[44]

As a result, the *Táin* has become the story of Medb's relentless pursuit of the Brown Bull for her own selfish purposes, leading to the eventual defeat of Connacht at the swords of Ulster after wholesale slaughter on both sides. But the bulls are not mentioned further in either version of the epic until half way through the story, when Connachtmen search for the Brown Bull in Cuailnge, and again at the end in a separate section once the battle is over, when the bulls fight each other. Of course, it could simply be that a page of the story giving Medb's reasons for the raid is missing from the older manuscript, but there is an alternative explanation for the differences in the opening sections. The mythical significance of bulls as symbols of wealth and virility emerged when herding and agriculture became the primary means of livelihood; their stories abound from Europe to Asia and all points between. They are just as likely to be metaphorical in the 'original' account of the *Táin*. At the end of the epic, the bulls fight for days, trampling all Ireland in their struggle for supremacy. Eventually, the Brown Bull kills Finnbennach, scattering from his horns bits of the carcass which confer place-names along his route back to Cuailnge. But before he reaches it, he dies of exhaustion. While neatly symbolising Ulster's final victory – though both armies lose half of their warriors in the process – this closing section leaves a cautionary message on the double-edged nature of power to be immensely destructive as well as constructive.

Cúchulainn, however, is the real hero of the *Táin,* though not without faults. His back-story relates his immense strength as a child, taking up weapons at the age of seven, going to the boy-camp to challenge them in their games uninvited and responding to their rejection by beating them up. His original name was Sentanti; he acquired the nick-name 'Cúchulainn' (literally 'Hound of Culann') after killing a valuable but murderous guard dog in self-defence.

Cúchulainn after killing the hound

The character of a swaggering, conceited youth given to unprovoked violence emerges in the main story along with his heroism, but the larger part of the text relates his invincibility in single combat, defending Ulster alone while his fellow Ulstermen are indisposed. Each of his encounters is described in depth: his ability at shape-shifting, to 'warp' his body to inhuman dimensions in battle-rage; his beauty when dressed to impress the women of Connacht and his honour as a warrior. Only he is assisted in battle by supernatural forces. His chariot, fitted with sickles when he wreaks destruction on the Connaught army in revenge for the death of Ulster's boy fighters, is cloaked in magic that renders it invisible, and Lugh, his spiritual father, emerges from the *sidhe* to heal his extensive wounds.

In many ways, Medb is a foil for him. She alone is blamed for flouting the rules of war by trickery, ambush and bribery during the struggle, yet her husband Ailill is equally involved in these decisions. In the final confrontation between Cúchulainn and Medb, she is placed in the most humiliating circumstances – squatting to relieve her bladder during her menses. Having already killed two of Medb's female healers, and a woman he mistook for Medb, Cúchulainn now spares her, saying, "I do not kill women."

After Ulster's victory, Medb comments on the shame and shambles of the defeat, to which Fergus replies: "We followed the rump of a misguiding woman. It is the usual thing for a herd led by a mare to be strayed and destroyed" – despite the fact that he and other exiles betrayed her at critical moments of the raid, ensuring Connaught's defeat. Medb is also criticised for being unyielding, although retreat in battle was not an honourable act for a warrior. Even the White-Horned bull was said, at the beginning, to be ashamed to be owned by a woman. An odd statement given that a woman's rights to own and inherit land and livestock were long enshrined in the Brehon Laws.

Other 'anti-woman' references are numerous but some of these are likely to stem from different origins. When the war goddess, Morrigan, in her guise as a young temptress propositions Cúchulainn, he spurns her: "It wasn't for a woman's backside I took on this ordeal." And when Fergus and Medb are spied *in flagrante delicto* in the forest, Ailill's aide steals the sword from his scabbard, rendering Fergus without arms (and symbolically emasculated) for which Medb is also blamed. But these latter instances represent the ambivalence of fighting men towards women as objects of desire potentially dangerous to male virility – an ancient fear. In many cultures, taboos are imposed on sexual activity around times of combat, a precaution emulated by many rugby coaches today for the same reasons. We cannot blame the monks for this specific gender conflict, but nonetheless, Queen Medb appears in the *Táin* to have been set up as a means to ridicule the power that women wielded in pre-Christian Celtic society.

The equivocation of scribes in compiling and copying the old Irish stories is clear in the comments at the end of the *Táin* in the later Book of Leinster version. In Irish is written a caution which would have been familiar to the *fili* (the old Druid storytellers): 'A blessing on everyone who will memorise the Táin faithfully in this form, and not put any other form on it.' But in Latin, for the eyes of the educated minority, is a disclaimer: 'I who have copied down this story, or more accurately fantasy, do not credit the details of the story, or fantasy. Some things in it are devilish lies, and some poetical figments; some seem possible and others not; some are for the enjoyment of idiots.'[45]

In their ardent calling to save the souls of unbelievers from eternal damnation – a concept that did not exist in Irish paganism – missionaries have always lassoed the most popular indigenous heroes and heroines, constructing narratives to turn them into saints or at least to convert them to the new religion. In one such story, Saint Patrick visits Tara to preach to King Laegaire mac Niall, fourteenth in succession from King Conchobar the foster-father of Cúchulainn. Laegaire says he will only believe Patrick if he recalls the great hero Cúchulainn out of the *sidhe* into his presence. Cúchulainn appears with all splendour, driven in his gleaming chariot, convincing Laegaire of his identity by relating his victories over demons and serpents, but he states that, despite all of this, the champions of Ulster lie in the pains of hell: "Believe in God and holy Patrick, O Laegaire, that a wave of earth may not come over thee."

The *Ollamh,* Oisín (Ossian), a member of King Cormac mac Art's elite bodyguard the Fianna, and son of its leader, Finn, is also recruited to the Christian cause. In the *Agallamh na Seanórach* (The Colloquy of the Ancients), Oisín returns from a visit to the Otherworld after 300 years, so he is alive, though ancient, during Patrick's time. Oisín and a fellow warrior, Caílte mac Rónáin, relate the deeds of the Fianna, defending their values as generous champions of those in need of protection. Nonetheless, Patrick confirms that they all now reside in hell, not having heard the gospel.

In another tale, King Conchobar's mother is told by a Druid that if her son is born on the following day, it will coincide with the birth of Christ taking place in the East: she sits firmly on a stone to delay the birth. And Brigid, daughter of Dagdha, was so prominent in traditional Irish culture – indeed a goddess ubiquitous among Celtic peoples all over Europe – that she was transformed into Christ's foster-mother as well as a saint. Her pagan festival of Imbolc, the first day of spring celebrating sun and fire, is subsumed in the Christian feast day of Candlemas held in February.

It was Pope Gregory's policy to adapt and incorporate local deities and myths into the ideology of Christian saints, a practice achieved all over Europe and in South America – everywhere missionaries were active. And the monks were skilled storytellers: it was Irish missionaries who revived Christianity in post-Roman Britain colonised by pagan Anglo Saxons, and who travelled on missions all over Europe. Preachers retained sufficient traditional elements in their tales as a convincing bridge from old beliefs to the new, and to entertain their listeners the better to influence them. This has been the case in proselytising all major religions, not only Christianity. All stories have the potential to affect us deeply, to influence our attitudes and behaviours, but the transmission of ideas and beliefs has ever been a dedicated role of myth, exposing Story to manipulation and co-option.

We can understand myths as idealised history, possible even if improbable; as cultural heritage recalling elements of shared experience; as explanation of natural and human phenomena; as moral or ritual instruction; as rationalisation of beliefs and behaviours past and present, and in any of these ways, as propaganda. Indeed, they may all be present in a single myth. Their power lies in combining an element of recognisable experience with imagination, expressed in language and imagery that appeal to deep human consciousness. They are metaphorical in the sense that, like masks, though appearing to hide something, metaphors reveal meaning in new and more vivid ways that penetrate our psyche, perhaps even to vestiges of archaic ancestral memory. Because of this, and despite some myths having truly ancient, even pre-historic origins, they are as fluid and transformable as language itself, especially when transmitted orally. Myths are interpretations of truth as understood at the time – through the prism of the present in each epoch – but they had also to entertain. If the story does not enthral, the myth achieves no purpose.

Myth is special to Story, among her earliest productions of deep truths: the vulnerability and inevitable mortality of humans, our experience of fear and uncertainty, and the need for reassurance and instruction on appropriate action. The universe, and our human society within it, is in a constant state of transition towards a future, and possibly a purpose, which we fail to fully comprehend: a disturbing situation upon which we endeavour to impose some stability. Much of what we 'know', though scientifically reasoned according to each age, is rationalisation mythology.

In this quest, our personal and cultural identity, our place in the present as legitimised in the past, has always been essential to our survival. The current search for roots and forbears – digging around the Internet for missing links in genealogies, no doubt hoping for heroes rather than villains – is a comparatively recent craze in the West. Elsewhere, from the ancient Sumerians to present day Polynesians, ancestors have always been traced back to where time's mist transforms them into gods. So it was in ancient Ireland; mythical figures such as Cúchulainn, Medb, Lugh, and Conchobar were likely real people, perhaps as long ago as 1000 BC, whose lives were celebrated and their adventures glorified and enhanced as much for the joys and thrills of storytelling as for cultural transmission. Coming from the same heritage, the monks understood this process well. But to promote their one supreme deity, their retelling of history more often turned heathen gods into people, as they do in *Lebor Gabála Érenn* (the Book of Conquests) where Macha, a war goddess, becomes a descendant of Noah.

This eleventh-century compilation of prose and verse is an origin myth, constructing a history of Ireland since the Creation. It appears to have two main purposes: to create a common source of pride in heritage which could further Irish unity, and to incorporate pagan gods into a Christian pedigree. Both are legitimised by synchronising events with those in the Old Testament, supported by sightings of such key real happenings as comets, eclipses, and extraordinary weather conditions. Using fragments of stories gleaned from documents spread over a few centuries, the account suffered the corrosion of all its kind, but because it was written principally as Christian propaganda, myths and heroes are slotted in with even more than usual muddle and contradiction; it was, as quoted by one of its authors, 'stitched together' for a purpose. For all that, The Book of Conquests provides the most comprehensive surviving collection of Irish myths, heroes and customs: everyone who is anyone, from the ancient earth goddesses to the High Kings at the time of Patrick, has a role in the action. Described also are the origin and workings of such cultural practices as the '*Boramha*' (the tribute in cattle imposed on Leinster in vengeance for trickery), the various weaves and colours of clothing that denoted social status, and the first occasion that hirelings were paid a wage.

Authenticity is claimed through the mythical figure of Fintan (aka Tuan mac Carrell) one of the first to arrive in Ireland, who survived plague and Noah's Flood and, by transforming himself into various animal forms, lived until Patrick's time to relate his story.

The Book of Conquests is not, of course, reliable history, but the broad brush-strokes of the myth provide a colourful and adventurous illustration of archaeological facts. Three women – the earth goddesses Banba, Fódla and Ériu, all ancient names for Ireland – and their husbands representing, respectively, the hazel (a spiritually significant tree), the plough, and the sun, are already in Ireland when the men and women of the Partholóns arrive from the sea. These immigrants clear more land, invent ale and cooking, and divide the island into four provinces before they die of plague (all except Fintan). Throughout their time, they are repeatedly attacked by a race of dark, crude, misshapen beings they call the Fomorii, led by the giant, Balor – he of the slaughtering eye.

Later, families of Nemeds from Scythia land on the shore in the only vessel to survive from a fleet that sailed from the Caspian Sea. They clear more plains and build forts to fend off the Fomorii who, nonetheless, overwhelm them, extracting swingeing tribute in produce and progeny. In a final battle, most of the Nemeds are killed, the survivors escaping by boat.

After a couple of hundred years, the Firbolg, Gailioin and Firdomnann – the former, supposedly descendants of the surviving Nemeds – arrive in their fleets, and divide Ireland between their five chiefs. Nine kings rule the land before the mysterious presence, out of a deep mist on a mountain, of the Tuatha Dé Danaan under their leader Nuada.

The Tuatha Dé Danaan ('the people of Dana', their founding goddess) came from 'cities in the north of the world' bringing with them highly skilled artisans, poets, physicians, and all the Druidic arts. Among their chiefs are Dagdha with his cauldron and Lugh bearing his invincible sword. In a series of battles – the Magh Tuireadh – they overcome the Firbolg and their associates, granting them the province of Connaught, and later, they defeat the Fomorii, who appear to have inter-married with the Danaans because one of their kings is half Fomorian, and another is the grandson of Balor. Peace reigns for 150 years, until blond warriors – the Sons of Mil or Milesians – sail from Iberia to invade Ireland's southern shores.

These Sons of Mil, say the authors of the Book of Conquests, were the Gaels. The leader of their first ship is killed; they send a second, massive force to take Ireland in revenge. Success in battle and magic between the Sons of Mil, and the combined forces of the Danaans and the Fomorii, swings back and forth. Eventually, they agree to divide Ireland between them: the Sons of Mil occupy all the land above ground, while the Tuatha Dé Danaan will remain below ground in the *sidhe,* the Otherworld.

Although it is feasible that boats of Gaels, or Gauls, from Galicia in Iberia landed in Ireland from time to time, there is no evidence for this final major invasion of Gaels. Having demoted the old pagan gods into human heroes, the Milesians were probably a way for the monks to despatch them from the scene. In an attempt at final annihilation, one of the poet-authors of this origin myth declares that whoever in his heart believes that the Tuatha Dé Danaan still exist in the *sidhe*, will not go to heaven because the belief is displeasing to Christ.

But apart from this, the myth paints on Ireland's canvas, swathes of bright pigments: successions of settlers arriving from the sea, each depositing different skills, artefacts and customs, merging with indigenous peoples (the Fomorians?) and with each other. And it bears a strong family resemblance to the portrait drawn by archaeology.[46]

Once the last ice age receded and the land recovered from subsequent flooding – about 9000 BC – hunter-gatherers moved into Ireland, migrating across land-bridges to most of the country over the next four-thousand years. After them, people of Neolithic culture began to arrive with their livestock and settled-farming way of life. Copious Neolithic rock art of astronomical information in the Boyne Valley, in County Meath, was engraved around 5000 BC and shortly afterwards they began to build their great stone tomb at Newgrange.

Sea trade back and forth brought innovations and the arrival of skilled artisans around 2400 BC. Their work is recognised as the burgeoning Bronze Age in Ireland, an exploitation of resources that requires organisation and social differentiation. In time, high artistry in gold and silver indicates a culture rich in skills and material possessions. Such wealth and power must be protected and from around 1100 BC, there is evidence of a warrior class of high status – Cúchulainn hears his cue and comes raging across the stage in his chariot.

As an intriguing aside: Cúchulainn's original name, Sentanti, was also the name of a Celtic hill tribe inhabiting what is now Lancashire. It was common for people to be known by the name of their tribe and some of their members *could* have crossed the sea to Ulster quite easily.

Since 5000 BC the land-bridge from Britain to Europe had been completely inundated by ice-melt and rising sea levels. People in Europe expanded their horizons by sea travel, not only the fleets of the Greeks and Phoenicians and the earlier, mysterious 'Sea Peoples' that have been recorded, but scholars, traders, adventurers, and families of refugees displaced by conflict, disease, natural disaster and climate change. Sea journeys, though dangerous and often ending in tragedy, criss-crossed the whole Atlantic fringe from the southern tip of Spain to Denmark, southern Norway and Sweden, embracing the coasts of Scotland, Britain and Ireland: ample opportunity for numerous landings and 'conquests' either by intent, serendipity, or shipwreck.

And it now appears certain that many of those peoples who arrived on the Atlantic fringe had migrated there from eastern Europe and beyond the Caspian Sea as Irish mythology relates: in an exciting new development at the end of 2015, Irish scientists sequenced the genomes of a Neolithic woman (3343-3020 BC) from a tomb in Ballynahatty, near Belfast, that revealed her origins from the Near East, and sequencing the genomes of three Early Bronze Age men (2026-1534 BC) buried on Rathlin (a tiny island off the northernmost tip of Ireland) showed a genetic heritage from the Russian Steppes – a wide swath of grasslands to the north and east of the Caspian Sea.[47]

Story followed all of these migrants and is generous and inventive in letting us share their fading tales of oral history, each generation understanding them in their own light, in literature, film, art and poetry.

Historical records from the eighth century leave no doubt about the intentions of much later invaders: Norsemen who found such rich pickings in Irish monasteries and kings' coffers that they set up permanent forts along the coast from which to launch their raids. By 842 AD they had established the town of Dyflinn (Dublin) and ruled over other parts of the country. Finally overcome in the Battle of Clontarf almost 200 years later during the reign of Brian Boru, the first king of all Ireland, their descendants became absorbed into Ireland's medieval Christian history. To hear their skalds – their ancestral poets – tell their own sagas we will have to brave the treacherous currents and icy blasts of the North Sea.

Chapter Five

The fates of champions in long-ships

Story takes to the waves in Norse long-boats, raiding and trading from the Atlantic seaboard in the west to the Caspian Sea in the east and to Iceland in the north, leaving a stream of sagas in her wake to be gathered up by Snorri Sturluson in the Edda.

Unknown raiders from the sea took on a terrifying aspect.

5

But when Thorolf was twenty years old, then Kveldúlf
[his father] made him ready to go a harrying.
Kveldúlf gave him a long-ship, and Kari of Berdla's
sons, Eyvind and Aulvir, resolved to go on that voyage,
taking a large force and another long-ship; and they
roved the seas in the summer, and got them wealth,
and had a large booty to divide.

[Egil's Saga[48]]

K veldúlf (Night Wolf) had made his own fortune from sea-
raiding. Heavily-built and far stronger than other men,
when angered he burst into uncontrollable rages; they
called it *hamrammr* (shape-shift). One of his sons, Skalla-Grímr, a
blacksmith, had this same characteristic and so did *his* son, Egil, who
had inherited his grandfather's physique. Egil was a precocious child,
clever at making up verses, but unruly and wilful even as a three-year-
old. He enjoyed sport and liked to win. Once, when he was beaten at a
ball game by an older boy called Grim, Egil showed temper at losing,
so Grim wrestled him to the ground to prove who was stronger while
the other boys jeered. Egil stomped off the playing field. When he
returned later, he put an axe through Grim's head; he was seven years
old. His mother, Bera, said he had the makings of a freebooter and
should be given a long-ship when he comes of age. But Egil insisted
on joining his elder brother on his raids the following summer.

To its victims, the sudden violence and plunder of unknown raiders from the sea took on the terrifying, almost supernatural, aspect recorded in the Anglo Saxon Chronicle in 793 AD.

> 'This year came dreadful fore-warnings over the land of the Northumbrians, terrifying the people most woefully: these were immense sheets of light rushing through the air, and whirlwinds, and fiery dragons flying across the firmament. These tremendous tokens were soon followed by a great famine: and not long after, on the sixth day before the ides of January in the same year, the harrowing inroads of heathen men made lamentable havoc in the church of God in Holy-island, by rapine and slaughter.'[49]

This first recorded raid on Lindisfarne Abbey, in England, became grist to the Christian mill of conversion as evidence of God's wrath for the local inhabitants' evil ways. With their double-bowed ships, designed for speed and manoeuvrability in narrow fjords, the predators came and went with alarming agility. The English had seen nothing like it. Unpredictable and seemingly invincible, such heathen sea-raiders formed the stuff of nightmares and myths. And so it has been in European folk memory over the centuries: we came to call them 'Vikings'; we fancied dragon figureheads and red-striped sails adorned their ships; we put horns on their helmets. They were 'pagan devils' incarnate and Story, understanding our dread, indulged our imaginations. Since then, Vikings have inspired a multitude of legends, songs and dramas and, becoming fashionably heroic since the nineteenth century, spawned political ideology, wishful descendents, and tourism. But barbarous and bloody as these marauders were – though no worse than their contemporaries – 'the Vikings' were not the homogeneous 'race' rendered in the crucible of folklore.

Apart from an occasional use of the word in Icelandic sagas, no one called them 'Vikings' until the nineteenth century when Romance writers in Western Europe and nationalists in Scandinavian

Europe did so for their different purposes. To the beleaguered Irish at the time they were simply 'foreigners'. Only later did the Irish differentiate them into 'white' (Norwegians) and 'black' (Danes), perhaps on account of their distinctive shields, recognising the armoured menace disgorged from each ship as its fighting crew of thirty to eighty men leaped ashore through the surf. To the Gauls in mainland Europe, they were 'Danoi', fierce tribesmen who invaded much earlier – in the sixth century – attacking from seas and rivers.

These seaborne marauders were Scandinavians from wild and dangerous northern lands later to become Norway, Sweden and Denmark – nations who also raided and fought each other for supremacy. After Norsemen had settled Iceland and the northernmost islands of Scotland, around mid 800 AD, they launched their long-ships from these places, too. Icelanders and Orcadians were among the crews that fought the Irish at the Battle of Clontarf.

Norse migrants and warriors took their stories with them, and it is from Iceland that we learn of the ancient mythology and history of Scandinavia, the heritage shared by Viking raiders. Our principal storyteller is Snorri Sturluson, scholar and gifted poet or 'skald', born in 1179 at Hvammur in western Iceland. Snorri wrote a history of the Norse kings (*Heimskringla*) as only a skald could: the life of each king is told in his own saga and includes many traditional Norwegian tales – history as story to feed our imaginations and emotions. Snorri probably wrote *Egil's Saga*, too. It tells the tale of Skalla-Grímr's family, one of the first to settle Iceland, taking their pillaged wealth with them; old grandfather Kveldúlf died at sea on the way there. They had all fled from Norway after a dispute with King Harold Fairhair (aka Finehair) during which the king had killed Kveldúlf's other son, Thorolf. Friction between the family and successive kings of Norway continued over the years, with a feud between Egil and Eirik Blood-Axe. The dangers of consorting with royals echo Snorri's own personal history – a 'saga' in itself.

Snorri's father, Sturla Thordarsson, a quarrelsome and ambitious chief of noble birth, had acquired much of his wealth from the settlement of law suits against other rich traders and chiefs. In one such case, the defendant's wife attacked Sturla in court with a knife, cutting his cheek. Sturla's compensation demands were exorbitant and the most eminent noble in the country, Jón Loftsson of Oddi, intervened to reduce the sum, offering, as part of the deal, to foster Sturla's three-year-old son. It is open to interpretation whether this arrangement was a sweetener for Sturla, or whether young Snorri was a 'hostage' to ensure that the court's decision held. Either way, Snorri could not have had a better education for a scholar and a skald because Oddi was the foremost centre of learning in Iceland. The school had been set up by Jón Loftsson's grandfather, Saemundr the Learned, after returning from study in Paris, no doubt bringing with him in his long-ship a precious cargo of books and manuscripts well wrapped in sealskins to protect them from the spray.

At Oddi, young Snorri studied ancient Norse poetry and sagas in addition to the lessons on Latin and theology which were customary for the times. And he had acquired significant kinsmen: Jón Loftsson was related to the kings of Norway as well as being a power in Iceland. Snorri spent two years in Norway from 1218, being well received by the fourteen-year-old King Hákon Hákonsson IV and his regent, Skúli the Jarl, both of whom awarded Snorri gifts and honours. Relations were so good that the Jarl gave him the ship on which he sailed back to Iceland. But fate has a habit of allotting double-edged favours – this Norwegian orientation, absorbed from childhood, carried within it the seed of Snorri's ultimate destruction.

Fortunately for us, this came later in Snorri's life and not before he had written his most famous work, *The Prose Edda*[50]; so called because he recreated in prose much of the mythology in poems and songs that existed in a collection called *The Poetic Edda*. This is also referred to as *The Elder Edda,* because the oral traditions it records were written down between the ninth and tenth centuries – at least a couple of hundred years before Snorri's time.

Drawing on this ancient lore, Snorri enthrals us into Asgard, the world of an extraordinary complex pantheon of Aesir (gods) and

Asynjur (goddesses), all with multiple names and powers: the one-eyed Odin or Allfather also known as Tyr, god of war and father of all the gods, and his wife Frigg; Thor, wielder of the thunder hammer with his magic belt that doubles his strength; Loki, fickle mischief-monger and father of falsehoods of gods and men; and the Valkyries, Odin's select maidens who choose which champions inhabit the great celestial Hall of Valhalla. The gods have their own long history of tangled relationships and conflicts resolved by magic or violence or both. Their stories reveal deep characters and mixed motives, each of their various guises changing in the different tales like morphing dream sequences. Only gentle Báldr, a son of Odin but a god of goodness and peace, rarely appears in sagas – where there is no conflict, there is no story.

Bragi, chief among skalds, is god of poetry in his role as Odin's official skald, in the way that great chiefs, kings, sultans and potentates throughout history have been praised, entertained, and even advised by their court poets (an appreciation reflected in Britain today by the appointment of a poet laureate). Although the term 'bragi', denoting 'poet', can apply equally to male or female skalds, 'Old Bragi', whose verses Snorri quotes, is believed to be the Norwegian skald Bragi Boddason, court poet to a line of Swedish kings in the early ninth century. He wrote a praise poem to Ragnar Lodbrók ('Hairy-Breeches') famous for his Viking exploits. Bragi was remembered and deified centuries after his time, much as, in a different era and culture, Shakespeare might have become the god of drama.

And we should not overlook the gods' splendid horses, especially Sleipnir, Odin's eight-legged steed, and Hoof-Tosser which Frigg's messenger, the goddess Gná, rides over sky and sea to perform Frigg's errands. All of the Aesir ride horses except Thor, who wades through rivers; presumably there is no steed strong enough to carry this great god's weight.

Distinct from Asgard is Midgard, the dwelling of mortal man, with Bifrost (the 'rainbow'), forming the bridge between them: it is well-guarded but unreliable because the gods did not build it in full sincerity. In addition, there are the gods' relatives and attendants as well as Rhime-Giants (generally a bad lot), numerous dwarves, and the Norns: female spirits who determine each human's fate according to the Norn's own character – noble or evil.

Snorri wrote his *Edda* as a guide to Norse mythology and as a manual on 'poesy' for skalds wishing to improve their craft. The middle section, *The Beguiling of Gylfi,* relates how Gylfi, King of what is now Sweden, is tricked by one of the Aesir's kin into giving land to Denmark. Conned despite his great knowledge and skill in magic, Gylfi journeys to Asgard to find the source of such cunning and acquire it for himself. Calling himself Gangleri and requesting lodging for the night, he is admitted into the vast Hall roofed in golden shields. The three important men who greet him – King Hárr, Jafnhárr, and Thridi – agree to answer his questions so he might increase his wisdom. Through the ensuing dialogue, Norse mythology is explained and illustrated with stories.

> 'Then said Gangleri: "Where is the chief abode or holy place of the gods?" Hárr answered: "That is at the Ash of Yggdrasill; there the gods must give judgement every day." Then Gangleri asked: "What is to be said concerning that place?" Then said Jafnhárr: "The Ash is greatest of all trees and best; its limbs spread out over all the world and stand above heaven."'[51]

The three roots of Yggdrasill (the Life-Tree) extend into different parts of the cosmos. Beneath one of them is the well of wisdom guarded by Mimir, who is wise in ancient lore because he drinks the well water from the horn of Heimdallr, the Aesir's watchman. One day, Odin came to Mimir, begging for one draught from the well, but he was only allowed it if he left one of his eyes in pledge, so he remains a one-eyed god, though a wise one. Although Odin is the supreme deity, Allfather and ruler over all place and time, even he, it seems, must bargain with life forces. Thor is the strongest of all gods but not the wisest. We create the gods we deserve, investing them with the same bright and dark potential found within ourselves.

In the *Skáldskaparmál,* the final section of *The Prose Edda*, much of the dialogue is abandoned to greater brevity and urgency in the instructions on metaphors and periphrases (*kenning*), creating stories from the myths that give rise to them and illustrating their correct use in skaldship with excerpts of ancient poems from the *Poetic Edda*.

Poetry itself is described with such periphrases as: 'Ship of the Dwarfs'; 'Mead, Gift, or Find of Odin', and 'Kvasir's Gore' – all deriving from its mythical origin when Kvasir, the wisest of all the gods, was killed by dwarves. They mixed his blood with honey, and whoever drinks the resulting mead acquires the skald's craft. Snorri uses the *kenning* 'Odin's mead', in *Egil's Saga*: Egil, the sea-raider whom we met earlier, pursues his grudge against Eirik Blood-Axe of Norway by taking his fighting skills to England in support of King Athelstan, but since Egil is also a skald, he chants a simple lay about the event:

'The Prince requires my lore,
And bound his praise to pour,
Odin's mead I bore
To English shore.'[52]

Although we have only the saga to recount his life, Egil Skallagrimssom was well-known in tenth-century Iceland as a gifted skald; another side to his complex character – he was capable of killing brutally one day and weeping with tenderness the next. This contradiction reflects the fact that Odin, god of war, was also patron of poetry. Skalds may be called 'Vidurr's Shape-Smith', 'Gautr's Gift Finder', or 'Yggr's Ale Bearer', in which all three proper names are variants for Odin from different myths. Story is almost giddy with all the names she can call her own. At times, the periphrasing is so obscure as to defy interpretation; perhaps this was intentional, like the 'deep language' of Druidic bards.

Not surprisingly, metaphors for a ship are rich and numerous: 'Otter of the Sea-Waves', 'Sea-Hart', 'Bear of the Stay', 'Deer of the Sound'. A ship is also called a horse: 'Steed of the Gunwale', and 'Horse of the Leek' ('leek' means 'mast'). The figureheads of long-ships were far more likely to have depicted horses' heads than the 'dragons' of European folklore.

Snorri's enthusiasm for Norse tradition is evident on every page. As if carried away, himself beguiled by the Aesir and unable to resist writing just one more story, he launches into myths and songs even when they seem not strictly necessary to understand a periphrase. He was raised a Christian, and after cautioning aspiring poets against changing metaphors chosen by the ancient skalds, he adds: 'nor, on the other hand, ought Christian men to believe in heathen gods …'[53] But one cannot help speculating whether, on occasion, he wondered about the character of the Norn who had bestowed his destiny: despite his favourable childhood at Oddi, his personal life was overshadowed with problems.

Snorri was still a minor when his father, Sturla, died, and it seems he inherited nothing from his biological family. Instead, in his nineteenth year, his foster-brother and his brother arranged for him an advantageous marriage to Herdís, the only daughter of Father Bersi the Wealthy, the chieftain of Borg. The couple remained at Oddi, and when Herdís' father died four years later, Snorri inherited the Borg estate and chieftainship, acquiring from this power base additional estates and wealth. But his marriage was unhappy. After eight years, he moved to Reykholt in the west, abandoning Herdís and their two children at Oddi, and soon became entangled in a number of love affairs, fathering three other children with different women.

However, Snorri's public life flourished at this time. His growing prosperity and political power led to his appointment, from 1215–1218, as Law Speaker at the *Althing*, Iceland's outdoor judicial assembly where laws were tested and cases heard – a position he held again in 1222 for at least another ten years. Such political clout greatly interested both the young King Hákon and the Jarl in Norway, who anticipated Snorri's support in their colonial ambitions over Iceland.

During these successful years, Snorri expanded his power base by arranging marriages for his three daughters to the most powerful families in the land – a traditional form of alliance featured frequently in the sagas and, as frequently, with disastrous results. But Snorri was then at his zenith: widowed the previous year, he remarried in 1224 'the richest woman in Iceland', Hallveig Ormsdóttir, which proved an affectionate relationship. By this time, Snorri had probably completed his *Prose Edda* and had composed perhaps the most brilliant praise-poem ever made to Norwegian rulers – the *Háttata* of over a hundred stanzas honouring both King Hákon and the Jarl – for which he was rewarded with a sword, a shield and a coat of mail; ironic gifts that sat unused when Snorri later had need of them to defend himself against the giver. But, for the moment, we leave Snorri in his short-lived ascendancy, because around this time, an anonymous skald was drawing upon the same ancient pagan sources in the *Poetic Edda* to create one of the best-known Icelandic tales, *The Saga of the Volsung*. It inspired not only the German folklorists Wilhelm and Jacob Grimm and composer Richard Wagner (for his opera *The Ring of the Nibelung*), but also countless storytellers since.

When it comes to defining form, Icelandic sagas are in a class of their own. Displayed in the *Volsung* story are epic features: miraculous birth, cursed treasure, heroic dragon-slaying and tragic love. But it also contains mythical qualities of supernatural interventions and cultural god-heroes, and there are even aspects of legend in the adventures of later historical figures – epic, myth and legend all woven into an enthralling tale. A partly fanciful account of the Volsung ruling dynasty and its allies and enemies, the saga is not short on drama: some thirty-eight deliberate killings of named characters are perpetrated. But motivation and consequences matter most to Story and these are fostered by personal relationships and their ambiguities – over half of the killings are of in-laws.

The saga begins with Odin – the traditional 'mythical ancestor' of Scandinavian ruling families – and the exile of his son, Sigi, after he was outlawed for murdering a thrall; the killing was an act of jealousy because the man was a better hunter than Sigi.

'Then Odin guided Sigi out of the land on a journey so long that it was remarkable. They continued until Odin brought him to where some warships lay. Sigi next took to raiding with the troops his father had given him before they parted, and he was victorious in the raids. Matters progressed until in the end Sigi was able to seize a kingdom to rule.'[54]

Sigi's Viking career echoes the real history of Scandinavian involvement in Europe. He seizes his land some time during the fifth century in the restless theatre of aggressive kingdoms, migrating tribes and greedy empires competing for land in a continental Europe intermittently ravaged by barbarian incursions from the east. This latter pressure came from a variety of tribes for which the generic term 'Huns' is often used, and whose brutality is laid – probably with justification – at the tent flap of the warlord, Attila. From the south, the weakening Roman Empire launched military campaigns and political intrigue to hold onto its dominion and, in between, ambitious leaders of disparate groups such as Visigoths, Ostrogoths, Gauls, Franks, Burgundians, Saxons and Slavs, sought wealth and power through alliances or by making forays into each others' territory and that of the Romans. The fortunes of each waxed or waned with the vicissitudes of battle and treachery.

Some kings in the *Volsung* saga – for example the Burgundian ruler, Gjuki, (father of Gudrun), and King Atli (Attila the Hun) – were historical figures, though distances and dates are conflated: individuals who lived hundreds of years apart become contemporaries; kings from distant tribes are neighbours. The Icelandic author certainly took liberties with the detailed complexities of European history, but his listeners would have cared not one jot. The saga was not intended as a history lesson. The political atmosphere is real enough, the action representative of the age, and the recruitment of infamous characters such as Attila the Hun give an exciting resonance to the story in a similar way to King Arthur's frequent appearances, often in equally dubious circumstances, within English literature.

Three major themes threading through the saga express not only pre-Christian, pagan beliefs, but also cultural mores that would have existed since our earliest history: the rule of fate, the necessity of vengeance, and the treachery of in-laws.

At the core of the saga are the emotions and motivations of people struggling against predetermined destinies to achieve their personal ambitions. Their desires are thwarted when gods intervene: Odin determines the outcome of critical combats; he also ends the saga, revealing to their enemies the one vulnerability of the last two surviving Volsungs, thus ensuring their deaths. And supernatural forces influence characters' effectiveness by selectively conferring powers of sorcery and prophesy or magic weapons and horses. For men, striving to achieve their goals is straightforward: combat is the answer to almost everything. But strong women in the saga use a wider variety of means: both combat and emotional manipulation employed by Brynhild; witchcraft by Grimhild; cunning by Signy; and the dogged determination of Gudrun who also takes up arms at the end. Even Sigurd's victory over the dragon to gain the treasure does no one any good: the treasure had been cursed during Loki's conflict with the dwarf who made it, the die already cast. The saga ends badly for all of them – as Gudrun observes after killing her husband and her two children by him, and before throwing herself onto their funeral pyre: 'No one can withstand their fate.'

In the Volsungs' world, avenging a death is not a simple matter of spite, of getting one's own back, nor is it entirely explained as a moral notion of 'honour'. Alacrity in avenging a family death is a measure of character. Signy, King Volsung's daughter, has both of her young sons killed because they are too weak to avenge the death of her father and brothers. Deciding that only her own blood line, the offspring of Volsung, could produce an heir valiant enough to perform the deed, she lies with her only surviving brother, her twin, Sigmund, to conceive a son. The boy, Sigurd, is then raised secretly by Sigmund as a future avenger, living in the forest dressed in wolf skins to symbolise the aggression to follow.

Avenging a death demonstrated the courage and skill required of a successful leader capable of protecting his family and defending tribal land. In an age of petty kingdoms and warlords competing for territory and resources, the survival of family and tribe depended on strong men, and it was invariably their mothers and wives – the bearers and sustainers of families – who goaded their men to kill in revenge. Such mettle indicated a good potential husband. Later in the saga, Brynhild praises Sigurd, to whom she is secretly betrothed: 'He was still a boy when he killed the sons of King Hunding and avenged his father and Eylimi, his mother's father.' Brynhild, herself a warrior – perhaps a human portrayal of a Valkyr, for she also has the power of foresight – asks that her marriage settlement be paid in slain men. She cites further proof of Sigurd's vigour in his killing of the dragon, Fafnir, and thus gaining the vast treasure he had guarded. Even in present-day Europe, there are communities where revenge is the only justice.[55]

And troublesome relatives? We should not be surprised by the number of killings involving in-laws. It still remains a tricky relationship capable of stirring 'murderous' thoughts repressed in a multitude of mother-in-law jokes. Exogamy – marrying outside the relative security of one's own circle of kin – was one of the most risky imperatives for early human survival. Essential not only for 'new blood' to continue the lineage, but for alliances with other families and tribes to foster a less threatening political environment, strengthen defence capacity, and increase the potential for seizing scarce resources from weaker groups.

Nonetheless, exogamous marriage, especially among the ruling classes, was a delicate social and political affair fraught with dangers (never mind the personal emotions of the couple concerned). In-laws were putative kin; they had access to one's own hearth with the potential to become the enemy within. If either the marriage or the politics turned sour, treachery was sure to follow. Understandably, the social rules and safeguards for achieving this relationship are many and complex in most cultures. The seeds of disaster are sewn in the *Volsung* when these rules are made ineffective. Grimhild, wife of the Burgundian king, plies Sigurd with spiked mead to make him forget his love for Brynhild and marry her daughter, Gudrun, instead. To cement the union, Sigurd exchanges an oath of blood-brotherhood with Gudrun's three brothers, creating obligations of loyalty as binding as those of a full brother. Later, when rivalry between Brynhild and Gudrun leads to serious tensions, Gudrun's brothers choose their youngest brother – too young to have been a party to the pact of blood-brotherhood – and instruct him to kill Sigurd. In a pragmatic rather than a heroic act, he stabs Sigurd with a sword as he lies asleep in Gudrun's arms. In due course, Gudrun is obliged by her ambitious mother to marry King Atli to boost family prestige, and the conflict-revenge cycle begins again; this time, generated by Atli's envy of Gudrun's brothers, who had commandeered Sigurd's vast stash of gold after arranging his death.

The people we called 'Vikings' knew such old songs and stories of gods and heroes, heard them told by grandmothers at the fireside and chanted by skalds in long-ships and chief's halls. The same heroic characters and themes – with variant names and plots – were known to many of the people they raided or with whom they traded, because the oral origins of their stories were ancient, part of a history of migration and struggle shared all over Europe for more than a thousand years.

A scholar in Northumberland, an Anglo-Saxon, writing perhaps in the eighth century or a little later, drew upon the same heritage for his epic poem *Beowulf*. The setting of the story is early sixth century, roughly the same as the *Volsung*, within what Seamus Heaney described as 'a pagan Germanic society governed by a heroic code of honour, one where the attainment of a name for warrior-prowess among the living overwhelms any concern about the soul's destiny in the afterlife'.[56] In *Beowulf*, petty kingdoms of Swedes (Shylfings), Danes (Shieldings) and Geats (tribes in what is now southern Sweden), along with Franks and Frisians, play out their tragic political history in cycles of feuding and marriage alliances as each grasps wealth and power. Kings are praised by court poets; leaders gain loyalty through their generosity as 'ring-givers' – the throne in the great warrior hall is called the 'treasure-seat'– and heroes slay monstrous creatures:

symbols of the primordial fear of darkness and deep waters. Beowulf, the Danish hero of the poem, performs this feat three times: he overpowers the brutal Grendel in the dark of night, kills Grendel's even more vicious mother in her underwater cave, and in his old age, he kills the fire-breathing serpent, the earth-scorcher guarding its hoard of treasure. But this is not a 'happy ending': Beowulf is mortally injured by the serpent. The poem ends with praise for his life around the funeral pyre, and his people's fearful recognition of their vulnerability now that he is dead.

Like the Icelandic sagas, *Beowulf* depicts unyielding courage in the relentless contest to survive in an unforgiving world, although fate is viewed rather differently. Personal fates dispensed by Norns in Icelandic myth are replaced in *Beowulf* by a common fate – what Tolkien described as 'the undiscriminating cruelty of fortune' – a struggle for life shared by all humanity which can only end in ultimate defeat. Despite other similarities to Nordic saga, the gods are absent. The anonymous author is clearly a Christian – the omniscient Christian god is an underlying presence – but the story neither proselytises nor preaches. Instead, it appears to retrieve and preserve enduring human truths from a distant pagan past.

As usual in epics and sagas, *Beowulf* and *The Saga of the Volsung* tell us only of ruling families. No doubt many of those who took part in Viking expeditions *were* blood-thirsty, gold-hungry chiefs, or high-status exiles displaced by local feuds and power struggles. Snorri records in his history that the 'giant' warrior-commander, Gangr Hrolf, was exiled by the Norwegian king, Harold Fairhair (aka Finehair), and took to sea-raiding in Western Europe. But they also included displaced men banned from society for some crime; the disinherited seeking their own fortunes, and young men, even boys, proving themselves in risky adventure. Such a spirit of exploration led Eirik the Red to colonise distant Greenland, and his son, Leif, to brave north Atlantic currents to the Labrador Sea around 1000 AD and to establish a short-lived settlement they called Vinland (possibly along the St. Lawrence estuary or on present day Newfoundland).

Leif Eiriksson sights the North American coast they called Vinland.

Yet others sought to relieve poverty with the prospect of winning enough silver to buy land on their return. It was not uncommon to launch raids as an annual summer event to supplement a meagre income from the land. The same urge was felt in the windswept islands of Orkney and Faroe as described by the modern skald, George Mackay Brown:

'There were the peasants in every island, a host of them – Mans, and Sigurth and Amund – of mixed Norse and Pictish blood, who year after year dug and drained and reclaimed a new bit of tilth and pasture from the grouse-haunted hills. They, too, suffered a sea change in summer, and were generally at the sacking of some Irish church or English seaport, and came home with wounds and bits of silver on them.'[57]

From around the fifth century, the Scandinavian homelands were being carved up between powerful chiefs, sons of the aristocracy who wielded religious and political authority over swathes of productive land – a limited commodity in a harsh climate over rugged topography. Each community owed allegiance to its chief in return for his protection, especially if they were his tenant farmers or his estate workers – *house-carles* – and many would have had the opportunity, perhaps the duty, to crew his long-ships. Some of these raids were probably small hit-and-run ventures with two or three ships, but later, Norse kings launched massive fleets carrying whole armies to expand their realm and claim tribute, notably the Danes who ruled north-eastern England for fifty years.

Viking forces invaded the Frisian coast (present day Netherlands) and Frankland (France), holding Paris to ransom in 845 AD, and so starting a lucrative protection racket extorting high payments – *Danegeld* – in exchange for peace. Somewhere among that force was the exiled commander, the 'giant' Gangr Hrolf, and he negotiated control over parts of northern France as liegemen to the Frankish king. Better known to us as Rollo, he became a Christian, and established the dukedom of Normandy. Four generations later, his Norman descendants – led by William the Conqueror – turned against England in 1066 for one final, enduring victory. But we are sailing too far ahead of our tale.

Not all Norsemen were 'Vikings' and not all captains of long-ships were pillagers. Norwegian ships loaded with livestock, tools, seeds and families, took settlers to Iceland, Greenland and the Scottish islands. Swedes in their long-ships traded – with and without menaces – in furs, slaves, honey and amber along the Mediterranean as far as Italy, and via the northern route along the Dnieper River to Constantinople, and down the Volga to the Caspian. In this part of Europe they were known as 'Rus', described in 922 AD by Ibn Fadlan (an Arab diplomat of the Baghdad Caliphate serving in the Volga)[58] as 'the filthiest of god's creatures […] they are as stray donkeys.' But if their personal habits offended Arab fastidiousness, they did have other impressive features: 'Never had I seen people of more perfect physique; they are tall as date-palms, and reddish in colour.' Ibn Fadlan comments on the large wooden houses they built on the river bank during their trading missions. 'Ten or twenty of them may live together in one house, and each of them has a couch of his own where he sits and diverts himself with the pretty slave-girls whom he has brought along to offer for sale.' Inevitably, one wonders if Ibn Fadlan was in the market for 'pretty slave-girls' to replenish the harems of his masters. Archaeologists found more than 100 coins from this period in Tisso in Denmark, most of them Arab or Byzantine. Al-Mas'udí, the tenth-century Arab traveller and chronicler also from Baghdad, records Rus raiders fighting their way through the kingdom of Kazarh to trade at Baku on the western shores of the Caspian Sea.

And long-ships plying all of these routes took passengers back and forth between Scandinavia and Europe, not only visiting merchants but also scholars such as Saemundr the Learned, the grandfather of Snorri's foster-father – the one who had studied in Paris.

Through cultural exchange that can result from such extended contact, and not willing to take any risks with their souls, Norsemen began to adopt Christianity and take the new religion back to Scandinavia. Later travellers hired themselves out as mercenaries in the Varangi, the special guard of the Byzantine Emperor, or went on pilgrimages to Rome. Such experiences feature frequently in the old sagas. In the *Orkneyinga Saga*, Rognvald Kolson, Earl of Orkney and an accomplished poet as well as an adventurer with a bloody past, went to even greater lengths in defence of his newfound salvation. He set sail in 1151 with a crew of Norwegian and Orcadian warriors to join the Second Crusade as Christian knights against the Moors in Spain.

By the thirteenth century – deemed by scholars the height of skaldic creativity – Icelandic saga-writers were keenly aware that their society was in transition and incorporated this perspective, along with a measure of the new Christian morality, in a different kind of saga. The outcome of these stories does not depend on gods, magic weapons or spells. *Hrafnkel's Saga,* for example, is a realistic tale told in simple prose. Though written in the thirteenth century, it refers – with varying degrees of historical accuracy – to events around 930 AD before Christianity was widely adopted. In these tales, Story weaves a homespun cloth beside the domestic hearths of Norwegian settlers in Iceland, revealing life's everyday struggles to wrest a living from the landscape while managing relationships with kin and neighbours. *Hrafnkel's Saga* is certainly not a gentle tale – and it centres on the roles of men rather than women – but revenge and succour, loss and gain, or foolishness and wisdom, play out in settings where men sleep in their own beds at night and demand breakfast in the morning; where humble shepherds guard sheep in high-meadow summer grazing, and gossip-women pound clothes at the river bank.

> 'It was in the days of King Harald Fine-Hair that a man called Hallfred brought his ship to Iceland, putting in at Breiddale east of the Fljotsdale District. On board were his wife and their fifteen-year-old son Hrafnkel, a handsome and promising youngster.'[59]

Hard work brings success. Hrafnkel's father expands his property and becomes a leading chief, and soon, his ambitious young son, who has been exploring the area, asks his father to give him the fertile but uninhabited valley on the other side of boggy Fljotsdale Moor.

With productive harvests and good grazing, Hrafnkel prospers, building a large house at Adalbol for his wife, two sons, and his servants. By controlling new settlement in the valley, granting land and protection in exchange for loyalty, he becomes a powerful chief in his own right, imposing his authority also on the adjoining district of Jokulsdale. Though a good manager of his own men, he is a bully, becoming embroiled in many duels and never paying the legal compensation for the men he kills. In his priest-role, Hrafnkel offers sacrifices to the gods and erects a temple to Frey, the god of sun, rain and fruits of the earth, to whom he feels special gratitude. He dedicates to the god his prized possession – a light-dun horse with a distinctive black mane and markings – naming it Freyfaxi (Frey's horse).

Within Hrafnkel's district lives Thorbjorn, a poor farmer with a large family, who reluctantly tells his skilled elder son, Einar, that he must leave home and support himself. Late in the season, the only work available is the lowly, unenviable job as a shepherd living at the shieling (primitive seasonal shelter) in the upland pastures, for which Hrafnkel agrees to hire Einar, warning him that he can ride any of the horses grazing with the sheep except Freyfaxi, because he has sworn an oath to kill any man who rides Freyfaxi without his permission.

A few weeks later, searching for missing sheep, Einar finds Freyfaxi easier to catch than the other horses, and rides him hard all day. Hrafnkel learns of this and, bound by his oath, he kills Einar, burying him informally at the shieling.

Thorbjorn asks Hrafnkel for legal compensation for his son's life, but Hrafnkel refuses because that procedure would place them as social equals. Instead, he offers generous provisions for the family and support for Thorbjorn when he wishes to retire. Thorbjorn rejects the offer, determined to seek formal arbitration.

Everyone warns Thorbjorn that he will face humiliation; he was a fool not to accept Hrafnkel's offer because no one has ever won a case against Hrafnkel. Even Thorbjorn's wealthy brother refuses to become involved because he does not consider himself Hrafnkel's equal and states: "'He's a wise man who knows himself.'" Eventually, Thorbjorn persuades his lawyer-nephew, Sam, to take his case to the *Althing*: the annual assembly of chiefs where cases are heard and new laws passed. No local chiefs are willing to support the case, but two brothers, Thorkel and

Thorgeir Thjostarsson, chiefs attending the *Althing* from distant Westfjords district, agree to sponsor Sam's efforts.

Sam competently presents his case before the appointed judges at the Law Rock as people throng the fields around it. To everyone's surprise (and the secret joy of many) they win their case with support from the Thjostarsson's followers. Hrafnkel is outlawed by the court, becoming a 'non-person' in society, and he rides back to his valley in a fury. A few days later, following up the 'confiscation' procedure, Sam and the two brothers arrive at Hrafnkel's house at dawn, drag him out of bed and, cruelly, suspend him and his men from a beam by their heels. Ignoring the brothers' advice to kill Hrafnkel while he has the upper hand, Sam gives him a choice: death, or banishment with only the few goods Sam will determine. Though it involves great humiliation, Hrafnkel chooses to live, so Sam takes over Adalbol and all Hrafnkel's wealth, installing his uncle Thorbjorn in Sam's own farm further up the valley.

At this point in the story, we may feel some satisfaction that a bully has received his comeuppance, although shown mercy, and that the law has upheld the rights of the meek – even if the outcome did profit the lawyer more than the plaintiff. But our complacency would be premature. We should not expect 'happy endings' from Norse storytellers and this saga is nothing if not a gripping tale of realism – we have yet to arrive at the final climax.

Many seasons pass. Hrafnkel clears forest and labours hard on the small farm at the head of the Fljotsdale valley to which he was banished. He hears that Sam killed Freyfaxi and destroyed the temple, but he accepts this and stops offering sacrifices, saying: "'I think it's a vain thing to believe in the gods.'" Though quieter and wiser, he soon controls the entire district, becoming even wealthier and more powerful than before.

Around this time, Sam's brother, Eyvind, returns from seven years of foreign travel, trading, and serving in the Varangi Guard at Constantinople. He is everywhere admired for his success and outstanding character. Sam sends men and horses to help Eyvind unload cargo from his long-ship and cross Fljotsdale Moor to join him at Adalbol. Later, when she sees Eyvind's party riding by, a woman in Hrafnkel's employ taunts her boss as a coward if he does not avenge himself on such a worthy target as Eyvind.

Hrafnkel takes eighteen fighting men and soon catches up with Eyvind, whose pack horses are delayed in the moor's treacherous bogs Hrafnkel knows so well. Eyvind is warned of his approach by a servant, but refuses to flee from someone to whom he has done no harm. Without a word, Hrafnkel kills Eyvind and all his companions, losing some of his fighters in the skirmish. Sam arrives with his own men, but Hrafnkel has gone too far across the moor for Sam to chase him with any chance of success.

Next morning, Hrafnkel arrives with a large force at Adalbol, drags Sam from his bed, and offers him a choice: death, or leave Adalbol with all its possessions and return to his old farm, living in servitude to Hrafnkel's authority. Sam chooses to live. He is allowed to take with him Eyvind's cargo, but Hrafnkel will pay no compensation for killing Eyvind, because of the cruel revenge Sam took for Einar's death.

A year later, Sam journeys to Westfjords to ask the Thjostarsson brothers for their help. They say that they are too far away. Sam has lost it all by sparing Hrafnkel's life against their advice and, as they expected, Hrafnkel proved cleverer than he was. They are unwilling to risk their position again, but offer Sam land in Westfjords, to live under their protection. Calling them 'small-minded men', he refuses this offer, and their parting gifts. Sam never did avenge himself on Hrafnkel, living in thrall for the rest of his life.[60]

Obviously, a bare summary of plot lacks the emotional depth of the original, which is rich in character, feeling and motivation as well as vivid depictions of place, but the social context of the tale is clear. Justice is not entirely arbitrary in this story: Einar had been warned of the oath, although the punishment seems disproportionate; legal procedures of the *Althing* are followed and, despite Sam's use of torture, mercy is shown by both Hrafnkel and Sam in giving each other a choice of death or banishment. However, the workings of a new judicial 'democracy' through the *Althing* are challenged by the power of individual chiefs, especially one bound by vows to the old faith. And the revenge killing of an innocent man because he is successful and Sam's brother, harks back to ancient blood-feud customs. The story is full of tensions between old traditions and a new moral code. There is no trickery, no use of magical powers or intervention from the gods. The story relates, with remarkable perceptiveness, that power is acquired, not from fate as in the ancient pagan sagas, but through personal responsibility, hard work and shrewdness, but it can be corrupted into maintaining itself at all costs, even by wanton killing, because the powerful can afford to flout the law. A social problem Story knows well and one to which we have still found no certain solution.

Though the saga is set in a period shortly after the *Althing* was inaugurated in the ninth century, Hermann Pálsson, in his translation, suggests that the plot was based on recent events known to the thirteenth-century author, involving the killing of his own nephews in a situation similar to that of Sam and Eyvind. Sagas were usually written anonymously, but because of certain stylistic features and a close resemblance of story details, Pálsson is almost certain that the author was Abbot Brand Jónson, a leading scholar and churchman who played an important role in arbitrating disputes. As a member of the prominent Freysgydling family, the Abbot tried to mediate in a series of fatal family conflicts – events with remarkable parallels to *Hrafnkel's Saga*. It seems that, even by the mid-thirteenth century – in Snorri's time – forceful families in Iceland could operate in near anarchy, disregarding the rule of law and even using the new religion to bolster their positions. In the early days, churches were built and administered by the chiefs as 'temples' had been in pagan times; the first to be ordained as Christian officiates were the rich and dominant men. Snorri's foster-father Jón Loftsson had been ordained as a deacon, as were some of his older sons. Churches began to come under separate ecclesiastical authority only during Snorri's youth.

Another, much shorter prose tale, *Thorstein the Staff-Struck*, also addresses changing values, especially the qualities expected in a chief. Old, truculent and nearly blind, Thorarin is a retired warrior – 'a fierce Viking in his younger years' – supported by his son Thorstein, a strongly-built and even-tempered man who works as hard as three men to maintain their small horse-breeding farm at Sunnudale under the chieftaincy of the wealthy and powerful Bjarni of Hof. Bjarni also keeps horses, tended by his steward, Thord – an arrogant man who affects the reflected glory of his boss.

Thord and Thorstein arrange a horse-fight – a popular sport – and when Thorstein's stallion looks like winning, Thord gives it a vicious blow on the head with his goad-stick. Thorstein retaliates by hitting Thord's horse. In fury, Thord strikes Thorstein with the stick, wounding him over the eye.

Thorstein does nothing, enduring the public humiliation of his new nickname, 'Staff-struck', but his father finds out about the incident and taunts him: "'I'd never have thought I could have a coward for a son.'"

Thorstein goes to the stables at Hof and challenges Thord to say whether his blow was accidental or deliberate, claiming compensation if the wound was intended. Thord jeers at him, and Thorstein kills him. Bjarni has Thorstein officially outlawed by the court for manslaughter, but takes no action to expel him, leaving Thorstein to continue his livelihood and look after his father.

Until, that is, later that year when Bjarni overhears

his two younger brothers gossiping as they work on the sheep. They recount Bjarni's past rigour – killing his own kinsmen when necessary – and question why he now destroys his honour by letting the outlawed Thorstein live. The next day, without divulging what he had overheard, Bjarni instructs his brothers to ride out and return with Thorstein's severed head.

The two men entice Thorstein out of his house into the meadow on an innocent pretext, and first one, then the other, attacks him. But they return to Hof strapped to their horses – Thorstein has killed them in self-defence. Bjarni buries them and all remains peaceful for a few months.

But Bjarni's wife, Rannveig, urges him to take a force of men and avenge his brothers to save his reputation. His followers now doubt his ability as a chief to protect them. He is reluctant: '"No one seems to learn from another man's lesson. Thorstein has never killed anyone without a good reason – but still, I'll think about it."'

Bjarni decides to go to Sunnudale alone, to challenge Thorstein to a duel. Hesitant to take on an opponent so much more experienced and skilled than himself, Thorstein offers to banish himself from the country instead, putting a friend in his place to support his father. Bjarni rejects the idea but allows him to consult the old man – who gives him no sympathy: '"Anybody who offends a more powerful man in his own district can hardly expect to wear out many more new shirts. Defend yourself the best you can."'

The fight is a prolonged and honourable affair during which they break for Bjarni to relieve his thirst, and again to tie his shoelaces; Thorstein replaces their shattered shields, and lends Bjarni a sharper sword of his father's, suspecting the one he brought is not his best. Fate favours first one, then the other. But when both are once again without shields and it is Bjarni's turn to strike, Thorstein asks him to settle the matter finally between them with a fatal blow if necessary. Bjarni replies: "'It would be a great mistake in one stroke both to throw away good fortune and do wrong. In my opinion, I'd be fully paid for my three servants if you took their place and served me faithfully.'"

Thorstein accepts and moves to Hof to work for Bjarni, who installs slaves to run Thorstein's farm and look after his old father.[61]

In this tale, Bjarni's followers challenge his ideas of justice – his preference for pragmatism and compassion rather than blood-revenge and endless feuding – and he has to compromise to retain his chiefly-reputation, but ultimately, his way is influential. The skald ends the story by telling us that after the duel, Thorstein's courage and integrity were respected, and that Bjarni held onto his following as a strong and trustworthy chief. In later life, Bjarni became a devout Christian, meeting his maker while on a pilgrimage to Rome. He was remembered as an exemplary chief with distinguished progeny and he figured in many Icelandic sagas.

Of particular interest to Story is the genealogy attached to the end of *Thorstein the Staff-Struck,* which lists Bjarni's descendants through the female line. In the seventh generations we find our storyteller, Snorri Sturluson, and his two brothers, Thord and Sighvat.

Snorri was much more ambitious and less wise than Bjarni, although fate does seem to play a role in his involvement in Norwegian politics. We left Snorri managing his estates, enjoying political influence and worldly success, but his destiny was about to take a downward turn. Like his father, he initiated a number of court actions, some against members of his natal family; he lost most of them, and made enemies. He had lost his favourite son, Jon, and then in 1236, a number of his relatives launched an armed attack on him at Reykholt, led by his nephew, Sturla Sighvatsson. Snorri had been involved in physical combat in his youth and had developed a distaste for it, which Sturla interpreted as cowardice. Snorri fled to Nes, and the following year, made another visit to Norway.

It was sixteen years since Snorri's last visit and King Hákon was no longer a youth. He now wanted complete control over his kingdom, while Skúli, the Jarl, was loath to yield the power he had wielded for so long as regent. Attempts at reconciliation had been made in the traditional manner – Hákon accepted Skúli's daughter, Margrete, in marriage, and promoted him to Duke – but civil war was imminent and Snorri was caught between opposing sides. Though fêted by both in the past, Snorri's relationship had been closest with Skúli, the older man, and on this visit, he spent two winters staying first with Skúli's son and later with the Duke himself, who quietly conferred an earldom on Snorri, presumably anticipating his allegiance in the power struggle. Suspecting duplicity, and no doubt disappointed that his expectations of Snorri's support in Iceland had not been met, Hákon forbade Snorri to leave the country.

If Snorri felt his danger in Norway, the situation at home had improved as far as his interests were concerned. Earlier that year, his nephew, Sturla, had been killed in combat along with three of his brothers and their father. With this threat removed, Snorri ignored Hákon's orders and returned straightaway to run his estates in Reykholt. From there he would have heard the news of Skúli's election as king by the assembly of earls and the civil war that followed. But Hákon won the decisive battle, and Skúli, now an outlaw, was ferreted out of his hiding place some months later and killed. Snorri might have thought that was the end of the matter, but that would have been naïve.

Whether Snorri had genuinely intended to promote Norway's ambitions over Iceland is unclear; in his Norse history he had championed Iceland's independence. Either way, he had played a dangerous game. But he was not the only Icelander in the pocket of the Norwegian crown. Gissur Thórvaldsson had received an earldom from Hákon, and it was to him that the king wrote in the autumn of 1241, calling Snorri 'a traitor' and instructing Gissur to send him back to Norway – by force if necessary – failing which he should be killed. Gissur had been Snorri's son-in-law, an alliance long overtaken by enmity, and he wasted no time in sending a henchman, Árni Beiskur, to Reykholt. We will never know whether

Snorri was given the option to return to Norway. When Árni found him, unarmed, in the cellar of his home, he felled him with an axe. Snorri was aged sixty-two – an old man for the time, but he might have left us many more stories.

Kveldúlf's advice to his grandson Egil, which Snorri wrote in *Egil's Saga,* seems ironic: 'Just take care not to be too ambitious. Never try to compensate with men greater than yourself, but never give way to them either.'

While acknowledging Snorri's genius as historian and storyteller, the translator of his *Prose Edda*, Arthur Brodeur, is hard on his personal character, dismissing him as either weak, 'or both weak and treacherous', depending on our interpretation of his motives. In this opinion, he draws heavily on the family history, the *Sturlunga Saga*, which has barely a good word to say for Snorri, but it was written by members of the family which became his enemy. And Brodeur was an American, writing in the early 1900s from within a staunchly patriotic nation. Neither national unity nor effective recognition of central authority had been achieved in Snorri's Iceland.[62] Nowadays we have a rather ugly word – 'presentism' – to describe such judgments made in hindsight: it is surely right to praise men and women for the originality and courage to act beyond prevailing mores, but how can we condemn others for following a moral compass set on the same bearing as their contemporaries?

It was an ignoble end to Snorri's temporal life, but his words live on, and there is more yet for Story to share with us from his *Prose Edda*. Through the dialogue in *The Beguiling of Gylf* (*Gylfaginning*) that we looked at earlier, Snorri describes the creation of the world from the Yawning Void to the streams of ice that froze the evil dripped by the Rhime-Giants, and the dismembering of the giant Ymir to form the earth – all following faithfully the original mythology of the *Poetic Edda* in the poems which Snorri recreates in prose. But further to his warning that Christians should not believe in heathen gods, he is careful to set Norse mythology as a whole into an outer frame of Christian history, which he does in the *Prologue* to the *Edda* by giving the gods (the Aesir*)* human origins. He states that

God (i.e. the Christian God) made heaven and earth in which the mythical gods began as human descendants of Noah after the Great Flood. These men became important chieftains in 'Turkland' – an area of Asia somewhere around the Black and Caspian seas. Many generations later, one of their descendants, Odin, had a premonition that he would be the most famous of all kings if he migrated to the northern part of the world. With a large entourage of families and goods, Odin and his people journeyed across Europe attracting a reputation for splendour 'more like gods than men'. They settled for some time in Saxland – in north-western Europe – where Odin set up his sons to rule different parts. Frankland was ruled by Sigi, ancestor of Sigurd, whom we met in *The Saga of the Völsungs*. In similar manner, Odin was welcomed in Jutland, Sweden and Norway, establishing other sons as kings; they took local women for their wives and established their own dynasties. Their success and fame led their Scandinavian descendants to revere them as gods.

If some of this sounds familiar, it is reminiscent of the Irish origin myth in the Book of Conquests: the descendants of Noah, the long wanderings of the Nemeds from the Caspian Sea across Europe and finally to Ireland (except that the Irish monks never admitted to their being gods). It is tempting to dismiss these parts of the myth as a fanciful invention of medieval chroniclers, or as monkish re-writing of indigenous mythology to impose Christian foundations. But Snorri, though a Christian, was no cleric with an alternative agenda. His deep knowledge and love of ancient Norse culture is evident in the vivacity of his storytelling throughout the *Edda;* his intention was to ensure that old traditions were remembered. But his *Prologue* is significant because it supports another intriguing possibility offered by the Norwegian adventurer, ethnographer and story-maker, Thor Heyerdahl.

Archaeological evidence of prehistoric boats dates to at least 8000 BC, but Heyerdahl was fascinated by the similarity between petroglyphs of sickle-shaped boats from around 3000 BC found in caves in Gobustan in Azerbaijan, near the western shores of the Caspian Sea, and those found in Norway carved during the first century AD. He spent many years pursuing his theory that widespread exploration and colonisation of western and northern Europe was undertaken by boat-building peoples who originated from this part of Asia, where complex civilisations already existed in 3000 BC. Navigation of the Volga River from its estuary on the Caspian coast at Astrakhan, offers an almost continuous route to the Baltic Sea and Atlantic shores beyond (the exact reverse of Viking passages hundreds of years later). Heyerdahl cites Herodotus' description of boats along the shores of the Caspian in 500 BC: made of hide stretched around a wooden frame which could be dismantled and carried over land when portage was necessary, boats large enough to carry not only a crew and cargo, but a donkey or two to carry the boat when dismantled. Among the skaldic instructions in *The Prose Edda*, Snorri relates that 'the best of ships' was *Skídbladnir*, made by especially skilled dwarves and given to Freyr, son of Njordr god of the sea. 'It is so great that all the Aesir may man it, with their weapons and armaments … but when there is no occasion for going to sea in it, it is made of so many things and with so much cunning that then it may be folded together like a napkin and kept in one's pouch.'[63]

Vikings carrying their boat

Matching dates with other evidence, Heyerdahl suggests that Odin's travels across Europe to Scandinavia could have taken place during the first century; the listed generations of his descendants would bring us to 800 AD when the historical records of Norse kings begin. With a generous allowance for skaldic exaggeration of the napkin-sized folded vessels, it seems that we could profitably review both Irish and Icelandic origin myths as emanating from the much earlier oral storytelling of an ancient past – storied cultural memory of distant but conceivable histories of migration from the Caspian Sea to western Europe and Scandinavia.

Features shared in both Celtic and Norse myths are common also in many other mythologies: the significance of fire, of runic inscriptions as spells, of treasure guarded by dragons or serpents, and of trees – oak for the Irish, ash for the Norse – and the possession of a cauldron of rejuvenation, even a mention of mistletoe (which does not grow in Iceland). In addition, critical episodes in their stories take place in woods and forests. All of which suggest surviving strands of archaic beliefs formed from a pre-historic desire to understand and ameliorate the natural world. Story weaves those common strands into the diverse myths and tales of each people because they have sustained them over generations in life's unending struggle to inevitable oblivion. And tribal histories bear special significance for populations undergoing migration – an experience fraught with conflict and uncertainty in new environments. Anchoring their past in shared narratives creates links to their places of origin, reinforces identity, and lends legitimacy to the power of their leaders.

The Saga of the Völsung achieves all of these, and it became extremely popular as an oral tale throughout Europe as well as Scandinavia. Of Sigurd, the dragon-slaying hero, the saga-writer says: 'His name is known in all tongues north of the Greek Ocean.' And indeed, it is.

Wherever people move through land and seas be they slaves, fishermen, soldiers, traders, missionaries, refugees, or the insatiably curious, their stories go with them: boasted in taverns; crooned over cradles; traded for lodgings in hovel and palace; and murmured across hammocks on long turbulent nights below decks. Given the irresistible pastime of storytelling, it is not surprising that after hundreds of years of Norse raids, trade, and settlement, we should find common threads from all of Western Europe and Scandinavia woven into the fabric of our stories. Settled enclaves, each ruled by petty kings with allegiance to one Norse power or another, were scattered along the shores of the Irish and North Seas. Ocean currents did not divide these seafarers; they linked them together as communication channels supporting a tight network of alliances or enmities, depending on the politics of the time.

Some historians place the end of the 'Viking Age' in 1066, when

Norwegian forces invading England were decisively destroyed by
Harold Godwinson's army at the Battle of Stamford Bridge and
King Harald Hardrada was killed. But that was not the end of the
story. Fighting on the Norwegian side at Stamford Bridge was
Godred Covan. Of mixed Gaelic-Norse ancestry, he had brought
a contingent from Dublin, but instead of returning to Ireland after
the defeat, he sailed to the Isle of Mann, whose king was probably
a relative – perhaps even an in-law. The Island, Christian for some
500 years, had long been under Norse influence and settlement, its
judicial system – the *Tingvollr* (present day Tynwald) – equivalent to
Iceland's *Althing*. After the king died, Godred seized power himself,
becoming King of Mann and The Isles – i.e. the southern islands of
Scotland. From this strong position he continued harrying, regaining
a hold on Dublin which gave him control of lucrative trade routes
plying the Irish Sea. And he dabbled in local power struggles in
Scotland and Wales – the King of Gwynedd was probably another
relative. Godred's dynasty held power for some 200 years and he
became a figure of legend: King Orry, who slew a dragon that had
plagued the island of Islay.

Recognising the strategic importance of Mann, the Norwegian
king, Magnus Barefoot, later based himself there with almost 200
ships, planning further forays into Ireland. Not until 1265, when
Scottish forces threatened to invade the Island, and King Hákon
failed in his attempt to beat the Scots at the Battle of Largs, did
Norse power come to an end in the North Sea.

So the 'Viking Age', in this part of Europe at least, did not
properly end for another two centuries. But naming it as the 'Age'
seems a British-centric view; Anglo-Saxons were, understandably,
pre-occupied with these 'horned devils', but there was a great deal
going on elsewhere in the world which was equally significant and
bloody. During roughly the same period, Muslim war lords and
competing Caliphates waged war on 'the infidels' from Spain in
the west, to the borders of China in the east. At the same time,
Christian Crusaders' attempts to beat back these 'heathen invaders'
and recapture the Holy Land were thwarted, at times, by Genghis

Khan's Mongol Hordes bent on their own rampage from the opposite direction.

With so many 'heroes' obsessed with their destiny to rule the world, we cannot avoid further slaughter in the tales they have to tell, but for a while at least, Story is heading into Arabia to indulge in marvellous delights inside Bedouin's tents and pashas' palaces.

Chapter Six

1001 tales and as many knights

Story saves Scheherazade's life, and as they reminisce about old Bedouin love stories and popular Chinese tales they become caught up in the Islamic expansion, the Crusades and the Mongol hordes. But they survive to tell their tales to the troubadours.

Scheherazade was renowned not only for her beauty,
but also as a scholar of philosophy and literature.

6

*I wonder, sister, says Dinarzade, where you learn so
many fine things. – You shall hear a great many
others to-morrow, replies Scheherazade, if the sultan,
my master, will be pleased to prolong my life farther.
Schahriar, who longed, as much as Dinarzade, to hear
the sequel of the story of Douban, the physician, did not
order the sultaness to be put to death that day.*

[Arabian Nights]

The power of Scheherazade's storytelling saves her life. The
characters, too, often gain redemption through telling
their own stories. Even Schahriar, the sultan who holds
Scheherazade's life in the balance each day, is freed from his self-
defeating obsession against women by listening to her stories.

On the 'one hundred and twenty third night', Scheherazade
begins the humorous tale of little Hunchback, the favourite buffoon
or court-jester and storyteller of the sultan of Casgar.

> 'There was in former times at Casgar, upon the utmost
> outskirts of Tartary, a tailor that had a pretty wife whom he
> doted on, and was reciprocally loved by her. One day, as he
> sat at work, a little hunch-back came and sat down at the
> shop-door, and fell to singing, and playing upon a tabor.
> The tailor took pleasure to hear him, and resolved to take
> him into his house to please his wife.'[64]

Hunchback's sudden and mysterious death implicates the tailor, a Jewish doctor, a Mussulman (Muslim), and a Christian merchant, each of whom believes he inadvertently caused the death, and secretly offloads the corpse to the unsuspecting other. The sultan, fond of his little jester and eager to whip off the head of his murderer, is so enthralled by the extraordinary account from each of the 'accused' that he exonerates them. But the story is extended for sixty-two nights by frames within frames, as a barber and each of his six brothers take up aspects of the event and continue convoluted tales of their own. This is all deemed to take place around the corpse of the unfortunate Hunchback. Eventually, the ancient barber rubs vigorously at Hunchback's neck with a special balm and he is revived, coughing up a fish bone that had lodged in his throat as a consequence of arriving at the tailor's house drunk and accepting the hospitality of a fish dinner – Arabian audiences of the Middle Ages preferred happy endings to their tales of uncertain fortune and rolling heads.

And so, Scheherazade's life is saved for another day, but in the outer frame of the stories we learn that her storytelling arises from a far more heroic motive than self-preservation in a tight spot. We are told in the prologue that she was renowned not only for her beauty and virtue, but also as a scholar of philosophy and literature and one of the best poets of her day. Being the eldest daughter of the sultan's grand vizier and chief administrator, Scheherazade was aware of the disaster that had befallen the kingdom, leading its citizens to despair.

> Schahriar, hitherto an exemplary and popular sultan, had discovered that his wife had been unfaithful. Indeed, he had returned unexpectedly one day to see her and her attendants indulging in a sex orgy in the palace gardens with her black slaves. A similar betrayal had also recently been suffered by his brother, sultan of Samarkand, who happened to be visiting him. Commiserating with each other, the two brothers convince themselves that 'there is no wickedness equal to that of woman'. Yet marriage is

necessary. So Schahriar hits upon a somewhat drastic plan to reassert his self-esteem and protect himself from betrayal by future wives. He decrees that he will marry a new wife each day and have her strangled the following morning.

The grand vizier is ordered to procure the young brides: first the daughters of generals, then those of lesser officers, and finally, as the supply of higher status women runs out, the daughters of ordinary citizens all meet their fate of a one-night marriage. Saddened by this terrible loss of young women's lives, Scheherazade asks her father to offer her as a bride to the sultan. The vizier is appalled at the thought of losing his beloved daughter and, even more horrible to think of, it is he who has to strangle the wives each morning. He tries to dissuade her with the wisdom of two old animal fables to show the folly of her request. Though listening respectfully, Scheherazade insists on the marriage, hinting to her grieving father as he takes her to the sultan that he may rejoice rather than regret the deed – for Scheherazade has a secret scheme of her own.

She asks the sultan for the company of her younger sister, Dinarzade, to sleep in their bedroom – a perfectly reasonable request to which he agrees – and, as the two girls have planned, it is Dinarzade who wakes her sister well before daylight, asking her to tell a story, until Schahriar is hooked on hearing what happens next. As the arrival of each dawn leaves a story suspended at a crucial point, Schahriar delays Scheherazade's death until the next day.[65]

When we discover the ancient storytelling heritage that gave rise to these tales, we better appreciate their enormous popularity in the East and later in the West, which still continues. Though not intended as children's stories, for many, Christmas is incomplete without Sinbad the Sailor, Aladdin's magic lamp, or Ali Baba with his gang of forty thieves transported, as if by a mischievous *jinni*[66], from the medieval caravans and caravels of Arabia onto the stage of the local Palladium. Our journey is a long one, starting with those caravans raising dust along the Silk Road.

Story had long wandered through the lands of Asia with migrants and travellers, with traders, slavers and pirates coast-hopping between India and the Mediterranean. But when the Royal Road was established by the first great Persian Empire (the Achaemenids) around 500 BC, and extended laterally as the empire grew, Story had a fast route from northern Persia to Turkey, south through Mesopotamia (Iraq and Syria) to Egypt, and east to India. We saw in an earlier chapter that animal fables from India, Persia and Greece had bumped into and influenced each other; many of them would have trotted along these paths. Herodotus was greatly impressed by the Persian courier service which had post-houses at regular intervals along these roads for changing horses while their riders, no doubt, entertained the local populace eager for news and tales from afar. Efficient though this communication system was – and it lasted a couple of centuries – the empire became too vast to hold intact, and after Darius III decentralised his government, the empire was unable to resist the predations of Alexander the Great.

Alexander continued to protect the Royal Road, finding it equally convenient for trade and conquest, and even after his death, his influence and that of his generals and successors spread east to the borders of China. Commerce is ever the infiltrator of barriers, and it was the Han Dynasty, reaching out to export its silks, spices and perfumes in the second century BC, which incorporated the Persian Royal Road as a main artery in an extensive network of routes from the cities of northern China, across central Asia and the Middle East, and through to the Mediterranean, sending goods to Europe, India and Africa, and establishing the route that became known to us as the Silk Road (or Silk Route).

Silk was highly prized in the West. Rome's appetite for the new sexy textile seemed insatiable, despite certain macho views of the fabric as 'poncy'. Being sharp traders, Chinese merchants increased their prices, inciting what is perhaps one of the earliest instances of industrial espionage: that sly emperor, Justinian, is said to have despatched two spies disguised as monks to penetrate the Chinese administration and smuggle back silk worms. From such nefarious beginnings arose a profitable Byzantine silk industry.[67]

In the meantime, as long as the main circuit of the Silk Road and its by-ways were secure from barbarian banditry, trade flourished; a wide range of goods were bought and sold – and stories told – at towns all along the routes. Those merchants of Arabia who lived in coastal towns were no novices to travel and trade by land or sea, and they took full advantage of the burgeoning commerce all around them. In the Arabian interior, Bedouin traded between the desert oases and ports, and sometimes further afield. With their tented, semi-nomadic lifestyle, they followed grazing and water for their sheep, cattle, camels and horses, and perhaps sowed a casual crop of millet. Though the strength and support of extended families was essential for survival, it was insufficient for security, so they affiliated their clans into independent tribes each ruled by a dynasty of chiefs. Tribes forged alliances with other tribes for mutual protection, or broke them when offence occasioned revenge: as elsewhere, marriage could create allegiances or accumulate unreliable in-laws. For this reason, marriage within the tribe – between paternal cousins – was a favoured arrangement. New blood was brought in by female battle trophies enslaved as second or third wives whose children, if they were lucky and accomplished, might be freed and accepted into society.

Such were the origins, according to his own verses, of one of Arabia's best known pre-Islamic warrior-poets and storytellers, 'Antarah ibn Shaddād al-'Absi ('Antarah, son of Shaddad of the Absi tribe), born in the middle of the sixth century. As in Celtic and Nordic cultures, for gifted men to be both poet and warrior was not unusual. From later compilations of his work, we inherited the stories and romantic poems brought together in *The Romance of 'Antar,* elements of which have since found their way into many other tales still told today.

As the preferred form of storytelling passed from clan to clan and generation to generation was oral, we might never have known

'Antarah's story except for the chance that one of his poems, a long epic of war and love based on his own life, was preserved in a collection of seven (in some editions ten) prized Arabic poems entitled *al Mu'allaqat* – literally, poems 'suspended' or 'hanging'. Several legends claim to account for this title, but the most likely interpretation is that it implied the metaphor of jewels dangling on a string; the poems lingering, in similar fashion, in the mind.[68] It is largely from this 'autobiography', no doubt spiced with poetic licence, that we learn the poet's own story as well as details of Bedouin life in sixth-century Arabia. Pre-Islamic religious beliefs encompassed a number of deities and spirits, some of whom would have been specific to particular tribes. The Ka'abah, the ancient black granite and marble polytheistic temple built in the form of a cube in the centre of Mecca, was a popular site of pilgrimage drawing worshippers of its various gods from tribes within Arabia and beyond. Communities of Christians, Jews and Zoroastrians (the state religion of the Persian Empire) had also settled in towns and cities in and around Arabia, principally as merchants or artisans.

> Shaddād, 'Antarah's father, was an influential member of his tribe, the Banu Abs; his mother, Zabibah, was an Ethiopian slave taken in war. By custom, her son took her status as a slave, a lowly position compounded in that society by inheriting her dark complexion. Perhaps to counter this double disadvantage, 'Antarah becomes a skilled fighter, hardening his body while working in the hills with livestock. In his tenth year, he kills a wolf that is attacking his father's sheep, and recites a poem about the event. Soon, he kills another slave for insulting a helpless old woman tending her flock; a deed that wins praise from the tribal chief for 'defending women's honour', and admiration from female relatives, including Ibla, his paternal cousin with whom he falls deeply in love. He composes many verses extolling her beauty and the passionate anguish it arouses in him, describing her in

traditional images as 'an amorous fawn', 'like the moon at its full', and compares her radiance to that of the sun: 'The sun as it sets, turns towards her, and says: "Darkness obscures the land; do thou rise in my absence."'

In his determination to win his freedom and claim Ibla as his bride, 'Antarah performs many noble and daring deeds in hunting and war, gaining the respect of his tribe's warrior elite, and he asks his father to release him from slavery. Shaddād, angered, draws his sword against him, forcing 'Antarah to win further battles and renown until his reputation as 'the father of horsemen' can no longer be denied. Ibla returns his love and they are betrothed, but her father's hopes of avoiding a penniless ex-slave for a son-in-law are clear in the massive dowry he demands in silver, livestock, slaves, and a rare breed of camel owned by a fierce tribe in the north.

Many challenging encounters follow 'Antarah's attempts to gather the dowry by raids and ambushes far afield, while back in his tribal lands, treacherous acts by his future in-laws seek to keep him from his bride-to-be. After vanquishing an enemy for King Chosroe II (Chosroe, or Khosrow, was King of Persia, Egypt and Syria from 590–628 AD), the king rewards him with gold, gems and other goods to more than complete the dowry. 'Antarah returns home and gives his entire fortune to his father and uncles; his generosity and nobility know no bounds – not that it prevents further devious moves by Ibla's family to stop the marriage. Eventually (after almost 1,500 pages of trials and adversity), a glorious wedding feast is held to which all 350 Arab tribes are invited. Much gift-giving and celebration precedes the arrival of the bride:

'And now Ibla was clothed in the most magnificent garments, and superb necklaces; they placed the coronet of Chosroe on her head, and tiaras round her forehead. They lighted brilliant and scented candles before her – the perfumes were scattered – the torches blazed – and Ibla came forth in state.'

A traditional happy ending, though with a bitter note in the last line:

'All present gave a shout, while the malicious and ill-natured cried aloud, "What a pity that one so beautiful and fair should be wedded to one so black!"'[69]

'Antarah and some of the other poets featured in the *Mu'allaqat* were probably still living – though advanced in years – when Islam was revealed to Muhammad through visions of the archangel Gabriel beginning in 610 AD. Three years after the gradual revelation of the Qu'rān began – and it took twenty years of intermittent meditation in the desert – Muhammad started to preach in his home town of Mecca, supported by a small following from among his family and members of his clan, Banu Hashim. Banu Hashim was allied to the powerful Quraish tribe which ruled over Mecca and was custodian of the Ka'abah, from which it gained considerable income from pilgrims. Opposition of Quraish leaders to Muhammad's new monotheism became open persecution, and he fled north with a group of followers – a flight known as the *Hegira* – to Yathrib (present day Medina) where he built his first mosque. During these years of exile inter-tribal conflict increased, with Muhammad's followers launching revenge raids on Quraish trade caravans and on their clans. Violence escalated to an assault by the Quraish on Medina with a large force in 629 AD (8 AH in the Islamic calendar which dates from the *Hegira*). By this time, Muhammad, in his sixtieth year, had gained sufficient converts among other tribes in Arabia to defend Medina and retaliate with a bloody conquest of Mecca, breaking the power of the Quraish and their Jewish allies. Muhammad died three years later, naming his cousin and son-in-law, Alī, as his *walī* and executor of his will. The word '*walī*', which implies granting authority, can mean either 'friend' or 'saint'; such unfortunate narrative ambiguity has led to centuries of conflict and bloodshed between Sunni Muslims, who interpret his action as a purely administrative, family matter, and

Shi'i Muslims who believe that Muhammad gave Alī the authority to succeed him as a prophet.

Muhammad would have been raised with the old Bedouin stories – a small boy sitting respectfully at the back of the tent with his young cousins, listening to their elders until the boys' eyes grew heavy and sleep overtook them where they sat. Allusions to traditional stories appear in the Qu'rān, only briefly because everyone would have known the tales. Although 'Antarah's stories and poems have been extended, embellished, re-interpreted and almost re-written since his time – not least by Muslim storytellers – we are able to delight in their original flavour thanks to the eighth-century scholar, Al-Asma'ī.

A gifted teacher at the Basra school of philology, Al-Asma'ī compiled the collection *The Romance of 'Antar* through the efforts of his students, but more significantly, he was dedicated to the preservation of authentic pre-Islamic literary traditions. His other works included over fifty treatises on natural science, ethnography and literary criticism – a work load likely to leave a fellow isolated with little time for social relationships and he remained a bachelor, despite the efforts of a friend to alleviate his loneliness by buying him a slave girl as a gift. According to this story, the girl refused to stay with the unfortunate Al-Asma'ī because he was too ugly. But romance was clearly not absent from his lonely academic soul: he preserved for us the fated love between Khaled and Djaida. The story has some similarities to that of 'Antarah and Ibla, but in this case, the lovers' separation is caused by a family feud and their own pride. And it reveals a different aspect of Bedouin womanhood: Djaida is strikingly beautiful and accomplished in the arts, but she is also a champion fighter excelling the skills of any warrior in her tribe, and the two mothers play pivotal roles in achieving the union – 'Antarah was a staunch supporter of women.

'Moharib and Zahir were two brothers, by the same father and mother; the Arabians call them "germane". Both were eminent for their courage and daring. But Moharib was chief of the clan, and Zahir was his minister, subject to his authority, giving him counsel and advice. It happened that a violent dispute and quarrel arose between them. Zahir retired to his tent, sorrowing and not knowing what to do. "What is the matter with you?" demanded his wife. "Why are you troubled? What has happened? Has anyone displeased or insulted you – the greatest of Arabian chiefs?"

"What am I to do?" said Zahir; "he who has injured me is one I cannot lay hands on, or wrong; my companion in private, my brother in the world. Oh, if it had been another, I would have shown him what kind of man he was at odds with, and made an example of him before the chiefs of our people!"

"Leave him in the enjoyment of his possessions," cried his wife, and, to persuade her husband to do this, she recited verses from a contemporary poet, dissuading a man from accepting an insult even from his parents. Zahir accepts the advice of his wife.'

Zahir leaves with his pregnant wife to settle with an allied tribe. When their child is born, they keep secret the fact that their baby daughter, Djaida, is a girl so that Moharib will not have cause to gloat over them. They publicly name the child Djonder, and Zahir trains her in the skills of war, exposing her to the hardest experiences until, in her male disguise, she can win any trial of combat. Meanwhile, Moharib's wife has a son, Khaled, who turns out to be a handsome boy, a dedicated warrior, spending his time riding through the desert with his tribe's champions.

Khaled hears of Djonder's fearsome reputation and learns that he is his cousin, but not till his father's death are he and his mother free to make a reconciliatory visit to his uncle Zahir accompanied by many gift-laden camels. After a warm welcome and some days of sociability and sport, Khaled greatly admires the character and martial prowess of his cousin (who retains her male identity). But in her tent that night, Djaida confesses to her mother that she is deeply in love with Khaled; "'If my cousin should leave without taking me with him, I shall die of grief at his absence.'"

The mothers confer and agree that the two cousins make a perfect match. Khaled's mother tells him Djonder's true identity as Djaida, and of her love for him. "'Nothing is so perfect as she, nothing lovelier and more attractive. Hasten, my son, to see your uncle and ask him for his daughter in marriage. You will be happy indeed if he grants your prayer.'"

Khaled, confused, accustomed to a warrior's life and with no desire for 'the weakness of a woman' astonishes his mother by fleeing back to his tribe.

After such a rejection, Djaida is heart-broken and indignant in equal measure. Seeking revenge to calm her anguish, she waits till her father is absent on a campaign, and rides out in fighting gear and further disguise to participate in military exercises at Khaled's tribal camp. Accustomed to strangers visiting for this purpose, they ask no questions, and she triumphs in all her combats. With her identity still unknown, she finally challenges Khaled as the leader of the warriors. Both protected by visors and body armour, a fierce contest continues all day, ending inconclusively and not doing Khaled's reputation much good. Next morning, Khaled passes his unknown opponent who is ready mounted, and begs to know who he is. Djaida lowers her visor: "'I am your own cousin Djaida, who offered herself to you; but you refused her – from the pride you felt in your passion for arms.'" Vindicated, she turns her horse and speeds back to her own lands.

Regretting his earlier churlish behaviour and now helplessly smitten with Djaida, Khaled seeks help through his mother and aunt, but Djaida replies to them: "'Never.

I would rather taste the cup of death. What occurred at his tents has quenched the fire of my grief and unhappiness.'"

At his mother's suggestion, Khaled gathers a large troop of allied sheiks and warriors, explains to them the entire Djonder-Djaida situation and, waiting until his Uncle Zahir returns from his expedition, they ride out to tell him what has happened in his absence, that the secret of Djonder is now known, and Khaled demands the hand of his daughter in marriage. Zahir, ashamed of his deception, recognises that matters must now be put right. '"She shall be married to her cousin as soon as possible, for of all the men I know, he is most worthy of her."' And he sets a reasonable dowry of five-hundred brown, black-eyed camels, and a thousand camels loaded with the choicest products of Yemen. Under pressure from her father's expectations, Djaida assents to the marriage, adding a condition of her own: '"I shall not enter into his tent until he undertakes to slaughter at my wedding a thousand camels among those which belong to Gheshem, son of Malik, 'The Brandisher of Spears.'"' [and traditional enemy of her tribe].

Undaunted, Khaled performs all that is asked of him. All is now set for the wedding. But on the first day of festivities, Djaida discovers that Khaled has gone with a party of slaves to kill lions for the banquet and she delivers her final test.

Dressed in military gear, she challenges him at the cave – the lion's lair where he is about to hunt – and overpowers him. Uncertain of her motives, Khaled asks: '"Have you come here merely to prove to me the extent of your valour?"' And she replies: '"I came solely with the purpose of helping you hunt wild beasts, that your warriors might not reproach you for choosing me as your wife."' And with this, Khaled finally understands the character of the woman who will share his life. With united purpose, they both successfully bag their prey, and Djaida returns swiftly to her tent, leaving Khaled to take credit for the kill.

The feasting is magnificent; amid great rejoicing the pair are married, and both men and women exalt the name of Djaida.[70]

In a fascinating comparison, a couple of centuries after Al-Asma'ī, a post-Islamic writer took key features from both of these well known traditional stories – 'Antarah and Ibla, and Khaled and Djaida – to tell a different love tale, that of Miqdad and Mayasa in which resolution is achieved, not by extreme bravery or by overcoming personal pride through mutual understanding, but by conversion to Islam. (There is an echo here of the distortion of traditional Irish myths by Christian monks.) As in the originals, poems feature frequently among the prose and often at length – warriors even chanting verse as they charge into battle – but we can identify Islamic elements and characters as they crop up throughout the story.

The hero, Miqdad, is poor and of low status, not because he was born a slave like 'Antarah, but because his father died leaving him no inheritance and he is brought up 'by his old mother'. (Muhammad was orphaned at the age of six and although brought up by his Uncle Talīb, it seems he was never a wealthy man – one of his traditional sayings is: 'Poverty is my pride'.)

Miqdad harbours a secret passion for his beautiful cousin Mayasa, the daughter of the tribal king. Mayasa was not raised as a boy like Djaida, but had been taught martial skills as well as horsemanship and writing: 'She emerged as a brave and skilful fighter and an admirable poetess'. When a party of powerful Quraish warriors from Badr (site of the historic battle and final victory of Muhammad over the Quraish) arrives in camp for military contests in a bid for Mayasa's betrothal, Miqdad begs his mother to borrow fighting gear from his aunt so that he can take part. He is Mayasa's paternal cousin and no one can deny his right to compete for her hand. The Quraish warriors mock Miqdad's old nag of a horse: "'This fellow is riding a bull!'" He charges them, roaring a war-cry that scatters them all. Then he challenges Mayasa who is mounted and competing in the combat, but the process is different from Khaled's battles with Djaida: after a long duel, Miqdad unseats her with the butt of his spear and sends her sprawling. She accepts defeat at the hands of such a skilled and heroic cousin and declares her willingness to be his wife if he fulfils her father's conditions.

As happened to 'Antarah, her father is angered at her choice of a 'penniless youngster' over the distinguished leaders of the Quraish and, hoping to prevent the match, he demands an extortionate dowry including a special breed of camels, huge quantities of gold, silver, and rare perfumes of musk and camphor. Like all good heroes, Miqdad accepts the challenge and goes off to secure this fortune by one means or another.

And now, King Chosroe is also brought into the story. Miqdad hijacks a caravan of rich trade goods belonging to the king as it approaches the city. Furious fighting ensues with guards and sheiks sent by the frantic vizier of the royal court to trap the raider, but when Miqdad is eventually captured and taken before Chosroe, he tells the king his life story. Love and valour are irresistible. After testing the hero's bravery against hundreds of his own crack troops, the king is so overcome by admiration and sympathy that he lets Miqdad off, even adding massive amounts of his own wealth to help the young warrior secure his bride.

An amusing new detail not in the other two stories reveals that, then as now, those with the power to do so are neither slow nor subtle in manipulating the market to their advantage. The reason for the vizier's anguish is that he has already closed the shops, forbidding merchants to sell anything until the king's trade goods arrive – when the caravan is hi-jacked, he stands to lose his commission if not his head.

Miqdad has been away longer than anticipated and as he approaches his tribe's camp, he learns that Mayasa's father, assuming (and hoping) he is dead, has sent Mayasa away to be betrothed to Malik, another tribal chief. Miqdad chases off into the desert to intercept her caravan with its armed escort and, against all odds, ambushes them, rescuing his promised bride. During the long camel trek back to their tribe, Miqdad is celebrating his victory with poems to his love – and not a few boasts of his own strength – when an armed rider emerges from the desert dust and Miqdad challenges him. "'Not so fast young man! I am the Meccan champion who uses his sword to fight in the holy war, Abu'l-Hasan 'Ali.'" (Muhammad's son-in-law and cousin.) At his name, our brave hero trembles and Ali soon has him at his mercy, but promises to spare Miqdad if he converts to Islam.

However, more treachery awaits them at home. Miqdad and his uncle are tricked and tied up by Mayasa's father so that Malik can kill them in revenge for ambushing the caravan, and then marry Mayasa himself. The resolution to this major disaster is the fervent praying of Miqdad's mother as she mounts a camel to ride to Medina for help. God hears her 'and folded up the desert for her' so that she reaches the Prophet in his mosque and tells him her whole story. He sends Ali to their aid. The two captives are freed and fight alongside Ali in a fierce battle which routs their enemies (echoing Muhammad's conquest of Mecca with the support of Ali and his Uncle Talīb). Both Malik and Mayasa's father refuse to convert to Islam and are beheaded.

A 'happy ending', but not with a wedding celebration, about which both 'Antarah and Al-Asma'ī would probably have been disappointed; instead, we are told that Miqdad became one of the Prophet's companions and fought in the 'Holy War'.[71]

The enmeshing of fantastic and magical deeds would have been exciting to a medieval audience, as it is to many modern ones, and especially to Muslim listeners and readers because all amazing and marvellous events, natural or supernatural, are acclamations of the omniscient power and excellence of Allah. Fantasy and fact routinely mingled.

Miqdad and Mayasa's tale is in a collection of stories in a much weathered and incomplete manuscript – a fourteenth- or possibly sixteenth-century copy of an earlier original – discovered by chance in 1933 in an Istanbul library. The first English translation, by

Malcolm C. Lyons, was published by Penguin Classics in 2014 as *Tales of the Marvellous and News of the Strange* – using as a title the heading at the beginning of the manuscript in the absence of a lost title page. In his introduction to the translation, Robert Irwin suggests that the original stories may have been written in the tenth century in either Syria or Egypt, and a later compilation commissioned by a high official whose Arabic name, unfortunately, is no longer legible.

The name of the compiler, too, is absent, but the manuscript is described intriguingly as a collection of forty-two tales (half of which are now missing) 'from a well-known book' – we can only guess which book it might have been. For Miqdad's story, the author clearly drew upon *The Romance of 'Antar*, adding subplots and details, but only a few of the tales are focused around Bedouin conversions to Islam; others are stories of merchants, caliphs (Muslim rulers), seamen, *jinn*, and women temptresses and tricksters: vibrant characters inhabiting a much earlier collection which may have been the 'well-known book'. This older collection known as *Alf Layla wa-Layla* ('A Thousand Nights and One') contains stories in Arabic which were derived and translated from original tales in Pehlevi (Middle Persian). At least eight of the stories in *Tales of the Marvellous* are variations on tales in *Alf Layla,* but in *Marvellous* they lack the elaborate, overarching framing of stories by Scheherazade's predicament: each tale, though it may contain stories within it, is entirely separate. Some of the tales, too, incorporate known historical figures, including Miqdad in the tale above and even a Christian saint, along with references to knowledge only a well-educated author or compiler would possess: it seems that the collection was put together for a cultivated patron rather than for popular storytelling, and we can leave it as a fascinating by-way along the trail of our search for the dawn of those Arabian nights.

So where did *Alf Layla wa-Layla* and the character of Scheherazade come from? The historian and traveller Al-Mas'ūdī (893–956 AD) – native of Baghdad and Arabia's answer to Herodotus – mentions a Persian work which he describes rather censoriously as 'full of untrue stories' titled *Hazār afsāna* ('*A Thousand Tales'*), and that it had been translated and adapted from stories in Sanskrit, Syriac and even Greek. Among the original Sanskrit tales were those from the *Panchatantra* and the cycle of stories about Dr Bidpai and the irascible King Dabschelim whom we already met. There were not, in fact, 1,000 stories, more like 200 because others were contained in the framing – stories within stories within stories – which was a characteristic feature of these storytelling traditions. One of the Persian adaptations appears to have been the introduction of Persian characters for the outer frame. Scheherazade is a Persian name, '*Šīrāzād*' ('nobly born'), and legends link it to royal genealogies over centuries; the names of the sultan, Schahriar, '*Šahriār*' ('prince-king') who rules Indian and Chinese territories, and his brother '*Sāhzamān*' ('king of the age') king of Samarkand are also Persian.[72] Their story is set in the time of the Sassanid Empire, the last Persian dynasty before its conquest by the Abbasid Arabs around 640 AD. And like the original Sanskrit stories, they were used for education as well as enjoyment; there was even a claim that Alexander the Great knew the *Hazār afsāna* and noted its value for instruction. As a boy he had been tutored by Aristotle, remember; he knew the power of Story and he loved books as well as conquering as much of the earth as he could reach.

Arab translators and writers in Cairo and Baghdad retained the framing characters of the Persian editions, but made so many adaptations and added such a wealth of new stories that *Alf Layla,* and especially later versions of *A Thousand and One Nights*, are justly considered to be Islamic literature. Scholars have continued to argue through the centuries over which of the tales were Indian, Persian or Arabic in origin, but that was of little concern to avid audiences of the time: *Alf Layla* had been circulating through eager hands in the Arab world since at least the ninth century. We know this because of a dedicated and diligent bookseller of Baghdad, Muhammad ibn Ishaq al-Nadim (who died around 995 AD).

Al-Nadim, a respected scholar, bibliophile and copyist, took over his father's bookshop in Baghdad, one of over a hundred in a city which had become a significant cultural centre with a flourishing book trade under Abbasid Islamic rule. Selling books was not simply a matter of buying in stock: first they had to make the books, meticulously hand-copying manuscripts and binding them attractively for sale. Paper from China had already been fluttering along the Silk Route for several hundred years, recycled as wrapping to protect delicate merchandise from the convulsions of caravan transport, and then for writing because it was so much cheaper than silk or vellum. Whether or not the legend is true, that the secret of paper making was wrung out of Tang Chinese prisoners after the Battle of Talas in 751AD, mass production techniques were developed in Baghdad's own paper factories soon after this date. Notable scholars in the city had well-stocked libraries of books when they were still expensive and rare in Europe.

Al-Nadim's great contribution to literature, and to the biography of Story, was his creation of the *Fihrist al-'Ulum*. To call it a 'book catalogue' woefully underestimates this treasure and the painstaking labour it must have entailed. He not only listed, but also summarised and sometimes critiqued the contents of every book in the Arabic language that existed during his lifetime, adding author biographies and provenances. Entries cover every conceivable subject, including – with tolerance unusual for the age – works by minority sects, Christians, Jews, and other religions and cultures, as well as works of ancient Greece and Rome translated into Arabic (incidentally preserving valuable knowledge that might have been lost to us forever if these Arabic texts had not found their way to Europe and been translated back into Latin). Significant letters, leaflets and documentary fragments did not escape the *Fihrist* either.[73] It was the first time such an undertaking had been achieved and it allows us a fascinating glimpse of Story's tenacity in bringing us the spectacular adventures of *The Arabian Nights*.

Al-Nadim knew the *Hazār afsāna*, describing it as 'truly a coarse book'; the same opinion was held of *Alf Layla* by intellectuals of the time, not because its tales of fantasy, love, travel, crime and humour were often racy but because, apart from poems and a few narrative passages, the language was colloquial rather than the learned style of 'literature'. These were stories for the people and demand for them outstripped supply, encouraging others to tap the vigorous story trade. Al-Nadim mentions one such writer, Al-Jahshiyari who, perhaps thinking that the promise of a 'thousand stories' in *Alf Layla* when in fact it contained less than 200 was cheap market hype, set out to put together a full measure of 1,000 stories from the same varied sources, but doing away with the framing structure. Unfortunately, he died before he had reached beyond 380 tales and his anthology has since been lost. Perhaps, like the manuscript of *Tales of the Marvellous*, it will one day be found among cobwebs in a forgotten library cupboard. Any librarians reading this would do well to have a look in the far corners of the basement.

But who were these avid ninth- and tenth-century readers and what was the great attraction of these tales? Even for those who could read for themselves, oral storytelling was a feature of Arabic culture, a favoured pastime and an inspiration; professional storytellers snapped up the opportunity for new wonders to captivate their audiences in coffee houses, in alcoves of bazaars and around their pitches outside mosques. The stories of *Alf Layla* depicted a magical past, a relief from daily toil, but also a glimpse into a glorious heritage which people could only imagine from the surrounding dusty ruins of ancient civilisations they sometimes used as sources of building stone. The histories of the pyramids in Egypt and of the palaces of Palmyra on the ancient caravan route through Syria, for example, were not known to the people who drove their donkeys and camels past them or sold their wares alongside them; they could only guess at the incredible wealth they suggested – the subject of covetous speculation. And there was comforting familiarity and humour in the absurd or wicked deeds of cunning merchants, wily doctors, and ingenious artisans; the unpredictable power of sultans and caliphs; the mischievous *jinn*, conniving old ladies and sensuous young girls. These were more exciting for urban audiences than simple desert love stories.

*Illustration of
Arabian Nights tale
'Abu Hassan and the
Caliph'.*

The same emotional core was still there – love, conflict, jealousy, treachery, and the envy of unimaginable riches – but characters were more urbane, settings more varied at sea and in cities, women more stereotyped, and fate immutable. And they were funny as well as wondrous. Plot possibilities came from far and wide: Arab merchants, diplomats and scholars travelled throughout the known medieval world, and many wrote of their experiences – Ibn Battuta, Al-Mas'ūdī, Ibn Rustah and Ibn Fadlan to name a few. Their accounts of foreign exotica were eagerly sought after and no doubt woven into existing tales.

And the misfortune of others at the hands of fate – to which all are equally subject – was a source of great amusement for it also held hope: fate could just as easily deprive a king of his power or grant a fortune to an idle good-for-nothing. All is at the hands of Allah. The darkness of night was not so much the domain of monsters as of magical transformations, and in daylight, endings are invariably 'happy'. This is a different kind of fatalism to that in Icelandic sagas where personal fates are predisposed by the Norns and stories often end in tragedy; in the Arab society of *A Thousand and One Nights*, fate can neither be negotiated nor resented, but must be accepted with good grace and the formula uttered at every personal disaster: 'God is great'. A belief in predestination was not confined to the devout; it is a recurring theme in the verses of the eleventh-century Persian poet, Omar Khayyâm, who was a man of science, a scholar of Greek and a religious sceptic.

> 'The Moving Finger writes; and
> having writ,
> Moves on: nor all thy Piety nor
> Wit
> Shall lure it back to cancel half
> a Line,
> Nor all thy Tears wash out a word
> of it.'[74]

Despite the frequent repetition of Allah's greatness, the *Nights* are not overtly moral tales with dramatic conversions to Islam, except in the diffuse and more relaxed sense in which Islam was ingrained in the tales as it was in real life. *Jinn*, too, were 'believers'; if naughty pranks ventured into wickedness they could be restrained within their own hierarchy. Christians and Jews tended to be typecast, though depicted with no great rancour; sometimes the butt of jokes – but so are Muslims and even caliphs on occasion. No tale was too fantastic: the more awe and wonder, the greater the credit to Allah. Because 'fiction' was not a recognised genre of Arabic writing at the time, fantasy merged with fact, especially to a credulous populace. The feats of the *jinn* on glamorous islands or in strange cities held equal plausibility to those of human characters.

Street storytellers probably ended a session at a critical point of tension in a story, as the authors of *Nights* had done, so that their audience would return for further 'tellings' which could go on almost indefinitely. Even after the sultan in *Nights* finally realises that his hatred of all women is misplaced and abandons his murderous scheme, choosing instead to take permanent delight in Scheherazade, an inspired storyteller would invent further beguiling tales. We can imagine his listeners, their day's work over, the cacophony of the market silenced, clustered around him with upturned faces in the cool dimness of evening, a single hanging oil lamp glancing light on the storytellers features and gestures as he animates each character. Late-comers sidle in from nearby alleyways, a stray dog curls up under a wall, and Scheherazade entices the sultan with another intriguing tale that might preserve her life for one more day.

Varying editions of the *Nights* continued to appear in the East well into the fourteenth century. Europe had to wait a few hundred years more for Antoine Galland, a French scholar of classical and oriental languages, to translate and publish *The Tale of Sinbad the Sailor* from a manuscript he chanced upon in Constantinople. Fairy tales being all the rage in France at that time, *Sinbad* was so popular that he quickly published twelve volumes of *Les mille et une nuits,* issued between 1704 and 1717 (the last volume posthumously).[75] English translations immediately followed which, like Galland's, edited out 'immoral' elements, and cut out poetry that had interspersed the original prose. Not until 1885, when Sir Richard Burton privately printed the first volumes of his own unexpurgated translation, could Victorian readers brave enough to do so in the seclusion of their own boudoirs appreciate the full flavour of the *Nights*. Few were better qualified for the task than Burton: among other accomplishments, he was an explorer, ethnographer, linguist, diplomat and spy extraordinaire – his erudition spiked with a generous measure of imperialism. He spoke fluent Arabic, having spent many years in the Middle East and India disguised as a Muslim, even completing the *hajj*, the pilgrimage to Mecca and Medina, in 1853.

Circulating a private printing issued by a formal institution was the only way to avoid the fate of publishers who had already fallen foul of the Obscene Publication Act of 1857; Burton set up the Kama Shastra Society for the purpose and got away with distributing 1,000 sets, each of 17 volumes (comprising *The Nights* and *The*

Supplemental Nights), though they were poorly printed abroad and full of typos. Burton had a consuming interest in cultural sexual practices; while anthropologists of the day measured the width of heads, he measured the length of penises. With his translation of the erotic 'how-to' volumes *Kama Sutra* and *The Perfumed Garden*, his reputation took on legendary proportions with claims of homosexuality and murder – none of it true, though gossip he often encouraged by his own egoism. So he was no shrinking violet in such matters, and keenly aware that in Islamic society, sexuality and every other bodily function was treated as a natural occurrence, another gift of Allah and not something to be smirked at or hidden. In regular editions of *Nights*, a woman's maidenhead is 'abated'; in Burton's edition she is 'shagged' or 'futtered' (a word of Burton's own invention from the French, *'foutre'*).[76]

Victorian society cultivated double standards in love and lust, though it was not all Queen Victoria's fault. She was probably more fun than the stuffy times allowed known. Although she is unlikely to have owned a copy of Burton's translation under the censorious eyes of her royal household, it would be pleasant to think that, feeling the absence of both Albert and John Brown, she allowed Abdul Karim, the Muslim Indian secretary she befriended, to entertain her with his own renderings of Scheherazade in the cosiness of her study.

Although the excitement of *Nights* tended to overshadow other Arabic writings, Story was enjoying her freedom in new, home-grown, prose short stories: a form called '*maqama*', literally 'standing', which suggests they were intended for oral recitation. Like *Alf Layla,* these appealed to ordinary people rather than to the intelligentsia, written for entertainment but with a light-hearted message for 'self-improvement'. Most included some verses, perhaps to give them a bit more 'class', and they were written as a series. Principal among these storytellers was Al-Hariri (1054-1122) of Basra, with his fifty short tales of the likeable rogue, Abū Zāyd al-Sarūyi, and the narrator who tries to reform him and convert him to Islam. Abū Zāyd is an educated man and a master of disguise, going about town as a luckless tramp, using his eloquence to con money out of people he meets. His ingenuity results in surprising and humorous adventures with a large cast of characters, the last story showing him in old age finally giving up his disreputable life-style.

The series was a bestseller. Al-Hariri personally signed 700 copies and there would have been many more unauthenticated volumes – a considerable demand for a book copied by hand in the absence of the god of marketing and his social media attendants. Although a well-known *adīb* – a connoisseur of literature and languages – Al-Hariri's *maqamat* may have been inspired by characters met during his day job: he was head of intelligence and communications for the secure courier network that operated throughout Islamic states. Story-forms spread through the same extensive web; *maqama* appeared in North Africa, Spain, Sicily, and some were even written in Hebrew.

The demand for 'fantastic' stories, in a culture where 'fiction' as a category did not yet exist, encouraged another narrative form – *risāla*: first-person narratives composed as 'personal correspondence'. Initially, these related sporting and warring escapades but soon expanded in both content and imagination, blurring the boundaries between *risāla* and *maqama*. Listeners and readers wanted amazing stories of 'real life', preferably humorous ones – they still do – and the means to satisfy them diversified and thrived. Authors freely purloined verse, prose and proverb from any sources available to them without thought to crediting originals; numerous collections overlap in content, the authorship of each piece too muddled to verify with any certainty, and fantasy jostles promiscuously with fact.[77] Some modern popular magazines, and certain newspapers it is not necessary to name, follow an ancient tradition in this regard.

Quite independently, new forms of prose short stories for *hoi polloi* flourished in the towns of eleventh-century China, too. In the *Hangchow* – the 'multi-media' entertainment quarter of cities, usually beside the marketplace – people could enjoy drama, music, acrobatics and puppet shows, or they could listen to old Buddhist tales and dynastic histories amply seasoned with ghosts, magic and other flights of imagination. And they could challenge the *shuo-hua*, the itinerate teller of tales, to improvise a story on a theme called out by a member of the audience – interactive storytelling in which smart repartee was expected. *Shuo-hua* performed in a highly competitive profession: only the most agile acting, tension-filled plots, and intriguing originality would draw a crowd willing to throw enough coins on the cloth to make a living.

But in China, fiction was not a new genre, although since the third century it had played a specific and limited role in the culture. Known as *hsiao-shuo*, literally 'small talk', it was applied to fables and anecdotes in a similar way to ancient Greece: to illustrate highbrow discussions on philosophy. According to a writer of the time, Chuang Tzu, scholars were 'winning honour and renown by means of *hsiao-shuo*'[78], but it was not for entertainment and the tales were gleaned from traditional sources, including India, because intellectuals disdained to write such frippery.

The first emperor, Shih Huang-ti, had taken a dim view of all writing: in 213 BC he attempted to burn every book in the land. But the Tang Dynasty (618–907 AD) brought something of an 'enlightenment' to literature and language, reviving the older, more compact and direct Confucian forms of expression in which brief stories – *ch'uan-ch'i* – were submitted for the 'composition' paper in the official imperial examinations for those seeking to qualify for the civil service. Students were required to demonstrate their narrative skills and command of language by creating *ch'uan-ch'i*. These romances, so concisely structured that they resemble modern short fiction – even flash fiction – escaped from the examination halls. In the eighth century, they became popular fiction in their own right among the educated minority, branching out to include adventure and satire as well as love themes.

By the eleventh century, after 200 years of woodblock printing had made books cheap and accessible, and literacy of the general population had been actively encouraged, stories in a vernacular, colloquial style became stories for the people. They had been developed orally by itinerate storytellers, collected originally into

*A student before the
Chinese examinations Board.*

hua-pen – 'story prompt books' – and were revived, adapted with new plots and characters, and published to a wide readership.[79] Story's freedom would later be curtailed, but for the time being, she flourished in a China that, since the Tang Dynasty, had exerted huge influence over Central Asia. China had further developed international trade by sea and silk routes; established diplomatic relations with the Tibetan and the Abbasid Empires; and hosted within its cosmopolitan cities, communities of traders and scholars of many states and faiths.

But beyond the Chinese frontiers, Islam rose unabated. By the twelfth century, Islam in one form or another had spread by adoption and conquest to occupy an area bounded by China in the east and Spain in the west, and from the Caspian Sea in the north to the Horn of Africa in the south. Because of its all-encompassing doctrine, Islam – literally 'submission' – had a profound effect upon cultures and their stories. 'Submission' was originally intended to be spiritual, to the will of the Master, Allah the Merciful, as the one omniscient god, but where there is no distinction between sacred and secular, submission becomes inseparable from domination by worldly power under masters less merciful. Possibly, the consequences are less for a culturally homogeneous population, but towns of the medieval period, especially those along the Mediterranean and east-west trade routes, were fast becoming multi-cultural communities. In the early years of Islamic rule, other religions were tolerated, though subject to additional taxes and other restrictions. But later, while praise of Muhammad and

Allah blossomed into new poetry, art and music, old traditions were destroyed. The intellectually open, rational, science-oriented principles of the Abbasid Empire, which had saved so much ancient European scholarship by translations into Arabic, began to wane under caliphs with a narrow religious vision. Stories were re-written and new legends created in the inevitable desire to control the narratives that define people's lives.

One of those narratives is the righteousness of blind obedience to the 'just cause' of violence against other faiths – a theme frighteningly familiar and contemporary – but Islam had no monopoly in this respect.

Western Europe only took notice of what was happening in Asia when the Byzantine Emperor asked Pope Urban ll for help to stem Seljuk Turkish invasions. Ironically, the Turks had converted to Islam even as they plundered and conquered Arab-held territories and were charging into Christian Byzantium – the eastern remnants of the Roman Empire. In 1095 AD, at a speech in the Frankish (French) Kingdom directed at church dignitaries and the powerful nobility, the Pope asked for their support against the Turks, adding the desirability of 'rescuing' Jerusalem which had been under Muslim control since the seventh century. Jerusalem was the lost chord that called the Crusaders into existence and to arms. But it all began in a murderous shambles.

Few events in European history have created more legends and fantasies than the Crusades. The mission to launch a Holy War against 'the enemies of Christ', variously called Turks, Tatars, Muslims, or Saracens, captured the imaginations of a religiously superstitious population, most of them poor and oppressed in a feudal system in which wealthy, powerful nobles grabbed land and intrigued against each other and the monarch of the day. The populace barely knew in which direction lay Jerusalem, but a deep well of frustration was tapped and turned into violent hatred by the impassioned preaching of a French cleric from Amiens known as Peter the Hermit. Before the nobility had had time to complete preparations and provisioning for the first Crusade, Peter the Hermit was leading a rabble recruited from across Europe to defeat the Turks with sticks and pitchforks. Impatient for action and beyond their instigator's control, they reached no further than Germany before finding unsuspecting scapegoats and began murdering Jews. Without provisions of their own, they pillaged towns en route – many were killed by incensed locals. Unsurprisingly, the hardy remnants of this People's Crusade that finally penetrated into enemy territory were annihilated by well-armed Turks in the Battle of Civetot.

This much is fact, but it has been glorified and imaginatively elaborated in legends over the centuries. One set of stories depicts the so-called Children's Crusade in 1220, shortly after the fifth official Crusade had failed to capture Egypt. Two young heroes feature in these legends, both of them, by coincidence or by pious association, were said to be shepherds. Nicholas from Cologne intended to convert Muslims to Christianity by peaceful means, expecting that the sea would part to allow him and his companions to enter The Holy Land for this purpose. His followers, youths and adults, reached no further than Genoa where the sea remained intractable, by which time the majority had died on the journey, the rest returning home or settling where they were. Stephen, from Cloyes in France, claimed to have a letter from Jesus for the king of France. Many who joined him believed they, too, could perform miracles, but enthusiasm fizzled out in Marseille and most returned home, disillusioned. Many versions and copies of these stories have been written since, often with strong pious intent to offer examples of Christian heroism and sacrifice, although there is no certainty that such crusades took place.[80] More likely are gatherings and marches by poor, disaffected youths rather than children. Legends of Children's Crusades express the religious righteousness of the times and perhaps a need for heroes of common clay – Story weaving a place in events for the peasantry whom history too often forgets.

The recapture of Jerusalem during the first official Crusade in 1096 was romanticised in the poetic style of the period in *Chanson d'Antioche*. According to legend, the poem was begun by Richard de Pélerin while taking part in the eight-month siege, but the original has been lost and the story remains only in a later collection of *chansons de geste* compiled in the twelfth and fourteenth centuries. Although four French nobles led their knights and armies on the first crusade into The Holy Land, the *Chanson d'Antioche* – as epics tend to do – established one of them, Godfrey of Bouillon, as the hero of the hour, the Christian knight par excellence. His heroism continued to attract popular attention and in the late thirteenth century, a shortened prose edition of his story was aimed at a wider and less patient readership because, according to the author, 'it seems to me that rhyme is beautiful but very long'[81]. A significant departure from the supremacy of verse, this was one of the first works of prose 'fiction' in France, a form that would soon become popular elsewhere in Europe.

Godfrey became the first European head of an Eastern state, ruling over Palestine as Defender of the Holy Sepulchre. The second crusade was a failure, but later attempts (the ninth and last official crusade was launched in 1291) had some successes, although early gains were lost during the Islamic counter-campaigns. It became harder to fund and inspire new crusades; much of the religious fervour was diverted by the temptations of wealth, trade and power, as knights turned into petty kings of the feudal states they had established for themselves in the Middle East. These 'Crusader States' seem to herald later colonial aspirations, although by 1291, they had all been re-conquered by Muslim leaders.

Nonetheless, Story had embedded a popular image of courtly knights in shining armour as icons of all that is

Guy of Warwick, a legendary knight.

gallant and virtuous, defenders of faith and country, slaughterers of dragons, and rescuers of maidens in distress; a motif which influenced literature and storytelling for centuries, defining the age of chivalry. Historical facts are less romantic. The legendary superiority of mounted knights in battle – a belief cherished by the nobility because it entrenched the feudal system that supported their private armies – was not borne out in practice. The realisation that disciplined ranks of bowmen and pike-men were more effective in warfare than mounted swordsmen opened a crack in the shield of feudalism.[82]

A restraining factor on the success of later crusades was the increasing hazard of crossing areas in the east under threat of the last bloody climax of this era.

Like a malign typhoon from the mountains, gaining momentum across the wild, open, steppes of Central Asia, Genghis Khan led his Mongol warriors on a rampage across Asia, and eventually to the rich grassy plains of Hungary and Lithuania in Europe. Before the fifth crusade, Mongol armies had already conquered Turkistan in one direction and crossed China in the other. These dedicated horsemen of the plains were less successful at sea. In 1274 and again in 1281, Genghis' grandson, Kublai Khan, sent huge fleets to conquer Japan, but his attempts were thwarted by storms; their wrecked boats are now being discovered off the coasts of Kyushu and Takashima Islands.[83] But for raging seas, the prose and poetic writings of Kamo no Chomei – his famous essay *Hojoki* and his *Hosshin shu* stories of hermits like himself – and Murasaki Shikibu's novel, *Tale of Genji*, might have been destroyed and lost forever along with other early Japanese literature.

Baghdad, the cultural centre of Islam where Al-Nadim had catalogued every work of learning, had no such protection from the Mongol Horde. Story wept as the waters of the Tigris ran black with ink from thousands upon thousands of books and manuscripts tossed into the river. The city of books was burnt to the ground; some sources claim a million inhabitants were slaughtered.

But the Mongol terror was not a war against particular religions or cultures: Genghis' faith was in the story inside his head – a personal destiny he believed sanctioned by the supreme spirit, Khökh Tenger, 'Blue Heaven'. He believed it his divine fate to rule the world; his purpose, absolute power. Wealth was secondary. This boy – Temujin of the once-proud Borjigin tribe – was raised in poverty with a widowed mother deserted by her male relatives as a result of a family feud. That the depth of his self-belief could command such loyalty and establish the largest empire the world had known then or since, seems incredible. But standing in the vast openness of the Mongolian steppes, fringed in the far distance by purple-hued mountain peaks, a fleeting insight into his inner narrative is possible. Looking up, the heavens are indeed radiantly blue, but there is no visible 'sky' as such, no capping, enclosing element: only a pure translucency into the eternal space of an infinite universe. Such a boundless environment does not imprint upon a strong personality an awareness of human smallness; on the contrary, like the deserts of Arabia, it allows the soul to soar to boundless heights. A destiny conceived here could empower an ambitious ego to expand without limit over heaven and earth.[84]

Genghis' mission required blind obedience to his ascendency: resistance was certain death, be it that of opponents on the battlefield or unarmed populations of cities. His story is told in *The Secret History* which is part myth, part legend, part history, and holds a significant place in world literature. Secrecy over Genghis' death and location of burial added to the extraordinary force of his story which continues still. *The Secret History,* more so than other stories inspired since by Mongol heroes and victories, provides a narrative nourishing a current revival movement in Mongolia which deifies Genghis Khan: a sustaining symbol of identity for a nation that suffered years of Soviet oppression under the same limitless blue heaven.[85]

Story lays long warp threads through time and space to weave her tales in various guises: here a sari, there a *hijab,* somewhere else a coat of armour, a shepherd's smock, or a pair of jeans. And before we leave this tumultuous period, so productive of diverse narratives that stretched Story's warp from end to end of the medieval world, we should glance at the rich weft of tales that interlaced it when that warp reached the *jongleurs* and troubadours of Europe: in northern Italy, southern France, and Cataluña in Spain – the three regions where the *Occitan* language was spoken in the Middle Ages.

Troubadours (*'trouvères'* in France) performed chivalric and romantic songs of their own composition in their vernacular *Occitan* tongue, and as the form spread, many became travelling *jongleurs* – performers of the songs, dramas and verse-stories of others in the local vernacular. Few people could read but anyone in the street could enjoy Story's company, hearing her speak and sing in their own dialect. Troubadours were not merely wandering minstrels: aristocratic patrons invited them to their courts and castles; their members were drawn originally from the nobility both rich and poor, including knights, lawyers, even a judge and an abbot. Later, merchants and artisans were attracted to the calling, sons and daughters sometimes following their fathers in the art – skill in music, verse and performance became more important than status.

As history favours the powerful, troubadours' names that have come down to us include Bertran de Born (Viscount of Hautefort and its vast estates) renowned for the quality of his poetry, and his liege lord the Duke of Aquitaine (Richard the Lion-Heart and son of Henry II of England), who was one of the earliest troubadours. Bertran was an accomplice in Richard's violent opposition to his father. After Richard became king, Bertran accompanied him on the Third Crusade which ended in a truce with Al-Adil-Saphadin (governor of Egypt and younger brother of Saladin), and composed many verses about his experience. Peire Lunel de Montech, a prominent lawyer and politician from Toulouse and a *trouvère* in his youth, composed in 1326 perhaps one of the last songs of the genre – *Ensenhamen del garso* ('Instructions to the boy') giving advice on composition to a young poet.

By the thirteenth and early fourteenth century, the troubadours' repertoire of characters and tales included Saracen sultans, French knights fresh from the battle fields (who sometimes became mixed up with King Arthur and his 'Round-Tablers'), and Asian desperados as well as serene romances and commentary on current issues. Richard de Pélerin, who began penning the *Chanson d'Antioch* outside the walls of the besieged city, was himself a *jongleur* when not fighting in crusades.

War always makes good stories, yet it is generated principally as a sport of the powerful, the wealthy or those obsessed with desire for both. A change of master over a single kingdom may have made little difference to the majority of its citizens, but these protracted, widespread conflicts ravaged land and people, leaving both too weak to withstand poverty and survive natural calamity. This was unfortunate, because Story was soon taken up by another rampant killer, one lacking conscious purpose and entirely without prejudice as to race, religion, or identity.

Chapter Seven

Plague and plagiarism

The golden age of exploration and wealth brings with it the Black Death. Story adopts Chaucer and Boccaccio to bring cheer to ordinary folk with saucy stories in the vernacular that everyone can enjoy while they admire the knights and laugh at the friars.

Geoffrey Chaucer from the frontispiece of Caxton's 'Canterbury Tales' (c. 1478)

7

Reule wel thyself that other folk canst rede,
And trouthe thee shal delivere, it is no drede.

[Chaucer, 'Truth'[86]]

D id the two great storytellers of the early Renaissance –
Giovanni Boccaccio and Geoffrey Chaucer – ever share a
flask of wine in a sunny loggia and talk of love and men of
letters? Did Boccaccio advise the young poet, pass on gems gleaned
from his friend Petrarch, or lend him copies of his own poems *Teseida*,
and *Filostrato* perhaps? Chaucer did make at least two protracted visits
to Italy. The first, in 1373, was to Florence and Genoa. Boccaccio
was sixty-years old then (Chaucer's senior by thirty years) and not in
good health, although he was indeed preparing a Florentine series of
public lectures on Petrarch: he died in Certaldo, three years before
Chaucer's second Italian mission in 1378. They are unlikely to have
met – except figuratively: for their lives and their stories interweave
in the intricate tapestry of the period.

It was a time of movement and flux. Mongol hordes continued
their customary barbarity in Asia; England and France began a
hundred years of war; France meddled in Italy; the fortunes of Italian
city-states waxed and waned with the intrigues of powerful ruling
families like the Medici and d'Este, and popes appropriated estates
to provide income for their illegitimate offspring. But learning
was revered. Books were still laboriously hand-copied; a personal
library of gilt-edged volumes spoke of the owner's affluence and
influence. These same wealthy nobles were patrons of the arts and

sciences, supporting scholars in their study of both: knowledge was not divided into 'disciplines' as now, scholars gained competence equally in classical languages, astronomy, philosophy, law, science, music and poetry. Some added archaeology, alchemy and geometry to the mix. And everyone seemed to be writing, not only learned treatises but stories of daily life for fun and entertainment. Even Machiavelli, that doyen of political strategy, wrote stories and dramas. His short story, *Belphagor*, part fantasy, part kitchen-sink drama, graphically portrays the timeless theme of domestic politics in which the husband's scheming fails – the wife prevails.

But in the big picture, two developments of particular significance transformed the lives of rich and poor in Europe between the thirteenth and sixteenth centuries: enormous wealth from international trade and conquest, and devastating loss of life from the 'Black Death'. Story, forever busily weaving identity from the strands of past and present, fed her shuttle with threads of gold and black and wove new textures into her history.

Political expansion and the opening up of new shipping routes spurred a burgeoning trade across the known world. Commerce became an essential prop to state treasuries and gave merchants access to traditional circles of influence at court; in some cases, through judicious marriages, their descendants even dressed in the mantle of nobility. An ascendant merchant class with access to education produced brilliant storytellers from among its ranks: Boccaccio and Chaucer were the sons of banker and merchant respectively.

On the general wave of exploration, travellers like Marco Polo – another merchant – helped to popularise tales from the Orient and Central Asia. Collections such as the anonymous Chinese tales *Kin-Kou-Ki-Kuan* (*Marvellous Tales Ancient and Modern*), stories by the Brahmin, Somadeva, in *Kathasaritasagara* (*Ocean of the Streams of Stories*), and *Hazār afsāna,* the collection of Persian tales which we saw earlier and were probably the original source of *The Thousand and One Nights,* were all brought westward and have since found their way into every medium of mass entertainment. Gathered up from fragments of much older oral tales and written down during the ninth and tenth centuries, they made their way across Asia and Europe in the mouths and panniers of travellers, traders, diplomats, and soldiers. And their influence appears in the stories of Boccaccio and Chaucer.

All major European nations plied the sea trade, but in the Mediterranean, the city-state of Venice was pre-eminent, challenged only by her rival, Genoa. A republic governed by an aristocracy of powerful bankers and merchants, Venice faced the sea and her trade routes, focusing resolutely on her destiny. She had equipped the Fourth Crusade that sacked Constantinople in 1204, her knights returning with rich spoils and a small empire of strategic island bases. Her wealth and splendour she displayed in grand architecture, incomparable art and libraries of beautifully illuminated books that were the envy of Europe. Gold was next to godliness.

So exalted was Venice's self-image, that a fetid hummocky swamp, dotted with the impoverished huts of Veniti fisher-folk, and crowded later with refugees fleeing yet another wave of northern barbarians, was not a fitting pedigree for its latter-day inhabitants and was swiftly forgotten. Instead, Venetians wrote their own creation myth: the birth, on 25 March 421 AD, of an independent, already Christian city-state on pristine lands. A city favoured by the patronage of St Mark (whose remains would be housed in the basilica that bears his name). Fully formed, Venice was immaculately conceived: a virgin city. Such is the power of Story.

Another tale of the time surrounds one of Venice's most famous sons – Marco Polo. *The Travels of Marco Polo* (originally titled: *Livres des merveilles du monde*) recounts the adventures of Polo and his travelling companions during their twenty-year excursion into Asia, Persia, Cathay (China), and Indonesia from 1271 to 1291. Most notably, it records his exploits as advisor to the court of the redoubtable Mongol leader, Kublai Khan, the grandson of Genghis. According to legend, Marco Polo dictated his experiences to an Italian romance writer, Rusticello da Pisa, when they shared a prison cell in Genoa during one of the recurrent spats between Genoa and Venice. Later, da Pisa wrote up the travelogue in Old French and it has been a popular and much translated book ever since. It is currently fashionable to doubt the veracity of Polo's account, especially his relationship with Kublai Khan. At this distance, such carping seems churlish when 'faction' plays such a prominent role in modern travel writing. In every story is the possibility of more than one kind of truth – as in real life. These tales have remained popular because views of the world have continued to expand; the strange and distant, the 'other', has somehow to be accommodated with the known and understood at a safe distance. People have always enjoyed stories of travel for this reason, as well as for the adrenalin rush of vicarious danger and adventure.

But these new channels of contact brought other vectors, carriers of darkness that had a huge impact upon literature, culture and society in general: they brought the plague, known to us as the Black Death. From 1347 to 1350 epidemics of plague swept through Europe and returned several times over the next 300 years. It killed millions of people and changed the social landscape forever. Believed to have started in China, plague spread, ironically, via those same trade routes that brought material prosperity: along the Silk Road from the East and by merchant shipping carried, it is now thought, not in a bubonic form on the backs of rats harbouring infected fleas, but in the coughs and sneezes of travellers, traders and sailors in a highly infectious pneumonic plague. Estimates of fatalities from the disease vary; in Europe and the Middle East, it could have wiped out up to sixty per cent of the population. Invasions, wars, and famines that preceded it in various parts of Asia and Europe no doubt made people in these areas more susceptible to the plague's effects. Not since the sixth century – in the Plague of Justinian – had disease wrought such devastation.

Boccaccio may have been away in Ravenna during the five months that plague surged through Florence, killing more than half the population, but his father was believed to have been at that time employed by the city government and involved in efforts to cope with the disaster. His father might even have caught plague himself, because he was dead by the time the epidemic ended in 1350, enabling Boccaccio to survive on his small inheritance and focus on his writing. Present or not, Boccaccio would have learned in detail the ravages of the epidemic.[87] It inspired the structure for his best-known collection of stories, *The Decameron*. In the first story, 'The First Day: The Storytellers', Boccaccio captures the effects of plague on local citizens:

> 'The peasants and their families, with neither servants nor doctors to care for them, died like animals in the field, on the farm and by the roadside. Like the people of the city, they abandoned their usual industrious lives and threw caution to the winds. Behaving as if they expected each day to be their last, they neglected their crops and animals completely.
>
> The city became a ghost city. Imagine the grand palaces and stately houses, once filled with the talk and laughter of lords and ladies, children and servants, now left deserted.'[88]

From this introduction one might think *The Decameron* a gloomy read but nothing could be further from the truth. The plague, which had ravaged the city only a couple of years before, was a frame for stories of a very different kind:

> '...a hill beyond which lies a lush and beautiful plain. The pleasure the sight of this will give you will more than adequately compensate for the difficulties of the climb, just as tears lead to laughter and sadness must eventually give way to joy. ...But since without this look at the past you could not understand how the events that follow came to happen at all, you must have the one before the other.'[89]

The context of the plague established a reason for ten young Florentines of good family (seven women and three men) to leave the infected city and spend ten days on their country estates.

To amuse themselves, they each tell a story every afternoon – resulting in the 100 tales of the collection. Each day, a different member of the group 'reigns' and sets the theme for that day's stories. Boccaccio thus set a fashion for framed tales that other writers all over Europe emulated for several centuries, including Chaucer in his *Canterbury Tales*.

The framing idea was not entirely original, of course, Boccaccio would have been aware of previous stories within stories, but he built a more substantial structure, placing his tales vividly and uniquely within Italian culture and experience. Even though many of the plots were derived and recast from older sources – as was the custom – *The Decameron* was innovative in being entirely in prose, and written in the vernacular (a trend started by Dante).

Like Dante and Petrarch before him (and Chaucer after him) Boccaccio's principal medium was poetry – considered then to be the highest form of expression – which he usually wrote in Latin. That people reserved prose for more pragmatic (indeed, 'prosaic') purposes, is not to say that stories were rare: stories flourished but they were still told in verse. In Boccaccio's time, although the move towards the vernacular was strong, prose fiction was not highly regarded by his scholarly contemporaries; the *Decameron* would have been called 'pulp fiction' had they known of such a phrase. He is obviously aware of this in the defensive comments he writes before the fourth day's stories of disastrous love. Addressing his readers as 'Dearest ladies', he refers to 'these little stories, written as they are not only in the vulgar Florentine, and in prose, and without dedicatory flourish, but also in as homely and simple a style as may be' confessing that his critics say he is too fond of the ladies and should not waste his talents composing 'these idle toys.'

Boccaccio shows a sympathy for the restricted lives of 'society women' that was unusual for his times. Marriages were arranged, often from childhood, and a married woman's life was largely confined to her own house and courtyard, or those of relatives. As education was not encouraged except in religious orders, few upper-class women would have been fluent in Latin, but they would have been literate in the vernacular Italian – one of their few private pleasures, to read and dream of love.

Perhaps more significantly for Story, the hundred tales Boccaccio composed for *The Decameron* paint a picture of changing social mores after the plague: people lived for the moment and made the most of personal freedoms, loosening the institutional authority of state and church. Up to this time, the church in Europe had dominated literature, music, even science and law. The aftermath of the plague opened up a crack for the expansion of humanist thought and a gradual secularisation of stories and music for sheer fun.

Boccaccio's stories were meant to be read aloud, as the original young storytellers told them, allowing their listeners to share their delight 'as tears lead to laughter.' The majority of his tales are racy and often farcical accounts of sexual exploits and chicanery, where mistaken identities and scabrous motives may find characters in the wrong bed, or entirely the wrong country; tales where monks deflower maidens under pretence of religious instruction, and dim-witted friars are exposed as fools. He began putting the collection together as the plague slowly withdrew from Florence, almost as if it was a way of marking the city's recovery. The use of young survivors as the storytellers, the inclusion of well known stories giving continuity with the past, and the humour and adventure in the stories themselves, all seem to suggest a spirited return to life – a revival. His choice of vernacular prose also implies a wider audience. Boccaccio hints at this when he declares he intended the collection as an amusing diversion to ease the misery of disappointed lovers, an experience with which he was painfully familiar.

We know for certain neither Boccaccio's place of birth nor his mother's identity, only that she was French and disappears from the record after his birth, but he was born in 1313 and spent his youth in Florence where his father – still a bachelor – was a merchant banker with the Compagnia dei Bardi. Boccaccio was seven years old when his father married into the distinguished Mardoli family. His illegitimate start to life, though hardly unusual, did not prevent Boccaccio benefiting from a sound classical education. After spending six years in Paris, training under a merchant, he returned to Florence, but when his father became head of the Neapolitan branch of the Bardi bank, the family moved to Naples and Boccaccio joined the bank as an apprentice. His father introduced him into the court of King Robert of Naples where he entertained the courtiers with his poems and stories, promptly falling deeply and hopelessly in love with Maria d'Aquino, an illegitimate daughter of the King, who was already married to a Count. She appeared as characters in his verses and stories throughout his career – a life in which he never married although it seems he fathered three children.

According to Boccaccio, it was the pain of unrequited love, or rather the desire to ease such pain of others with humour, that inspired the stories of *The Decameron*. In the introduction, he refers to his own wretchedness, relieved by sympathetic friends, and his belief that women suffer the more because they have less freedom in diverting themselves from their heartache:

Giovanni Boccaccio

'To compensate, therefore, for the injustice of Fortune, which gives least support to those who are weakest, I offer these stories to all ladies in love (others can fill their minds easily with their household tasks).'[90]

The love stories are not only about princes, sultans, and noble gentlemen, but ordinary folk who can be just as licentious and devious as the couple in Filostrato's story told on the seventh day:

A mason of Naples has a handsome young wife, Peronella, who regularly entertains her lover, Gianello, in the house when her husband leaves for work. One day the husband returns early and Gianello conceals himself by jumping into a barrel. The husband has returned because he has found a buyer for the barrel. Quick-witted Peronella tells him she already has a buyer; he is at that moment inside the barrel inspecting its condition. Gianello then leaps up and declares the barrel sound but in sore need of cleaning. The conscientious husband gets into the barrel to scrape and scrub it thoroughly, while Peronella and her lover continue to make the most of their opportunity; Gianello finally purchases the barrel and takes it home.[91]

Among his sources for the more ribald stories would have been traditional *fabliaux* – brief, comic and often lewd tales in verse that were particularly popular in the thirteenth century and a significant part of the troubadours' repertoire.

The establishment gets a wigging too – the fifth story on the eighth day tells how two youths succeed in debagging an incompetent judge while he is trying a case at the bench. Fifteen of the stories satirise widespread corruption by servants of the church, whether priests, monks or friars. In the tenth story on the sixth day, Friar Cipolla ('Brother Onion') is depicted as an avaricious trickster who tries to con simple country folk into believing that a feather was from a wing of the Archangel Gabriel, left behind after the Annunciation, and a heap of coals were the ashes of the roasted martyr Saint Laurence. The selling of fake religious relics, or charging people to touch them as a cure for illness, was a common practice in the Middle Ages that preyed on the superstition and credulity of the uneducated; a practice of which Boccaccio strongly disapproved.

His professional life ran no more smoothly than his love life: after persuading his father to release him from apprenticeship at the bank, he spent six years studying canon law – the church's own judiciary system. But he found that a legal career held no appeal for him either, although at various times he carried out diplomatic missions on behalf of the Florentine Council as far afield as Venice and Padua – duties he found increasingly irksome with age, involving long, saddle-sore journeys avoiding bandits on the road by day and bedbugs in the inns by night. Ultimately, he immersed himself further in the study of science, humanism, and literature, and found his vocation in poetry.

Although scholars and nobles read copious volumes during this period, oral storytelling was still the popular medium whether in royal courts or the market place. The thirteenth century Italian prose collection, *Cento Novelle Antiche* ('A Hundred Ancient Tales'), draws on a huge range of sources; stories feature knights of King Arthur, Italian aristocrats, and Asian despots as well as classical heroes. Many of these tales are incomplete or very short like *The Bell of Atri* (number 14 in the collection and little more than 200 words), which suggests a collection compiled as a catalogue of plots, or a sort of *aide-mémoire* for narrators to embellish in their own style at each telling.[92] The *Cento Novelle Antiche* bears no author's name; one likely origin is the songs and verses of the troubadours and *jongleurs* who contributed so much to early European literature. Nor did these and many other tales of the period originally have titles: in keeping with oral traditions, they began with an introductory paragraph to set the scene and settle the audience. (Editors for various publications have added titles over subsequent years.) Stories in *The Decameron,* too, have no titles; they are identified by the names of the storytellers for each day and they begin with brief descriptions of the plot.

For his own plots Boccaccio dipped into ancient collections of tales, or later interpretations of them, including the *Cento Novelle Antiche*: for example, the story of the three rings in which Saladin, who has recently conquered Egypt, borrows money from a Jew.[93] Throughout the Renaissance, new plots and characters for stories were rare. Rather than plagiarism in the derogatory sense we use the term today, it was accepted practice to seek continuity with the classics and other popular sources by adapting old legends and myths, retelling and interpreting them in new ways. Storytelling was the main source of entertainment; whether in a cottage, tavern, or noble salon, people enjoyed the familiarity of favourite tales as well as new twists and contemporary details added by each storyteller.

But more than a score of Boccaccio's stories are entirely original. One group narrates astute wit in evading awkward situations (perhaps a reflection of his legal training), while others lampoon the behaviour of well known characters: in both cases, the situations and characters are all Italian and local. Amongst them are Bruno and Buffalmacco, real people – early Renaissance painters better known for their practical jokes than their artistry – and Calandrino, also a painter, with the reputation as a dullard on whom Bruno and Buffalmacco play hilarious pranks. On one occasion, they convince him he is pregnant and con money out of him for medicines to cure him.

Unlike the framing of the *Arabian Nights*, stories are not suspended until the next night. The storytelling in *The Decameron* continues all afternoon and evening sitting around the fountain in the garden simply to pass the time of their temporary evacuation in pleasure, so ten complete tales are told each day. An occasional ghost appears in the tales but no equivalent to *jinn* or spirits; instead of magic and fantasy, the listener is entertained with people's foibles, cunning tricks, stupidity, and earthy human weaknesses, so prevalent throughout the social hierarchy that it undermines the authority of those in charge. We hear one saucy example in the second story of the ninth day:

> A pretty young nun is spied upon by her fellow sisters who notice late one night that she is in her cell with her lover, and not for the first time. They rush off to knock on the abbess' door to report her. The abbess, dressing hurriedly in the dark in case someone enters her room, claps onto her head what she thinks is her headgear when in fact it is the breeches of the priest who is *her* secret lover. While the abbess admonishes the sinful young nun, calling her 'accursed of God', the girl draws to her attention the nature of her headgear. Caught red-faced, the abbess switches principles and declares that such rules are impossible to obey, and that each should take her pleasure where she can.[94]

Chaucer tapped many of the same sources as Boccaccio, as well as some of Boccaccio's own poems and stories, and although Chaucer continued to write in verse rather than prose, after his visits to Italy he followed the trend of writing in the vernacular. In his *Canterbury Tales*, he even went to the extent of a realistic country dialect for the Miller's Tale, to which the next storyteller, Oswald the Reeve (farm manager) takes offence and comments: 'Right in his cherles termes wol I speke', ('I'll talk in his own bumpkin language').[95] Before Chaucer's time and the Hundred Years War against France, the official language of state in England was French – the language of the Norman invaders. English had survived, spoken by ordinary people, but it began to recover its original dominance from 1363 when the Lord Chancellor took the bold step of opening parliament in English instead of French. He did not go so far as to replace the word 'parliament' however, despite its origin from the Old French *'parlement', 'speaking'.*

Chaucer also brought to life in his verse the realities of existence for common citizens. Whether folk could read or not (and most could not), they could now hear some of the best stories ever written, in their native tongue and about issues that affected their own lives. These were plots and characters they could recognise, identify with, or laugh at. Because Chaucer wrote in English, we can appreciate some of his original writing and it is fun to decipher words and realise how meanings have changed or remained much the same, but few of us can read Middle English well enough to enjoy his stories as fully as his fellow countrymen did; fortunately there are translations. Like all poetry, the rhyme and metre of Chaucer's original verse add to the meaning and humour of his tales; verse translations are available, as well as prose through which we can enjoy Chaucer's tales in the form in which we read short stories today – a 'literary immortality' of which Chaucer would no doubt approve.

Although Chaucer drew on Boccaccio's work for some of his tales, and similarly adopted a framing device – a pilgrimage to Canterbury is the frame within which pilgrims tell their stories to amuse each other on their arduous journey – Chaucer's *Tales* is uniquely English. It was also the first time such a socially inclusive tale, so diverse in content and character, had been written in England and it became immensely popular. Realistic dialogue, more complex plotting, and deeper characters than traditional stereotypes, were all Chaucer's own elaborations in storytelling and were innovative for his time. Boccaccio's ten storytellers are all of the same age and class, and little interaction takes place among them: each of Chaucer's storytellers is a well-defined character with his or her own story; they cover virtually all sections of society and their gritty exchanges contribute to the humour and context of the stories. The *Canterbury Tales* is rich in unforgettable personalities and distinctive voices, portraying sordid facts of medieval life in equally explicit language, underpinned as it was by conflicts between social classes and within the church – and all told with coarse good humour. Much of this conflict reflected the massive social impact of the Black Death, which it was Chaucer's first piece of good fortune to avoid.

He was about the age of six or seven when plague arrived in London, but the family had already moved to Southampton where his father was engaged in business for the King. On their return, the main danger had passed, though other outbreaks would follow. Chaucer's full and varied career placed him in an ideal position to appreciate and share with us the nuances of life after the plague. His professional duties kept his finger on the pulse of the nation; he even lived for some years in apartments over the Aldgate – a main entrance into the walled city of London through which begging friars, rioting citizens and wagons of merchandise alike would trundle through the mud and offal of the streets below his window.

Like Boccaccio, Chaucer was a poet and scholar, rising to eminence from a family heritage of trade and commerce – his father was a successful wine merchant in London, supplier to the Royal Household of Edward III and holder of official status at court. The wine trade did not appeal to Chaucer any more than banking had to Boccaccio, but the diplomatic and administrative functions he carried out for the state throughout his life were more extensive than Boccaccio's. Chaucer even had a brief spell as a prisoner of war in France and was released for a ransom of sixteen pounds. So well did he fulfil his duties that the King granted him an additional boon of a daily *lagena* of wine – approximately a gallon – probably supplied by Chaucer's father. Both Boccaccio and Chaucer received the benefits of participation in court life, but in Chaucer's case, it was more an apprenticeship in manners and statecraft that prepared him for a life of public administration and diplomacy; the literary career seems almost an alter ego.

From his early teens, Chaucer became a page in the royal household of Elizabeth de Burgh, Countess of Ulster and daughter-in-law to Edward III. He was dressed in short doublet and black and red hose, and travelled constantly with the royal retinue between their numerous establishments. Apart from grammar, languages, and writing, he learned such niceties as to hold meat with only three fingers of the left hand when slicing it (forks were not yet in use), and to break bread rather than cut it (a piece of dining etiquette observed still, by those who care about such things). With his fellow pages, he would have learned the aristocratic sports of hawking and hunting, and the court accomplishments of singing, dancing and playing musical instruments. Not only did pages serve at table, run errands, and pen memoranda, they entertained the royal household and their guests.

The concepts of 'courtly love' and the heroic chivalry of knights, in and out of battle, were still important elements of stories and verses in England as elsewhere. Dramatised, mimed, and animated narrations of King Arthur's exploits, the epic Trojan Wars, and the broken hearts of languishing maidens, all delighted princes, ladies in waiting, and legions of court servants and hangers-on: there was little else to do, after all. In these stories, love – especially unrequited love – moved men and women, even the gods, to exquisite heights of feeling that generated extraordinary deeds of valour and self-sacrifice for the vicarious enjoyment of their audience. Love, in fiction at least, was a matter of the soul. Young Chaucer's involvement in these spectacles may even have inspired him to write his own stories.

The mature Chaucer spurned the fashionable doublet and hose in favour of a more dignified plain long gown. He had weightier matters to consider. With the population halved by the plague, wages in the towns rose, and land cleared of dwellings after the epidemic was cheaper, but the fabric of the economy had been ripped apart and the numbers of poor and unemployed increased. Among the structures to wobble after the predations of the plague was feudalism: while it denied serfs any rights, it had ensured a basic livelihood. Taxes from shattered estates and bankrupt traders no longer reached the treasury. The king, perpetually in debt exacerbated by disruptions to trade and the costs of war with France, despatched Chaucer to Florence to arrange further bank loans; a task in which Chaucer, the wily negotiator, succeeded despite the sovereign's history of default. As Chaucer spoke fluent Italian as well as French, he was able to take full benefit from this first visit to Florence and immersion in the cultural heritage of Dante, Petrarch, and Boccaccio.

Geoffrey Chaucer

Chaucer's second Italian mission and the most important – from Story's point of view – was six years later (in 1378) to negotiate an alliance between the newly crowned English King, Richard II, and the despotic ruler of Milan, Bernabo Visconti – later immortalised in *Canterbury Tales* as 'the scourge of Lombardy'. It is fortuitous for English literature that not only had Petrarch stood as godfather to Visconti's son, but Visconti's library was one of the most comprehensive in Italy. If Chaucer was as competent as usual in negotiation, it is possible that Visconti rewarded him with a book of Italian literature from his collection, or at least gave him access to his library. It is after this visit that literary scholars have identified the strongest influence of Dante and Boccaccio on Chaucer's writing; passages in *The Knight's Tale* in particular being almost translations from Boccaccio's romantic poem *Il Teseida*. Without this literary awakening, Chaucer might never have been inspired to write *Canterbury Tales*.

Two major events have yet to take place in England before all the ingredients for the *Tales* are assembled. Economic and social displacements that followed the plague became a groundswell for political protest by the tax-paying yeomen of England – misnamed the 'Peasant's Revolt' – led by Wat Tyler. After the collapse of traditional structures of patronage and employment, it was harder than ever to scratch a living: desperate people sold anything, including their daughters, and made whatever gain they could by fair means or foul. The fourteen-year-old King Richard II faced down Tyler's mob assembled on the green sward of Smithfield, but notice had been given, and taken, that the populace could no longer be fleeced with impunity whenever the treasury ran dry.

A similar spirit of independence fuelled challenges to the spiritual hegemony of the Catholic Church, a movement led in England by John Wycliffe, who wanted people to read the Bible in their own native tongue, and to speak directly to God without the intercession of priests. Wycliffe was fed up with the corruption of church officials and the shameless activities of successive popes. A problem compounded by the existence of two rival Popes – one in Rome and another in Avignon – each with their militant supporters. This extraordinary situation lasted for some thirty years.

The church dominated every aspect of life all over Europe, and a variety of church functionaries appear in *Canterbury Tales*. Pardoners sold 'papal indulgences': a substantial payment that reduced the time sinners spent in purgatory. Summoners – a sort of religious police – used their own network of spies to seek out infringements of church law, particularly non-payment of tithes and fornication; on-the-spot 'fines' could keep sinners out of court – and fill the purse of the Summoner. One of Chaucer's tales describes a Summoner who protects a whore in order for her to inform on her (other?) customers. The Limiters, or 'begging friars', each had their own beat – their Limit – in which they solicited funds for their abbeys. And they all competed with each other in their efforts at extortion. Add to this that priests charged fees for baptisms and funerals and sold access to fake relics, and we begin to understand the strength of fear and superstition that allowed such protection rackets to reign for so long. People's understanding of God and the Bible was determined by stories told them by the priests and friars. The Bible was in Latin: even the few ordinary people able to read could not read Latin. What they heard and saw of their religion they had always integrated in various ways with the old pagan stories – still relevant to the seasonal cycles and rhythms of life – and they believed that the condition of their lives was ordained by God. But life was a harsh struggle. To whom could they turn for reassurance? Who could they trust?

The stories of both Boccaccio and Chaucer lift the wool from the eyes of their audience. In the prologue to one of Chaucer's stories, rivalry and suspicion within the church is explicit: the Summoner relates how a friar dreamt he was visiting Hell and seeing no other friars there, is reassured by the fact, but the angel in charge takes him to the depths where Satan himself lies in the form of a dragon, and the angel says to Satan, "Lift your tail!", as Satan does so, the souls of thousands of friars fly out of his *erse* like demented bees.

Not all those disenchanted with the Church were Lollards, as Wycliffe's followers were called; Chaucer seems to have been among those who wanted the Church to improve its performance rather than to adopt a different creed.

In *Canterbury Tales*, Chaucer ridicules the church's servants as licentious dissemblers and confidence tricksters, like a court jester whose witty darts hit home, yet the frame of the stories is a springtime pilgrimage to Canterbury cathedral, a site of holy relics since

The Summoner

199

the sixth century when St Augustus was Archbishop and baptised King Ethelbert. A pilgrimage was a genuine act of faith, but it was also a popular jaunt in Chaucer's day. Absent from these tales are fasting, scourging of flesh or bruising of knees; instead, much food and wine are consumed, while normal social constraints are lifted – much like the average tourist in the Costa Brava – a situation perfectly suited to Chaucer's sense of irony and fun. Yet Christian principles recur in many of the stories, especially the pious tales of the Second Nun, and the Parson's tale – a sermon in prose because the cleric denounces rhyme and fable on moral grounds. Chaucer's description of the parson is even-handed: he recognises that many clerics from humble origins work poor parishes with dedication, but they lack resources because these are channelled to the monasteries. It is more than likely, though, that Chaucer intended the idea of pilgrimage as a metaphor for the journey of life in general with all its variety and challenges.

The narrator, Chaucer himself, is staying at the Tabard Inn in Southwark in preparation for his own pilgrimage when he meets twenty-nine other pilgrims each in a different occupation ('sondry folk'), all gathered there by chance, and decides to join them. The inn-keeper and their host, Harry Bailly, offers to accompany them all on the pilgrimage as their guide and master of ceremonies; it is he who calls upon each to tell their tale on the journey and crudely mediates their squabbles. In the general prologue, Chaucer describes in vivid detail the appearance and personality of each character. Of the Friar he says, with his usual irony:

'A Frere ther was, a wantowne and a merye,
A lymytour, a ful solempne man.
In alle the orders foure is noon that kan
So muchel of daliaunce and fair langage.
He hadde maad ful many a mariage
Of yonge women at his owene cost.
Unto his ordre he was a noble post,'[96]

In David Wright's prose translation:

> 'A begging Friar was there, a gay, pleasant Limiter with an imposing presence; nobody in all the four Orders was so adept with flattery and tittle-tattle. He had had to pay for the marriages of a good many young women; still he was a noble pillar of his Order.'[97]

> (Payment for young women's marriages indicated that he had already deflowered them.)

But Chaucer's description of the Knight is wholly complimentary, defining the hero of the time since the crusades:

> 'The Knight was a very distinguished man. From the beginning of his career he had loved chivalry, loyalty, honourable dealing, generosity, and good breeding. He had fought bravely in the king's service, besides which he had travelled further than most men in heathen as well as Christian land … He wore a tunic of thick cotton cloth, rust marked from his coat of mail; for he had just come back from his travels and was making his pilgrimage to render thanks.'[98]

The Knight's Tale is by far the longest; written some time before the other tales. It relates themes of adventurous challenges to love and loyalty that would have been familiar favourites to Chaucer's audience.

Other characters are duplicitous in their attempts to make money or trick others; the Reeve cheats his master, the Miller cheats his customers, and the Summoner cheats everyone. In good humour, Chaucer includes himself in the banter: when it is his turn to tell a tale, his deliberately gauche rendering of the ballad of Sir Topaz is interrupted by the Host: 'No more of this…your shithouse rhyming's not worth a turd!'[99] Having demonstrated his lack of skill at verse, Chaucer is asked to tell a story in mere prose.

The rich drama of *Canterbury Tales* leads us to imagine their animated retelling – with all the different voices, dialects and gestures – on long dark evenings before a crackling fire. They were written in the last few years of Chaucer's life, almost a summation of his life's experience. After his overseas diplomacy, he had been Clerk of Works for the Crown, a magistrate, and a Member of Parliament for Kent until he returned to London to retire. As a measure of his material success, Chaucer owned sixty books – a formidable personal library for the times. On retirement he leased a property in the garden of the Lady Chapel of Westminster Abbey, close to the White Rose tavern also within the abbey's grounds – an irony he no doubt enjoyed. Chaucer died in 1400 of unknown cause – possibly of plague which had recurred at that time – leaving the *Tales* incomplete, a collection of fragments in no definite order.

None of Chaucer's original manuscripts for the *Tales* has survived, but it is testimony to its popularity that many contemporary copies were made, despite the laborious and expensive process of hand scribing. An elaborately illustrated copy was collected in the private library of the Earls of Oxford and sold in 1741 to what is now the British Library. The usually accepted sequence of various tales is that established by the philologist, Walter William Skeat, who prepared an edition for publication by the University of Oxford in 1894.

Boccaccio may have viewed the *Decameron* tales as 'idle toys', but they became hugely influential in European literature for their humanism and quality of prose. He never repeated this style, however, concentrating in the future on serious scholarship and writing only in Latin. This might reflect the reversal in his playful appreciation of women, demonstrated in the acerbic wit of *Corbaccio* – a bitter satire of a widow who had jilted him – written a couple of years after *Decameron*. Despite his criticism of clerics and friars, Boccaccio was not against church doctrine. He had taken minor orders earlier in his career and, during a spiritual crisis later in life, had considered entering a monastery. His friend Petrarch dissuaded him, advising him to purify his life within the day-to-day world as a more humanist approach to his difficulties. Boccaccio's last years were spent in poverty, eking out a poor living by teaching and scribing – copying his own work and that of others. He died in the village of Certaldo in 1375.

Although the stories of Boccaccio and Chaucer were threads tightly woven into the fabric of their times, they remain popular because they display the true storyteller's art: to show us the wealth of human nature through which we can find our own way regardless of period or place. Their tales were among the first to be printed by the new moveable-type technology fifty years later, heralding a time of excitement, fear, defiance and revolution in which Story played an important role.

Chapter Eight

Let the presses roll

In China, books have been printed from blocks for centuries, but Johannes Gutenberg invents the printing press, and Story joins Wyllyam Caxton in his study encouraging him to translate her favourite tales into English vernacular. Together they pore over the Golden Legends, wonder at King Arthur's round table and chuckle at the antics of Reynard the Fox.

*If we listen carefully at the door of Caxton's candle-lit study
cluttered with books and papers …*

8

It is not written with pen and ink as other books be …
For all the books of this story …
were begun in one day and also finished in one day.

[Wyllyam Caxton 1474, on his first book printed in English.[100]]

To catch a glimpse of the first time movable type was applied to a writeable surface, we must imagine ourselves in the warm sunny Mediterranean rather than cool damp northern Europe or the far away Orient. If we wander between ornate pillars, cross a shadow-striped courtyard and peep through an opening into an artist's workshop, we see a young artisan busily at work – we will call him, Minolis. Beside him sits a wooden tray holding forty-five small dies or seals, each representing a mirror image of an ideographic sign of a writing system. Minolis picks out a die and carefully presses it into a disc of soft clay which is supported on the bench in front of him. Neatly, selecting each sign, he fills the disc with a spiral of impressions, starting from the outer edge and ending in the centre. Reddish in colour, the disc – though not a perfect circle – is about sixteen centimetres in diameter and is to be embossed on both sides; it is delicate work, so we must leave quietly so as not to break his concentration.

The earliest evidence of a movable type being employed to create a written text is the Phaistos Disc from Minoan Crete dated around 1600 BC. Apart from that fact, the rest is mystery that has continued to intrigue archaeologists and scholars of ancient languages since the disc was unearthed in a collapsed outbuilding of the Palace of Phaistos in 1902. Only the one disc has been found, and there are no other examples where this exact set of signs has been used; without other samples for comparison, scholars are still unable to decipher the script, although many interpretations of the text have been offered. Because of the pattern of repetitions in the groups of signs, one suggestion is that the text is a lyric, a hymn or a song, and we can only wonder at the story it might tell.[101]

Was the disc purely for ceremonial purposes? And from what material was the type made? The Minoans could have carved each piece in stone, ivory or, more likely, used moulded metal; they already made bronze alloys and knew the art of lost-wax casting for intricate artefacts and jewellery of gold and other metals, and they manufactured decorative dies to emboss their fine, elegant pottery. The Minoan economy – based on sea-going trade and local production – was sufficiently complex that the need for a writing system had already been recognised. And yet, having invented this method of printing, which would have been much faster than hand-scribing each sign, the technique is never seen again. Why? There are many possibilities, but perhaps, like Johannes Gutenberg 3,000 years later, Minolis was experimenting in secret with a creation of his own, his efforts forestalled possibly by a fatal earthquake.

Our young artisan had probably seen, or at least knew about, the cylinder seals which the Sumerians had been carving into stone and impressing onto wet clay since about 3500 BC. Pictorial scenes from Gilgamesh – a hero depicted fighting a bull – were among these early impression printings. Later, the cylinder technique was used to print blocks of text in cuneiform script onto clay tablets. The libraries of the ancient Mesopotamian city of Nippur stored some 30,000 such clay 'books'.

From around 650 AD, the Chinese also devised block printing, not from cylinders, but from slabs of carved wood and copper plates pressed onto paper, silk or other fabrics. As with the Sumerians, the first printings were of images for signature seals and religious charms, some including brief texts. Although we cannot be sure when printed books were first produced, the earliest survival is a copy of the *Diamond Sutra* (a Mahāyāna Buddhist text) dated 868 AD, printed on seven sheets of paper glued together to make a scroll – the traditional form for presenting texts. The printing had been commissioned by an individual, Wang Jie, in honour of his parents. By the next century, the Song dynasty in China was mass producing anthologies, dictionaries, learned texts and histories through the National Academy. Publishing became an important state enterprise.

During this period, at least one Chinese printer experimented with moveable type. Pi Sheng carved individual characters onto small pieces of clay and hardened them in a kiln to create type. He found that carved wooden type was more durable, but it absorbed ink unevenly. Wang Zhen encountered the same problems in 1298, and they both faced an additional major challenge: because of the ideographic nature of Chinese script, they needed several thousand dies to represent all the characters (*hanja*), and numerous copies of each to compile one complete text – it took Wang Zhen six years to carve thirty-thousand characters. With these difficulties it is little wonder that the easier technique of 'block printing' was preferred for the next 300 years. Successive Chinese emperors began to gather their literary heritage from centuries before, preserving in printed collections not only the *hua-pen* – the storytellers' prompt books – and putting them into general circulation, but also the short fiction and anecdotes which were extremely popular among the literati. Especially sought after were tales of the strange and the marvellous, part of a genre the studious Chinese referred to as *biji,* 'jottings'. Despite this unflattering label, they were written in classical Chinese and with a sense of humour, as seen in this little tale from a fifth-century anthology:

'On many occasions, under the influence of wine, Liu Ling would be completely free and unrestrained, sometimes even removing his clothes and sitting stark naked in the middle of his room. Some people once saw him in this state and chided him for it. Ling retorted, "'Heaven and earth are my pillars and roof, the rooms of my house are my jacket and trousers. What are you gentlemen doing in my trousers?"[102]

While China continued to produce many thousands of books from block printing, the challenge of producing a moveable type strong enough to withstand repeated pressings was met by Korean printers in 1377, who manufactured type from cast bronze to print Buddhist texts. But their script was derived from Chinese, so they shared the problem of reproducing thousands of different characters. The far-sighted King Seycong recognised the potential of printing and instructed his scholars to create a new script to make it easier. From the fifteenth century, Korea's distinctive Hankul script – closer to traditional spoken Korean – became the national writing system and the basis for a state printing industry using both block and moveable type.

By this time, too, block printing had spread to Europe where small presses produced mostly pamphlets, religious texts and illustrations. Germans printed pictures of the saints for the devout; Italians produced sets of playing cards for the debauched. But in fifteenth-century Europe, everything was ready for innovation and a more efficient method of production: parchment was available and cheaper than vellum, and was already being replaced by paper, which was even cheaper once it was milled in Nuremberg and a few other European cities; demand was created by the ecclesiastical establishment's desire for a standard, error-free, edition of the Bible and other texts for the increasing number of grammar and monastery-run schools. A new class of educated laity was emerging from among the minor landed gentry and merchants, for whom book ownership was a fashionable status symbol, and, despite political upheavals and continued territorial wars, trade and manufacturing produced a burgeoning economy in which craft guilds gained power in towns expanding with urbanisation.

The city and province of Mainz, in central Germany, was particularly well placed beside the Rhine for cheap transport of heavy raw materials and bulky output. Here lived Johannes Gensfleisch zur Laden zum Gutenberg, a younger son of a town councillor. Young Gutenberg, a small-scale entrepreneur with a fascination for metal-working, had conceived the idea of making metal moveable type for mass printing. The Roman alphabet was easy: only twenty-six letters which, allowing for upper and lower case, punctuation and sundry symbols, would require a minimal set of a hundred or so individual pieces of type to be duplicated, rather than thousands. Developing the techniques and finding the funds proved the difficult part. Before he could start, he had to create a metal alloy that could be cast with accurate detail and without uneven shrinkage, an oil-based ink that would adhere to metal and not fade, and a means of exerting an even pressure of the right force, not to mention working out the whole production process of sequencing and collating pages printed from several presses simultaneously.

Gutenberg's first business venture had been making decorative metal plaques and badges as souvenirs for pilgrims. Pilgrimage to sites of religious relics was a popular pastime not only in Chaucer's Canterbury but all over Europe. In the German territories, Aachen, the burial place of Charlemagne was the major attraction. But Gutenberg had already been experimenting with the technology he required for his printing idea, and he must have realised that he was not the only one trying to work out how to satisfy this new demand, because he kept his trials secret in his workshop out of town in St. Arbogast. When his business partners – three up-coming artisans and guild members – discovered this, he persuaded them to invest in the idea and they borrowed money to do so. Gutenberg was already in debt and visiting pawnbrokers to fund the construction of a heavy press to his own design. His secret almost came out when one of his partners died and the man's family sued for the return of his investment. Gutenberg hurriedly dismantled all his equipment, but the matter was settled in court without divulging the exact nature of the project.

Gutenberg then moved to Strasberg, the centre of metal craft at the time, and then comes an intriguing question. We learn that

Gutenberg paid his taxes in Strasberg in 1444, but for the next four years there is no record of him. What was he doing, and where? Did he travel somewhere? The mystery is ripe for a story but we know little of his personal affairs. He seems to have focused his entire life on his passion to print and is not known to have married, or even produced offspring, although a dubious case of breach of promise was brought against him by a woman who claimed he had promised to marry her daughter – perhaps she, too, had a good eye for business.

When we catch up with Gutenberg again in 1448, he is in Mainz, borrowing money and inheriting the family home after his elder sister's death; it is in this house that he lived and set up his first commercial press. He experimented with a short German text but the main market was for Latin – still the language of learning throughout Europe – so he printed a twenty-eight page book of his old school grammar, the *Ars Minor* of Aelius Donatus. This was a good choice: it ran to twenty-four editions, each with a print run of over two-hundred copies.[103]

Continued Turkish attacks on the Holy Roman Empire and its capital, Constantinople, provided another bread-and-butter line for Gutenberg: Pope Nicholas V had issued a letter offering indulgence to anyone who donated money to John ll of Cyprus to pay for defence against the Turks – Gutenberg printed thousands of them. But being a jobbing printer was not his goal.

He had the skills, the vision and the dedication to start a revolution in printing for which the time was right, but these attributes were not enough. In the same way that the development of writing had been spurred by commercial needs, so the progress of printing in the west depended on a merchant class ready to invest. Printing in China and Korea had been state sponsored, but Europe's ruling elites were preoccupied with power politics, and they were too impoverished by war to show much interest in industrial innovation other than as a source of taxes. Setting up a printing press required private capital. Gutenberg had few assets and little money, but he had a big idea which demanded new type, heavier presses and a larger workshop.

He found an investment partner in Johann Fust. Though Fust was a newly wealthy metal worker and merchant, he had to borrow the capital. With Fust's backing, and still keeping his techniques secret, Gutenberg printed a standardised edition of St Jerome's original translation of the Bible into Latin (the Vulgate), using four presses simultaneously and taking about two years to achieve the total run of copies. It became known as 'the Gutenberg Bible'. As was still customary for hand-copied books – a craft that continued for a further four centuries – the first printings of the Gutenberg Bible were unbound and without coloured chapter headings and illustrated letters: purchasers hired their own illustrators, rubricators, and bookbinders to finish books to their own requirements.

Fust, with a merchant's acumen for marketing, took copies to the autumn Frankfurt Trade Fair to stimulate advance orders (a forerunner for the Frankfurt Book Fair). Wandering around the fair, when he should probably have been attending to more serious duties, was a Papal Legate, Aeneas Sylvius Piccolomini, who was so impressed by the printed Bible that he wrote to Cardinal Juan de Carvajal urging him to order copies, telling him that 'buyers were lining up even before the books were finished,' and assuring him that the print was so clear he would be able to read it without his spectacles.[104]

The book was an undoubted success, but waiting for payment while continuing to fulfil orders caused financial strain. Fust sued Gutenberg for the interest on his loans and return of the principal sum. Gutenberg lost the case and had to hand over his workshop, equipment, production, everything, to Fust, who thereafter continued as a successful printer. He employed Gutenberg's techniques and types, and took on his calligrapher, Schöffer, as a new partner and master printer.

Sensibly, and probably to maintain a steady income, Gutenberg had continued to operate his smaller jobbing press. He started again in his mid-fifties, training more technicians and inventing a new type for his most ambitious project: printing the *Catholicon*, an important ecclesiastical reference work containing a grammar and dictionary, which extended to over 700 printed pages. As an interesting footnote, when Fust published a lavish edition of the *Mainz Psalter* (for which Gutenberg had already completed most of the preparatory work), it was printed with the colophon or printer's trade mark, 'Fust & Schöffer'. Gutenberg only used a colophon once, in 1460 for the *Catholicon*, and it did not name him but gave the credit to God: 'By the help of the most high [...] who often reveals to the lowly what he conceals from the wise.'[105]

Johannes Gutenberg in his print-shop

Gutenberg's was an extraordinary achievement, an idea requiring the sort of originality that might have led Leonardo da Vinci to a similar outcome; he, too, later learned the craft of metalwork but in Gutenberg's time he was yet a toddler. And Gutenberg had been right to keep his early experiments secret: once he lost control of the technology to Fust, competition quickly established in Mainz, especially from craftsmen he had trained in his own workshop. But work was plentiful: two rival archbishops in Mainz were both distributing their propaganda on printed leaflets. Other printing presses spread rapidly along the Rhine, and war in Mainz accelerated the spread to other European cities as exiled printers settled in Italy, France, Switzerland and Spain. Story had waited impatiently while religious texts hogged the limelight, but now this migration out of Germany coincided with the dispersal *into* Europe of Greek scholars from Constantinople as the city was threatened by Turkish invasion. Refugees from Constantinople brought with them 'lost' treasures of classical Greek literature, including Homer. Among them were many scribes, some of whom settled in Venice and joined the printer, Aldus Manutius, founder of the great Aldine Press, to produce editions of the Greek classics eagerly sought after by Europe's humanist literati.

So keen was competition that pirating was rife. In the preface to his 1518 edition of *Livy*, Aldus warned readers that 'some Florentine printers, seeing that they could not equal our diligence in correcting and printing, have resorted to their usual artifices'; they were marking their inferior works with Aldus' colophon of a dolphin wrapped around an anchor. Aldus advised that the head of their own dolphin turned to the right, whereas in the counterfeit it turned to the left.

If Gutenberg's initial inspiration to print arose from his technical genius and inventive mind, that of Wyllyam Caxton, the first to print in England, was his enthusiasm for literature. For Story, this was a bonus because Chaucer's *Canterbury Tales*, Aesop's fables, Malory's King Arthur, and the Flemish tales of Reynard the fox, were among the books Caxton chose to publish; some he translated into English for the first time, making them available to anyone who could read in the vernacular. Of course, in order to succeed commercially, both Gutenberg and Caxton had to make business decisions about what to print, but Caxton was already a prosperous and influential merchant with political, indeed royal, connections. As a businessman rather than a skilled craftsman, Caxton's printing never reached the artistic and technical quality of Gutenberg's, nor would he have claimed to be a scholar – he was extremely modest about his abilities. But he was a member of the rising merchant-gentleman class, had received a sound classical education, enjoyed reading, and had the patience to translate works from Latin and French into English. Of approximately eighty-seven separate works Caxton is known to have printed, he had translated more than twenty of them – a difficult task because there was no 'standard English' either in meanings or spellings. Regional dialects were often mutually incomprehensible. Caxton commented in one of his prologues that, compared to French, English, especially Old English, was a crude language in which it was often hard to find equivalent terms, and at times so broad he barely understood it himself. But like any good publisher, he knew his readers and aimed each of his works accordingly.

'Some gentlemen which late blamed me, saying that in my translations I had over curious terms, which could not be understood of common people, and desired me to use old and homely terms in my translations […] certainly it is hard to please every man because of diversity and change of language. For in these days every man that is in any reputation in his country will utter his communication and matters in such manners and terms that few men shall understand them. And some honest and great clerks have been with me and desired me to write the most curious terms that I could find; and thus between plain, rude and curious I stand abashed. But in my judgment the common terms that be daily used be lighter to be understood than the old and ancient English. And forasmuch as this present book is not for a rude uplandish man to labour therein ne read it, but only for a clerk and a noble gentleman that feeleth and understandeth in feats of arms, in love and in noble chivalry'.[106]

In addition to the 'clerks (scholars and clerics) and noble gentlemen', his wide circle of merchant friends and royal patrons were his main customers. In recognition – or perhaps as an astute bit of marketing – he dedicated his translation, *The Order of Chivalry* to the reigning monarch, Richard III.

Cy apres selupt la tierce
partie de ce preset traictie la
qlle parle des drois darmes
selon les loix et droit escript.

uremon entendement assez tra
uailie de la pesateur de la matie
ou labeur des precedetes partie
Adone surprins de somme en m

From Caxton's Faits d'armes et de chevalerie (1489).

The book he refers to above as 'not for the rude uplandish man' was *Eneydos* (Virgil's *Aeneid*), an epic poem in which Virgil recruited the

Trojan hero, Aeneas, as a founder of ancient Rome, reinterpreting the legends of Troy – both the *Iliad* and the *Odyssey* – and by doing so he was, perhaps, attempting to trump Homer as well as to establish respectable Greek origins for the Roman republic. Such revival of old legends – reinterpreted with a mixture of wishful fiction to create legitimacy – became a feature of literature during the fifteenth and sixteenth centuries, enlisting Story to strengthen ruling dynasties and perpetuate religious doctrines.

With his usual self-deprecation, Caxton declared he was too 'ignorant' to translate such a classical work alone, and asked John Skelton at the University of Oxford to edit and correct his efforts. Despite his modesty, Caxton's success in steering a path through the 'plain, rude and curious' made a major contribution to stabilising written English, which became increasingly differentiated from the spoken word.

While oral stories continued to breathe and evolve with each new relationship between storyteller and audience, enriched by the time and place of their performance, the act of printing, of producing and distributing hundreds of copies, created a 'definitive text' of a story. And editors or printers often made up titles for stories because traditional oral storytellers did not specify a title – they began with a brief introduction to the tale. Most of these early printed works originated from old hand-copied manuscripts that contained numerous scribal errors or existed in several different versions. A discerning printer sourced more than one manuscript and made editorial decisions on authenticity. An added complication arose because 'writers' were not yet a distinct profession: members of the educated and leisured classes – gentlemen, nobles, clerics, successful merchants, and members of parliament – wrote or translated as a pastime according to their incidental interests. This was especially the case with fiction, for which it was still the custom to re-write and reinterpret traditional legends and classical mythology, borrowing freely from others. Authorship was often difficult to define. Printing began to change this as its potential for spreading knowledge, scientific ideas, and both religious and political propaganda was better appreciated. Identity of authors and 'ownership' of texts would become increasingly important.

Although Caxton was a translator rather than a writer of books, he indulged himself freely, and often wittily, in his lengthy prologues and epilogues to the works he published. It is in these that we learn of his being born and educated in the Weald in Kent, and spending some thirty years in the Low Countries – notably in Bruges, Ghent and Cologne – as a merchant and diplomat. It was here that he later became a member of the household of Margaret, Duchess of Burgundy (Margaret of York, sister to Edward IV and Richard III of England). Caxton received an annual fee from Margaret (possibly for financial services), and she was the connection which inspired him to learn the art of printing.

Caxton's date of birth is uncertain, but was probably around 1422. In his mid-teens, he was apprenticed to Robert Large, one of the foremost mercers in the country, trading in cloth and luxury goods between England and Europe, especially Bruges – which had become a vibrant commercial centre and where, incidentally, the famous Stella Artois brewery had been inebriating the inhabitants since 1366. Robert Large held office in the Mercer's Company (the powerful regulating institution of merchants), was Sheriff of London in 1430, and Lord Mayor nine years later. Caxton could hardly have had a better introduction to high-level trade, and he must have put these influential contacts to good use because he soon became a successful merchant in his own right, setting up an import-export business in Bruges before the age of thirty.

Caxton became a leading figure among the growing number of English merchants in Flanders and, in 1462, Edward IV appointed him Governor of the English Nation in Bruges, a role which required him to protect English merchants' interests, resolve disputes between them, and perform ambassadorial duties in trade agreements. Quite likely, he was also involved in negotiating Margaret of York's marriage to Charles the Bold, Duke of Burgundy, which was a significant political alliance for her brother in securing support for further war against France.

However, in the fluctuations of England's Wars of the Roses – between Yorkist Edward IV and Lancastrian Henry VI – by 1470 Edward was in temporary exile in the Hague and Caxton was in Cologne apparently with time on his hands: 'I have now good leisure, being in Cologne and have none other things to do at this time.' And he spent his time in the service of Story.

Before he travelled to Cologne, Caxton had been reading a recent French book, *The Recuyell of the Historyes of Troye,* and enjoying it so much he began to translate it into English. Despairing of his skills in French, he put his translation aside for some time, but when he showed early chapters to his patron, 'my Lady Margaret', she corrected his mistakes and urged him to continue.

The book was of special significance to Margaret because it was compiled by Raoul le Fèvre, chaplain to the duchy of Burgundy. Le Fèvre had followed the duchy's traditions by interpreting the Greek heroes, Hercules and Jason, as chivalric figures and mythical ancestors of the House of Burgundy into which Margaret had married (one is reminded of the *Song of the Völsungs* and other Icelandic sagas that sought ancient mythical founders for their ruling families). A dramatisation of Hercules' life had been performed as part of the festivities at Margaret and Charles' wedding. Tales of Greek and Roman history, the more fanciful and entertaining the better, had become extremely fashionable all over Europe. King John of France had ordered a French translation of Livy more than a century before; clerics and lay writers eagerly gleaned snippets for their poetry and collections of anecdotes, as they did from Greek texts when these became more widely available.

Raoul le Fèvre was not the only story-writer pandering to royal pretensions. In Europe's mutating theatre of small friable kingdoms challenged by forceful, greedy neighbours, destinies were played out in recurrent wars and the ancient practice of alliance by marriage. Court poets were expected to support their patron's legitimacy with appropriate compositions. With so many changes in partners and fortunes, this could become a tricky task. Margaret of Burgundy was Charles the Bold's third wife; he had been married at the age of seven to his first bride, the twelve-year-old daughter of Charles VII, King of France. She died six years later. For seekers after wealth and political power, sons and daughters were pawns to be placed at best advantage on fate's chessboard. No wonder the fictions of courtly romance and love-yearning ballads of the troubadours were so much in demand: real love – amorous glances at harvest supper and courting along country lanes in anticipation of marriage – was a luxury enjoyed only by the peasantry.

During Caxton's stay in Cologne, he completed his translation of *The Recuyell of the Historyes of Troye* and seems to have used this opportunity also to investigate the printing industry in the city, which was rapidly overtaking Mainz and Strasberg in book production. After the massive task of translation, to have made hand-copies for all those who had asked for Raoul le Fèvre's celebrated story would have involved years of labour. To resolve this, Caxton, now in his early fifties, decided to become a printer.

> 'My pen is worn, my hand weary and not steadfast, mine eyne dimmed with overmuch looking on the white paper, and my courage not so prone and ready to labour as it hath been, and that age creepeth on me daily and feebleth all the body, and also because I have promised to divers gentlemen and to my friends to address to them as hastily as I might this said book, therefore I have practised and learned at my great charge and dispense to ordain this said book in print.'[107]

And ever the merchant, he writes elsewhere that he thought it a good business proposition to have the book available in English. He may already have been buying and selling books as part of his luxury goods trade (unlike other products, there was no tariff on trading books), but they would have been in Latin as most new printed works were. Publishing a book in a vernacular language was still rare and a risk: such readers were a small local market, whereas a book in Latin could be sold all over Europe.

Caxton tells us he went to great expense and effort to learn printing, though not where or how, and it is curious that while in Cologne he commissioned the printing of an encyclopaedia in Latin – *De proprietatibus rerum* by Bartholmaeus Anglicus ('Bartholomew the Englishman') – from the printer Johan Schilling. Possibly, Caxton thought he would find a ready market for the book among scholars, but it would have been an excellent opportunity to have watched the entire printing process, ask questions, and perhaps pay an additional fee for Johan Schilling to teach him the techniques. Caxton was, after all, a well-respected figure in commerce and would hardly be refused such a request.

However it was, on his return to Bruges in 1473/4, Caxton made contact with Colard Mansion, a prominent scribe and illuminator who had recently set up a printing press in two rooms over the porch of St Donatus Cathedral. It is not clear how personally involved Caxton was in the actual printing, but with Mansion's help, and with type probably designed by David Aubert of Ghent (a scribe well known to the Burgundian Court), Caxton published *The Recuyell of the Historyes of Troye,* the first book printed in the English language.

As his first attempt, it was far from perfect – one commentator claims there were 360 misprints – but Caxton was as pleased with the new technology as a child with a brand new Lego set, declaring in the epilogue that it was not written laboriously with pen and ink like other books, but was begun and finished in one day. He dedicated the volume with gracious enthusiasm to his Lady Margaret of Burgundy, pointing out that she had insisted he persevere with the translation and had handsomely rewarded him for his efforts – adding that he hoped she would continue to do so in the future. In the uncertainty of the times, royal patronage was an essential security.

Misprints or not, one of only twenty copies known to have survived the last five-hundred years was sold at Sotheby's on 15 July 2014 for over a million pounds, despite doggerel verses and animal doodles scribbled in some of the margins and recipes copied out on the blank portion of a back page; as the auctioneer's catalogue points out, these are all part of the book's rich history.[108]

After his years of translating the book and learning the new technology to print it, this first successful publication must have caused much celebration in the Caxton household, along with some serious thinking on the business potential: how and where he could best develop it. He seems to have been confident in the growing market of readers in England and keen to produce literary works in his own language – the second book he translated and printed in Bruges was *The Game and Playe of the Chesse*. Although a man like Caxton undoubtedly played chess, this treatise concerns a different kind of gamesmanship. The text is a thirteenth-century allegorical work by Jacobus de Cessolis, who employed chess pieces and short exemplar stories from classical literature to demonstrate social responsibility and good governance – a role we saw Story playing many centuries earlier with animal tales to instruct 'dim-witted' young princes. Caxton's diplomatic role in Bruges ceased as the political scene changed, and this probably had some bearing on his decision to set himself up as a printer, because by 1475/6 he was renting property at Westminster in the grounds of the abbey (coincidentally, near where Chaucer had lived after retirement).

A few years later, Caxton also rented a loft over an archway leading to the abbey's almonry. This may have been an expansion for his printing press and bookshop: in a broadsheet he printed in Latin to advertise his *Sarum Pye* – a booklet listing the order of church services and commemoration of saints' days – he directs its readers to this building, distinguished by the sign of the Red Pale. (Although 'pale' can mean 'fence', as in 'paling fence' and 'beyond the pale', the sign is more likely to have depicted a single paling: a red, vertical stripe, probably against a shield background.) Under the advertisement he asks: 'I pray let this paper stand', so perhaps he had them pinned up in the neighbourhood – the first printed broadsheet in England.[109] He would be surprised to know that, though they no longer 'stand', two originals still exist – one of them in the Bodleian Library in Oxford.

Caxton's assistant, appropriately named Wynkyn de Worde and variously described as Dutch, Alsatian, or French, probably met Caxton in Bruges. Together they issued as the first printings from Westminster, a series of pamphlets including Chaucer's *Anelida and Arcite* (a verse story of love and betrayal from Greek mythology), and three poetical works of Dan John Lydgate (a Suffolk priest, admirer of Chaucer and prolific writer on history and morality), all works which Caxton no doubt knew well and admired. We can imagine his pleasure – and not a little pride – when his royal patron, Edward IV, came to his print-shop to see for himself this remarkable machine brought over from Bruges, and marvelled at a whole page of script being stamped out in seconds.

Caxton in his Almonry print-shop demonstrates the press to Edward IV.

Having run-in his press and, presumably, ironed out any technical problems, Caxton launched immediately into publishing books. From his list of printings,[110] he seems to have drawn on his own literary taste as well as what was popular at the time; among his early publications were Chaucer's *Canterbury Tales* and another best-selling manuscript, the *Legenda Aurea*. This thirteenth-century Latin text was compiled by the Dominican preacher Jacobus de Voragine, who later became Archbishop of Genoa (aka Giacomo de Varazze – one has great sympathy with Caxton's vexed comment elsewhere that, 'Names in these days have diverse equivocations, after the countries that they dwell in').[111] Jacobus narrates often fanciful and miraculous stories of the saints, arranged in the order of the liturgical calendar and interspersed with religious discussion; he probably wrote it to liven up his lessons for priests and students in monastic colleges. However, many of the stories were already favourites in the oral folk heritage of ordinary people and were popular among the educated laity, often inspiring settings and ideas for the guilds' passion plays and pageants.

Jacobus' work epitomised much of the literature of the time in combining Catholic doctrine with the persuasiveness of 'romancing' individual lives of the saints in story- form. Another much read work with similar purpose was the *Gesta Romanorum* ('Deeds of the Romans'). Although a few saints' stories are the same in both collections, *Gesta Romanorum* focuses on tales involving Roman emperors or, more frequently, 'a certain king who had a beautiful daughter ...'. The stories' origins are mixed, but principally from Arabic literature (*Arabian Nights)*, Aesop's fables, and Roman 'history'. The latter was extremely flaky in its facts: in one story, Socrates marries one of those 'beautiful daughters', and is a contemporary of both Emperor Claudius and Alexander the Great. Some stories are so short they are little more than *aides-mémoire*. It seems to have been compiled for the edification and amusement of monks and clerics, because at the end of every one of over 100 stories, moral lessons are stated in a section headed: '*Application*', which draws belaboured and often tortuous allegories between the story characters and precepts of the Church.

Of the two collections, Caxton chose to translate *Legenda Aurea*, published as *The Golden Legend* in 1483. It was his most ambitious production and certainly his largest at almost 900 pages on extra large 'Royal' paper. His book contained many woodcut illustrations because, as he explains in his Preface, he intended it for the education of the unlettered as well as for other readers.

The more fantastic tales of *The Golden Legends* and the *Gesta*

Romanorum were also a rich source of plots and characters for writers. Both Boccaccio and Chaucer had dipped into the tale of Saint Julian the Hospitaller which appears in both collections.

> The night of Julian's birth, his father has a vision that the child is destined to kill its parents. He would have destroyed the baby except for the mother's resistance, and they keep the curse secret.
>
> Raised with the attributes and pursuits of a young Christian nobleman, twelve-year-old Julian is hunting one day when a stag at bay tells him he will kill both his parents. Horrified at the thought of such a terrible act, he travels as far away as he can from his home and finally reaches Galicia, where he eventually marries a wealthy woman of good character and settles down.
>
> Twenty years later, his parents travel all over the country in search of him, praying at churches and asking after him. By chance they seek lodgings with Julian's wife while he is out hunting, and when she discovers who they are, she takes special care of them and lets them sleep in her own marital bed.
>
> But the devil whispers to Julian that his wife has a lover in their bed. He rushes home in a rage, bursts into the bedroom with his sword raised and slays the two sleeping figures in the bed.
>
> As he leaves the house swearing never to return, he is surprised to see his wife talking to some women. She tells him that his parents have arrived and she has settled them in her and Julian's bed.
>
> Julian is distraught at what he has done and wishes himself dead, but his wife comforts him and urges him to have faith in God's mercy. After he prays [i.e. the *Paternosta*] and repents, an angel confirms his forgiveness, and the couple use their wealth to build lodging houses to provide care and hospitality for poor and weary travellers.[112]

In *Canterbury Tales*, Chaucer draws on Julian for the character of the Franklyn, described as a typical provincial squire but one with an epicurean taste for wine and food, both of which he willingly shares with anyone who visits him. And it shows how well the Saint Julian story must have been known that, to emphasise the Franklyn's hospitable nature, Chaucer makes only the briefest reference: 'An householdere, and that a greet was he; Seint Julian he was in his contree'.[113]

Boccaccio's tale in the *Decameron* (the second story on the second day) is less devout and tragic than the original, as one would expect.

> Rinaldo d'Asti, a merchant of Verona, is returning on horseback from a trip to Bologna when he falls in with three fellow travellers. In conversation, he reveals that every morning when on a journey, he recites the Paternoster and an Ave Maria for the souls of Saint Julian's parents, and prays to the saint to provide him with a good lodging that night.
>
> This fact provides additional piquancy to his three companions when they later rob him of everything in a deserted spot, leaving him in only his shirt as darkness gathers.
>
> He walks to the nearest town, Castel Guglielmo, but the gates are locked by the time he arrives, so he shelters under the balcony of a house overlooking the castle walls, where his shivering and moaning is heard by the lively young widow who lives there.
>
> She takes pity on him, providing him with a warm bath, a suit of her late husband's clothes, a hot dinner, and the pleasure of her bed – a good night's lodging for which Rinaldo duly thanks God and Saint Julian. And next day, the robbers are caught and Rinaldo's possessions returned.[114]

Filostrato, the character who relates this, introduces it wittily as 'a story in which are mingled things sacred and passages of adverse fortune and love, which to hear will perchance be not unprofitable, more especially to travellers in love's treacherous lands'. [115]

The emphasis is clearly on romance rather than morality and these raffish tales were obviously meant to titillate a wider general readership. As printing proliferated, authors began to insert forewords into books, expressing their intention that readers should learn moral rectitude from the pit-falls and misdemeanours of others: the ruse did not fool the censors for long.

Not that the religious community was above titillation. The favourite story in a saints' legendary, compiled by a Dominican monk in German prose around 1400 (*Der Heiligen Leben* – 'Lives of The Saints'), was that of Gregorius Peccator ('Gregory the sinner'). Gregory was a young knight born of incest who inadvertently committed the same sin with his mother. Life-threatening penance, for which he chained himself to a rock for seventeen years, led to his forgiveness and his becoming a bishop or, in some versions, a pope. (The same tale is in *Gesta Romanorum* and found its way into a later Icelandic saga, but is not in the more staid *Legenda Aurea*.) This entire German collection of over 200 legends was read probably more than any other in Europe – a 1502 edition had a print-run of 1,000 copies.[116]

For Caxton, producing *The Golden Legend* would have been a good commercial proposition despite the great expense and effort it entailed. And exercising a publisher's prerogative, he left out some of the original accounts and added about sixty other saints' stories drawn from traditional English and Irish sources and the Old Testament. Printing tales from the latter was as close as he would dare go towards enabling people to read the scriptures in their own language: it was still forbidden to publish the Bible in English. With his usual good humour, he writes that he would have given up on the task but for the encouragement of 'my lord William, Earl of Arundel, which desired me to proceed and continue the said work, and promised me to take a reasonable quantity of them when they were achieved ...' and, as a further boon, 'during my life to give and grant me a yearly fee, that is to wit, a buck in summer and a doe in winter'[117], a promise which Caxton alludes to again at the close of the Preface as a polite reminder. As the Earl, William Fitzallan, was Master of the Chase and able to deliver such bounty, it is pleasant to think of old Caxton enjoying free venison steaks for the rest of his days, perhaps with the occasional cask of wine from Margaret's Burgundian court.

In Caxton's chatty prologues and epilogues, he is as a storyteller relating the tale of each publication in the context of his times and revealing the favourite stories of the period.

Influential readers and friends sometimes suggested books he should publish, and he admits to being scolded for translating and printing *The History of Godfrey of Boulogne* – the famous French crusader who led the conquest of Jerusalem – but neglecting the history of England's own hero, King Arthur. He printed *The Noble Histories of King Arthur and of certain of his knights'* in 1485 and, perhaps to make amends for his earlier neglect, his long preface begins with justifying Arthur's fame and popularity, which he points out had been written about more in Europe, especially France, than in England. Caxton describes Arthur as a widely recognised member of those popularly hailed as 'the nine worthy and best men' of the world.

His identification of these nine men provides an insight into the heroes of the period and the stories they inhabited, from the crudest oral tales to sophisticated histories and learned treatises. 'The three Paynims', i.e. pagans or pre-Christians are: Hector of Troy, Alexander the Great, and Julius Caesar – embodiments of Greek and Roman cultures which had found their way into stories in Europe and would continue to be influential. 'The three Jews', also 'before the incarnation of our Lord', are Joshua, King David, and Judas Machabeus, whose stories are told in the Bible and heard by generations of rapt listeners. The Christian heroes he lists as Charlemagne, Godfrey of Boulogne – whose history he had already printed – and King Arthur whom he describes with patriotic fervour as 'first and chief of the three'.[118]

This looks like a sop to his readers, because when first asked by his 'noble gentlemen' friends to produce Arthur's history, he questioned whether Arthur had really existed. Scandalised by his scepticism, the noble gentlemen quoted overwhelming 'evidence' which Caxton details in the preface, including various supposed remains such as Gawaine's skull in Dover Castle and the Round Table in Winchester. That his readers took these so seriously is symptomatic of the culture of saints' relics the friars had encouraged for so long to their own advantage.

Arthur, a Celtic war leader defending what is now Wales against the advancing Saxons, is referred to as a hero of the recent past (perhaps around 500 AD) by the sixth-century Welsh bard, Aneirin, in his poem *Y Gododdin*. Arthur is also mentioned by the Welsh monk, Nennius, in his history of Britain written sometime in the ninth century, though neither Nennius nor Aneirin describes Arthur as a 'king'. These are the only early mentions of Arthur. Later, his name becomes mingled with various legends of saints and heroes until 1133, when another Welsh monk, Geoffrey of Monmouth, wrote his *Historia Regum Britaniae* including Arthur as a heroic Celtic king. Geoffrey claimed that his work was historically accurate and based on ancient Celtic accounts, which he never identified.

These accounts probably no longer existed, but remnants of oral Celtic legends did, and Geoffrey found in them the name of Arthur, a warrior about whom little was known other than his valour during the early Saxon invasions. This must have suited Geoffrey's purpose: a Welshman coming to terms with the Norman colonisation of his country. It seems he wanted to provide an alternative history to the chronicles being written at the time – notably by William of Malmesbury, of mixed English and Norman parentage – which generally started with the Saxons or the Normans, entirely ignoring the island's Celtic past. Geoffrey had to accept that the Britons were ultimately vanquished by the Saxons, but the assertion that this had not been a walk-over – that the Celts had been ruled by a courageous, charismatic leader who led twelve successful battles against the invaders – provided leverage for a history to restore national pride. But written in

Latin, it was little read in England until translated into French and much embellished in 1155 by Maistre Robert Wace, clerk to the court of Henry II of England; and Wace probably added the 'Round Table' to the tale.

From then on, the story grows by accretions like galls on an oak. Many of these contributions or interpretations are still hotly contested by an army of devotees on the Internet, but it is traditional to credit the next major enhancement of the tale to another Welshman, Walter Map, a scholar and diplomat, ambassador to the French court of Louis VII, and a dedicated priest. Map, though captivated by Arthur's passion, apparently felt that a spiritual dimension was lacking, and incorporated the old legend of the *Holy Graal* in a series of prose romances, including the death of Arthur in which Arthur advocated a righteous life dedicated to the love of God. Map had been strongly against the crusades, complaining that they diverted men from their responsibilities at home, so it was left to other writers to develop the theme of chivalry for Arthur and his band of knights.

It was an appealing legend, especially to the French rather than the Saxons (by then vanquished by the Norman invasion), and like any popular story, it was soon taken up by poets and embroidered with each retelling. The French poet and *trouvères,* Crétien de Troyes, created Lancelot and wrote five new 'episodes' focused around chivalry and courtly love – fashionable motifs of his time in the midst of crusade fever. He is also credited with the story of Yvain the Lion Knight which echoes Aesop's fable of the injured lion. And Robert de Boron from Burgundy is believed to have added the *Romance of Merlin*. Not until 1200 was the story written in English, by a priest who claimed that Arthur did not die, but only rested on the Isle of Avalon (identified by devotees as Glastonbury Abbey) to return at some point in the future. Each writer elaborated this original partly-pagan legend with his own culture and purposes – poetic, political or religious – creating strong Christian, chivalric, or moral aspects. The story we know today was compiled by Sir Thomas Malory in 1470. Malory drew mainly from earlier French sources, and he added the relationship between Arthur and his sister, Morgan la Fée, but the social and environmental setting is firmly in his own time.

If Arthur – whether warrior, tribal chief or king – did exist, and there is good reason to suppose he did, his life and those of his fellow resistance fighters would bear little resemblance to the legends since written about them. Caxton appears unconvinced by the relics: 'to pass the time this book shall be pleasant to read in, but for to give faith and belief that all is true that is contained herein, ye be at your liberty.' Believe it if you will. However, he praises the story for its examples of gentle, virtuous deeds, acts of humanity, friendship and love – in the latter part of his life, Caxton was even more a sucker for the chivalry of old. As to the cowardice, murder and hate that are also in the tale: 'Do after the good and leave the evil.' And as a wise publisher must satisfy his readers, he produced a handsome edition comprising 'twenty-one books, which contain the sum of five hundred and seven chapters'.[119]

Caxton was right. As Story knows well, facts are irrelevant to her power; her 'truth' is far more subtle. In Monmouth's time, the recognition of past glory, and a Celtic identity that predated Saxon and Norman invasions, was important in the struggle between English and French cultures taking place in Britain. And from the quill of Malory – an unabashed romantic writer – the combination of a quest, a strong hero with moral authority, and plenty of adventure and love interest has proved irresistible to readers and listeners for the last 600 years and shows no signs of abating.

Malory's own identity is contested but he was almost certainly a knight. It seems he offended someone in authority because, in signing himself as author, he prays to be released from prison (a predicament he shares with a later romance writer of knightly tales, Miguel de Cervantes). Whoever he was, his instinct as a storyteller led him to focus not only on the rise and fall of action, but especially on the relationships between the characters and the conflicts created by betrayal. The legend echoes the essential human dilemma since the dawn of consciousness: our need as social beings to balance individual with group desires, trusting others despite making ourselves vulnerable in the process.

Wondrous aspects of the story, and whether or not it was 'real history', would not have been a concern for most people in that period, so it is interesting that in our own time debate about the truth of Arthur raises such passion and intensity.[120] It can only deepen since a Reading University archaeological team recently discovered that the monks of Glastonbury Abbey, desperate for a source of income after the abbey and all their fund-raising relics were destroyed by fire in 1184, invented the grave of King Arthur and Queen Guinevere to draw pilgrims. Apparently, previous archaeologists had either misread or hidden such subversive evidence. Perhaps, living in a rational age, we can only satisfy our need for this story comfortably if it is 'true' – so we have to convince ourselves that it is so. Two key aspects of legends of all kinds that made them hugely popular were their claims to roots in history – however speculative – which gave them the allure of possibility, and the 'personal hero' that encourages emotional engagement between readers and listeners. Together they allow the acceptance of 'wonderful and extraordinary' deeds that enter our subconscious and mingle with our own narratives.

Morte d'Arthur was one of the last great chivalric stories. Times were changing. The swell of discontent with corruption among religious functionaries and the arbitrary powers of princes and kings – illuminated in the stories of Chaucer and Boccaccio and the learned treatises of the humanists – had been gaining ground all over Europe in a move towards reform. The extravagances of chivalry and courtly love were giving way to a new rationality. Printing played an important role in spreading these ideas, especially when translated into vernacular languages. Caxton had already translated an established best-selling book critical of church and state, *The History of Reynard the Fox*, which he published in 1481, making it available for the first time in English – clearly another good business decision, because it was followed by a second edition a few years later.

Casting human satires around animal characters had been

a tradition since before Aesop's fables and, as with the legend of Arthur, many writers have worked on the Reynard cycle of stories. From at least the twelfth century, writers produced versions in both German and French verse and prose, developing parables from a blend of local folk-tales and oral Greco-Roman traditions, and adapting them to each generation and to all classes of readers. Caxton apparently worked from a prose edition printed in Flanders in 1479, producing a translation described by Henry Morley as 'free, vigorous and lively … full of homely wit'.[121] Such a style of translation would be in keeping with the earthy humour of this scathingly realistic and deeply moral tale; if we listen carefully at the door of Caxton's candle-lit study cluttered with books and papers, we hear him chuckling at both the coarse jests and the underlying subtleties as he searches for just the right turn of phrase to convey the spirit of the story.

The gist of the tale, set with delightful rural details in Flanders, is that Reynard the fox is a trickster: he steals from the other animals, cons them out of their rights, lays devious traps which lead them into trouble or kill them, rapes their wives, and manipulates his accusers with lies and flattery.

> Lion, King Noble with absolute power over all the animals, summons all his subjects to a gathering at Whitsun. Reynard disobeys the instruction because he has a guilty conscience and, in his absence, each of the animals lays complaints against Reynard to the king. Bruin the bear is sent to bring Reynard to the royal court to answer the charges. Reynard feigns cooperation, but tricks Bruin into thinking there is honey inside the cleft of a tree, in which Bruin gets stuck and is beaten by the farmer. Tybert the cat is sent next, and Reynard entices him with mice into a gin trap.
>
> On three later occasions, Reynard confesses his misdemeanours to his nephew, Grimbert the badger, and comes before the king's court, but wriggles his way out

of trouble by claiming sympathy for invented wrongs or by blaming others. The other animals, especially the powerful ones, are not innocent of crime either.

During one of Reynard's court trials in which he is threatened with hanging, he sets the king's sycophantic lords and councillors against each other by fabricating a plot to make Bruin king.

His tricks are so clever, his lengthy and devious arguments so plausible, that even the reader is duped; we can only marvel at his audacity and laugh at the absurdities he orchestrates.

When Reynard makes a pilgrimage to Rome to seek absolution for all his sins, he gains it by conniving with the Cardinal of Pure Gold – whose concubine is Reynard's niece.

Extricating himself from another scrape, Reynard tricks the Ape's wife, Dame Rukenaw, into speaking up for him at the King's Council and putting pressure on the lesser animals to support him. Before a set battle with his rival, Isegrim, the wolf with a monk's tonsure, Rukenaw shaves Reynard all over and oils his fat body so that wolf cannot grip him, and gives him the following advice on tactics:

'Ye muste now drynke moche/that to morowe ye may the better make your vryne/but ye shal holde it in tyle ye come to the felde/And whan nede is and tyme/so shall ye pysse ful your rowhe tayll/and smyte the wulf therwyth in his berde/And yf ye might hytte him therwyth in his eyen thenne shal ye byneme hym his sight/that shold moche hyndre hym/but ellis hold alway yow tayle faste bytwene your legges that he catche yow not therby/and hold doun your eris lying plat after your heed/that he holde you not therby.'[122]

Which may be freely translated – drink a lot tonight so that you have a full bladder tomorrow, then at the right moment, piss on your tail and swipe it in the wolf's face. Aim for his eyes to blind him, but otherwise keep your tail between your legs so he can't catch you by it, and keep your arse down to stop him grabbing you by the …

> With more such brilliant advice, these sly manoeuvres eventually outwit wolf's superior strength and Reynard wins the vicious and bloody fight. While Reynard's erstwhile enemies now fawn on him, he continues his cynical duplicity, so beguiling the king and queen that he is promoted to the position of king's Justice and hailed by all.

There is no redemption in this tale; neither repentance nor final victory of good over evil. The German root of the name 'Reynard' means 'hardened', as in 'hardened criminal'. In his epilogue, the unnamed author tells his readers that though the book is full of jests it also contains wisdom, and if they recognise any of these faults in themselves, it is up to them to improve their ways. He blames no specific persons, but states that the courts of popes, kings and emperors everywhere are full of lords and bishops who practise such lechery, lies, and greedy deceits to get the better of each other at the expense of the powerless. And since clerics even go to Rome and Paris to learn Reynard's craft –'there are more foxes than ever.'[123]

In Caxton's own prologue (an unusually short one for him), he offers the book for the profit and pleasure of any who can read it or hear it and understand it, that they may avoid such evil deeds, and he obviously felt it necessary to point out the story's subtlety, suggesting that the more times it is read, the better it will be understood. The adventures of Reynard were read voraciously all over Europe; Thomas Carlyle described it as 'for some centuries, a universal household possession and secular Bible, read every where in the palace and the hut.'[124] As it was customary for the next two or three hundred years for favourite story-characters as well as notable persons to find their way onto shop and tavern signs, foxes, and especially the Fox and Goose, were popular public-house signboards in England, and in Paris in 1540, a bookseller, Jean Rouelle, traded under the sign of the Fox's Tail. Reynard's story is an entertaining read, and its parody of humanity contains a core of truth that makes it still relevant in our own time.

Wyllyam Caxton's book business continued to flourish. He worked until his death in 1491 after seventeen years of printing – his last publication, touchingly, was his English translation of Savonarola, *Art and Craft to know how well to die,* a preparation for death to the benefit of the soul. One hopes he achieved it.

Wynkyn de Worde carried on the print-shop in Westminster for a few years before moving to London, where he operated from a workshop with the sign of the Sun in the parish of St Brides in Fleet Street – the first printer to do so – and later received a patent as the king's printer. It is in one of his publications, in 1495, that a paper mill in England is first mentioned as being established by John Tate near Hertford, which de Worde records with 'joy' in a brief epilogue. Another of Caxton's assistants, Richard Pynson, worked for de Worde for a while before setting up on his own account, also in Fleet Street.

Printing had already spread from Germany throughout Europe, north and south, and was carried by trade and political dominion from various centres to the Americas, Turkey, North Africa, and Asia. Each nation's earliest publications reflected both their cultural significance and the ownership of the printing press: in 1530, the first press was brought to Hólar in Iceland by a bishop and was run by the church for the next 200 years, publishing a vernacular New Testament in 1540; in North America, the *Bay Psalm Book,* produced in Massachusetts in 1640, was probably the first printed book from a press brought by missionaries, and in India, *Shâhnâmeh Firdusi*, a traditional epic poem printed in Bombay in Persian was followed by the *Ramayana* in Sanskrit. China had continued prolific block printing, but by 1729, China's state printers were using moveable type to print *Gujin Tushu Jicheng*, a massive collection of almost the entire literary and artistic heritage of the empire from the earliest times, covering some 800,000 pages.

Along with a generation of others in Europe, Caxton had been translator, editor, publisher, printer, book seller and, judging from the length of his prologues and epilogues, a writer, too, but commercial drive in the printing industry quickly overtook the literary-gentleman type of printer. Although Wynkyn de Worde produced on his own account some 500 titles, he remained strictly a printer and stationer, advancing his craft by using italic type for the first time in England and printing music with the new technology. The capital investment required to set up a new print-shop was considerable. Technical specialisation, and increasing volumes of production for a fast-growing market, began to divide the process into separate professions with different objectives that influenced which stories were made available to the general reader.

From the sixteenth century, the changing nature of 'authority' challenged the supremacy of sacred texts (which only a small section of the population could read) in favour of more accessible popular propaganda and stories. This process had begun much earlier with the vernacular tales of Chaucer and Boccaccio, exposing the worst aspects of the church as an institution with its snout in the trough of worldly corruption – decadence shared by those in governance. Opposition to Roman Catholicism, which Wycliffe and his Lollards had attempted in England, was more successful in Germany. Martin Luther, now with the aid of print to disseminate his message, wrote such a profusion of pamphlets and treatises, along with a translation of the Bible into German, that by the time he died in 1546, he had authored a third of all books being printed in Germany. By that time, too, half of the country was out of Rome's control and establishing the new Protestant religion.[125]

One of Luther's first publications ridiculed the fictions and fantasies promoted by the Roman church, which he claimed were meant to dupe the people. He targeted especially legends of the saints. Employing one of these stories as his own propaganda, Luther published an edition of the legend of St John Chrysostom, a particularly fantastic tale in which a maiden is carried by the wind up to his hermit's cave; he seduces her and, overcome with guilt, pushes her off a cliff. After years of living like an animal in penance, the saint sees the woman with their child, miraculously saved. Luther discredits the legend in an afterword, and points out absurdities in marginal notes: where the saint withdraws into a life of poverty and solitude 'because temporal goods are injurious to the soul', Luther comments tartly that not even the Pope would believe that. The episode is not in *The Golden Legend,* which depicts John Chrysostom as so upright and austere an archbishop that he makes enemies among the clergy; Luther took the story from the more sensational German collection, *Der Heiligen Leben*.

Printing spread new ideas and stories too far and too fast for the Church to suppress them. But the interlacing of politics and vested financial interests in religion stirred up thirty years of religious wars in Continental Europe. Books were destroyed, heretics and 'witches' burnt at the stake. In Spain – unique in its historical legacy of large Muslim and Jewish populations – the Supreme Court of the Inquisition had been established since 1478 to protect the Catholic 'old guard' from rising humanism, and especially from the growing wealth and power of ex-Jews who had converted en masse to Christianity in response to oppression. The Court's focus changed over time to concentrate more on the censorship of books and on sexual morality, but it was not finally abolished until 1835.

Story trod warily but bravely among these factions and wars in Europe, for she had much work to do there.

Chapter Nine

A clash of two ages amid gargantuan change

Amidst Rome's violent suppression of humanism and Protestantism in much of Europe, Story is claimed by all sides and her protégé threatened and tortured. Rabelais pens scurrilous satire in a call for freedom as Marguerite of Navarre tries to protect him and other free thinkers who demand reform of the Catholic Church.

Marguerite was already known for her intellectual gifts and her kindness

9

Let us always remember this tender Queen of Navarre,
in whose arms our people, fleeing from prison or
the pyre, found safety, honour and friendship. Our
gratitude to you, Mother of our Renaissance!

[Jules Michelet: *History of France*]

Joggled in her mule-drawn litter along the stony, potholed country roads of southern France, Marguerite, Queen of Navarre, bade her lady of honour grasp the escritoire more firmly so that she could write upon it with greater ease. She wrote quickly and fluently in vernacular French, the witty, satirical stories that would become known as the *Heptameron*. They told of the scandalous doings of the aristocrats and royals she knew so well, of others' amusing domestic skirmishes, and of the notorious lechery of friars – all discreetly disguised in the characters of her tales.

She was better placed than most to write on such matters. A member of France's royal house of Valois, she was also known as Marguerite d'Angoulême, after the name of the duchy in which she was born in 1492. She and her brother, Francis, two years her junior and heir presumptive to the throne, studied under the best scholars of the day. Bright, eager pupils, they showed an aptitude for Latin, Greek philosophy, literature and, of course, divinity, probably reading the lives of the saints in the original Latin. Together they enjoyed the usual past-times of music and drama, chess, archery and tennis, Marguerite watching Francis in his jousting at the tourney

– they were inseparable. Their widowed mother raised them at the Chateau d'Ambois under the guardianship of Louis XII, and in their early teens, they both moved to Louis' court to prepare Francis for his future role as monarch, a position reinforced by his marriage to Louis' daughter, Claude.

As the pendulum of relations between England and France swung from war to alliance by marriage and back again, Marguerite nearly became part of the English Tudor household: after the death of Elizabeth of York, the forty-seven-year-old Henry VII was a suitor for twelve-year-old Marguerite. Negotiations faltered, and three years later, she became Duchesse d'Alençon through her marriage to the duke, Charles – a politically expedient match to a man who shared none of her learning. But as her soldier husband spent most of his time away fighting, Marguerite oversaw the administration of the duchy, and when her brother became King Francis I of France in 1515, she became his confidential advisor along with their mother.

Marguerite was already known for her intellectual gifts and her kindness. She gathered around her a circle of France's notable poets and writers: François Rabelais, whom we meet soon; Bonaventure Despériers, who later became her secretary; Étienne Dolet, a scholar and printer; Anthony le Maçon, another of her secretaries, and Clément Marot, court poet who accompanied Francis on military campaigns as poets had done since the days of Celtic bards.

All of these intellectuals, along with Marguerite their patron, espoused much of the humanism of her friend, the Dutch priest and scholar, Desiderius Erasmus. They favoured reform in the church, but not necessarily the austere Protestant religion that Martin Luther was successfully forging in Germany and that John Calvin preached in Paris before his exile. One of the great scholars of the Reformation, Erasmus led the humanist search for original sources of philosophy and faith to be found in the study of antiquity, including newly available Greek texts which gave a fresh perspective on history. He greatly admired the second-century AD Syrian satirist, Lucian (who wrote in Greek) and said of him: 'he has a way of mixing gravity with his nonsense and nonsense with his gravity, of laughing and telling the truth at the same time' – a style elaborated by Rabelais. Erasmus, too, wrote satires as well as erudite treatise and translations, and he was optimistic. In a letter to a friend in 1517 he wrote, 'I am led to a confident hope that not only morality and Christian piety but also a genuine and purer literature may come to renewed life or greater splendour.'[126] And in an amusing give-away on attitudes towards erstwhile 'barbarians' he adds, 'Polite letters which were almost extinct are now cultivated and embraced even by Scots, Danes and Irishmen.'

But Erasmus' optimism was misplaced. His claim that church institutions had debased true Christianity, and his call for greater personal freedom of worship within the Catholic faith proved too much of a challenge; the religious establishment saw such intellectual freedom as a major threat to its authority.

In France, Italy and Spain, resistance to this new movement was severe; political power and wealth of church and state were too tightly entangled to admit reform. The slightest deviation from Catholic doctrine – even eating meat during Lent – could be punished by imprisonment. 'Free thinkers' without powerful contacts to save them were burnt at the stake. For as long as she could, Marguerite used her influence as the king's sister to protect from persecution not only her literary circle but also reformist bishops. Her own long devotional work in verse, *Miroir de l'âme pécheresse* ('Mirror of a Sinful Soul') which spoke of her spiritual, personal relationship with God and omitted the standard references to saints, martyrs and miracles, was deemed by the theologians of the Sorbonne to be 'unorthodox'. They demanded it be burnt. To protect his beloved sister, Francis had her most outspoken critic, Noël Béda, thrown into a dungeon at Mont St Michel from which he never emerged.

As well as Marguerite's significant political and diplomatic role at the French court, her strength and tenderness made her a principal nurturer to her family. When Francis led a major campaign against Italy in 1525, he set his mother to rule France as Regent and, since his wife was in a critical condition with tuberculosis, left his six children in Marguerite's care. With the exquisite timing of children, they all promptly fell sick together and she lost her favourite niece. That same year, she also lost her husband, Charles, who died in her arms from battle injuries. Though it had not been a particularly satisfying union for her with Charles' long absences, in her copious writings she expresses an enlightened attitude towards marriage in which love is an essential part of a conjugal relationship.

> 'I call perfect lovers those who seek some perfection in the object of their love, be it beauty, kindness, or good grace, tending to virtue, and who have such high and honest hearts that they will not even for fear of death do base things that honour and conscience blame.'[127]

Marguerite had no sympathy for wives who indulged their husband's infidelities, although she tolerated with good humour her brother's multiple mistresses. And again, Francis needed her help. With his Italian expedition defeated at the battle of Pavia, Francis languished, dangerously ill, in a prison in Madrid. Marguerite travelled there to nurse him at great personal risk, while engaging in tricky negotiation with Spain's king and Holy Roman Emperor, Charles V, to ransom Francis. Having difficulty influencing the lawyers, nobles and bishops who held sway, she also appealed to their wives, mothers and daughters. Marguerite finally succeeded in obtaining promises of her brother's release in exchange for his two oldest boys as hostages. She returned to France barely escaping imprisonment herself. The 'safe pass' she had been granted was due to expire; in haste, she rode hard on horseback with her entourage rather than in a customary litter.

Emperor Charles had been so impressed by this tall, dignified widow who, though no beauty with her long nose and large mouth, possessed such wit and charm as well as great intellect, that he contemplated marrying her. But Marguerite had another offer. For the second time, she was propositioned by a Tudor king. England's Henry VIII proposed a marriage alliance with her, preparatory to divorcing Katherine of Aragon – a liaison that did not appeal to

Marguerite. A wise decision. Instead, she pressed Francis to arrange a marriage for her with the brave and dashing heir to the throne of Navarre, Henry d'Albret. She had known him since her youth and nursed a secret affection for him.

Henry had also fought at Pavia and been taken prisoner in the fortress there. He escaped by leaving a page as a sleeping decoy in his cell, and scaling the outside walls of the castle by rope during the night. In his twenty-fifth year, Henry was eleven-years younger than Marguerite and proved to be a philandering, neglectful husband. Nor did he care for tedious state administration: that was left to his new wife, now with the title Marguerite, Queen of Navarre. She accomplished the task with efficiency and grace, setting up public works and schools to benefit the disadvantaged in their realm.

The province of Navarre, on the French side of the Pyrenees, had been contested for generations between France and Spain, but at this time it was under the patronage of France. So much so that Francis whisked away Marguerite's three-year-old daughter, Jeanne, to be carefully educated in France for her future role as heir to the throne of Navarre. Francis' action could not be challenged, but it must have been hard for Marguerite whose first-born, a son, had already died in infancy. Francis arranged a marriage for Jeanne when she was nine years old; a sickly child, so weighed down by heavy jewels and her bridal gown of gold-threaded brocades that she was unable to walk. A cleric carried her into the church to make her vows.

But Marguerite hardly had time to feel deprived of mothering her own daughter. In addition to her duties in Navarre, she continued active in French affairs, spending as much time as she could with her brother in Paris, while attending to matters in the Duchy of Alençon and other lordships which Francis had given her as dowry. Through her deep involvement in mediating between opposing religious extremists, she saved the lives of many reformist clerics as well as intellectuals, providing them a safe haven at the Castle of Nérac. She even found energy to translate parts of the New Testament to construct tragicomedies, engaging top actors and musicians from Italy to entertain the court. With her attention stretched between the extreme north and south of the country, she led the life of an itinerant, finding in the arduous days of travelling sufficient time and opportunity to write.

Returning again to that joggling litter in which sat the Queen of Navarre and Louise de Daillon – the attendant holding her escritoire – we find them going home after visiting the popular Pyrenean hot springs at Cauterets, and not for the first time. The healing qualities of the hot mineral mud in autumn were well known; now in her fiftieth year, Marguerite found it a great restorative after the aches and minor ailments that overtook her occasionally, and she chose this location as the framing device for her collection of stories.

She describes a party of upper class patrons who had spent most of September benefiting from the springs at Cauterets. As they prepared to leave, there was such a continuous deluge that flooding made roads impassable; they were driven to crossing the Pyrenees into Spain and hiring a boat to return to France. Mid-sixteenth century travel was dangerous at the best of times. On this occasion, one woman's husband was murdered by brigands in league with the innkeeper, and the men escorting an elderly widow, Oisille, were killed by marauders. The ten survivors – the two widows, a married couple with their servant, a pair of boisterous cavaliers, two flighty young ladies, and a retired knight – eventually met up at the Abbey of Notre Dame de Serrance. Having persuaded the abbot to grant them shelter, they spent the first evening sharing their horrendous experiences of travelling there.

As the weather worsened, they realised they would be trapped for some time, so Oisille suggested that, after allowing sufficient time for personal devotions, they should meet in the gardens every afternoon to entertain each other with stories. The resulting entertainment was so alluring that some of the monks were discovered listening from behind a hedge; vespers sometimes began late.[128]

Some critics decried Marguerite's stories as mimicking Boccaccio's *Decameron* – which she had certainly read because she asked one of her secretaries, the poet Anthony le Maçon, to translate it from Italian

– but mutual storytelling to pass the time was integral to French culture; she borrowed only the framing idea of stranded characters. Her storytellers show greater variety and complexity than Boccaccio's, their dialogues more revealing. With one or two exceptions, all the tales are original – with the life she led, Marguerite hardly needed to plagiarise other's work – and most are elaborations of real events known to her. They unveil the society in which she lived with explicit humour, which later generations found offensive, especially from a woman. But the stories all portray how the application of honesty, virtue and quick-wittedness can defeat the venality and deceit of others, as in the tale below, in which 'Grey Friars' refers to the Franciscan Order (reviled also by François Rabelais, who was one of their number for a short time).

'At the haven of Coulon, near Nyort, there lived a boatwoman who, day or night, did nothing but convey passengers across the ferry.

Now it chanced that two Grey Friars from Nyort were crossing the river alone with her, and as the passage is one of the longest in France, they began to make love to her to relieve the dullness of the trip. She returned them the answer that was due; but they, being neither fatigued by their journeying, nor cooled by the water, nor put to shame by her refusal, determined to take her by force, and, if she clamoured, to throw her into the river. She, however, was as virtuous and clever as they were gross and wicked, and said to them, "I am not so ill-disposed as I seem to be, but I pray you grant me two requests. You shall then see that I am more ready to give than you are to ask."

The friars swore to her by their good St. Francis that she could ask nothing that they would not grant in order to have what they desired of her.

"First of all," she said, "I require you both to promise on oath that you will inform no man living of this matter." This they promised right willingly.

"Then," she continued, "I would have you take your pleasure with me one after the other, for it would be too great a shame for me to have to do with one in presence of the other. Consider which of you will have me first."

They deemed her request a very reasonable one, and the younger friar yielded the first place to the elder. Then, as they were drawing near a little island, she said to the younger one, "Good father, say your prayers here until I have taken your companion to another island. Then, if he praises me when he comes back, we will leave him here, and go away in turn together."

The younger friar leapt out on to the island to await the return of his comrade, whom the boat-woman took away with her to another island. When they had reached the bank she said to him, pretending the while to fasten her boat to a tree, "Look, my friend, and see where we can place ourselves."

The good father stepped on to the island to seek for a convenient spot, but no sooner did she see him on land than she struck her foot against the tree and went off with her boat into the open stream, leaving both the good fathers to their deserts, and crying out to them as loudly as she could, "Wait now, sirs, till the angel of God comes to console you; for you shall have nought that could please you from me to-day."

The two poor monks, perceiving that they had been deceived, knelt down at the water's edge and besought her not to put them to such shame; and they promised that they would ask nothing of her if she would of her goodness take them to the haven. But, still rowing away, she said to them, "I should be doubly foolish if, after escaping out of your hands, I were to put myself into them again."

When she had come to the village, she went to call her husband and the ministers of justice that they might go and take these fierce wolves, from whose fangs she had by the grace of God escaped. They set out accompanied by many people, for there was no one, big or little, but wished to share in the pleasure of this chase.

When the poor brethren saw such a large company approaching, they hid themselves each in his island, even as Adam did when he perceived his nakedness in the presence of God. Shame set their sin clearly before them, and the fear of punishment made them tremble so that they were half dead. Nevertheless, they were taken prisoners amid the mockings and hootings of men and women.

Some said, "These good fathers preach chastity to us and then rob our wives of theirs."

Others said, "They are like unto whited sepulchres, which indeed appear beautiful outward, but are within full of dead men's bones and uncleanness."

Then another voice cried, "By their fruits shall ye know what manner of trees they are."

You may be sure that all the passages in the Gospel condemning hypocrites were brought forward against the unhappy prisoners, who were, however, rescued and delivered by their Warden [the Father Superior], who came in all haste to claim them, assuring the ministers of justice that he would visit them with a greater punishment than laymen would venture to inflict, and that they should make reparation by saying as many masses and prayers as might be required. The judge granted the Warden's request and gave the prisoners up to him; and the Warden, who was an upright man, so dealt with them that they never afterwards crossed a river without making the sign of the cross and recommending themselves to God.'[129]

The detail that the minister of justice gave up the prisoners to the Father Superior is significant: it illustrates a major contention of humanists and reformers that canon law was encroaching too far into civil affairs and impeding justice in secular crime by protecting religious functionaries.

Tale IV of the *Heptameron*, which also tells of an attempted rape, is largely autobiographical. Marguerite's first husband was living at the time of this event, so she disguises her identity by making the heroine a twice widowed princess, 'of the most illustrious lineage of Flanders', whose brother, the Prince, is lord to the handsome and over-ardent 'hero' of the tale. This lusty fellow is not named in the story and is referred to only as 'the gentleman', but we learn from the memoirs of Pierre de Brantôme, who was raised in Marguerite's household and was the grandson of Louise de Daillon – the 'holder-still' of the escritoire – that he was in fact William Gouffier, Lord of Bonnifet.[130] William had grown up with Marguerite and Francis, enjoying an affectionate relationship with both. He held important offices when Francis was king, including that of admiral, but he must have abused his privileged friendship with Marguerite, giving rise to the story summarised below:

The Princess, a discreet and honourable yet fun-loving young widow, lives in the household of her brother, the illustrious Prince. Among the Prince's courtiers is a handsome gentleman who shares the Prince's sporting interests and is a great favourite, spending so much time in the family's company that he develops a deep love for the Princess. One day, he takes the bold step of declaring his love. She refuses him, and while she forgives his presumption, asks him never to mention it again.

Her would-be lover grows more ardent, convincing himself that if he could gain some advantage over this lively young woman, he would overcome her reserve. He invites the Prince to hunt the best season's stags on his estate. The invitation is accepted and the Prince brings his family to stay at the gentleman's house in the country. The Prince and his wife are given rooms in one wing of the house, the Princess placed in another. Her room is richly appointed with tapestries and with thick floor matting (which conceals a trapdoor in the floor beside her bed). The room beneath is occupied by the gentleman's elderly mother, but since she suffers with her chest, and her coughing might disturb the Princess, she exchanges rooms with her son.

After a few days of conviviality, the gentleman and his mother spending much time in the Princess' chamber, entertaining her with sweet-meats and conversation, he keeps her up very late one evening. When she finally bids him leave, he returns to his room, dresses in his finest gold-threaded, perfumed shirt, and arranges his embroidered nightcap until he is confident that his charms and grace are irresistible. There he waits until silence tells him that the Princess and her lady of honour are asleep in the room above.

He enters stealthily through the trapdoor unnoticed in the darkness, and overcome by impatience he clambers immediately into the Princess' bed. On being so violently awakened, she scratches and bites the unknown intruder with such ferocity that he flees back to his room without accomplishing his desire, his face badly cut, his best shirt stained with blood.

The Princess and her lady of honour, finding no way an assailant from outside could enter the room, begin to suspect their gentleman host since no one else in the Prince's entourage would dare attempt such an act. The Princess wants to report him to her brother, but the lady persuades her against it, saying that his shame and failure will be sufficient revenge and he is unlikely to tell anyone. Whereas if he is punished, it will become public knowledge; people will assume her virtue was taken, that there must have been encouragement on her part and her reputation will be ruined. She advises the Princess to say nothing, but to gradually withdraw her friendship from him.

When the Prince's party are ready to take leave of their host the next day, they are told that he is too sick to bear the light or be spoken to and they depart without seeing him. The Princess rightly guesses that he is afraid to have the telling marks on his face seen by anyone.

An intriguing little twist to the original incident, given in Pierre de Brantôme's memoir, is that Marguerite's worldly-wise lady of honour on this occasion was the wife of Cardinal Jean du Bellay,[131] whom we meet again because he was François Rabelais' principal patron. Circles of power and influence were, indeed, tightly drawn.

Pierre de Brantôme is worth a brief diversion as a good example of the kind of corruption in the Catholic Church people complained about. The third son of a baron, de Brantôme spent his childhood in Marguerite's household in Navarre – where both his mother and grandmother were employed – and completed his education at the University of Poitiers. Both Marguerite and Francis had died by this time, so he presented himself to Francis' son and successor, Henry II of France. Henry awarded him an abbey and lordship and several benefices. Brantôme, neither priest nor monk but destined to be a professional soldier, drew on the rents and church tithes of the abbey and parishes for income, no doubt supplemented by bounties and loot from the various wars in which he participated all over Europe. Church rents and tithes, ultimately generated by an over-worked and under-fed common populace, were routinely awarded in this way to anyone whose loyalty was sought for political ends.

Marguerite died in 1549, her collection of stories published posthumously. Although we saw the benefits of printing over hand-copying – faster, cheaper, no copying errors and wider distribution – Story is at the mercy of a printer, and in the absence of the author, a bowdlerized text may become fixed in type to Story's detriment. The first publication of Marguerite's collection, in 1558, was by Peter Boaistuau, under the title *Histoires des Amans Fortunez*. Boaistuau not only referred to the unnamed author as 'he', and edited the manuscript someone had given him 'to cleanse it of a multitude of errors', but he also cut out stories, added others and completely changed the form of the whole work. For the enjoyment of Marguerite's tales we are indebted to another printer, Claud Gruget, who recognised the travesty of the first version and did what Caxton would have done: he gathered several hand-copied versions for comparison, and produced an edition as close as he could to Marguerite's original content and structure, giving her full credit as author. It was Gruget who gave it the title *Heptameron* ('Seven Days Work') indicating multiple stories on each of seven days, comparing her work favourably to that of Boccaccio's *Decameron*. In fact there are seventy-two tales: on an eighth day, only two are told because Marguerite did not live long enough to complete her plan for a hundred stories.

Amid the general violence and repression that pervaded social institutions throughout Europe during the fifteenth and sixteenth centuries, patronage was essential for survival. Marguerite had saved many lives, but during the latter part of her life, her power to protect the persecuted greatly diminished. Among those who had been in her circle, Clément Marot was imprisoned several times – initially for breaking Lent – and then hounded from one country to another until he died in exile in Turin. Bonaventure Despériers' suicide in 1544 is believed to have been his way of escaping almost certain death at the stake. And the printer, Étienne Dolet – apparently an outspoken man who kow-towed to no one and made enemies in both religious camps – defiantly published both Calvinist tracts and a work by Plato. Theologians at the Sorbonne had Dolet condemned, tortured, and burnt alive.

François Rabelais was more circumspect. He wrote his first two books of gritty satirical prose, *Pantagruel* and *The Great Gargantua,* under the anagrammatic pseudonym 'the late M. Alcofribas Nasier', and in the prologues and epilogues of all five books, he insists that he tells these jokes and funny stories merely to amuse his readers: 'Mirth's my theme and tears are not, for laughter is man's proper lot.'[132] However, he hints at deeper meanings in his second book: 'the subjects here treated are not as foolish as the title on the cover suggested.'[133] His instincts to dodge impending trouble, his powerful patrons – Marguerite and her brother, and Jean du Bellay, Bishop of Paris (later Cardinal) – and his value as a physician all protected him, although they did not prevent the Sorbonne from condemning his books.

Rabelais' date and place of birth are uncertain – with the raging religious wars and eventual revolution that followed, it is a wonder any documents at all survived – but he was born sometime between

1583 and 1594, and probably in Chinon where his father was a successful lawyer holding public office. Being the youngest of four children, with two older brothers and therefore unlikely to inherit, he would be expected to seek his livelihood in the church, and he attended a Franciscan school. Later, he enrolled as a novice at the convent, in due course taking his full vows. But Rabelais' passion was learning and he found the Franciscans too restrictive. Local tutors, whom the young monks found to teach them Greek, had links with humanist scholars and the word 'heresy' was being whispered around the musty cloisters. Rabelais obtained the Pope's permission to rescind his Franciscan vows and transfer to a Benedictine monastery nearby. In his new abbot, Geoffroy d'Estissac, he found a long-term supporter.

With his studies probably funded by the Benedictines, Rabelais went to Paris and Montpellier to read medicine. By the early 1530s he was lecturing and in practice as a physician. Around this time he wrote his first book of allegorical fantasy, *Pantagruel,* describing this giant's youth with his father Gargantua, his education, and 'his terrible deeds and acts of prowess' as king of the Dipsodes (not an accidental pun on 'dipsomania').

François Rabelais

In Rabelais' choice of setting and characters, he rode the slipstream of an extremely popular tale made widely available in 1532 in small, cheaply printed 'chap book' editions. Published anonymously, *The Great and Inestimable Chronicles of the Enormous Giant Gargantua* draws on traditional French folk-tales about the giant of that name, combining them with another favourite legend in France, that of our old friend King Arthur and his knights. In the *Chronicles,* Merlin fashions a giant, Grandgousier, from the bones of a male whale mixed with a phial of Lancelot's blood, and makes him a wife from the bones of a female whale and ten pounds of Guinevere's nail clippings. The two giants produce

Gargantua whom Merlin takes to Arthur to assist in his battles. Arthur has a massive iron club made for Gargantua, with which he destroys the army of Gog and Magog and subdues Dutch and Irish rebellions.[134] We need not worry about the muddled history if we remember Story's trait of adopting tales and adapting them to local culture and current affairs.

Gog and Magog in British legend were the two survivors of a ferocious tribe, descendants of the daughters of Emperor Diocletian who slew their husbands. Giants are prolific inhabitants of myth and story. The Greeks had the sons of Uranus and Gaea, and the Old Testament cites the Anakim and Rephaim tribes of giants in Jordan before the Israelites. To add to a delightful confusion, Geoffrey of Monmouth (the originator of the King Arthur story) mentions a commanding giant in Cornwall by the name of Goemagot. In ancient folk histories giants often account for features in the landscape: the Giant's Causeway in Ireland, and Stonehenge which, according to Geoffrey of Monmouth, was transported from Ireland by Uther Pendragon's troops under instructions from Merlin. But it was not all fancy: there have been many documented giants of believable size. The third-century Roman Emperor, Maximus I, was said to be 8 feet 6 inches tall, and Charles I employed a porter, William Evans, who measured 8 feet in height. In choosing Gargantua as a character, Rabelais was following a popular story tradition, but he might also have been making fun of the credulity of those who believed the Old Testament literally, including the story of OG, King of Bashan, claimed to be the 3,000-year-old giant who walked beside the Ark during the Flood.[135]

In his prologue to *Pantagruel*, Rabelais lavishes praise on the *Chronicles* and is well aware of its success, commenting that: 'more copies of it have been sold by the printers in two months than there will be of the Bible in nine years.'[136] Without actually claiming authorship of the *Chronicles*, Rabelais would not be above gaining a bit of leverage by association, and he continues its chronology by inventing Pantagruel as the son of Gargantua, making him a mock-chivalric hero with a couple of dubious 'knights' in attendance.

Prose fiction in the vernacular was already being written in France, but such sustained phantasmagorical satire was an innovation.

Pantagruel's friend, Panurge, is described as: 'A bit of a lecher [...] a mischievous rogue, a cheat, a boozer, a roysterer, and a vagabond if ever there was one in Paris, but otherwise the best fellow in the world.'[137] Their companion, Friar John, is an arms-wielding maverick and heavy boozer, notable for his flask disguised as a breviary – a popular novelty at the time; apparently Rabelais owned one himself.[138] The action consists of a series of sometimes-connected happenings in the sketchiest of leaky plots, and characters are little more than cardboard caricatures inconsistent from one book to the next. But Rabelais is not concerned with literary finesse. His imagination drives his writing with a sort of mad energy. In absurd verbal burlesque, his characters tumble, often clumsily, across the pages. The speeches, stories and dirty jokes they tell each other are vehicles for Rabelais' distinctive cocktail of bawdiness, erudition and invective through which his characters literally piss on the self-serving cant in the public life he so despises.

Among a host of other adventures in this first book, Pantagruel defeats 300 giants, and his friend Panurge brings back to life one Epistemon, whose head had been cut off. Epistemon tells them about the devils he had seen while in hell.

'They don't treat them as badly as you'd think,' said Epistemon. 'But their way of life is most strangely altered. For I saw Alexander the Great darning breeches for a miserable living.'[139]

All the great Greek and Roman heroes of history and mythology are similarly lampooned, and he takes a swing at past popes, allotting them various occupations in hell: a pie seller, a skimmer of pots, a rat-catcher, and an anointer of pox sores.

Rabelais is especially critical of the out of date and restrictive education methods of the Sorbonne. Pantagruel studies in Paris and Rabelais writes a six-page list of spoof books to be found in the university there; many are punned Latin titles, but for a few examples of others: 'The Handcuffs of Devotion', 'The Tipplings of the Bishops', 'The Kiss-My-Arse of Surgery', 'The Codpiece of the Law', and 'The Maidens' Shittery'. The humour of many other references to local people and current events of his time is now lost in obscurity.

And he derides the pomposity of lawyers and theologians. While in Paris, Pantagruel comes to a judgement on a convoluted and difficult case he is asked to deal with: 'Then in the Sorbonne he argued with the theologians for the space of six weeks, from four in the morning till six at night […] But not withstanding their ergos and sophistries, he made fools of them all, and conclusively proved to them that they were just calves in petticoats.' [140] This is followed by a long letter to Pantagruel from his father, Gargantua, which is a serious statement about education policy.

It was this kind of ridicule that enraged the Sorbonne. They banned his book. Rabelais escaped the furore by accompanying Bishop du Bellay to Rome as his physician, leaving the manuscript of his second book to be published in Lyon a few months later. *The Most Fearsome Life of the Great Gargantua* goes back in time to give us Pantagruel's ancestry from his grandfather Grandgousier and his father Gargantua, before launching into more episodes of Pantagruel and his friends. Much of the description at the beginning is the same as in the *Chronicles*, but the major part is original and in the same style as *Pantagruel*. His second book was as popular as his first and the Sorbonne condemned this book, too.

When religious hostilities broke out while he was in Rome, Rabelais bolted without permission. The situation soon settled, however, and du Bellay recalled him, his unauthorised departure forgiven – du Bellay was now a cardinal with considerable influence. He appreciated Rabelais' skills as a doctor, as did many other prominent people including the Pope. Most people still believed that diseases such as the plague were caused by sin, a superstition encouraged by preaching friars and pedlars of absolution. Quacks abounded, selling remedies often worse than the ailment. But under humanist influence, medical schools were beginning to question the thousand-year-old wisdom of Galen and Hippocrates on which their teaching was based. Legally and illegally, corpses were being dissected, and enlightened individuals began giving direct observation more credence over ancient theory. By the same method, Leonardo da Vinci had already discovered much about human anatomy. And the use of artillery in warfare resulted in new forms of injury which stimulated better surgery. Rabelais would still have used many traditional treatments – notably blood-letting – as was the norm, but he was keenly interested in these new developments and no doubt applied them when he could. In recognition, the Pope appointed Rabelais a secular priest, enabling him to travel more freely, but he would pursue a cat and mouse game with the politics of religious condemnation for the remainder of his career.

Rabelais completed advanced medical studies at Montpellier and then became physician and secretary to the Governor of Turin, Seigneur de Langey (du Bellay's brother), a position he held until Langey's death in 1543. Back again in France, he was keen to publish further work despite increasingly harsh censorship laws. King Francis issued him a six-year licence to print his books, but Francis was strongly against reform, seeing the spectre of Protestantism in any shift from traditional practice. Aware of this, Rabelais sent his printer expurgated editions of his first two books, together with the manuscript of his third, *The Heroic Deeds and Sayings of the Good Pantagruel,* written for the first time under his own name with the designation 'Doctor of Medicine'.

In error, the printer re-issued the original, unexpurgated editions. The authorities' response sent Rabelais scuttling back to Italy to the protection of du Bellay's relatives where he probably continued writing, because when he returned to France in 1547, his fourth book was almost ready to publish. Once again, he was engaged as Cardinal du Bellay's physician, and en route with him to Rome, he left the manuscript of book four with his printer friend in Lyon, François Juste.

Rabelais's third and fourth books contain more anecdotes and complete little stories, and they begin the long sea journey of Pantagruel and his companions on their quest – not for the Holy Grail, but for the 'Oracle of the Holy Bottle'. The question they seek to settle is whether Panurge should marry, and if he does, will he be cuckolded?

Every country and island they encounter, each with uniquely weird inhabitants and environments, provides opportunities for mocking almost everyone, but attacks on specific institutions are toned-down. Still, the Sorbonne's theologians remained intransigent.

With all four of his books still officially banned, Rabelais hoped for better fortune under Francis' son, Henry II. Henry had fallen out with the Pope, so he gave Rabelais a ten-year licence to publish whatever he chose, also granting him two properties near Paris. Rabelais must have been elated at this new security and freedom, no doubt celebrating with not a few flagons of wine. He added a stinging parody of Papal Law to book four and had it printed in 1552.

But immediately after the book was distributed, Henry made up his differences with the Pope and this book was condemned along with the rest. Rabelais was aging – he was approaching fifty-nine years, or sixty-nine depending which date of birth you choose – and his health began to deteriorate.

Rabelais' literary inheritance had included the French *fabliaux* – ribald verse tales beloved of the troubadours – and he shared this typically lewd, 'gallows humour' aimed, as often as not, at clerics and women. In his Gargantua and Pantagruel stories he took such coarseness to a high art, deliberately exaggerating it – Marguerite's work was demure in comparison: often explicit, she was never crude. With Rabelais, body effluents and genitalia of inordinate dimensions feature on practically every page, and farting is pandemic. Even allowing that he was a medic, that these matters were discussed more openly in his time, and that he often applies them cleverly in parody, superficially his stories abound in the sort of gratuitous smut to send pubescent novices sniggering behind the monastery stables. But these were not his intended audience. Rabelais wrote for sophisticated readers whom he addresses familiarly as 'dear fellow boozers'. Wine and drinking are a constant theme – the Oracle's revelation is 'DRINK' – and though there is undoubtedly literal truth in this, at a deeper level, drinking can be read as a comic code for imbibing the new questioning individualism of humanist thought. Rabelais was drunk on the possibilities of this new learning. The grossness of his humour was designed, perhaps, to amuse his contemporaries while disarming his critics. And he wrote, very likely, with a good deal of wine in the ink (a claim he makes repeatedly himself). What comes across above all is the huge pleasure he derives from playing with words and ideas for their own sake.

Every aspect of social vanity is grist to Rabelais' satirical mill, even the cod-piece – ubiquitous in the Pantagruel stories and employed with astonishing originality. In Rabelais' time, cod-pieces as large as possible – or impossible – were the height of court fashion, along with the bloated double doublet with its 'layered look' of slashed sleeves – presumably, for the same sort of testosterone boost that led to the exaggerated shoulder pads of the late 1950s' Teddy Boys. Story is as fashion conscious as anyone else.

Gargantua

Less palatable is Rabelais' misogyny. The deceit and trickery of women was a stock topic guaranteed to excite readers, but the intensity of his barbs against them seems almost pathological. In one example, he begins with Aesop's fable of the injured lion and its subsequent gratitude – a favourite legend of the saints in which Saint Jerome is the lion's friend, a story Rabelais certainly knew – but he degrades the fable into his own fantasy of grotesque female abuse. Though his vows forbade him to marry, he fathered two illegitimate children while in Paris and another in Montpellier[141] – few knew better than he the truth of his biting wit against fornicating friars.

Yet occasionally, he includes thoughtful anecdotes which are little gems of stories in their own right. For example, when Pantagruel is persuading Panurge to consult the Fool on his marriage plans on the grounds that kings and countries have been saved by the advice and predictions of fools, he says that is why, 'when the strolling players distribute their parts, the role of the fool and jester is always played by the most skilful and perfect actor in the company', and he tells this story:

> In front of a Parisian cook-shop by the Petit-Chatelet, a porter ate his bread in the steam coming from a roast-meat stall, and found it made his bread very tasty. The cook watched him finish his bread and then demanded payment for the steam from his roast. The porter claimed he had taken nothing since the steam was evaporating anyway, and he was therefore not in his debt. The cook threatened to confiscate the pack-hooks the porter carried on his back if he was not paid. Whereupon the porter drew his cudgel to defend himself, and as the argument heated, a gaping crowd gathered. Among them was Seigny John, the town fool. The cook asked the porter if he would accept John's arbitration of the matter, to which the porter willingly agreed.
>
> After hearing the claims of each side, John told the porter to hand him a piece of silver and the porter gave him an old coin. Taking his time, John weighed the coin on his shoulder, rang it on his palm, tried it with his teeth, and examined it minutely. The mob was silent while the cook watched with confidence, the porter, in despair. Finally, the fool rang the coin several times on the counter of the stall.
>
> Drawing himself up to magisterial dignity, pulling his fur hood over his head and giving a few loud authoritative coughs, the fool gave his decision: "'The court declares that the porter who ate his bread in the steam of the roast has civilly paid the cook with the sound of his money. The court orders that each shall retire to his eachery, without costs. The case is settled.'"
>
> Pantagruel concludes that no fairer judgement could have been given and that Panurge would do well to consult a fool.[142]

Rabelais' style swings from low obscenity to high intellectual virtuosity of genuine erudition, frequently quoting ancient philosophers or making adroit allegories on the development of language – an intellectual concern at the time. Some of these quotes, though, are simply bait to tease the reader – Rabelais' ghost is probably looking up at us, enjoying a last laugh at the literary pedants who toil to attach profound meanings where he intended only nonsense. The Greek scholar he mentions most often is Diogenes Sinope: a member of what is called the 'Cynic' school, extolling an austere morality of self-sufficiency which included disregard of laws and customary authority – a personal anarchy which probably appealed to Rabelais, but perhaps without the 'austere morality'. In the life-style of Thélème, the 'ideal abbey' with echoes of Camelot that Gargantua built as a reward for Friar John, monks and nuns marry, dress in finery, eat and drink of the best, and follow faithfully the one rule of the order – 'Do what you will'. One has the feeling that if Rabelais did have the makings of an anarchist, it was not the sort that blows up buildings, but one who, given sufficient funds, would be more of a libertine.

Through Rabelais, Story reveals a pressing desire for freedom, as well as dissatisfaction with the corruption and authoritarianism of public institutions. People could not work, travel, marry, or worship freely; their lives were held in the vice-like grip of interlocked state and church. Europe's emergence from medieval superstition was not a sudden switch like putting our clocks forward an hour. The interplay of Renaissance and Reformation ideas made a slow, shuddering transition felt variously in different places – many of our institutional rituals, and even personal beliefs, are still intrinsically medieval. By enabling wider distribution of new ideas, printing gave momentum to popular frustration, and Rabelais made full use of its potential. His main concern appears to have been personal freedom based on humanist thought; he was certainly no Protestant. His life was surprisingly orthodox, to the extent of supplementing his income later in life with church benefices, drawing revenues from parishes he may never have visited even as he lampooned the hypocrisy of others.

Rabelais died in 1553. His fifth book, with the same title as the third, was published nine years later, inevitably raising doubts over how much of it he wrote himself. The question seems largely academic: the wondrous 'Oracle of the Holy Bottle' is reached after typical Rabelaisian adventures which, to the average reader, appear written in the same imaginative style as his earlier books. As free as he was with his criticism, Rabelais never spiked his benefactors. He acknowledged the recently deceased Marguerite in his third book with a brief verse, *To the Spirit of the Queen of Navarre,* suggesting she might like to come down from her well-deserved place in heaven to read the next adventures of Pantagruel.

Marguerite's daughter, Jeanne, had assembled all her mother's writing after her death – over 400 pages of elegies, translations, plays, stories, and poems that revealed her own religious journey along with the spirit of the age – and locked them away from prying eyes. They remained in an ornate iron casket for more than three centuries. Without this filial loyalty they might all have been lost, because in the violence that followed from both Protestants and Catholics, buildings were sacked and burnt, even Marguerite and Henry's tombs in the Cathedral of Lescar near her beloved Château of Pau were desecrated and completely destroyed.

But Marguerite's important devotional work, *Miroir de l'âme pécheresse,* had already come into the hands of an eleven-year-old girl in England, who studied the poem and translated it into English. It was a serendipitous moment. How she could have come by that poem is an interesting tale.

When Mary Tudor, sister of Henry VIII, came to France in 1514 as bride to the aging Louis XII, she brought in her entourage a promising young lady in waiting. Louis died the following year and Mary returned to England, but her young aide stayed on with the new queen in Francis' court, and it is more than likely that she joined Marguerite's household in the Duchy d'Alençon to continue her education. This vivacious fifteen-year-old would have been a pleasing companion and an intelligent student: pious, but competent to discuss theological issues, an interest no doubt encouraged by Marguerite who, with her customary generosity, almost certainly gave her attendant a copy of her *Miroir* to read and allowed her to make her own copy. With war imminent in 1522, the young English woman returned to London to continue serving at the Tudor court.

Fourteen years later, married and with a three-year-old daughter, she met an unexpected death. But her daughter grew into the studious young girl who translated the *Miroir* into English prose during her study of French. The child's name was Elizabeth – she would become Queen of England. Her mother, of course, was Anne Boleyn, Henry VIII's unfortunate second wife whom he executed.

In Elizabeth's translation, *The Glasse of the Synneful Soule*, she does not mention the French author and may not have known who wrote the poem, or that when she was little more than a year old, her father had proposed her betrothal to Marguerite's young nephew, heir to the French throne.

The young princess worked on her translation during her lonely year of banishment from court. She dared not write to her father, but learned from her step-mother, Katherine Parr, that Katherine mentioned her every time she wrote to the king. Elizabeth was no doubt grateful for her support and gave Katherine a copy of *The Glasse of the Synneful Soule* as her customary new year's gift. Elizabeth carefully wrote out a fair copy, bound it into a little book with a tapestry cover worked in blue silk, and decorated it with gold and silver braiding in an interlaced knot design enclosing Katherine's initials. In each corner was embroidered a pansy – the tiny purple, yellow and white 'heart's-ease'.[143] In the language of flowers they symbolised loving thoughts, a tradition which Shakespeare quoted fifty years later: 'it fell upon a little western flower, before, milk white, now purple with love's wound'.[144] – Spoken by Oberon in *A Midsummer Night's Dream,* a play which this great storyteller performed for Queen Elizabeth at her court.

In our eagerness for stories we have jumped too far ahead. Though fraught with religious and political tensions, Elizabeth's long reign was a period of relative prosperity where music and drama flourished. The play was the thing. But Story had spent a long time setting the stage for her secret lover, Will Shakespeare.

Chapter Ten

All the world's a stage

Story sips wine with a tipsy Dionysus recalling how she created the first drama in ancient rituals; memories that eventually lead to the Tudor Court in England where her secret lover, Will Shakespeare, is everyone's favourite bard ... until theatres are banned and Story skips across the Channel to join the Commedia dell'Arte.

Shakespeare's inspiration blossomed into a genius of extraordinary originality.

10

O that I were a fool!
I am ambitious for a motley coat.

[Shakespeare, *As You Like It*: Act II Scene VII]

Merry with wine, munching bread and olives, a noisy company of actors and dancers celebrate with their playwright, Aeschylus. The year is 472 BC and their play, *The Persians*, has won the drama competition at Athens' Dionysia – the five-day festival dedicated to Dionysus, god of wine and fertility.

Competition rules required each playwright to enter three heroic tragedies and one satyric drama. The latter, a burlesque usually written around a mythical theme, involved the half-man-half-beast satyrs and silens associated with the ancient cult of Dionysus. For his satyric play, Aeschylus had written a skit on Prometheus, the Titan who stole fire from the gods, in which one of the satyrs – all are known for sensual indulgence rather than intelligence – is so in love with fire he wants to kiss it and is warned that he will lose his beard.

But it was Aeschylus' tragic trilogy that won acclaim, especially *The Persians*, a popular theme commemorating the Athenian victory over the Persian King, Xerxes I, at the Battle of Salamis only eight years before. Aeschylus had fought in that battle. He had rewritten Phrynichus' play, *The Phoenissae,* which told the same story and had won the drama competition four years previously. Perhaps Aeschylus was inspired also by his earlier experience in fighting the Persians at Marathon in 490 BC, when a Greek force of 20,000 defeated a 100,000 Persians (or 10,000 Greeks defeated 25,000 Persians depending on which source you read). It must have been a bitter memory for Aeschylus because his beloved brother fought alongside him at Marathon and was killed.

Dramatised victories were always more popular than defeats. After Phrynichus moved the audience to tears and won the festival in 511 BC with *The Capture of Miletus* – a play about the sacking of this Athenian colony by the Persians – he was fined for evoking a devastating defeat. Future plays on this topic were banned by the city authorities. Drama offered a public model for popular ambition: heroic success was the desired example, not sorrowful failure.

This success with *The Persians* is the second time Aeschylus has won the competition; the first occasion, twelve years before, must have been especially pleasing for him, because that year he introduced some daring innovations. Instead of the usual set-up of a large singing and dancing chorus carrying most of the performance with one soloist-actor, he reduced the size of the chorus, added a second actor – both wearing masks to perform multiple roles – and told most of the story in dialogue. By 438 BC, more complex plots were made possible by stage devices to lift actors into heaven, trap doors to drop them into hell, and separate entrance and exit points. In later years, Sophocles would win, and continue to win more than twenty competitions after adding a third actor, a longer story, and scene paintings for more realism. Sophocles' last victory in 401 BC (awarded posthumously) was for *Oedipus at Colonus*, a play rewritten some 400 years later by the Roman philosopher, Annaeus Seneca the Younger, and which still influences writers. By Sophocles' time, rather than being members of a chorus of dancers and singers, performers had become actors speaking dialogue in iambic metre, creating 'Greek tragedy' as we know it and which, directly or indirectly, continues to inspire drama and storytelling.

Aeschylus' jubilant troupe is still sitting where it had performed, in the open-air circular *orchestra* or 'dancing area' situated at one end of the spacious *agora*, the civic and commercial centre of Athens.[145]

The wooden statue of Dionysus, that had headed the opening procession and stood to witness the five days of drama, dance and music, has been trundled back to the temple along with his carved phallus – so massive it required a separate wagon. The tiered seating which, an hour ago, had been crammed with more than 10,000 spectators – many of whom had travelled long distances to enjoy this major event of the year – now stands empty except for a few small knots of enthusiasts still discussing the performances in the warm spring evening. Most people are milling around the shops and food kiosks that line the *agora*, or making preparations for the all-night feast to follow. Refilling their goblets with good wine, our thespians, now joined by other actors, musicians and friends, reminisce about their theatrical traditions. We can loiter on the edge of their circle and eavesdrop.

The nocturnal orgy that night would evoke the ritualistic and mythical origins of Dionysus; even more so would the games and plays performed in rural areas around Athens during December and January, the 'Lenaea', celebrating wine's rebirth marked by the end of its fermentation. In his youth, Aeschylus had worked in a vineyard in his hometown of Eleusis and no doubt attended the Lenaea festival. He certainly had an interest in the occult, being a member of a local esoteric cult dedicated to the earth-mother, Demeter. The mystery of death and rebirth felt in nature's cycles of seasonal renewal – especially evident as the 'dead' stems of vines in winter bear luscious bundles of grapes in summer – are major elements in Dionysus myths. Celebrations of this ancient cult took place in woodlands where participants, women and men ecstatic on new wine, could imagine themselves gods as they re-enacted mythical scenes with choral verses – *dithyrambs* – accompanied by flutes, drums and cymbals, and all interspersed with wild orgasmic indulgence. Little wonder the cult was so popular.[146] We better empathise with their passion if we understand that the soil was poor; a good harvest required intensive effort and even then might fail for reasons beyond their control.

A drunken Dionysus supported by a friend

These early revellers took their noisy impromptu performances into the streets of Athens, brandishing fennel wands and huge carved phalluses. Unimpressed, the city's sophisticated citizens banished the drunken yokels back to the countryside. In retaliation, so the story goes, Dionysus cursed the men of Athens with 'phallic wilt' until such time as they adopted his cult which, understandably, they duly did sometime around the seventh century BC. Festival competitions at that time were for *dithyrambic* choral and dance presentations which gradually became more refined. According to tradition, the first tragic drama performed as part of the festival, in 534 BC, was written by Thespis, who won the competition and was awarded a goat – a symbol of Dionysus and his hoofed and hairy satyrs; even his female companions, the maenads, were frequently depicted wearing goat skins.

Dionysus had the power to bring people back from the underworld, and was himself resurrected. The story is told in

Euripides' winning play *The Bacchae*, which gives Dionysus a place among the Greeks' Olympian pantheon of gods. The mortal maiden, Semele, daughter of the King of Thebes in Egypt, is seduced by Zeus and becomes pregnant. In her jealousy, Zeus' wife, Hera, persuades Semele to insist her lover appears before her in his full godly glory as proof of his love. Zeus complies reluctantly, knowing that Semele, a mere human, will be instantly destroyed by his powerful thunderbolt, as indeed happens. But Zeus saves the unborn child, sewing it into his thigh. This child is Dionysus and his birth as a handsome, already full-grown young man so enrages Hera that she instructs the Titans to kill him. They tear him to pieces. But Rhea, ancient earth goddess and mother of Zeus, brings him back to life. The fact that Dionysus was part mortal encouraged his inebriated followers to identify more closely with him; like the daily rhythms of nature, he was a familiar, almost familial part of everyday life, much more so than any other of the gods.

Although the origins of his cult are unknown, Dionysus was considered even in ancient Greece as a 'foreign' god, said to have travelled widely to India, North Africa and all over the classical world with his satyrs and maenads. In his *Histories*, Herodotus claims that the Greeks learned of Dionysus from the Egyptians and associates him with the god Osiris. Archaeological evidence suggests Dionysus was worshipped by the Cretan Mycenae as early as the thirteenth century BC, but even they would not have been the first to dramatise ancient myths. For that we turn to the Egyptian story of Isis in which she fashions a golden phallus and becomes pregnant with Horus after the death of her husband-brother Osiris.

The mythical figure of Osiris, 'Ruler of the West' (i.e. 'of Eternity'), is likely based on a real king who succeeded in uniting Upper and Lower Egypt. He was certainly evoked by later pharaohs seeking legitimacy by adopting elements of his biography as their own – a political role of stories we have already seen elsewhere. In ancient stone monuments, Osiris is depicted as a giant, a frequent attribute of great men in legend. As often happens to great men, he is murdered by a group of conspirators who hack him to pieces (as

Dionysus was torn apart and scattered). Isis binds together the pieces of her husband's body; only the penis is missing, which she replaces with one of gold. She and her son, Ap-uat, avenge Osiris' killing in a bloody battle, and establish a cult in his name. Worshippers of Osiris re-enacted his story every year in many locations including Heliopolis (near modern Cairo) in Lower Egypt, and Abydos in Upper Egypt (about 80 kilometres by land north of Luxor).

An engraved stone tablet dated at around 2000 BC depicts such a performance in which one I-kher-nefert acted the role of Osiris. It represents the earliest known drama, foreshadowing later European 'passion plays'. The play ends with the resurrection of Osiris. Significantly, it conveys the same promise to his devotees: the longed-for immortality which eluded Gilgamesh at an earlier time in Sumeria, but which all major religions have since made a conditional boon.

In contrast to the Greek tragedies, whose playwrights avoided bloodshed on stage, the more ritualistic re-enactments of the Osiris cult appear to have favoured realism, since later chronicles record that actors often died of wounds inflicted while playing the parts of warriors in mock battles.

It is possible that the origins of dramatic storytelling go much further back to the earliest rituals of burial. Placing a body in a grave with personal possessions and provisions for the future enacts a narrative, a story of who they were, what has happened to them, where they are going, and how they will get there. We can see possible associations with the sun's daily burial below the horizon and the planting of seeds to germinate underground. Of course, not all societies bury their dead, but whatever form final rites take, they predicate a narrative of life and death – a 'storied' resolution of the ultimate mystery.

While up to now we have followed Story busy with oral and written verse and prose, she has been equally occupied with dramatic representations to answer the same vital human questions.

The boundary between ritual and theatre is nebulous: we may identify differences but there are many overlaps. It is a matter of emphasis rather than distinction, and forms a vast subject where we could wander about in circles forever – many scholars have groped around that particular labyrinth for their entire careers. But in a broad sense, ritual is designed to *make* something happen either now or in the future and requires belief in its efficacy; theatre is created to make us accept a reality happening right now in front of our eyes, which requires a certain suspension of belief. In theatre, as with all stories, there is also entertainment and the possibility of enjoyment on many levels; and theatre is accessible to everyone, depending on the price of tickets or deliberate social exclusion, it is public, whereas ritual may be private, sometimes secret. As an example reduced to a personal level, it is a little bit like the difference between 'ritual' exchange of rings and wedding vows to create an enduring relationship, and the 'theatre' of a couple keeping up appearances of conjugal harmony in front of others while saving their acrimony for the 'green room' of their own home.

Both ritual and theatre are embedded in narrative – mythical, historical or imaginative – and involve some form of transformation; and though transformation is more important in ritual than in theatre, in both it may be felt by members of the audience as well as by the performers. Greek philosophers were aware that drama creates an especially potent form of story, its actuality capable of releasing raw emotions without the mediation of a storyteller. During Plato's lifetime, 429–348 BC, Greek tragedy had reached the height of its form as serious theatre without the burlesque of early satyrs (comedy had become a separate genre). But the power of drama to stimulate the senses to irrational fantasies worried Plato; he considered it a bad influence on behaviour and inimical to human happiness. He would be appalled by today's horror films and violent computer games.

From a wealthy and influential family, Plato was a man of wide experience, having travelled for years throughout the Mediterranean region studying with the most famous scholars. There is even a story that he was captured by pirates before returning to Athens where he set up his Academy. Plato taught that rational thought was the ideal means towards a fully realised moral life, and that what we receive through our senses are merely ephemeral impressions of a changing and imperfect outer world, the world of mere phenomena. For him, tragic drama played on the senses to the detriment of reason.

Aristotle, a student of the aged Plato, agreed that drama had powerful emotional effects, but argued for different results. Aristotle had a scientific turn of mind, perhaps encouraged by his physician father. He valued the senses as a means to observe and understand phenomena, and had made significant contributions towards cataloguing Greek plant and animal anatomy. For him, inner reason and the outer world of matter were inextricably linked: the former gave meaning to the latter. Only by combining the two could one achieve the ideal. The emotional responses to drama that Plato considered sinister and morbid were, to Aristotle, a beneficial catharsis that flushed out natural feelings and resulted in better balance and health. In Aristotle's study of psychology – still relevant to much of the discipline – he identified the very essence of conflict within the human psyche: between the 'id', 'desire' and its force for gratification, and the 'ego', 'reason' which ameliorates indulgence by its awareness of possible future outcomes.

The essence of story-making is plotting outcomes as the consequence of a series of actions; Aristotle understood the power of inner feelings that drove human acts. Screen- and story-writers have ever since been exhorted to tap those mysterious inner sensations we call emotions. Story in her many forms, but perhaps especially in the realism of drama, allows us to play out our inner conflicts in a 'safe' place. That the emotional reach of stories also makes us vulnerable to manipulation is a potential danger which Plato might have recognised more readily than Aristotle.

Myths as dramatic representations remain popular today in religious street dramas, such as the Christian Oberammergau in Germany, and Hindu re-enactment of the Ramayana during Divali in India. In various ways their performance recounts cultural history and reaffirms identity and belief, and may incorporate topical concerns, even political propaganda. In eleventh-century Persia, farces and folklore epics were popular court entertainment.

Their characters – greedy merchants, lecherous old men, impudent servants, tricksters and buffoons – animated the favourite old stories we met earlier in *A Thousand and One Nights*, but as with the original stories, such plays were not considered 'literature'. Serious drama accompanied by music emerged around the sixteenth century in poetic form, notably the verse dialogue that gave gravitas to the cycle of Shiite Muslim passion plays recounting the martyrdom of Husain on his journey to avenge the death of his father, Mohammed Ali. Though religious and moral in content, these dramas gradually came to include heroic legends of Tamerlane and the popular love stories of 'Antarah. As there were no permanent theatre buildings, performances were offered by travelling troupes in tents, in the open, or wherever they were invited.

Similarly, we can trace English drama's origins back to medieval passion plays enacting biblical stories to educate the common people and instil into them Christian morality: an important means because the liturgy and Bible were only in Latin until the sixteenth century, their content inaccessible to ordinary people. It was, perhaps, a matter of 'if you can't beat 'em, join 'em', because the Church disapproved of the itinerant bands of '*mummers*' diverting the population with their distinctly secular entertainments. These improvised skits, tricks and jigs in the village square owed more to pagan than Christian traditions, especially when they mocked the friars. Village priests and their church wardens began to dramatise the more graphic elements of the liturgy – the Christmas nativity and Easter resurrection – and gradually involved members of the congregation in these performances.

By the fourteenth century, whole cycles of 'mystery plays' and pageants consisting of separate little dramas to mark episodes of the liturgical calendar were performed in towns, usually by craft guilds which then dominated town councils. Each guild jealously guarded its responsibility for presenting specific plays, often with a trade connection which offers an amusing foreshadowing of modern 'sponsorship'. In the York Cycle, for example, the Guild of Shipwrights performed the Building of Noah's Ark; the Fishers and Mariners Guild the Flood; the

Baker's Guild were responsible for the Last Supper; the coming of the Three Kings bearing gifts was performed by the Goldsmith's Guild.[147] Plays took place either on a mobile pageant-wagon or on a simple, easily erected static platform, and were delivered in rhythmic verse. Despite the seriousness of the plot, dialogue was not without humour as seen in the following exchange where Noah's wife accuses him of skiving from work after God has diverted him with an extremely long speech of instructions on building the Ark:

GOD: Noah, to thee and to thy fry
My blessing grant I;
Ye shall wax and multiply,
And fill the earth again,
When all these floods are past and fully gone away. (*God exists*)

NOAH: Lord, homeward will I haste as fast as I may.
My wife will I see and hear what she say.
I am afraid there will be some fray
Between us both;
For she is full testy,
For little oft angry;
If anything wrong be
Soon is she wroth.

(*Noah's wife enters*)
God-speed, dear wife, how fare ye?
WIFE: Now, as ever might I thrive, the worst is that
I see thee;
And tell me now at once where hast thou thus long been?
To death may we drive, or live for thee
In want indeed;
When we sweat and swink,
Thou dost what thou think,
Yet of meat or of drink
Have we much need.[148]

Costumes, props and real animals enlivened the scenes: stubborn donkeys refusing their exit cues to perform their own stage 'business', and cows nibbling hay from the nativity manger, spring to mind. This tradition of 'people's theatre' – complete with ham acting – continued well into the sixteenth century. By that time, plays had become more varied, often depicting sensational aspects of the lives of saints gleaned from Caxton's illustrated edition of the *Golden Legends.*

Soon, a new genre of 'morality plays' emerged. Though fundamentally religious and intended for moral improvement, they were not linked to the liturgical cycle or directly to biblical stories. Their sources included proverbs and old wives' tales and their 'characters' were personified virtues and vices debating human dilemmas in verse. Particularly popular with audiences were the vivid, often lurid, representations of the Seven Deadly Sins. But apart from these livelier scenes, morality plays contained long dialogues with little action or plot, and audiences, especially the growing town population, were ripe for something more entertaining and theatrical. The rule of the Tudors, from Henry VII in 1485, heralded a period of social change in which such theatricality flourished as never before. Henry had curtailed the power of nobles to pillage the countryside with impunity, and he amassed a fortune, leaving a worthy inheritance for his successors.

When we peeped in at young Princess Elizabeth embroidering that pretty cover for her translation (*The Glasse of the Synneful Soule*) as a gift for her stepmother, her father, Henry VIII, was already prising away the papal grasp on England and deflating the power of friars and monks, whose excesses Chaucer had so wittily lampooned a century earlier in *Canterbury Tales*. Despite a widely felt disillusionment with church functionaries, religion remained an essential part of everyone's daily life. Religious reform was a significant if often covert issue in Tudor England, but the divide between Catholicism and the new Protestantism widened and deepened. Henry's ascension as Head of the Church of England[149] – principally to enable a divorce from his first wife, Katherine of

Aragon – and the subsequent dissolution of monasteries provoked violent unrest among poorer communities in the north of England. Feeling the loss of alms and other support that the monasteries had provided, and suffering from harsh taxation policies, some 30,000 people mounted the armed revolt known as the Pilgrimage of Grace.

Henry and the aristocracy became the main beneficiaries of selling off monastic assets, but many of the rich donors who had previously supported the monasteries, redirected their funds to the endowment of more grammar schools. In theory, these were free to bright lads of whatever class, but poor families needed their children to work, not spend time at school. The majority of people could still not read or write; with the Bible now in the vernacular, it became the means for ordinary folk to learn basic literacy, but formal education was taught in Latin. Grammar schools to educate sons of the laity as well as the clergy had begun during the previous century and included the grammar school at Straet Ford (Stratford-upon-Avon), a chartered market town of productive craftsmen and a flourishing brewery. Monastic land bought by successful farmers and merchants strengthened the position of country squires, possibly increasing the assets of Robert Arden, the gentleman farmer of Wilmecote destined to become William Shakespeare's maternal grandfather. And continued efforts to control the dominance of nobles over local inhabitants, allowed the freer and more independent yeoman class to blossom; among them was Richard Shakespeare, tenant farmer at Snittersfield on the outskirts of Stratford, who would become William's paternal grandfather.

Despite repeated threats of war with France and religious tensions at home, Henry VIII held on to his crown for thirty-eight years. After his death, the population coped with a swing to Protestantism under regents who ruled in the name of his son, the boy-king Edward VI, followed by a zealous papist regime under Edward's elder sister, Mary Tudor, dubbed 'Bloody Mary' by Protestants to draw attention to the number of Protestants burnt at the stake during her reign.

By the time twenty-five-year-old Elizabeth became queen in 1558, her pragmatic Supreme Governorship over a compulsory state religion – a modified version of the Church of England her father had established – would have been a relief to many, but the compromise did not silence the dissatisfaction of ardent Roman Catholics and staunch Puritans, both of whom suffered oppression under her rule. But a new national consciousness was gaining ground and the vivacious young queen won her subjects' admiration and loyalty – boosted no doubt by her wise reluctance to increase taxes. There was, though, an ongoing concern for the future, which found expression in a play, *Gorboduc*, written in 1562 by two law students and future parliamentarians, Thomas Norton and Thomas Sackville.

Lawmen with political ambitions were the forerunners of England's tragic dramatists, their plays performed in the courtyards and halls of London's Inns of Court. Steeped in the classics and especially the first-century Roman philosopher, Seneca, it is not surprising that they drew upon his work for inspiration. Seneca rewrote almost forgotten plays of Aeschylus, Euripides and Sophocles, and retained many structural features of Greek drama. His favourite theme was revenge, the bloodier the better. His own end was a bloody affair. Emperor Nero accused Seneca of conspiracy and ordered his execution. Honour demanded that this should be self-inflicted and he was an honourable man. Seneca cut his own veins, dictating his memoirs while his thin, aged body slowly bled to death, a process finally hastened by his friends immersing him in a hot bath[150] – perhaps the memoirs had become a little tedious to listen to.

Norton and Sackville adapted Seneca's dramatic techniques to tell the story of a legendary British king, Gorboduc, who divided his realm between his two sons. The two princes quarrelled, the younger brother killing the elder. Their mother murdered the younger son in revenge, which so incensed the people that they rose up and killed both mother and father. With no heirs, the land was utterly devastated in civil war. The story plucked a chord of public unease at the beginning of Elizabeth's reign: an unmarried queen with no heir. As in early Greek drama, the play was in five acts, a chorus reinforced the moral and political lessons of the story, and killings were ameliorated by a 'storyteller', i.e. announced by a messenger rather than shown directly to the audience.[151] That squeamishness would change with later professional playwrights, but Seneca's use of blank verse remained the principal medium of English theatre.

And as evidence of changing public tastes and the death of 'the age of chivalry', another play, *The Misfortunes of Arthur* – written in 1588 by other law students also applying Seneca's style – portrayed the young King Arthur committing incest with his sister and being killed by their offspring, Mordred, who then seduces Queen Guinevere.[152] The knightly hero transformed into a villain, indeed. Poor Arthur.

People's worries over future succession were softened by the relative prosperity that flourished during Elizabeth's reign, its benefits felt by many in the countryside as well as in the towns. Sons progressed to higher status than their fathers, and daughters advanced by advantageous marriage. Richard Shakespeare's son, John, left his father's tenant farm to begin an apprenticeship with a glove-maker and tanner in Stratford, branching into commerce later to trade in wool and other agricultural products. Freed from Papal Law, interest on loans was legal, and at less than ten per cent it encouraged new ventures and competition. John Shakespeare became so successful that by 1557 he owned two properties in addition to his own house, held public office – including that of official ale-taster of the borough – and married Mary Arden, whose father, Robert Arden of Wilmecote, had left her money and a farm. It is unlikely that either John or Mary could read and write beyond a basic level, but when their son William was born in 1564, John was an alderman and entitled to free education at Stratford Grammar School for his children.

Four years later, John Shakespeare was mayor of Stratford; his position and wealth now that of a 'gentleman', he applied for a family coat-of-arms. Misfortune was to postpone this accolade for almost thirty years, but he might have been comforted had he known that his enterprise had already empowered one of his sons to be a world-renowned bard even five centuries later. How deprived Story would have been if John Shakespeare had stayed in the village and raised his family there or, having gone to Stratford, stuck to his tanner's trade and insisted his sons do likewise.

The growing *nouveaux riche* – the middle-class lawyers, doctors, clerks, merchants, squires, teachers and artisans – improved their standards of living: they ate from tin and pewter instead of wooden platters, constructed houses of brick with chimneys to burn coal rather than logs, hung tapestries on their walls and put glass panes in their windows; the wealthiest built cabinets to accommodate small private libraries and drank wine instead of beer. Those exposed to the classics at school wanted more diverse entertainment, and probably young Shakespeare joined the townsfolk flocking to the plays performed by groups of touring actors in the town square or courtyard of the local inn.

Scholars vied with each other to produce translations of Greek and Latin literature to meet the new demand. Among them was William Paynter, a graduate of St John's College, Cambridge, who published in 1566 the first edition of a collection of stories not only from the ancient classicists, but also more recent tales from storytellers in Italy and France whom we have already met – Bandello, Boccaccio, and Marguerite of Navarre. And as we saw earlier, some of *their* stories had even longer roots to Aesop's fables, Dr Bidpai tales and the Panchatantra. Paynter's collection, *The Palace of Pleasures,* ran to three editions, finally totalling over a hundred stories. As was traditional for university graduates, Paynter had been ordained a clergyman, but took employment in the civil service as a clerk of the ordnance in the Tower of London. Ironically for the times that were supposed to be changing for the better, this cleric lined his pockets with money filched from public funds. But no character is all bad and we should be grateful for his publication of *The Palace of Pleasures*: it inspired the new generation of dramatists such as John Lyly, Christopher Marlowe and Robert Greene, and later, William Shakespeare, Ben Jonson and their successors.

Elizabeth befriended Story in her royal patronage of the arts and literature and especially drama and music. A bit of a 'drama queen' herself, a fashion-leader with a penchant for rich brocades and fancy couture, Elizabeth nonetheless took a learned interest, and was known to have translated one of Euripides' tragedies from Greek simply for fun. Her Master of Revels operated as a sort of court impresario, organising masques, plays, music and poetry to please the queen and her noble entourage. Stories old and new, even current affairs, were heard in verses, songs and plays more often than read from the page; pedlars sold ballads by the dozen in the streets. 'I love a Ballad in print, a'life; for then we are sure they are true.'[153] All over London could be heard the pedlar's cries: 'Ye maidens and men, come for what you lack, and buy the fair ballads I have in my pack.'[154] All manner of products from food, fabrics and toys, to flea remedies and back-scratchers were cried by traders weaving their way around rubbish and sewage in streets so narrow they barely saw the light of day. The din in the city at all hours was so great that a law was passed to stipulate times when no noise was allowed on pain of imprisonment. Specifically forbidden was whistling after 9 p.m., affrays and outcries in the night, and beating one's wife … if it created a noise.

Other laws began to regulate the growing number of performers. Strolling players – successors of the itinerant *'mummers'* – were now deemed 'vagabonds' and were banned in 1572 to avoid spreading plague. (Later, all plays were forbidden within the city walls for the same reason, and all theatres in London were closed for a year in 1593 due to an outbreak of the disease.) Actors now had to belong to a group sponsored by a suitable patron. The Earl of Pembroke, the Earl of Derby, Robert Dudley, and the Queen herself were among those who sponsored their own groups of performers with names such as The Lord Chamberlain's Men, Leicester's Men, Pembroke's Men and Queen Elizabeth's Men. Fear of seditious elements may have reinforced the restriction on strolling players: a censorship law in the first year of Elizabeth's rule forbade the performance of any play that included heresy or profanity, or commented on national governance – religion and politics were touchy subjects throughout her reign, and in some social quarters are still avoided in 'polite conversation'.

From this time, too, permanent theatres were built in the outskirts of London. The first was The Theatre at Shoreditch built in 1576 by the actor James Burbage (whose son Richard also became an actor and a friend of Shakespeare's). Its neighbour, the Curtain Theatre, opened the following year. Over the next twenty years came the Rose, the Swan, the Globe, the Fortune and the Red Bull. Audiences (mostly male) filled the theatres during the day – lack of stage lighting prevented evening shows. All classes of people attended: the privileged on stools at the front under the protection of an overhang, while *hoi polloi* stood in the open centre exposed to all weathers expressing noisy appreciation for their penny-worth of entertainment. But performances were also commanded before her majesty in Whitehall and Richmond to a mixed audience of the court, and in later years at Nonsuch Palace in Surrey.

Globe Theatre

With new secular freedoms, schools and academies had begun to moderate education instead of the monasteries and guilds, and humour lightened the load of moral baggage. Nicholas Udall, headmaster of Westminster School in 1555, found a play written around 200 BC by the Roman comic dramatist, Plautus, and transformed it into the English culture of the time with his comedy, *Ralph Roister Doister*. The swaggering soldier hero of the title; his sidekick, Matthew Merrygreek; Dame Custance, the respectable widow they try to court for Roister Doister's wife; and her fiancée, Gawyn Goodluck whom they try to dislodge, are all typical Elizabethan 'middle-Englanders'. Typical also are the homely servants: the nurse, Margery Mumblecrust, and the two maids, Tibet Talkapace and Annot Alyface. Imagine what fun a bunch of schoolboys, some presumably in drag, would have made with such a play. The future playwright and Shakespeare's friendly rival, Ben Jonson, attended Westminster School some twenty years later – perhaps the pupils were still performing Udall's plays. More likely they were playing *Gorboduc* by that time.

As Ben started school in London, William was leaving Stratford Grammar where his studies would have included English composition, Latin, and classical Greek and Roman authors such as Plutarch, Seneca, and Ovid – all of whom were later sources for his plays. William left school at the age of fourteen, and the lack of any further formal education may have been prompted by the sudden downturn in his father's fortunes (about the cause of which we know nothing). Whether William worked to help family finances, wandered the forest of Avon with his head buzzing with stories, or stayed with relatives to continue informal studies elsewhere, we can only guess; all we know about his teenage years is that he married an orphan, Anne Hathaway.

Clearly, he somehow continued to develop his writing and acting skills. Actors were expected to master a large repertoire of roles, sometimes acting in two or three different productions a week, as well as to collaborate in adapting and writing plays. Perhaps he joined a touring group, because we learn no more of him until he is twenty-eight years old, has left his family in Stratford, and is in London as an accredited member of Pembroke's Men, a company which had already performed several of his early plays. Shakespeare was becoming successful enough as both actor and playwright by 1592 to provoke the jealousy of a rival: the dramatist, Robert Greene, wrote in an autobiography shortly before his death:

> 'There is an upstart crow, beautiful with our feathers, that with his Tygers heart wrapt in a Players hide supposes he is as well able to bombast out a blank verse as the best of

you; and, being an absolute Johannes Factotum, is in his own conceit the only Shake-scene in a country.'[155]

Ironically, this burst of spleen is the first written record we have of Shakespeare's theatrical career, and the profuse apology of Greene's editor, after Greene's death, confirms the high regard in which Shakespeare was held by others. And he was, indeed, a 'Jack-of-all-trades' involved in every aspect of drama, becoming part owner and manager of The Globe theatre. Shakespeare's friend and contemporary, Ben Jonson, gave a more appreciative portrait in his eulogy after the master's death:

'He was not of an age, but for all time!
And all the Muses still were in their prime,
When like Apollo he comes forth to warme
Our eares, or like a Mercury to charme!
Nature her selfe was proud of his designes,
And joy'd to weare the dressing of his time!'[156]

And indeed, so was Story 'proud of his designes'. Although Shakespeare's appeal *has* transcended time and place (allowing for sixteenth-century racial and religious prejudices) his success emerged as a son of his age: an age of new social and educational possibilities, of royal patronage, and with the presence in an established theatrical tradition of successful playwrights and actors from whom he learned his trade. And if Elizabeth's reign cannot be called 'peaceful', her subjects at least enjoyed the stability of continuity. It was a time, too, of national pride: the explorations of Francis Drake and Walter Raleigh, successful defence against the Spanish Armada (with a lot of help from the weather), and the first expansion of England's sea trade beyond Europe through a chartered company of English merchants called the East India Company. All provided opportunity and fertile ground for the imagination which, in Shakespeare's case, blossomed into a genius of extraordinary originality. He fell deeply in love with Story. He spoke to her in exquisite poetry and gave her other unique gifts which she shares with us.

Like all dramatists since the Dionysia, Shakespeare sometimes rewrote others' plays, and pilfered a plot idea from here, a character trait from there or a setting from somewhere else when writing his own. The sources available to him were greater than they had ever been. In addition to the Greek and Latin authors he knew, he seems to have drawn upon the *Chronicles of Holinshed* for his English history and on Boccaccio's stories in Paynter's *Palace of Pleasures* for several of his comedies. It is impossible to trace all that inspired Shakespeare as he wove his borrowings into the age-old themes of death, destiny, power, and love in his own distinctive way. An abiding muse was his devotion to his virgin queen; he would have taken special pleasure in acting before Elizabeth at her court in *A Midsummer-Nights Dream,* in which he had written a playful tribute to his devout sovereign – the 'fair vestal throned by the west', the 'imperial votaress':

'That very time I saw, but thou couldst not,
Flying between the cold moon and the earth,
Cupid all arm'd: a certain aim he took
At a fair vestal throned by the west,
And loos'd his love-shaft smartly from his bow,
As it should pierce a hundred thousand hearts;
But I might see young Cupid's fiery shaft
Quench'd in the chaste beams of the wat'ry moon,
And the imperial votaress passed on,
In maiden meditation, fancy-free'[157]

Shakespeare's last performance for Elizabeth was at Richmond Palace in 1603, seven weeks before her death. For those who seek deep analysis, much has been written about his works by scholars who have dedicated whole lives to the task. From Story's point of view, three qualities in his plays affected her deeply and influenced her future: Shakespeare's unique gift for portraying character, his appreciation of women, and his understanding of love.

Following Chaucer's example, character had gained significance in stories, and Shakespeare's contemporaries continued this trend; they were no longer satisfied with type-cast knights, generic heroes and stereotyped kings. Gone, too, are all those scurrilous saints and shallow moralists. Most authorities agree that Christopher Marlowe was particularly good on character. But Shakespeare excelled by creating 'individuals' on stage with the emotional complexity of fully realised human beings. Aristotle would have appreciated the psychology.

And among his deep characters is a wide ranging cast of females. In general, women had not fared well in formal fiction until Shakespeare. Depicted in a single dimension as war trophies, compliant wives, political pawns, drudges, bawds, or martyred saints, and even as goddesses and mythical earth mothers, the shallowness of their roles limited the nature of male-female relationships in stories. Often, female characters were little more than a foil to illuminate clever men and courageous heroes. Although Shakespeare was not immune from the sexism of the age, his women can be tender, waspish, forceful, devious or noble as a plot unfolds and their affections are courted or ambitions thwarted. They can take the initiative or succumb to their fate, but they are significant players and their wit and intelligence is on a par with men. The irony is that there were no real women on stage; they were played by youths trained to the roles. Perhaps, during those 'silent' teenage years when we have no record of young William, he was learning to play female roles with a touring company and realised how much better they could be portrayed.

Because of the fullness of female as well as male characters, Shakespeare is able to portray realistic, complex relationships and their consequences, in particular the bonds of love. In comparison to the distant 'courtly love' of chivalric tradition, whose essence was its *lack* of attainability, he shows us the warm, close entanglements and misunderstandings of genuine love that expects to last through a lifetime. And because his sweethearts are more eloquent than the characteristic tongue-tied lover, his poetry evokes our own emotional experience, or at least our hopes. Parental interference or disaster may still disrupt a relationship, and love sometimes results in disappointment and bitterness, but Shakespeare's depiction of love, intended as a mutual bond capable of enduring in conjugal affection through the ups and downs of marriage, was in contrast to the European cynicism of previous centuries and the Eastern stereotyping found in *A Thousand and One Nights;* Shakespeare's love feels closer to the Bedouin love stories of 'Antarah. In breaking away from tradition and following his own concept of drama, writing from his heart rather than his head, Shakespeare created stories that spoke not only to contemporary society, but to humanity in all times since.

Shakespeare's plays were even more in demand at the court of King James I (James VI of Scotland) who succeeded Elizabeth, becoming the first monarch over England, Scotland and Wales. James chose Shakespeare for his own playing company, the King's Men, and from 1603 to1606, he commissioned them for twenty-nine court performances, twenty of which were of Shakespeare's own plays.[158] This saved Shakespeare's company from possible ruin, because a virulent outbreak of plague had closed the theatres – by 1605 some 30,000 people, almost a third of London's population, had died of the disease – and the King's demands stimulated Shakespeare to write new plays, among them, King Lear, Macbeth, and Anthony and Cleopatra.

Whatever had caused John Shakespeare's financial downfall, it took him more than twenty years to recover, but he was eventually reinstated as an alderman and the family coat-of-arms had been approved in 1596 with the motto: 'not without right'. Granted in recognition of services rendered to Henry VII by John's grandfather, the motto is equally applicable to William Shakespeare's reputation as a poet, playwright and actor. How much contact Shakespeare maintained with Stratford during his London career is not known, but he had bought a large house there in which he later died from an unspecified sickness in 1616. Story mourned the fate that took her lover so soon.

During the forty years of Stuart rule[159] that followed Elizabeth, religious and political discontent festered, culminating eventually in civil war – so feared a hundred years earlier. The victory of Parliament and the Puritans ('Roundheads') over the Royalists ('Cavaliers') in 1649 resulted, among other things, in the suppression of all forms of fun. Under Oliver Cromwell's Protectorate, Sunday sports were banned and maypoles – remnants of pagan celebration – were cut down. As part of the crackdown, all stage plays were forbidden and would remain so until the Restoration of the monarchy in 1660 – we must travel to Europe for our merriment.

In Italy, a different kind of theatre – the *Commedia dell'Arte* – continued to flourish as it had since the fourteenth century, and it owed more to troubadour heritage than to literature. Music was as important as it had been in England, but Europe lacked the dramatists and theatre-building frenzy of the Elizabethans. Acting troupes performed in the mansions of their noble patrons and, unlike the English companies, they included female players. Uninhibited by English moral scruples, the whole purpose of *Commedia dell'Arte* was to create as much fun as possible, achieved through the actors' art more than the play itself. Partly improvised, performances required actors to respond smartly with witty and often bawdy repartee, switch identities at speed, and maintain the energetic momentum of farce. Acrobatics, clowning, juggling and mock fights were all part of the histrionics. The carnival atmosphere, lewd humour and general zaniness of the whole enterprise would have appealed to Rabelais, and it projects echoes of the drunken revels in the cult of Dionysus. But acting in the *Commedia dell'Arte* demanded too much skill to accomplish with a skinful of wine. As Rabelais pointed out, fools are always played by the best actors.

Storylines were set in advance – plots involving love intrigues, mistaken identities, trickery and treachery – leaving actors scope to improvise dialogue and stage 'business' within the general scenario. Although stock characters could be recognised by their costumes or masks, they played varying roles in different plays. Some are still with us: the rascally big-nosed villain, Punchinello, later crossed the channel to emerge on British beaches as Punch with his long-suffering wife, Judy. In colourful patchwork trousers, Arlecchino sometimes played a valet, or a jester, but he is always a prankster stirring up trouble and turning the plot; we know him as the clown, Harlequin or Pierrot, enlivening pantomime. And pert and pretty Columbine, teasing lover of Arlecchino and maid to the principal love-interest, Lucinda, has amused many a later audience in vaudeville with her mixture of sauciness and innocence.

Plots for the plays were gleaned from ancient tales and contemporary events, the two often entwined: stories of soldiers and sultans from the crusades; bits of folklore and racy *fabliaux*; tales of grasping merchants and wily widows who inhabited *A Thousand and One Nights*, and current gossip about the 'celebrities' of the times – the more salacious the better. At least one stock character came from the classics: the Roman comedy dramatist, Plautus. His 'braggart soldier', whom Udall transformed into the slightly more respectable and very English, Ralph Roister Doister, became, in Italy, a swaggering Spanish captain ridiculed wherever possible, because the Italians still smarted from the iniquitous activities of Spanish mercenaries during the Holy Roman Empire under Charles V. As we have seen before, borrowing is rarely direct: history and culture weave in and out of stories for each time and people, and through each storyteller's interpretation. In a similar way, although actors in the *Commedia dell'Arte* tended to play the same stock characters throughout their careers, they made their characters uniquely their own through voice, gesture and detail of costume and mask. One actor's Arlecchino was distinct from another's; audiences cheered their favourites and jeered others who did not make them laugh enough.

Joseph Grimaldi playing Scaramouch from the Commedia dell'Arte.

The fun and entertainment that the uninhibited European audiences wanted, and were willingly given, was the earthy vulgarity we saw earlier from the author of *Reynard the Fox* and from Boccaccio and Rabelais: all writers familiar with the ribaldry of *fabliaux* and some of the more scurrilous tales in the *Gesta Romanorum*. Some *Commedia dell'Arte* creations found their way into the formal stage comedies of the seventeenth-century playwright, Molière, or were recreated in operas by Rossini or Gozzi, and even into ballet, but their roots extend to folk traditions of village merrymaking, seasonal festivities and, ultimately, the art of living with nature and our fellow beings.

On a wider canvas, the extraordinary combination of intelligence and brutality that drove early human expansion has fashioned how humans relate to other groups of our species, and it largely depends on relative power. Subjugating others into slavery is an ancient practice which enabled the creation of many old empires throughout the world, including those in Africa, whose kings discovered that they reaped better rewards from foreign buyers. Until those chiefs, too, were overpowered. While drama flourished in Europe, the international slave trade was gaining momentum – what caused death and despair to millions brought immense wealth to others (but Story would help to end it, eventually). Not that the huge profits of trade brought peace: Portuguese, Spanish, English, French and Dutch fleets repeatedly grabbed at each other's overseas settlements and played lethal games of chase at sea. Anticipating a fortune 'when my ship comes in' was more a matter of '*if* my ship comes in'. But sailors returned with tales of wonder as well as plunder, and the Great Fire of 1666 had finally cleansed London of plague – posh parts of the city even boasted their first street lamps.

Agents of Enlightenment debated in coffee houses or gathered in fashionable *salons* to indulge in the latest luxury from the East – tea. Often to be seen in these circles – and the subject of scandalous gossip when not present – was a prolific English author, probably the first to make a living entirely from writing. And one with shrewd insight if this quote is anything to go by: 'Money is a language all nations understand.' So what was the scandal? – Largely the fact that the author was an independent woman. In addition to plays and poems, Aphra Behn wrote popular fiction. Her novella *Oroonoko* (1688), about an African prince enslaved and sold in South America, was one that Story threaded onto her shuttle as she wove her new indulgence: the proliferation of the novel. 'Proliferation' because, if we keep it simple and define a 'novel' as a long, prose story of fiction (though often based on fact), where multiple characters enact their lives, and through which authors may express the interests of their age as well as entertain, then novels had been written long before.

We need not dabble in the vociferous controversies around an exact definition – whether a novel can be in verse, for example. We already know that Story employs every form and combination of expression to suit her purposes. If we must have a 'first', we could choose the second-century AD erotic Greek romance by Parthenius Longus, *Daphnis and Chloe,* or one of the tragic Icelandic sagas of the eighth century, or Murasaki Shikibu's *Tale of Genji* (c.1010) in which she reveals the extravagant lives and seductive arts of the Japanese court. We could wait until the twelfth century, when Arabic scholar, Ibn Tufail, wrote *Hayy ibn Yaqdham* ('Alive, Son of Awake') in which a feral child alone on a desert island is raised by a gazelle, leading to a novel of philosophical and scientific discovery. Or plump for Spain's Miguel de Cervantes and his satire of medieval heroics in *Don Quixote* (1605). In England, we could choose Aphra Behn, but in our patriarchal society, that accolade is more often given to Daniel Defoe – merchant, prolific journalist and spy. Defoe had reached the age of fifty-nine before writing his first novel, the adventure tale *Robinson Crusoe* (1719); in contrast, his second, *Moll Flanders,* is a starkly realistic story of a young woman rising from poverty to wealth via prostitution – one of the earliest novels to focus on a female heroine.

Altogether, these represent a wonderful variety of creative innovations, which show the pitfalls of definitions and claims to primacy as clearly as they celebrate Story's rich ingenuity. In nostalgic mood, Story entwines all of these strands and braids them anew with folk-tales to create the motif for her next engagement with history.

Chapter Eleven

Once upon a time...

In an age of romanticism and swelling nationalism, ancient tales revive myth, chivalry and folklore all over Europe to nurture national pride and spark revolutions, while Story inspires Walter Scott to weave his Highland ballads into a historical novel and urges James Fenimore Cooper to write his own tales of America.

I care not who knows it – I write for general amusement.

11

Life could not be endured were it seen in reality.

[Sir Walter Scott 1771–1832]

His flaxen hair spilling over the river bank, young Walter slid his hand gently beneath the water. He was trying to tickle a trout – an old Highland poacher's trick taught him by his grandfather's shepherd. To catch a fish in this way requires total concentration. Walter's thoughts hovered elsewhere, his head full of ancient battles, his pocket full of ballads. The lucky trout escaped.

Walter rolled back onto the grass and took from another pocket the verses of Milton he had copied out with great labour, and not without a few blots and scratchings-out. Though he had seen only six summers he could already recite, with the passion of an actor, the poets of the day as well as those of his Scottish heritage; both heard first at his mother's knee. To cure the paralysis of his right leg – the results of an infant fever – he had been sent at two years old from his Edinburgh home to live on his grandfather's farm at Sandy Knowe in Tweeddale, on the Scottish Borders, where his bonnie appearance and cheerful chatterbox nature made him a great favourite.

> 'For I was wayward, bold, and wild,
> A self-willed imp, a grandame's child;
> But half a plague, and half a jest,
> Was still endured, beloved, carest.'[160]

Walter's most devoted 'henchman', Sandy Ormistoun, his grandfather's cow-baillie, carried him around the farm on his shoulders until he was old enough to ride his own Shetland pony, Marion. That full freedom of the moors and meadows of Tweeddale inspired much of Walter Scott's future writing, along with the folktales told him by his doting grandmother and aunts.

During Walter's absence from Edinburgh, his father's legal career grew sufficiently to enable the family to leave the crowded close which had seen the deaths of six of their infant children, (they had so nearly lost Walter too, but the 'fairy folk' must have kept an affectionate eye on him). The Scott family moved to a newly built house in George Square overlooking the Meadows. Scotland was becoming more prosperous – in the cities at least. The voices of home-grown scholars such as Adam Smith, David Home, Thomas Reid and Francis Hutcheson were heeded not only in Scotland but also in Europe as leading thinkers in the enlightened age. Despite some ninety per cent of the male population being able to read (universal education in Scotland was established in 1640[161] – way ahead of England) feudalism still prevailed, but as the eighteenth century raised its curtain, Scotland was poised to enter a new drama: the Act of Union with England. It had been a long and troubled betrothal.

The majority of Scotland's people lived on meagre subsistence of oats and kale with a scrawny cow or two for the lucky ones. With crafts and trade flourishing in England it was an uneven match, a marriage of necessity – almost a shot-gun wedding. Not all Scots wanted to be joined to England; approval for Union was hard-won with accusations of slush funds to buy parliamentary votes, but the act was passed in 1707. Influential Scots held prominent positions in the government of 'Great Britain', the new United Kingdom; the economy improved; Edinburgh dandies affected English gentility and accents, and the traditions of aristocratic barons in the Lowlands, and of powerful clan chiefs in the Highlands, began to erode.

In 1745, when Charles Edward Stuart, the 'Young Pretender', grandson of the exiled James II, came over from Europe to incite rebellion and return the British throne to the Catholic Stuart dynasty, it was already too late. An earlier Jacobite rising by his father, 'The Old pretender', had failed in 1715. In this second attempt, although Charles Edward raised an army of both Lowlanders and Highlanders, the English were no longer interested and Scots were ambivalent. Many gave Bonnie Prince Charlie their hearts, but their heads told them that their future lay not with reinstituting the past. His small force won early battles in Preston and in Falkirk; the English soldiers fleeing from the roaring kilted mob brandishing their broadswords and dirks – the wild Highlanders, Celtic warriors feared since Roman times. If the Celts no longer attached the heads of the vanquished to their saddles, they were still a terrifying sight. But under the leadership of Lord Cumberland, a reinforced army of English and Scots troops equipped with artillery and a new war device – the 'bayonet' – roundly defeated the Jacobites on Culloden Moor. In revenge for their earlier terror, Cumberland's forces slaughtered injured survivors, burning-alive those who had sheltered in a cottage, executed prisoners and randomly killed civilians encountered on their triumphant rampage into Inverness, the Highland capital. For good reason was he called 'The Butcher Cumberland'.

The handsome prince survived and went into hiding on Scotland's west coast, while for five months Cumberland's soldiers scoured every cove and hillside for the fugitive, offering thousands of pounds reward for his capture. No one betrayed him and he escaped to the continent – a romantic figure and the inspiration for many a ballad. Such was the history – within living memory of many – that filled wee Walter Scott's head while he wandered the rocky hills and glens around Sandy Knowe.

The traditional remedy of a fresh bloody sheep-skin wrapped around Walter's lame leg having failed to bring any improvement, his Aunt Jenny took him by sea to London and on to Bath for the healing spa waters. They stayed for a year. The main benefit seems to have been his enchantment with Shakespeare's play, *As You Like It*, which he saw with his uncle, Captain Robert Scott, who was on leave from the East India Trading Company. (So began a deep engagement with Shakespeare whom Scott quoted constantly in his later journal.) Though the treatment made little improvement to his leg, Walter's health was robust, thanks to the care and country air of his childhood, an idyll rudely interrupted in his eighth year by his return to Edinburgh where he had to fight his way through the pecking order in a family of four boisterous brothers, and begin formal schooling.

His early education having been 'free-range', Walter had to work hard to catch up with his class-mates. If the expectations of his staunch Calvinist father kept him to the grind with kind firmness, his mother encouraged his love of literature. Shakespeare and *Arabian Nights* as well as favourite Scottish authors were read aloud by the fireside in the evenings, and the children put on modest 'theatricals'; claiming the role of Richard III for one such performance, Walter observed that his limp would do in lieu of a hump. And on family visits to their numerous Border relatives, he absorbed the tales of ancient uncles whose memories stretched back to the rebellion of '45 and Bonnie Prince Charlie's fate. If nature dealt Walter a blow with his physical impediment, Story adopted him as a favoured son.

'As the sapling was then bent, so the tree was to grow. On a memory, which was wax to receive and granite to retain, had been impressed affections and interests which were to dominate his life.'[162]

In the gap between high school and college, Walter again spent time with Aunt Jenny who had moved to Kelso. Attending school there he met a local boy, James Ballantyne, beginning a life-long friendship that would bring fortune and calamity to both. Walter's peers already delighted in his impromptu storytelling. In our imagination, we can join him and his college friends on a long ramble over the hills to a favourite ruined abbey or castle, and sit on the sheep-grazed turf to read together the romantic chivalries of *Canterbury Tales, Decameron,* or *Mort d'Arthur.* And when the lads want their knights to survive for another adventure, we hear them joshing each other's attempts to spin their own yarns.

Such dalliance ceased when Walter began an apprenticeship with his father's firm and 'entered upon the dry and barren wilderness of forms and conveyances' while he studied for the bar, but the work provided pocket money for books and theatre tickets. He was ambitious to succeed for himself as well as out of love for his father and, despite wishing himself on the moors, he worked hard: 'When actually at the oar, no man could pull it harder than I.' – A prophetic statement.

Although Walter led the typically riotous life of a student, he won his advocate's gown in 1792 and served for five years at the bar. They were disturbing times; an almost perpetual state of war with France and rumours of imminent invasion kept garrisons in a state of readiness. Despite his gammy leg, Walter joined a volunteer cavalry unit, practising sword drills and polishing his kit with great enthusiasm. If there was romance in these echoes of chivalry, a darker reality lurked on the Continent. The French Revolution was at an early, idealistic stage during Walter's late teens, but over the next ten years, it entered one of the most destructive episodes of European history: the Reign of Terror, during which almost 19,000 people were guillotined. Many people feared the 'contagion' of revolt would spread to Britain.

When Walter gained an official appointment as Clerk to the Court of Session in Edinburgh, and later, additional responsibilities in the county of Selkirk as Sheriff (local judge), he continued his habits of travelling both in the Highlands and his native Border lands; he learned both history and human understanding among the diverse people he dealt with – from poachers to parsons, and from lairds and lords to fish-wives and farm labourers.

From his twenty-eighth year, Walter was well set up: while the court was in session he and his wife, Charlotte (daughter of a French émigré whom he met on a trip to the English Lake District), lived with their young children in an Edinburgh townhouse, the family occupying a rented country property when he worked in Selkirk. Though far from a scholar, Walter scribbled verses and continued to read widely including French, German and Italian from original texts. He read the early novelists, Henry Fielding and Tobias Smollett as well as the earlier poets, Shakespeare, Pope, and Dryden, and he was familiar with Norse sagas. Books he obtained from James Sibbald's circulating library in Parliament Square, or perhaps bought occasionally from Peter Hill's poky old bookshop in the High Street. There he could chat with the apprentice, Archibald Constable, until Archibald left to set up his own premises. Constable was four years younger than Scott and, along with Ballantyne, would be the other party to the financial disaster that awaited them all. But at this happy time, Walter followed his special interest in the traditional Scottish ballads that defined a folk culture fast receding and he continued, as he ranged over the landscape, to collect oral verses from anyone who could be induced by patience, kindness or a wee dram, to recall them.

While Walter rode the Scottish glens, the boy he would one day meet as a fellow novelist was growing up on the shores of Lake Otsego at the headwaters of the Susquehanna River, across the Atlantic Ocean in New Jersey. Ten-year-old James Cooper may not have known how to tickle a trout but he, too, loved to roam the river banks and forests that surrounded his childhood in Cooperstown, a remote frontier settlement which his father, William Cooper, had founded. At the time of James' birth, his family's fortunes had markedly improved. He was the eleventh of twelve children, seven of his siblings had already died in the harshness of earlier pioneering life. His mother, Elizabeth, was of Swedish stock; his father's Quaker forebears had arrived in 1679. Like Walter Scott, James Cooper came into the world following momentous political events. The thirteen colonies that comprised Britain's North American territories had won their own rebellion six years before James was born. The American War of Independence had rumbled and raged from 1775 to 1783, drawing in French, Spanish and Dutch government forces paying off old scores against their trading rival, Britain, by fighting in support of the colonists.

American colonists' smouldering resentment of British control had been sparked into war by the otherwise innocuous beverage, tea. In addition to exploiting the raw materials of her overseas possessions to stoke her industrial revolution, Britain cross-traded goods from one country to another, garnering middleman profits at every transaction and topping up the treasury with taxes on the local purchase of foreign goods. American resistance to paying British taxes when the colonists had no say in government became focused on a new tea tax. Designed to be unavoidable – by giving the East India Company complete monopoly of the trade – British politicians had calculated that the colonists would never go without their tea for a mere principle. They were wrong. The brew boiled over when three tea ships, held-over in Boston harbour awaiting payment of duties, were boarded by incensed protesters who smashed open the tea-chests and flung their extremely valuable cargo into the sea – an event since known as The Boston Tea Party. And they were thorough. In the morning, when tea leaves were seen floating on the surface of the water, they rowed out and dunked them with their oars. The ensuing conflict, which spread in one way or another to almost every corner of the colonial world, ended in a victory for the newly created United States of America.

Culturally, however, the mother country remained dominant. 'Of creative literature there was then very little of any value produced: and to that little a foreign stamp was necessary, to give currency outside of the petty circle in which it originated.'[163]

James learned his letters in Cooperstown village school, and for lack of a more senior establishment, was sent as a private pupil to a rector – the son of an English clergyman and graduate of an English University – in the town of Albany. His tutor impressed upon his charges the superiority of English manners and instilled in them the same education in classics and history that he had received in England. Unfortunately, he died before James was properly prepared for attending Yale College as a junior. The youngest Yale student at thirteen years of age, James excelled at Latin but seems to have gained little else and was expelled after two years for some prank. Without an authenticated account[164], the nature of the prank has ranged in biographers' imaginations from blowing a door off its hinges with explosives, to tying a donkey into a professor's chair.

It seems the fiery temper and unyielding nature that punctuated his later literary life were already evident. His father, by this time a congressman, would hardly have been pleased. Such lads were generally sent to sea to learn the lessons of life, and this was James' next adventure. After a tough training year before the mast in the mercantile marine, he joined the American navy as a midshipman. But he served for only four years.

As so often happens to the best laid plans, love intervened. James married Susan DeLancey; of French Huguenot descent, her wealthy and influential family had been Loyalists in the Revolution, and her father had served in the British navy. James' young wife insisted he leave the sea. His father having died two years before, he invested his inheritance in a country estate, dabbled in local politics and played a prominent role in New York high society.

This future author, whose stories would be hailed even more in Europe than in America, had passed his first thirty years without a thought of penning a single word, and spent the next thirty writing continually. His epiphany is said to have occurred in his parlour one evening when he thrust aside in disgust the English novel he was reading, declaring that he could have done better himself. Susan held him to his boast. With her encouragement he wrote his first novel, *Precautions*, which he published in 1820. Typographically it was a disaster, the punctuation so erratic as to be almost incomprehensible. By most accounts the content was little better. A story of English society, it was seen as a weak imitation of English style and manners – that rector had a lot to answer for. But Story gripped James by the scruff of his neck; his writing was about to be transformed.

Though poles apart in temperament and intellect, Walter Scott and James Fenimore Cooper[165] would both become prolific writers, and they were literary icons to their countrymen. And although Walter was eighteen years ahead of James and blazed the trail, they would each create the 'historical novel' in their respective countries – a significant influence in what has been called the Romanticism Movement.

Literary 'romance' was not of the Mills and Boon variety – although love was a popular theme, especially to Burns, Shelley and Byron ('mad, bad, and dangerous to know'[166]) – but more in the sense of 'romancing' as being fanciful, expressing sensual and original flights of fancy, and what Jane Austen might have called 'a certain delicacy of feeling'. And it included an interest in the mysterious and the magical. 'Movement', too, is a misleading label if it implies a co-ordinated body. This

James Fenimore Cooper

reaction against the rational thinking of the Enlightenment in favour of emotional imagination was subtle, arising gradually and unevenly in various ways and times in different cultures.

We saw how earlier humanist writers challenged the overarching power of the church; similarly, in the seventeenth and eighteenth centuries, scholars continued to promote independent thought and experimentation in advancing science, philosophy, and political theory. Old superstitions were questioned; educated people no longer believed that sickness of body or mind was caused by sin and demonic possession. They had called it the Age of Reason. But this enlightened rationality was led by intellectuals and governing elites: its formal orthodoxy sustained the old social hierarchies which a growing number of 'free thinkers' were beginning to resent.

Perhaps more importantly, human nature is not wholly rational, not even that of a scientist – many discoveries have been sparked by an irrational idea – and though human emotions may be repressed, they cannot be denied. In the eighteenth and nineteenth centuries, Romanticism took up the new individual freedom of thought, creating original art and literature that flowed from the senses. Instead of continuing to draw on the classics, writers turned for inspiration to idealised notions of nature, mythology, folklore, exotic tales of 'noble savages' and often to medieval chivalry and heroism. Many of the writers were, themselves, romantic figures leading flamboyant, eccentric lives leading to an early tragic death.

Especially significant was the enlistment of Romanticism in the widespread simmering of revolutionary and nationalist feelings. Folklore played a supportive role in this endeavour. We can get a feel for the relationship between politics and art at this period if we indulge in a whistle-stop detour through Eastern Europe.

Poland's national poet, Adam Mickiewicz (1798–1843), urged his countrymen to fight for independence from Russia and other major powers that had carved up Poland's territory; his narrative poem of medieval Lithuanian heroism, *Konrad Wallenrod,* called his young compatriots to action. Steeped in folklore as a child, Mickiewicz wove traditional stories into his own poems and dramas. They inspired the Polish composer, Frederick Chopin, to create a new musical form for piano, the *ballade*, with the same combination of drama and lyricism. Mickiewicz was a close friend of the Russian poet and short-story writer, Alexander Pushkin. During Pushkin's passionate life he killed a man in one duel and died young in another. Spurning the French dominance of Russian literature, Pushkin incorporated into his writing the concerns and traditions of his own people; his political activism on behalf of the serfs led to his exile. Both Mickiewicz and Pushkin were aware of Jacob and Wilhelm Grimm's collections of folk-tales and legends in Germany. Pushkin had an unlikely ally in a member of the notorious Russian Orlov family (one of whom bought one of the world's largest diamonds – known as the 'Orlov Diamond' and the subject of many romance tales). The Orlov brothers – talented and ambitious military leaders – orchestrated the palace coup in 1762 that placed Catherine II (aka Catherine the Great) on the throne, ousting her unstable husband, Peter III, who was murdered a few days later. Subsequently, the Orlovs – Grigory, Aleksey, and Fyodor – became extremely wealthy aristocrats. Grigory had been one of Catherine's lovers and remained her advisor (he also gave her the diamond). Fyodor's son, Prince Mikhail, befriended Pushkin and shared his liberal views. Mikhail supported the Decembrist Revolt in 1825, demanding a constitution and the emancipation of the serfs. That same year, an Orlov nephew, sixteen-year-old Count

Orloff-Davidoff, stayed for an extended period with Walter Scott at Abbottsford as part of his education. A few years later, while working in Europe, Fenimore Cooper struck up a friendship with Adam Mickiewicz and arranged a donation towards the Polish struggle for independence.[167]

We gain much by being aware of the intricate web of connectedness, even in this brief sample, because Story has a finger in everyone's pies, strudels and fairy cakes.

The 'revival' of folklore during the Romantic period was more of an appropriation by the intelligentsia because, in reality, folk-tales have never left our hearths since we sheltered in caves and jostled for a place at the communal fire. Some element of every tale Story has told us so far will have survived in various guises in later oral folk-tales. Remember the Egyptian story of the Book of Thoth hidden within all those boxes and guarded by a death-less serpent? Among the magical gifts it conferred was the ability 'to understand the language of all creatures.' The idea that special power is acquired from the knowledge of animal language has persisted for thousands of years. Italo Calvino notes that, 'The man who understands animal speech will be Pope…is an old European superstition', and he relates a traditional folk-tale from Lombardy:

A rich merchant sent his son, Bobo, to a tutor to learn languages. When Bobo returned able to understand the speech of birds and animals, the father believed his son had been taught witchcraft and instructed his servants to take the boy away and kill him. The servants let Bobo go but told the father he was dead. In subsequent adventures, Bobo saved lives through his ability to eavesdrop on animal speech. He arrived in Rome where a new Pope was to be elected. 'In those days they chose the Pope by letting a dove loose in St. Peter's Square, where crowds of people waited. The man on whose head the dove lit would be the new Pope.' The dove landed on Bobo's head and he was enthroned as Pope. When his father saw this he was struck down with remorse, 'and just had time to ask his son's forgiveness before expiring in his arms.'[168]

Folk-tales are told to amuse and to instruct in the art of living; retold by every generation, they are seasoned to the flavour of each locality with personal experience, history and gossip. And we have woven fairy tales, with their magic and spirit beings, since we became aware of the supernatural as an unknowable force with potential to help or harm. Sometimes, during centuries of retelling, magic was added to a simple, commonsensical folk-tale – perhaps to increase enjoyment and wonder or to plug a plot hole – and it became a tale of fairies. Such a process renders fine distinctions between 'folk' and 'fairy' tales difficult and largely academic, but classifying them and tracing their origins attracted a coterie of devoted scholars and still does; current research has traced the tale of 'Jack and the Beanstalk' to origins more than 5000 years ago[169] – we leave them to labour in Story's dusty archives.

Magical elements are especially useful in stories as a short cut to personal transformation, for example from poor to rich or from childhood to adulthood. The ancient oral wisdom of folk-tales and fairy stories became popular in the *salons* of the literati in sixteenth-century France, most famously through those rewritten by Charles Perrault. In an introduction to one story, he is conscious that writing simple tales – *contés* – may be considered by some as frivolous (he held important administrative posts in the court of Louis XIV).

'Some lofty persons seldom smile,
And cannot bear to give their time,
Regarding literary style,
To anything that's not sublime.'

But it is wise for men oppressed by work,
'To free themselves from reason's bonds,
And pleasantly be lulled to rest,
By some old tale of maids distressed,
Of ogres, spells, and magic wands'[170]

In Perrault's tale, 'Donkey Skin', a mighty king gave the greatest honour to his remarkable donkey, Ned:

> 'Nature had made the beast so pure,
> That what he dropped was not manure,
> But sovereigns and gold crowns instead
> (Imprinted with the royal head)
> Which every morning Master Ned
> Left for collection on his bed.'[171]

But there is a dark side to this story. On her deathbed, his queen made the king swear not to remarry unless he found someone more lovely and virtuous than herself (which she was certain was impossible). However, the king found his daughter fitted that description and proposed to marry her. The distraught girl sought out her fairy godmother, whose advice was to ask first for gifts which her father could not possibly provide, such as a dress the colour of the moon. The king provided this, and all the subsequent requests she tried. Finally, the girl asked for the skin of his exalted donkey. When this, too, was presented to her, she wore it as a disguise and ran away to a distant farmhouse where she was hired as a kitchen drudge. Eventually, she was noticed by a visiting prince and after much interplay of lucky chances, her baking for him a delicious cake clinched the matter. Their wedding was a glorious affair, attended by her repentant father.

The horror of the girl's situation is lightened by humour, but Perrault confirms the morals a child may learn from the tale: that suffering is better than doing wrong, that virtue will triumph in the end and that 'love deranged defies all sense: against it, reason is a poor defence'.

The basic story is an ancient one, perhaps warning of a common danger. More likely its ultimate origin lies in a kinship rule against paternal incest in our early hunter-gatherer days. As we might expect, there are many versions: different conditions set by the dying queen, various means of escape for the hapless daughter, and alternative endings. But a significant common element supports its origins in kinship rules: in almost every version of the tale, the only effective recourse for the daughter is to run away. In patriarchal societies, it is the women who leave their natal home to marry. Undoubtedly this would have involved hardships and the capacity to accept and adapt, encouraged by the promise of 'finding your prince' in the end. Above all, fairy tales are optimistic; they combine the everyday and the magical to achieve the impossible.

In a process we have seen many times already, a twelfth-century bishop appropriated this old story and transformed the girl into a martyr, St. Dymphna. She was supposedly an Irish princess who escaped from her predatory father by fleeing to Belgium with the help of a priest. Being a medieval Christian version there is no humorous donkey: the father tracks her down, and after her further refusal of him, decapitates her – a necessary ending for martyrdom.

The fifteenth-century Italian author and folklore collector, Gianfrancesco Straparola, retold the tale as the long adventure story, 'Doralice', in which the daughter of the prince of Salerno is helped by her old nurse to escape her father's attentions by hiding in a trunk and being shipped to England. There she marries a prince and has two children. Her father takes revenge on his in-laws by murdering the infants, but we have the satisfaction of knowing that he also meets a bloody end.

The donkey was clearly an invention of Perrault's sense of fun[172], but the Brothers Grimm gave it a nod in their version of the story, 'All Kinds of Fur', or 'Coat of Skins', in which one of the impossible gifts the king's embattled daughter asks for is a coat made from the skins of every kind of animal. When this is produced, she runs away and, similar to Perrault's tale, she is found in the forest and taken to work in a palace kitchen where she eventually meets her prince, wooed this time not with French cake, but with wholesome German soup in which she has dropped a gold ring.

The princess in the donkey skin hides in the forest.

That folk-tales involve so many wealthy and powerful kings, handsome princes and beautiful princesses is probably because they have the aura of wonder; they are more interesting than us humbler beings. Where peasants are heroes or heroines, it is usually because they become unaccountably rich – nowadays we have celebrities to enthral us: the princes and princesses of the screen. But from a child's point of view, kings and queens represented the powerfulness of adults relative to their own powerlessness. Whether by fathers, ogres, dragons or tyrant kings, dominance over others is a common theme of folklore, where bravery, wit or magic may tip the balance of power. Heard from the cradle and ingrained in the common psyche, folk-tales offer a potent source of symbolism for political allegory.

Varieties of the same stories are found all over Europe, but each nation makes its own claims to ownership in a swell of patriotism. The French Revolution had spawned General Napoleon Bonaparte whose pretensions to rule all of Europe threatened every smaller state; for them, strength through internal unity became a national imperative.

In Germany, Wilhelm and Jacob Grimm's interest in traditional tales was aroused while they studied law at Marburg University. Their professor, Friedrich Carl von Savigny, told them that the essence of law could be understood only by knowing ancient customs and language. At a time when Germany and Prussia were divided into numerous principalities ruled by quarrelsome despots, the unifying potential of shared cultural traditions was not lost on the Brothers Grimm. They were not collectors in the true sense of gathering tales directly from the peasantry – family and friends brought stories told them by their grandmothers and governesses – and Wilhelm substantially rewrote some to suit his moral purpose, but by 1818, they had published 156 folk-tales, and 585 legends or *marchen*. (They distinguished 'legends' as grounded in historical fact, however distant or unlikely.) Still pursueing a unifying German 'essence', they began work on an immense dictionary tracing the origin of every German word. The first volume was published in 1854; its 1,824 pages only reached as far as 'Biermolke'. Both Jacob and Wilhelm had died before they completed entries for the letter 'F'. Other German writers such as Johann von Goethe and Ludwig Tieck were also contributing to a sense of a German nationhood during the early Romantic period – a political unity not achieved until 1871. Later, this search for a 'common soul' would be corrupted into the myth of the Aryan race and the fascist atrocities of the Third Reich.

Scotland had begun the romancing of cultural roots much earlier, when a clerical scholar, James Macpherson, produced his translation of the ancient Gaelic bard, Ossian (whom we met as Oisin in Irish mythology). *Fragments of Ancient Poetry* created a literary sensation in 1760, not least because the high quality of the poetry from such 'primitive' forebears was both surprising and a source of national pride. That documentary fragments and oral tradition had preserved Ossian's composition over more than a thousand years was a cause for wonder. But wonder turned to doubt when Macpherson produced more: the eight-volume *Temora: An Ancient Epic Poem* published in 1763. Condemnation of the poems as frauds soon followed, no doubt louder from those who regretted their earlier public credulity. But others supported the work's authenticity in a controversy that brawled for half a century. Walter Scott wrote a paper on it for the Speculative Society – one of his debating clubs at law school.

The Ossian poems portray a past age in which chiefs and warriors of Ireland, Scotland and Scandinavia intrigued among themselves, invaded each other's lands in heroic battles and fell in love with each other's beautiful daughters. We meet what appear to be well-loved characters from Irish mythology, the great King Cormac, the Firbolgs, and the bard Ossian(Oisin), who is the narrator recalling exploits of his son Oscar, and of his father Fingal ('Finn' in Ireland). Spellings and details are often different to the Irish stories we saw earlier. Such poetic licence is usual in epics: like the *Saga of the Volsung*, times, places and characters may be conflated, but the Ossian poems are true to the spirit of the third century in the lands of its Gaelic and Norse heroes – even to the Celtic custom of honouring the valour of vanquished foes rather than reviling them in the manner of Homer.[173]

Macpherson was clearly an accomplished poet and storyteller; his error was in claiming he had translated found fragments of original verses composed at the time by the ancient bard. Macpherson undoubtedly collected oral material and probably acquired old documents, but these would have been remnants of Gaelic mythology shared by both Ireland and Scotland. Names and incidents had been changed over time in accordance with local characteristics as is usual with such traditions, and he changed some himself in his own reinterpretation. The poems could not be those of Ossian. But Macpherson's romantic epics revived a legitimate cultural heritage when every Celtic emblem of the Highlander had been forbidden after the defeat at Culloden. Ossian embodied all the elements that initiated Romanticism. Translated into most European languages, including Russian, Macpherson's work exerted huge influence over writers seeking to create a 'national literature' from their folk history, however 'romanticised'. And it was an inspiration to Walter Scott.

We left Walter collecting ballads, the 'sung stories' of Scottish oral traditions. While ballads may contain ghosts and uncanny acts of fairy folk, they more often relate events in the lives, loves and conflicts of local characters. Some would have been remnants of praise poems by 'court' bards, still retained by the more powerful chiefs into the eighteenth century. Others recorded regrets at unsuccessful forays into neighbouring territory:

> 'Now Liddesdale has ridden a raid,
> But I wat they had better hae staid at home;
> For Michael o' Winfield he is dead,
> And Jock o' the Side is prisoner ta'en.'

While we boned-up on Romanticism and folklore, Walter published his collection of ballads, *Minstrelsy of the Scottish Borders (*1802), to great popular acclaim. He was a national hero. His work stirred the general mood of nostalgia for a romantic past in Europe and America, and it restored Scotland's national pride. The work greatly influenced European writers and it was a favourite reading of Napoleon, even as he plotted to invade Britain. Walter had kept closely to the original oral material, contributing to it only to sew together fragments and fill gaps. Launched into fame, he embarked on narrative poetry of his own with *The Lay of the Last Minstrel, Lady of the Lake,* and *Marmion* (1808) which commemorated the battle of Flodden Field. The patriotism expressed in *Marmion* held special appeal with Britain under threat from invasion:

> 'Breathes there a man with soul so dead
> Who never to himself hath said,
> '"This is my land, my native land."'

Scott was offered 1,000 guineas by Archibald Constable – the Edinburgh book seller then a publisher – before Constable had even read the poem. Scott's works were first published by his old friend James Ballantyne who, finding too few clients as a solicitor, had launched a local newspaper and set up as a printer in Kelso. Walter encouraged him to move to Edinburgh and became a partner in the company, Ballantyne & Co. Together they launched into producing poems, stories and short prose, Walter writing or editing much of it, and offering openings for emerging young writers.

Even before *Marmion* was published, Walter had written the first six chapters of a prose work on the Jacobite Rising but had abandoned it. He came upon it again about eight years later when searching for some fishing tackle in an old cabinet. Perhaps persuaded by the popularity of contemporary novelists – Maria Edgeworth[174] writing on Ireland, and Jane Porter's *The Scottish Chiefs* (1810) – Walter decided to complete his longer prose work. It became his first novel, *Waverley – Sixty Years Since,* published in 1814: the forerunner of an extremely successful series of some twenty tales of adventure, intrigue and conflicting loyalties set in a picturesque Scottish landscape.

While historical truth always remained important to him, Walter delved into the motives of his characters, and rather than be constrained by the biographies of known contestants, he created as his hero the fictional cavalry officer, 'Captain Edward Waverley', a romantic, impressionable young Englishman of ancient noble family. Edward was born into conflict: brought up partly by his Loyalist uncle (secret supporter of the exiled Stuart dynasty), and partly by his father, staunch adherent to the current regime in which he held office. By this device, Scottish traditions are shown naturally as discovered by a stranger, while laying the ground for the three-way clashes that followed between Highland, Lowland and English cultures. With his prose and through the lives of his characters, Scott made for his readers an emotional experience of the past as vividly as Snorri Sturluson had with his Icelandic sagas, and William Shakespeare with his drama.

An opportunity for gentle humour is rarely overlooked and often at its best among Scott's minor characters. After a dinner hosted by The Baron of Bradwardine in which wine and whisky had been consumed by many a pint, he and his guests, Edward, and the Lairds of Balmawhapple and Killancureit, round off the evening in Lucky Macleary's, the best this remote Lowland locality could offer for a local 'tavern':

> 'Accordingly, in full expectation of these distinguished guests, Lucky Macleary had swept her house for the first time this fortnight, tempered her turf-fire to such a heat as the season required in her damp hovel even at Midsummer, set forth her deal table newly washed, propped its lame foot with a fragment of turf, arranged four or five stools of huge and clumsy form upon the sites which best suited the inequalities of her clay floor; and having, moreover, put on her clean toy, rokelay, and scarlet plaid, gravely awaited the arrival of the company, in full hope of custom and profit.'

(A 'toy' is a woollen head-covering extending onto her shoulders; 'rokelay', a cloak).

Following the initial triumph with *Waverley*, Ballantyne & Co. set up a business association with Archibald Constable and together they embarked on an ambitious programme of issuing novels in high quality bindings, usually in three volumes. Already, this was the era of the 'three-decker novel'. Scott took little interest in the business side of the enterprise and concentrated on writing. Despite the new popularity of prose, most novelists at that time were women – Jane Austen leading the van – and so were their readers. Intellectuals still considered epic poetry the epitome of literature. Conscious of the dignity of his post as Clerk to the Court of Session, Walter published *Waverley* anonymously – issuing his subsequent novels as 'By the author of Waverley'.[175]

Scott wrote as he spoke: with the strong narrative voice of an oral storyteller, using dialect freely, because social storytelling – often improvised – was still the prevailing Scottish culture. From the humblest to the haughtiest gathering, stories were told and the characters discussed as if they had been real people – which they often were. Scott's style was sometimes criticised, but he saw it as part of the story's authenticity and had no patience to correct it with what he called 'fine writing'. He knew what his readers wanted and crafted his work accordingly: 'No man shall find me rowing against the stream. I care not who knows it – I write for general amusement.'[176]

In the search for cultural and political identity, Story had unleashed a new genre: 'the historical novel'. It caught the popular fancy, fuelling a demand for long prose that made the nineteenth century the age of the novel. Everyone, it seems, wanted to sink their nose in historical romance. Everyone, that is, who did not think such frivolity beneath their dignity. The Americans, too, caught the craze.

An English visitor had suggested to James Fenimore Cooper that he should write about his own country. Perhaps this gentleman mentioned Walter Scott as a successful example, because in James' next novel, *The Spy* (1821), he followed Scott's lead and wrote an adventure arising from the American War of Independence. Encouraged by its success, he began a series of novels depicting the fast-disappearing pioneer culture he had known as a child on the banks of the Susquehanna. With the oral history of his family and surroundings, and heeding the example of *Waverley*, Cooper created the hero Natty Bumppo, a back-woodsman whose dress, gleaned largely from nature, won him the nickname 'Leather-Stocking'.

> 'A kind of coat, made of dressed deer-skin, with the hair on, was belted close to his lank body by a girdle of coloured worsted. On his feet were deer-skin moccasins, ornamented with porcupines' quills, after the manner of the Indians, and his limbs were guarded with long leggings of the same material as the moccasins, which, gartering over the knees of his tarnished buckskin breeches, had obtained for him among the settlers the nickname of Leather-Stocking.'[177]

The whole series, among them *The Pioneers*, *The Prairie*, and much later, *The Last of the Mohicans* and *The Deer Slayer*, became known as the 'leather-stocking tales'. Setting them in the conflict between old hunting life-styles of the forested wilderness and modern progress that could not fell trees fast enough, Cooper had produced America's first 'romantic novel' of authentic history. He was not the first well-known American author. Washington Irving, a lawyer from New York, had been publishing with great success since 1802: a number of essays, a satire and a collection of short tales – *The Sketch Book of Geoffrey Crayon, Gent*, which contained his best-selling stories, *Rip Van Winkle* and *The Legend of Sleepy Hollow*. But Irving had spent much of his working life as a diplomat in Europe and also wrote on European topics, publishing most of his work there. With several 'leather-stocking' volumes to his credit, Cooper, seldom backward in criticising others, challenged Irving to write about his own culture. Irving wrote *A Tour of the Prairie* in 1835 and *The Adventures of Captain Bonneville* two years later.

Cooper interspersed the production of his 'pioneer' novels with an equally successful series of sea stories drawn from his own experience. In 1825, he took his wife and four daughters to stay in Europe where he continued writing. Before his brief meeting with Scott in Paris, we must catch up with Walter; much has been happening since his success with the Waverley novels.

Scott was generous in his appreciation of others' writing, and modest about his own. He could not deny his success, however, and he enjoyed its benefits. Constable had gone into partnership with Hurst and Robinson in London, and Scott's work was selling all over Europe and in America. However, with no copyright control, 'pirated' versions in the USA gave him no benefit. In a buoyant economy, writers were well paid. Constable was generous with advances, and Scott drew heavily on his credit with Ballantyne & Co. Like most businesses at the time, transactions between publishers, printers and authors were generally in the form of notes of credit payable on demand – 'accommodations' as they were called – creating a network of mutual indebtedness, while cash flows were supported by bank loans. But it all seemed to work and Walter was more prosperous than he had ever anticipated, enabling him to invest in his own 'romantic lifestyle' in the Borders of his youth.

He bought Abbotsford, a country house in the Tweed valley, and whenever he was free of court duties, indulged in the abundant hunting and fishing the area offered and began to establish his own rural estate. Washington Irving stayed for several days with the Scott family (in 1817 when this enterprise was only beginning) and was taken on rain-soaked tramps to sites of historical interest and treated to the tales of local worthies. The experience encouraged Irving to incorporate folklore into his own stories – he and Scott remained friends, exchanging letters over several years.

Abbotsford House.

Abbotsford was extended so many times to accommodate visitors that it finally resembled a baronial castle with its wings and turrets. A steady flow of house-guests enjoyed Scott's lavish hospitality, exchanging tales over the dinner table while his piper, John of Skye, paced the terrace playing pibrochs. Wordsworth was a regular guest and other admirers visited from France, Italy, Russia, and even Persia. One acquaintance returning from Australia brought him back a pair of emus which, upon discovering what they were, he wisely declined: 'We will have no emuses here'. He continued to buy more land, build workers' cottages and involve himself in garden landscaping and planting several thousand trees. Walter still had to attend at Edinburgh when the court was in session, but Abbotsford was his passion.

After a morning's writing, and if there was no Sheriff's hearing, he inspected his estate on horseback or on foot, often accompanied by his trusty old retainer, Tom Purdie. He and Tom would have long arguments about the work to be undertaken, Walter usually worn down to giving way, only for Tom to come round to his view the next day. Walter explained to Washington Irving that his relationship with Tom was, "'as it was with an old laird and a pet servant, whom he had indulged until he was positive beyond all endurance. "This won't do!" cried the old laird, in a passion, "we can't live together any longer--we must part." "An' where the de'il does your honor mean to go?" replied the other.'"[178]

Walter's heart seemed to linger in the age of chivalry, where serving king and country defined an 'honourable life'. The ceiling panels in Abbotsford's hall were adorned with the armorial arms of his ancestors traced back some 500 years and he knew all their stories. He lived like a character in one of his own novels: an indulgent and genial laird who attracted equal loyalty from his followers; his estate steward, Willie Laidlaw – an accomplished man fallen on hard times whom Scott had persuaded to take on the role – was more friend than employee. And when Scott was awarded a baronetcy, news of the 'Sir' so delighted old Tom Purdie that the sheep, already painted with the owner's initials – 'W S' – all bore the mark 'S W S' by the following morning.

But in a dramatic plot twist worthy of Scott's own storytelling, he suddenly faces the prospect of complete ruin. His journal entries contemplate the loss of Abbotsford, the terrible blow to local families who depend on him, and even the future of his beloved dogs.

He was not alone in this predicament. Britain's industrial revolution was generating factories and a host of related enterprises and inventions from tin cans and oil lamps to the first steam railway. Such prosperity, especially at a time when coins and paper money were scarce, had led too many people to over-extend on credit. When bills were called in at the first signs of trouble, banks could not meet the demand, and as if hot coals had been tossed into a haystack, the whole system began to burn. At the final crash in 1825, many well-established business houses lost everything. It was worst in London, and Constable's publishing partner, Hurst and Robinson, pressed him to honour his notes of credit. Constable leaned on Ballantyne & Co. who did not have the funds, so Scott lent Constable £10,000[179] to ease the pressure. But there was to be no 'easing'. The economic crisis was national; the solution required structural change which would have ramifications for the future and not only in Britain. It was one of the effects which dampened Romanticism with a new realism, as we shall see later.[180]

Constable's filing for bankruptcy drew Ballantyne & Co. down with him. Scott was never quite sure how much Constable's own mismanagement was to blame, or whether Constable had in some way deceived him: robust sales and book stocks did not seem to tally with the present collapse. (Even in his lifetime, sales of Scott's work amounted to millions of copies worldwide.) Scott reconciled himself to the turn-about in their relationship. 'To nourish angry passions against a man whom I really liked would be to lay a blister on my own heart.'[181]

Though not all were directly his debts, as a partner in a bankrupt enterprise Scott took responsibility for £130,000 of what was owed to creditors. The Edinburgh townhouse and contents were sold and he took rooms in a lodging house to attend his court work. He was determined to avoid declaring *himself* bankrupt because he wanted to pay creditors in full, rather than the usually small percentage following liquidation. Most of all, he was desperate to hold onto Abbotsford. After many months of nerve-wracking negotiations, false hopes and new crises, a trust was set up by which he pledged his property, his existing literary works and all his future production until the debt was paid. In exchange, Abbotsford was saved, for the time being … if his books remained popular … if he could keep writing. He was optimistic: 'But adversity is to me at least a tonic and bracer; the fountain is awakened from its inmost recesses, as if the spirit of affliction had troubled it in his passage.'[182]

While completing his latest novel, *Woodstock*, he took on two new historical works each running to seven or eight volumes – *Chronicles of the Canongate*, and *Life of Napoleon* – and wrote reviews, articles and stories for literary journals, checking proofs and wading through copious correspondence between writing sessions. 'I will die a free man if hard working will do it'.[183]

Amidst this crushing pressure, his life's companion, Charlotte, died after a long debilitating illness. Now in his fifty-fifth year, Walter found the tremendous workload a strain, and working at night in candle-light hurt his eyes. He confided moments of frustration to his journal with characteristic wit: 'Methinks Duty looks as if she were but half-pleased with me; but would the Pagan bitch have me work on the Sunday.'[184]

And he passed over each new irritation with his favourite expression: 'Naboclish!' ('Never mind!') – Irish Gaelic he had picked up on a visit to Ireland.

In the autumn of 1826, Walter went to Paris for a couple of weeks to research for his *Life of Napoleon*, and his daughter, Anne joined him. The self-styled 'emperor', Napoleon Bonaparte, had met his Waterloo in 1815 by Prussian and British forces and had died in exile in 1821; Britain's patriotism ran high and his biography was expected to sell well. The outward passage to Calais was rough, but it seems their strong Scottish constitutions stood them in good stead: 'We ate and drank like dragons the whole way'. During a hectic schedule of visits, interviews and fending off enthusiastic French fans, Scott had two occasions to talk with Fenimore Cooper. Scott did not feel the same rapport with Cooper as he had with the more urbane Irving, and Cooper did not reciprocate Walter's compliments on his work. But Cooper did strongly advise Scott to self-publish his books in America 'as a citizen', to gain direct benefit. Scott was interested in anything that would increase sales, but pricing would be tricky because the Americans were accustomed to much cheaper books than the British.

Cooper faced financial pressures of his own on his return to America in 1833. He, too, had spent money while it flowed, and so had his five brothers, eating up their father's inheritance. When they died, Cooper took responsibility for their dependant widows and children, writing hard to amend his depleted fortunes. Fired by the struggles for democracy he had witnessed in Europe, he began a series of semi-political works that incensed critics at home and abroad. Disliking criticism, Cooper responded with gusto, becoming embroiled in a number of law suits. Like Scott, he turned to writing history and biography – in his case, of the American Navy – which met with a lukewarm reception. People preferred Cooper's fiction, which had always pleased ordinary readers rather than the critics; he regained popularity with his return to the 'leather-stocking tales' and Bumppo's back-story as a youth. *The Pathfinders* – for some reason especially popular in Russia – and *The Last of the Mohicans* were among his most successful books.

Later in life, Cooper returned to the Susquehanna of his childhood, living in Cooperstown and supervising the forested land he bought overlooking Lake Otsego. At his death in 1851, he had written almost 100 volumes, his latest was at the printers and the plan for another sat on his desk. A pioneer of home-grown fiction, Fenimore Cooper assured America of its first successful historical novel, but he and his writings remained controversial. Perhaps it is just as well that the spikiest criticism – Mark Twain's *Fenimore Cooper's Literary Offences* (1895) – was made when it was way too late for Cooper to retaliate.

Sir Walter Scott's *Life of Napoleon* was a notable success; of the initial 10,000 printed for the first volume, most were sold within days. During 1830, his journal is punctuated with scribbled notes of potential profits and liabilities as he tries to estimate how long it will take him to pay the creditors – he reckoned four to five years. He would not have been surprised to learn he would not last quite that long. Even though he retired from court work that year, the punishing schedule of new works sapped his aging strength. And he was less resilient: the unexpected death of old Tom Purdie after an outing together affected him deeply. He wrote through the pain of rheumatism that kept him confined to the house for days at a time, and castigated himself for 'idleness' when bouts of depression and a series of minor strokes prevented him from working. By 1831, approximately half of the debts had been paid, and his library of books, collection of antiquities, furniture, and even his cutlery, were released from bondage to his creditors – progress which greatly salved his pride.

The following year, he succumbed to his doctor's insistence that he spend the winter in a warmer climate. By this time, becoming a little confused about his affairs, he believed all his debts honoured; out of compassion, no one contradicted him.[185] In October, Walter set off on his last 'romantic adventure': a tour of the Mediterranean in a Royal Navy frigate, the *Barham* – courtesy of the government – and in the company of his eldest son. Mental confusion began to intrude more often upon his senses, and though he remained in good humour throughout their tour, he felt distracted and longed for Scotland and the home he feared he would not see again. When they heard news of Goethe's death in March – Scott had intended to visit him in Weimar – he said, "'He at least died at home. Let us to Abbotsford.'"[186] Returning overland through Europe, a fourth stroke left him virtually immobilised. On arrival at London in June, he was intermittently comatose and unable to travel further for several weeks.

As Scott's carriage finally rumbled up the drive of his beloved Abbotsford and he saw his old friend, William Laidlaw, waiting for him along with his dogs, some of his old spirit revived: "'Ha! Willie Laidlaw! Oh man, how often have I thought of you!'"

Walter's steady decline during 1832, tempered by day-dreaming in the library and wheeled excursions through the gardens, ended on September 17th surrounded by his family. Tucked into a recess of his desk they found a small package that had belonged to his mother: it contained six locks of hair, one from each of her dead infants. In his biography of Scott, John Gilbert Lockhart[187] chose as an epitaph a line from Homer's *Iliad*: 'There he lay, mighty and mightily fallen, having done with his chivalry.'

Almost everyone had 'done with chivalry'. Although Sir Walter's themes were heroic, he described in detail the often wretched lives of the humblest villagers, and so had Pushkin in portrayals of the serfs. Though writing in the romantic style, they were keenly aware of the realities of life, even if Scott did not share Pushkin's political agenda: the chaos of revolt was anathema to Scott's rational legal mind. American and European wealth had been boosted by slavery and exploitation, both at home and abroad; revolutions, rebellions and the final ending of the slave trade shook commercial complacency, and the world was getting smaller: an injury in one place bled in another.

Such realities became Story's focus. The growth of industry, urbanisation, greater access to education and the spread of lending libraries had supported a blossoming of newspapers, magazines and cheap 'chap book' editions of the ubiquitous novel, along with 'penny dreadfuls' and 'shilling shockers' of short pulp fiction hawked in the streets. During the nineteenth and early twentieth century, not only in Europe and the Americas, but almost everywhere, a new class of readers and writers emerged. And Story found herself penned into the corsets of 'literary form' – a form unwittingly foreshadowed by Walter Scott. For within his novels little gems of complete stories appear with the magic of silver sixpences in a Christmas pudding. In *Redgauntlet*, the gem is a tale combining the supernatural with feudal hardships told by a blind itinerant musician: *Wandering Willie* is tightly focused on a single theme that leads the reader from an intriguing opening, to a conclusion that satisfies yet leaves questions to ponder. If the novel was 'painted' in bold swathes of colour on a canvas wide enough for a multiplicity of shades, this short tale was a miniature portrait, perfectly toned without a single unnecessary brushstroke; a disciplined structure which literary scholars identify as the beginning of 'the short story'.[188] We turn a page of history to some harsh realities of life and a brief golden age of fame for Story – fortune would take a little longer.

Chapter Twelve

Tell it how it is

Story recruits some of her favourite storytellers in Russia, France and America to expose the stark realities of serfdom in the east and industrialisation in the west which, between them, oppress and enslave so many of her people. And with their endeavours, Story helps to overpower slavery.

*Chekhov chose to cross Siberia to investigate the
infamous penal colony in Sakhalin Island.*

12

I sit on a man's back, choking him and making him carry me, and yet assure myself and others that I am sorry for him and wish to ease his lot by all possible means – except by getting off his back.

[Leo Tolstoy][189]

An ass asked a nightingale to sing so that he could judge whether her talent was as good as everyone claimed. The nightingale sang and trilled in exquisite variations so sweetly that all the creatures in the wood were enchanted into silence as they listened; even the shepherd was diverted from courting his lover by the splendour of the nightingale's song.

'The singer ceased. The ass gave weighty speech and slow:
"Not bad at all," he said; "in fact, my boy,
It's music one can quite enjoy.
But how your heart would warm
To hear out cock perform!
Just think of all the tricks you'd learn
If for a hint or two, to him you'd turn."
But my poor nightingale, at verdict of this kind,
Dashed off, and left in flight, fields nine times three behind.

And God deliver us from critics quite so blind.'[190]

And not only from critics, but also from censors. Ivan Andreyevich Krylov (1768–1844), for he is the author of this delightful little tale, wrote fables because it was the only way he could beat the censorship that sought to silence opposition in Russia. Fables were the unassuming, popular medium by which his voice could be heard, as they had been for Aesop and Phaedrus. 'Anything in the way of racy criticism which the unintelligence of the censorship would sometimes let pass, was welcomed by the public with the relish of a forbidden fruit.'[191] Stories were read aloud and passed on as oral tales among those who could not read; it is much harder to censor oral stories – they form an alternative narrative of their own. Some of Krylov's fables mark significant national events, *Crow and Fowl*, and *A Quarttet,* for example, celebrate Napoleon's defeat in Moscow – one reason, perhaps, why Krylov was popular with the otherwise repressive tsar, Nicholas I, who would summon the fabulist to hear his latest tale. On one such occasion, Krylov slyly chose a fable that the censors had blocked, thereby gaining the tsar's authority to publish it.

Fables – a medium employed by earlier Romanticists – portray in Krylov's verses a harsh reality where a third of the population struggle under the yoke of serfdom (about half of the peasantry) and most of the rest suffer poverty and injustice. His stories were a mirror in which Russians could recognise themselves: a significant contribution towards a national Russian literature, because these were not mere re-runs of Aesop's stories. They were Krylov's own creations. His animal characters, though possessing universal human foibles, depict common Russian types he knew: greedy nobles, corrupt bureaucrats, inept officials, and the doughty serfs who suffered at their hands and sometimes got the better of them with a peasant's guile. And it was part of Story's guile to disguise her message in allegory. Krylov knew his subjects: although his father was a middling officer in the army, the family's forebears were serfs – Krylov wrote his fables in the peasants' earthy vernacular; his homely maxims became household sayings.

Ivan Krylov was ten years old when his mother became an

impoverished widow – his father had left only a box of books – and he worked as a clerk in the small town of Tver to help support the family. The limited education Ivan received had been fortuitous. It is possible that his mother worked in the household of the local landlord, Nikolai Lvov, and showed him her six-year-old son's poetry, because Lvov was so impressed with the boy's abilities that he allowed him to share the lessons of his children – an ambiguous situation in which young Ivan was no doubt made aware of his lowly status, but an experience that nurtured his desire to write.

When Krylov was transferred to St. Petersburg in his teens, he began to write plays and comic opera while supporting his mother and younger brother on his civil service salary. He was not yet writing fables. From 1780 he focused on journalism and discovered his bent for scorching wit, publishing a couple of monthly satirical magazines – *The Spirit Mail* ('Pochta dughov') and *The Viewer* ('Zritel') – lampooning the nobility and the bureaucracy he knew so well. Neither magazine lasted much more than a year, but his talent was recognised by two radical writers from among Russia's influential intelligentsia: Nikolai Novikov, a satirist, publisher and philanthropist with a deep interest in education, and Aleksandr Radishchev, a senior civil servant from a noble family, who wrote on the injustice and brutality of serfdom. During the late 1760s, when Catherine the Great had been in reform mode and lifted censorship, Novikov and Radishchev spearheaded the vogue for literary journals in emulation of those in England, and in 1789 they encouraged Krylov by engaging him as a junior editor.

But their collaboration was short-lived. A year later, Novikov was suddenly imprisoned without trial in Schlüsselburg fortress, and Radishchev, initially sentenced to death, was exiled to Siberia. France's Revolution – then in its second year of blood-letting – was sending spasms of dread into the Russian imperial court; Catherine sharply reversed her inclinations towards reform. Although she admired the enlightenment, such ideals were clearly too dangerous for public consumption. She was, in any case, pre-occupied with various campaigns against the Ottoman Turks in addition to expanding her own empire (military costs accounted for some fifty per cent of the national coffers). Krylov, with a peasant's instinct for survival, moved out of St. Petersburg and remained silent. In a curious circularity, he was employed for six years by Prince Golitsyn as his secretary and tutor to his children.

Not until his late thirties did Krylov discover the potential of the fable. He started by translating the French fabulist Jean La Fontaine – pretentions to French culture had long held sway among Russia's elite – but he soon turned against western influence and began drafting his own fables, while gaining popularity as a dramatist. By this time, Alexander I occupied the imperial throne. Although Alexander achieved little real reform, he was more liberal than Catherine and was sympathetic to dismantling serfdom, if only because of its crippling effects on the country's economic development. With an excellent sense of timing, Krylov published his first collection of fables in 1809 – it made him a national favourite. The tsar awarded him a pension and numerous honours for his contribution towards Russian literature, including membership in the prestigious Russian Academy.

Nineteen years later, when an ambitious teenager, Nikolai Gogol, arrived from his Ukrainian home to seek fame as a writer in St. Petersburg, and gazed in wonder at the imperial city, he might have strolled across Anichkov Bridge into Nevski Prospekt and found himself outside the Imperial Public Library – built in grand classical style on Empress Catherine's instructions.[192] It contained, among other treasures, the libraries of Voltaire and Diderot, and had been opened to the public five years earlier. Story would certainly have inspired the nineteen-year-old Nikolai to venture inside. When he did so, he was likely to have seen a fat old man lounging in his dressing-gown in a librarian's armchair: one of the honours bestowed upon Krylov was a life-long appointment to the library staff. It was largely a sinecure – Director Aleksey Olenin and his assistants did most of the work – and his characteristic response to a query was a languorous flap of his hand in the direction of one shelf or another. Though held in high esteem, Krylov had a reputation for gormandizing and indolence, but he did spend considerable time in the library and continued writing fables until he died in 1844 at the age of seventy-six. His last collection of fables accompanied the notice of his death sent to his friends and associates.

Nikolai Gogol, of course, gained world renown as a dramatist, novelist and short-story writer. Often dubbed the 'father' of the Russian short story, he is also credited with being the first Russian 'realist', though perhaps more in a literary than a political sense. Although the lives of Russian people are vividly revealed in his works, he made no declarations of support for freeing serfs and neither did his contemporary in the USA, Edgar Allan Poe, openly condemn slavery; whatever their private thoughts, neither of them wrote against their respective political establishments. By strange coincidence born within weeks of each other (in 1809), their short stories portray idiosyncratic, highly imaginative 'realities' with generous dashes of the demonic and surreal, and perhaps, not a little cynicism. Poe, one of the first great American short-story writers, shared Gogol's talent for the grotesque. They both wrote stories about a madman, and themselves hovered on the verge of insanity before meeting early tragic deaths – Poe in 1849, three years before Gogol. But we will return to the enigmatic Mr Poe later.

With a more advantageous background than Krylov, young Nikolai attended high school in Nizhyn, in northern Ukraine, as a boarder, since it was some distance from his family's small estate at Sorochyntsi near Poltava (then part of the Russian Empire). He grew up speaking both Ukrainian and Russian in common with those of his social class, though his mother was of Polish descent and his father's ancestors were Cossacks. When his father died, Gogol was fifteen years old and already attracted to the arts through his father's poetry and plays, and by participating in the amateur dramatics his father and uncle staged. But the aspiring young writer arrived in St Petersburg keen to escape his provincial roots: his first literary work, *Hans Küchelgarten* – self-published under the pseudonym, V. Alov – was an epic narrative poem in the grand German romantic style, which he had initially composed at high school. Later, in a moment of excruciating insight generated by caustic reviews, he burnt all the copies he could retrieve from the booksellers.

Gogol had intended to support himself with a civil service post – the usual career route for educated young men in his position – but found that without connections and money he would not achieve beyond the most menial employment. While drifting in and out of various jobs, including that of history teacher in a girl's school, he began to penetrate St Petersburg's literary life with a few stories published in magazines. He discovered that the current fad was for folklore, part of the flowering of national literature begun by Pushkin and Krylov, to be developed in different ways by Turgenev, Dostoyevsky, Tolstoy, and Chekhov. Ironically, the city's editors wanted exotic tales of Cossack traditions: heroic horsemen, village customs and picturesque rural merrymaking – the provincial culture of 'Little Russia' that Gogol had been so eager to leave behind. Gogol was ambitious to submit stories, and perhaps he regretted not paying more attention to local mores during his upbringing because first he had to write home to his mother:

> 'I expect from you in your next letter a complete description of the costume of a village deacon, from his underclothes to his boots … clothing worn by our village maidens, as well as by married women … a minute description of a wedding not omitting the smallest detail …'[193]

Without questioning how she could be expected to know about the deacon's underwear, these details she supplied, along with local superstitions, old wives tales and horror stories which found their way into Gogol's tale, *St. John's Eve*. The story relates how a poor young man whose eagerness to win a bride beyond his reach entangles him with witches, bloody murder, and mysterious bags of gold and indeed, the tale portrays 'a minute description of a wedding', along with costume descriptions right down to the last hair ribbon. (Interesting how often Story recruits mothers to her mission and how frequently history forgets them).

Gogol had found a rich vein of inspiration: his two-volume collection of Ukrainian tales, *Evenings on a Farm Near Dikanka*, were published in 1831/32 to great acclaim, followed three years later by *Mirgorod*, and a more varied collection of prose, *Arabesque*. But it was Gogol's later work that has since given him a lasting literary reputation, beginning with his comic drama *The Government Inspector* – a merciless attack on the absurdities of small-town officials, with an ironic side-swipe at himself as the dramatist.

> GOVERNOR: Not only do you get made a laughing-stock of, but some quill-driver, some paper strainer will go and put you in a play! It's maddening! He'll spare neither your rank nor your calling, and all will grin and clap their hands [...]The quill-splitters! Damned liberals! Devil's brood! I would scrag you all, I'd grind you to powder![194]

At the time, the play was less well received than Gogol expected: though performed at the command of Tsar Nicholas I who laughed heartily at his provincial administrators, bureaucrats did not take kindly to the playwright's venomous satire any more than 'the Governor' had, and Gogol spent the next twelve years in voluntary exile. He travelled through Europe, spent a winter in Paris with exiled Polish and Russian literati, and finally settled in Italy. In Rome he wrote diligently, producing his best known stories – *The Overcoat, The Portrait* with its supernatural terror, and the surreal tale, *The Nose* – and completed the first volume of his novel *Dead Souls* (Myórtvjye dúshi), which he returned to Russia to publish.

'*Dúshi*', 'souls', referred to serfs: tied to the property of their masters, they were a form of wealth; a landowner's status partly derived from the number of 'peasant souls' he owned, and they could be used, for example, as collateral for a bank loan. But the people in this novel are not merely caricatures of Russian types of the times; they also represent common human weaknesses: the protagonist, Chichikov, a venal character posing as a gentleman of business, manipulates provincial officials prone to flattery and self-interest, and cons suspicious but greedy middle-class gentry. Landowners paid taxes on their total number of serfs as on any other physical asset, a tax that was payable even if serfs had died since the last census, which could be ten or twenty years past. Chichikov's scam was to buy these 'dead souls' – which were nothing but a tax burden on their owners – for a nominal sum in deals that were to be kept secret. His own secret was that, on his return to the city, he planned to offer these spurious souls as security to buy an estate of his own. Nineteenth-century novels are considered too verbose for today's readers, but *Dead Souls* is still a rewarding read. The simple plot, apparently suggested by Pushkin, gave Gogol a vehicle to take Chichikov all over Russia interacting with countless citizens of all classes.

The novel opens on a due note of mystery with the appearance of a typical gentleman's conveyance at a country inn:

> 'To the door of an inn in the provincial town of N. there drew up a smart britchka – a light spring-carriage of the sort affected by bachelors, retired lieutenant-colonels, staff-captains, land-owners possessed of about a hundred souls, and, in short, all persons who rank as gentlemen of the intermediate character.'

The style is satirical, the same sardonic humour as in the *Government Inspector*. Pushkin loved humour, but *Dead Souls* did not make him laugh: 'As Gogol read it aloud to him from the manuscript the poet grew more and more gloomy and at last cried out: "God! What a sad country Russia is!" And later he said of it: "Gogol invents nothing: it is the simple truth; the terrible truth."'[195]

Gogol claimed that the comic was hidden in everything, waiting only to be brought out, but his seems an ambiguous, bitter comedy about which his critics were divided. Reformist intelligentsia saw his work initially as supporting their cause – they were soon to feel disappointed. Though Gogol was influenced by his friend Pushkin, and spent time in Paris with the Polish activist-poet we met earlier,

Adam Mickiewicz, he declared no ambitions towards constitutional reform. After the conservative establishment complained that *Dead Souls* portrayed Russia in a bad light, Gogol published *Selected Passages from Correspondence with My Friends*, stating unequivocal support for the ruling autocracy. But we should be cautious in surmising Gogol's true ambitions: during a reading of *Dead Souls* he once commented that the censor at least had the benefit of developing cunning in the writer.[196]

In fact, Gogol had intended two further volumes of the novel portraying redemption for Chichikov and his ilk. Either Gogol's creative powers had waned or he was incapable of writing in a more positive vein: after years of struggle with the manuscript he experienced a personal crisis, sought guidance from a spiritual councillor, and destroyed much of his work, including most of the second volume of *Dead Souls*. Perhaps he feared that the grotesquery and satires of evil deeds emanated from demonic laughter within his own soul because in his final year, Gogol subjected himself to rigorous self-deprivation, eventually refusing to eat, and died in 1852. The inscription on his grave read: 'I shall laugh my bitter laugh.'[197]

His passing was deeply mourned by fellow writers. Ivan Turgenev, creator of intimate tales of peasant life and whose first short-story collection, *Sketches from a Hunters' Album*, was published that same year, tricked the *St Petersburg Gazette* into printing an obituary which the censor had already rejected as too extravagant a praise of Gogol: 'whom we now have the right, the bitter right, to call great; a man whose name signifies an epoch in the history of our literature, a man of whom we are proud as one of our glories.'[198] The gesture cost Turgenev a month in a police cell, followed by eighteen-month's banishment from the city to the family estate at Spasskoe, where his movements were watched by state informants.

Turgenev's own deep compassion for the serfs stemmed from witnessing the cruelty of his dominating mother to the serfs she controlled. His liberal position drew criticism from both sides – caught between dissatisfied revolutionary youth and the defensive establishment – and after publishing *Fathers and Sons* in 1862, he left for voluntary exile in Europe, where we catch up with him later in the company of Gustave Flaubert and Guy de Maupassant.

A reading of Gogol's short story, *The Portrait* – which he continued to rework to the end of his days – suggests insights into his later state of mind: a gifted artist paints so vividly the evil eyes of his subject – a moneylender – that their force destroys him and everyone else who comes into contact with the portrait. Only by purifying himself through life-threatening penance is the artist able to recover his talent. Stories – perhaps all arts – have the power to fashion our humanity and construct our lives, but their effects for good or evil can extend beyond the intentions of their creators. Though impossible to gauge to what extent, undoubtedly the "terrible truth" about Russian society that both Gogol and Turgenev so graphically described nurtured the reformist movement.

The year following Gogol's death, Russia was preoccupied with the start of the Crimean War, involving hostilities with Britain and France as well as the old enemy, the Ottoman Empire. And in 1855, Tsar Nicholas died, succeeded by his son Alexander II. Not until 1861[199] was serfdom abolished, but its death throes were lethal. Alexander had passed his instructions to emancipate the serfs to committees of provincial landowners for implementation. The outcome gave landowners the right to decide which parts of their land (generally the poorest) they would sell to freed serfs at often inflated valuations. The poorest peasants could not acquire sufficient acreage for subsistence. Those who could not pay became landless peasants often worse off than before; those who could were likely to face generations of debt.

The whole process was slow and did little to stem social inequality or simmering unrest. Anton Pavlovich Chekhov – another 'father' of the short story – was born a year after emancipation was decreed; thirty-five years later, having attended a dinner to mark this milestone in Russian history, he wrote some caustic comments in his diary:

'February 19. Dinner at the 'Continental' to commemorate the great reform. Tedious and incongruous. To dine, drink champagne, make a racket, and deliver speeches about national consciousness, the conscience of the people, freedom, and such things, while slaves in tail-coats are running round your tables, veritable serfs, and your coachmen wait outside in the street, in the bitter cold— that is lying to the Holy Ghost.'[200]

Chekhov's grandparents had bought their freedom from serfdom long before emancipation. His father opened a grocery shop in Taganrog, where the Don flows into the Sea of Azov, and raised his family there; a life that provided a rich source of stories for *The Stammerer*, a humorous magazine the school-boy Chekhov produced to entertain his brothers. Although we may know him better as a dramatist – notably for *The Seagull, Uncle Vanya*, and his last play, *The Cherry Orchard* – Chekhov wrote screeds of short fiction. After taking up a scholarship to study medicine in Moscow, he churned out stories and humorous anecdotes under the pen-name of Antosha Chekhonte, and sold them to popular magazines such as *Fragments*, *Alarm Clock,* and *Dragonfly*. *Fragments* alone published 270 of his pieces between 1882 and 1887. The money Chekhov received was important because his father's business had been declared bankrupt and Chekhov's earnings helped the family struggling to make a living in Moscow. Chekhov published his first story collection, *Motley Stories* in1886, the year of two critical influences on his writing career.

Alexey Suvorin, editor of the prestigious periodical, *New Times*, invited Chekhov to submit work, suggesting he did so under his own name, and Dmitry Grigorovich, a writer and friend of Dostoyevsky, wrote to Chekhov telling him he had talent and should put more effort into the quality of his writing. In his reply, Chekhov described the letter as 'a bolt of lightning [...] until now I have approached my writing in a most frivolous, irresponsible and meaningless way. I cannot recall a single story on which I spent more than a day; indeed I wrote 'The Huntsman', which you liked, in a bathing hut!'[201]

Chekhov took the advice to heart. Following a nostalgic trip back to Taganrog and a tour along the Don, he wrote his long story *The Steppe*: a panoramic tale of the melancholy grandeur of these vast plains that challenge human occupation, told through the innocent eyes of a child. The work gained his first recognition of true literary worth. By a cruel twist of fate, the tuberculosis that would cut short Chekhov's life already inhabited his lungs.

Chekhov was not a revolutionary writer, not even an 'activist' in a strict sense. He seems politically naïve – 'I am neither liberal or conservative … I would like to be free and nothing else.'[202] – but a strong social conscience and deep fund of compassion illuminate his writing. Though invariably short of money, as a doctor he treated poor patients for a token fee or none at all, built local schools, organised famine relief after harvest failures in the Volga and, at the peak of his literary career, he made an extraordinary journey. A successful young bachelor might have been expected to jaunt in Paris, but in 1890, Chekhov chose to cross Siberia to investigate the infamous penal colony in Sakhalin Island without official backing or even permission.

Sakhalin lies off the east coast of Siberia in the Sea of Okhotsk where harbours may be ice-bound for seven months of the year: a long, narrow island that Chekhov described as 'one and a half times the size of Denmark'. His arduous 10,000-kilometre trek from Moscow, being bruised in bare wooden carriages and nauseated in filthy hostelries waiting for river steamers – the trans-Siberian railway would not be built for another thirteen years – took Chekhov two-and-a-half months. Frequent letters to his family and his friend and publisher, Alexey Suvorin, describe every detail (including his painful piles) with characteristic buoyancy and good humour. And the trip out was not devoid of fun. On arrival at Blagoveshchensk on the banks of the Amur River, Chekhov discovered one of the delights of Japanese culture – the 'always laughing' elegant prostitutes. But the observant writer is ever present in the letter he sent to Suvorin:

'The Japanese girl's room was very neat and tidy, sentimental in an Asiatic kind of way, and filled with little knick-knacks [...] She has an incredible mastery of her art, so that rather than just using her body you feel as if you are taking part in an exhibition of high-level riding skill.'

To his family, he wrote: 'I am alive and well, and I haven't lost any of the money. I'm saving some of the coffee for Sakhalin.'

For three months, Chekhov traipsed around this barren, barely habitable island, interviewing administrators, gaoled convicts, prisoners who worked in scattered communities in every form of hard labour, and free homesteaders – families accompanying exiles or those who had served their terms and stayed on to open small businesses. He was appalled by the conditions. Taking note of poverty and sickness, of girls prostituted from the age of twelve, of the degraded lives of women, and of brutal floggings, Chekhov wrote a detailed report[203] backed up with statistics – even down to the rations issued to convicts. But gifted storyteller that he was, we share the scenes and stories that made him call Sakhalin 'a Hell':

> 'Travelling with me on the Amur steamer to Sakhalin was a convict in leg irons who had murdered his wife. His daughter, a motherless little girl aged six, was with him. I watched him when he came down from the upper deck to the WC, followed by his daughter and a guard. While the convict sat on the WC, the little girl and the soldier with his rifle waited outside the door. When the convict climbed back up again, the girl clambered up behind, hanging on to his fetters. At night the little girl slept hugger-mugger with the convicts and the soldiers.' [204]

And the Zhakomin family – mother, father and son – though protesting their innocence, had been sentenced to exile for murder in 1878. The son was transported to Sakhalin by sea, but the old couple were marched with other prisoners across Siberia, through mosquito-infested swamps and across desolate frozen wastes of the *taiga* – a nightmare journey that took three years. Their daughter, who voluntarily accompanied her parents, died of exhaustion. When Chekhov met them in the remote settlement of Korsakov in the south of Sakhalin where they ran a small store, the mother and son had worked out their terms, but the old man, Karp Nikolayevich, was still a convict.[205]

Chekhov called his account of Sakhalin a 'census', perhaps to avoid problems with censorship: he makes recommendations but avoids direct criticism of the regime. However, we may read into a passing observation, a metaphor for the sheer waste of lives on the island: 'Near the guardhouse on the jetty there lies the skeleton of a young whale. Once it was happy, playful, roaming the expanses of the northern seas. Now the white bones of the giant lie in the mud, pounded by rain.' *The Island* was first published in serial form in 1893.

The following years were productive for Chekhov, despite his deteriorating health, and he continued with his social works. In 1897 he published *The Peasants*, a story in which the protagonist, Nikolay Tchikildyeev, having lost his job as a waiter in Moscow as a result of a permanently debilitating illness and spent all his savings on ineffective treatment, decides to take his wife and daughter back to their peasant village to live at 'home' among his relatives. After the first gladness at pure air and scenic space, they are overwhelmed by the squalor of the family hovel, the brutalising effects of poverty, and the extent of drunkenness and violence – features common to most of the village. Nikolay's old mother resents having to feed them and asks: who will pay for his funeral? In this post-emancipation village, the old men reminisce about the days of patronage when they were fed twice a day; a new order under freedom has not emerged and better-off peasants – notably the tavern keepers – exploit the weak. What little of the story the censor left uncut drew severe criticism from conservatives.

Grim political events – the massacre of Jews at Kishinev in 1902, the assassination of the Minister of the Interior by Socialist Revolutionaries the following year, and Russia's war with Japan – foreshadow the horrors of the twentieth century as Chekhov nears the end of his short life. But his letters to his beloved sister, Masha, always express hope and optimism. Masha (Maria) had long since abandoned her career and any hope of marriage in order to support Chekhov in all his endeavours – sacrifices he had selfishly encouraged. On 28 June 1904, he wrote to her from a German sanatorium in Badenweiler, complaining of the suffocating heat and asking her to find out about boats from Trieste to Odessa so that he could travel there: 'I don't feel I have had enough of a holiday yet'. He died four days later.

Characters, people and their dilemmas, are more important than plot in Chekhov's stories – perhaps a product of his professional calling – and, mimicking the ambiguities of real life, their endings are often inconclusive; more might be imagined to happen after 'the end' than had happened up to that point. This would not suit Guy de Maupassant, Chekhov's less literary contemporary in France, whose stories were tightly structured around a significant plot decisively resolved, often with a surprise twist in the last line. Maupassant (1850–1893) is yet another 'father' of the short story, and we must accept Story's unbridled passion with all of these 'fathers' because, with his prolific pen, Maupassant, more than anyone except perhaps Poe, gave the short story its popular modern form: life (and indeed, death) intensified, laid bare, keenly observed in a narrow beam of bright light, and honed down to nothing but the essential kernel of the tale. Maupassant published several hundred short stories as well as novels and travelogues; impressive, though less than the number of his sexual liaisons for which he was equally famous or rather, infamous. On his only visit to England, when taken out to lunch by Henry James, he horrified his host by pointing to a woman at a nearby table and in his husky French accent, asking James to get her for him.[206]

Once again, Story recruited mothers to encourage her favourites. Maupassant's parents were landowning gentry in Normandy. They separated, and after his thirteenth birthday, his mother sent him to a seminary school that accepted lay students. A hated experience he tolerated for five years before, as they say in the navy, 'working his ticket': ensuring his expulsion by calculated bad behaviour. While Maupassant studied law in Paris, his mother asked her friend, the prominent writer, Gustave Flaubert, to take an interest in him. Flaubert 'adopted' young Maupassant, tutoring and mentoring his early creative efforts, while Maupassant's father secured him a post in the civil service – that unsung prop of nascent writing talent – and he began to submit stories to local newspapers. He made his mark at the age of thirty with perhaps his most famous story, 'Boule de Suif' ('Ball of Fat'), in the anthology *Soirée de Médan* published by Flaubert's close friend, the novelist Émile Zola.

Maupassant had the knack of fixing human failings starkly to the page without moral judgement, like moths pinned in an etymologist's collection of natural facts. The entire action of 'Boule de Suif' takes place inside a carriage full of weary travellers and spans but a brief period on the journey. The hungry passengers behave amiably towards a prostitute, eyeing her basket of food which she generously shares with them. Shortly afterwards, a German officer among them stops the coach, refusing to let it continue until the woman has satisfied his lust. The other passengers pressure her to comply, and afterwards, shun her in contempt.

After this exposure, major newspapers such as *Le Gaulois* and *Gil Blas* courted Maupassant, who resigned from the civil service to write fulltime. Flaubert had already drawn his protégé into French literary circles. On Sunday afternoons, Flaubert and Turgenev – the two friends corresponded intimately for seventeen years – along with Maupassant and perhaps one or two others, gathered at Zola's country house near Médan on the banks of the Seine. In a letter to Flaubert, Zola described his rural retreat as a 'rabbit-hutch',[207] but it sprouted wings and towers and second storeys – much like Sir Walter Scott's Abbotsford – and became similarly stuffed with furniture, sculpture, paintings, and elaborate draperies. Amid such cultural clutter, Flaubert held forth to his small circle of literati; we can see him in our mind's eye, his great bulk filling the armchair and his copious moustache quivering with emphasis.

A keen observer of life around him, Maupassant's subjects

echo his own experience: he had been a foot-soldier in the Franco-German war, a bureaucrat, a boater and swimmer, a traveller, and a good-natured mixer in company whether with peasants, the bourgeoisie, or the upper classes with whom he spent increasing amounts of time as success brought him the wealth to do so. Maupassant claimed that the simplest of daily experiences offered inspiration: 'The least thing contains something mysterious. Find it.'[208] Perhaps in light of his own misfortune (his health was already affected by the syphilis which would eventually kill him), his stories also encompass fate: the same unavoidable fate found in the Icelandic Sagas, which thwarts all attempts to control our own lives. And like Gogol and Edgar Allan Poe before him, Maupassant wrote about insanity, but with characteristic clarity and precision that near the end of his life shows his own madness had not yet overwhelmed him.

Maupassant was the epitome of the realist. Joseph Conrad wrote of him: 'There is both a moral and an excitement to be found in a faithful rendering of life [...] This is the particular shape taken by his inspiration; it came to him directly, honestly in the light of his day, not on the tortuous, dark roads of meditation.'[209] Conrad might have been thinking of Gogol with his reference to 'dark roads of meditation', but the comparison would also fit the American writer, Edgar Allan Poe. As prolific an author as Maupassant, Poe wrote similarly concise, focused, precisely constructed plots fifty years before him, but his 'reality' was largely in his head and heavily influenced by his own tortuous life. The nature of Poe's highly inventive stories of mystery, crime, horror, satire, fantasy and often grotesque humour, earned him the description: an 'unromantic romanticist'. A poet at heart, Poe published his stories along with reviews and articles in newspapers and magazines as a means of earning a living after he discharged himself from the army cadet corps. Later in his career, he edited a couple of journals until he proved too unreliable, and twice made abortive attempts to launch his own periodical.

Poe seems fated to personal disaster from birth. His mother, a touring actress, died of tuberculosis and as his father had then disappeared, the two-year-old Edgar was fostered to the Allan family in Richmond, Virginia. When Poe was barely twenty years old, his adored foster-mother died, also of tuberculosis, and when later in life he married his cousin, Virginia, she too died of the same disease. He never ceased to seek motherly love in relationships that seemed destined to end in death or rejection. But it was his mother-in-law, his faithful Aunt Clemm, 'Muddy', who kept his household together and supported her 'dear Eddie' to the end. She was the home-maker and often the bread-winner during constant moves from one town to another, to cheaper accommodation or to better prospects, as Poe chased opportunities he invariably squandered on a whim or through the bouts of drinking that were seriously damaging his health.

Despite his personal catastrophes, Poe was not a 'victim': those who knew him described him as proud, passionate and optimistic; in later life such optimism became symptomatic of his sliding grip on reality. But one never knew when the inventive Mr Poe was telling the truth. Uncertainty and mystery hung over his death as it had over his life: he was found dying in an alcove seat of a tavern in Baltimore when he was expected to be in New York – no one knows for sure where he had spent the previous few days.[210] Although he was a controversial figure and made enemies with his vindictive reviews, Poe's genius was recognised in his lifetime by some of his contemporaries in America and his work was even more popular in Britain – his themes have an international appeal. But he never managed to escape poverty.

Poe's tales still send shivers through modern readers, but perhaps his most important legacy was his originality, which helped to wean American readers from dependence on the 'mother culture' of England. Publishers were still reluctant, even in Poe's time, to invest in local writers when pirated English works brought assured profits at minimal cost. And the Financial Panic of 1837, heralding six years of depression, made it even harder for America's own writers to survive.

The financial crisis was not the only trauma straining the Union: discussion on the morality versus the economics of slavery already divided the nation. And yet Poe seems to have written nothing explicitly for or against slavery[211] and slaves do not appear in his stories – the character Jupiter in 'The Gold-Bug' is a freed slave who stays with his master from choice. The omission seems strange, given that Poe was cared for by the household slaves of his foster-father, John Allan, who was a businessman in Richmond. Poe appears to have had happy memories from his childhood in the care of his black 'mammy', but as an adult he must have been aware of their cruel treatment at the hands of southern planters. Even Charles Dickens on his American lecture tour in 1842 – a transatlantic excursion encouraged by Washington Irving – made a point of visiting one of Richmond's tobacco plantations to witness 'the evil of slavery'. In his account of his tour, *American Notes*, Dickens devotes several pages to slave-owners' advertisements which appear in large numbers daily in the press seeking runaway slaves; descriptions of missing slaves include broken limbs, gun-shot wounds, lashing scars, clipped ears, and brand-marks burned into their faces.[212]

There was no shortage of literature on both sides of the debate. Harriet Beecher Stowe, a religious and social activist, was already publishing essays and sketches on the subject in her local press in Cincinnati, where opinion was evenly split on abolition. But her novel, *Uncle Tom's Cabin,* was not published until 1851, two years after Poe's death. The novel first appeared in serial form in the magazine *National Era* and as a complete two-volume work in 1852 at $1 for a paperbound edition. After that, there was no excuse for anyone to be unaware: the publisher, John J. Jewett promoted the novel with massive publicity, author events and commemorative products – Uncle Tom dolls, post cards, songs – like a 'bestseller' is planned and launched today. In the first week, 10,000 copies were sold. A year later, Jewett announced total sales of 305,000 in America, and at least as many sold in Europe[213] – such a response to a novel was unprecedented in the United States and its influence spread far beyond even Europe.

Early edition cover of 'Uncle Tom's Cabin'.

The Filipino polymath and nationalist, Jose Rizal (1861–1896), is said to have read *Uncle Tom's Cabin* while studying medicine in Europe and been inspired to write his own novel, *Noli Me Tángere* ('Touch me not') satirising abuses of the Spanish colonial government in the Philippines and corruption in its Catholic Church. Though published in Berlin in 1887 and banned in the Philippines, smuggled copies were widely read. The novel stirred a growing revolutionary movement among Filipinos for which Rizal was executed on his return to his country. His was a rare early voice from a colonised people.

Harriet Beecher Stowe had been writing sketches, essays and album pieces for almost twenty years, initially for pleasure and increasingly to supplement household income – as did Louisa Mary Alcott some years later – but *Uncle Tom's Cabin* was her response to the Fugitive Slave Act of 1850, which made it a crime to assist a runaway slave anywhere in the United States; an act that potentially made every American citizen an accomplice to slavery's inhumanity. Her story informed and heated up the debate on slavery, which was finally abolished in 1865, though it had taken four years of destructive civil war to achieve. If Poe did support slavery, he was on a robust side, and it would be almost thirty years before slaves were freed in Brazil. *Uncle Tom's Cabin* was a moral imperative for Stowe: as well as using her own experience in Cincinnati, she researched slave conditions elsewhere and read all the anti-slavery literature she could access, at the same time writing for periodicals, running a household and producing seven children between 1833 and 1851.

Other dedicated women and religious movements in Britain, especially the Quakers, had pressed to end the transatlantic slave trade as early as the 1760s and Story had helped them, too. Because slave ownership was not legal within Britain, it was easy to disregard the fact that slaves were owned in every corner of the Empire, extracting raw materials for British industry, and that British ships had traded probably four million slaves between Africa and the Americas in exchange

Harriet Beecher Stowe.

for luxury goods, especially sugar. Wealthy merchants, owners of overseas plantations and eager consumers – all of them well represented in parliament – were reluctant to acknowledge a bitter aftertaste of sugar in their tea. But when the captain of a Liverpool slave ship threw more than 130 slaves overboard in order to claim insurance for them, the ensuing court case and publicity made slavery impossible to ignore and public opinion turned to favour abolition.[214] The majority of people were way ahead of their political representatives whose sympathy ebbed with each story of violence by the oppressed – peasants in the French Revolution, a slave uprising in what is now Haiti, 'native' riots in India – but activists, notably William Wilberforce and John Newton (a reformed slave-trader and author of the hymn 'Amazing Grace') presented more than 500 public petitions to parliament and wrote their own pamphlets, books and stories. In 1788, the poet, William Cowper wrote several ballads and poems, his most famous, 'The Negro's Complaint':

'Men from England bought and sold me,
Paid my price in paltry gold;
But, though slave they have enroll'd me,
Minds are never to be sold.'[215]

The following year, Olaudah Equiano (aka Gustavus Vassa) wrote an autobiography, *The Interesting Narrative of the Life of Olaudah Equiano*, in which he tells the story of his kidnap as a child in what is now southern Nigeria, of being sold to a slave ship and ending up on a plantation in Virginia, and how he eventually managed to buy his freedom and travel to London. That some academics now quibble over various facts of his story is irrelevant: its popularity, in conjunction with Olaudah's own activism, exerted strong influence for abolition. As we have seen before, Story's 'truths' are often deeper and more meaningful that facts.

Although it was not legally sanctioned to own a household slave in Britain, in 1828, when Mary Prince was brought by her master from Antigua to England while he and his wife settled family matters, her attempts to be released from slavery failed. Mary had a husband in Antigua, a free man. Unless she was officially freed, she could not return to Antigua without being sold again and separated from her husband perhaps forever. Even knowing this, John Adams Wood refused either to let Mary buy her freedom from him or to sell her to another who would do so. He would let her leave, but not as a free woman. Mary Prince was then approximately forty years old and painfully rheumatic. Though Wood was not the worst of her three previous masters, she had endured thirteen years of beatings and deprivation under his roof.

In desperation, Mary walked from his house – a black stranger in London's crowded streets where the only person she knew was the shoe-black who came to the house to polish Wood's shoes. She found him and asked him to guide her to a Moravian church, a sect she had known in Antigua. People there helped her to find accommodation and domestic work, but she was still a slave outside of Britain.

Mary came into contact with Thomas Pringle, the secretary of the Anti-Slavery Society, and while she worked for him, she asked him to help her publicise her story: 'I tell it, to let English people know the truth' i.e. what life was like for a slave in a British colony. Mary's words were transcribed by a writer friend of Pringles, Susannah Strickland, and published in 1831 under the title *The History of Mary Prince, A West Indian Slave.* In this extract, she recalls being brought late in the evening to the house of her third master, after he bought her at a market. She was eleven years old:

> 'The house was large, and built at the bottom of a very high hill; but I could not see much of it that night. I saw too much of it afterwards. The stones and the timber were the best things in it; they were not so hard as the hearts of the owners.'

Mary's is a harrowing account – though uplifting in her compassion for the suffering of others, particularly one of her earlier mistresses treated almost as cruelly by her husband as Mary was herself – and the vivid descriptions of her and her siblings being forcibly separated from her mother and sold to different buyers, deeply affected the many women working for abolition.

Mary Prince's modest story was not a novel and could not receive the marketing hype bestowed on *Uncle Tom's Cabin,* but it nonetheless made a significant impact on the campaign to abolish slavery in the colonies – a proposal previously blocked by vested interests. Owning slaves in British Empire territories was made illegal in 1833; the government having to pay compensation – to the ex-slave owners, not to the ex-slaves. The East India Company was exempted from the slave-owning ban – a moral lapse corrected ten years later. But the 1833 act applied to Antigua, and it made Mary Prince a free woman. In the next century, Nigerian writer, Chinua Achebe would write: 'To be human, you must have a story.' But Story knows this is not enough: to be *seen* as human, your story must be *heard*.

Slave trading by British ships had already been officially banned by act of parliament in 1807, and Britain urged other European nations – France, Spain, Holland and Portugal – to do likewise. Whether this was on moral grounds or to ensure their competitors gained no economic advantage, slavery was a commercial trade governed by supply and demand: approximately three million more Africans were shipped across the Atlantic between 1807 and the late 1860s when this particular trade in men, women and children finally ceased[216] – once slaves were freed in America, the largest market for them had gone. European trading settlements were confined largely to the African coasts, Arab slave-traders continued as they had for centuries in the interior.

After the American civil war, the 1870s and '80s were marked by reconstruction and internal migration. Stiff competition and high unemployment left many people struggling with poverty while others 'got rich quick' – and frequently 'went bust' just as quickly. Witty and often satirical portrayals of such realities of life for ordinary Americans were the stuff of O. Henry's stories, and it was the general public rather than literary critics who loved them – humour is rarely appreciated by critics. O. Henry's readers could recognise themselves and their neighbours in the familiar predicaments of his characters, and in dialogue that did not shun the dialect and slang of each setting, from the backwoods of Tennessee and the pioneering shanty towns of the wild-west to the sophisticated city streets of New York.

O. Henry (aka William Sydney Porter) was a prolific story writer – for more than a year he wrote a story a week for the New York Sunday magazine *World* – and he began publishing his work in the same way that Poe had launched his entirely different tales: by submitting yarns and sketches to magazines and newspapers. Building on early successes, O. Henry started his own humorous periodical *Rolling Stones* in 1894 for which he wrote all the copy himself and, when that folded, he joined the *Houston Post* as a journalist and cartoonist. At the time, he wrote under his own name, W. S. Porter, or under various pseudonyms;

becoming 'O. Henry' a few years later was embedded in a secret he kept so well that even his daughter was unaware of it until after his death. But we should start nearer the beginning.

Although the country was in the throes of civil war when William Sydney Porter came into the world in 1862, there were no battles in Greensboro, North Carolina, where his father was a doctor and his mother, a college graduate, wrote poetry and painted. Her potential inspiration for the boy's writing and drawing talents was cut short by her death from tuberculosis when William was only three years old. Years later, William's young wife also died from tuberculosis.

Such parallels to Poe's experience may seem odd, but in nineteenth-century America, as in Europe, up to ninety per cent of the population carried the tubercular bacillus and eighty per cent of those who developed symptoms died from them. TB's prevalence was an unfortunate side-effect of rapid industrialisation, overcrowding and poverty, exacerbated by initial ignorance of its contagious nature. Diagnosis was made easier by the invention of the stethoscope in 1819 and of x-rays in 1900, but no effective cure was available until the advent of antibiotics in the 1940s. In the meantime, the disease remained another spoke in fortune's wheel of uncertainties.

William's widowed father went to live on his parent's farm, where the boy was raised by his Aunt Evalina – who also ran a school there – until he began work as a clerk in his uncle's small-town pharmacy and general store at the age of fifteen. The store would have been a modest plank building, fronted by a veranda and hitching posts for the settlers from miles around who arrived for their supplies in buggies, wagons or on horseback, while townsfolk came on foot, the more considerate stamping the dust from their boots before entering. From behind the long wooden counter his uncle sold dry goods as well as medicines, and a soda fountain encouraged customers to linger and chat. His uncle's store was the gathering place – the source of news, gossip and oral storytelling that entertained country folk – where William began his observations of life and its motley inhabitants. And the fresh-faced youth contributed his own tales and artistic talents; especially popular were his amusing caricatures of well-known locals.

Once out of his teens, William moved to Texas and took what employment he could: on a ranch, then as a pharmacist, and as a clerk in the Texas Land Office. He had met and married Athol Roach before he secured a post as a bank teller in the Austin branch of the First National Bank – a better-paid job that left him more time to write. All these experiences enriched his stories. And thanks to Aunt Evalina, he was well read, his yarns often contained references to the classics, to Shakespeare and especially to *A Thousand and One Nights* – English translations, suitably censored of 'immoral elements', had been available for at least three generations.

O. Henry's story, 'The Higher Abdication', opens with a hobo being kicked out of a bar:

> 'Curly arose from the gutter leisurely. He felt no anger or resentment toward his ejector. Fifteen years of tramphood out of the twenty-two years of his life had hardened the fibres of his spirit. The slings and arrows of outrageous fortune fell blunted from the buckler of his armoured pride. With especial resignation did he suffer contumely and injury at the hands of bar-tenders. Naturally, they were his enemies; and unnaturally, they were often his friends.'[217]

Curly is taken up by a boisterous party of stockmen on the loose from outlying ranches and treated in the town's run-down hotel for as long as it amuses them. Abandoned, stupefied by the unaccustomed excess of food and booze, Curly wanders around in the dark for somewhere to sleep, finally stumbling into an unattended transportation yard and burrowing under a pile of woolsacks, blankets and other cargo in the back of a covered wagon.

When he is rudely yanked from his nest, feet-first, Curly discovers he has slept through the wagon's journey. He ends up in a remote cattle ranch –'thirty miles from a railroad, and forty miles from a saloon' – where his appearance is distinctly out of place.

'As you gazed at him there passed through your mind vague impressions of mummies, wax figures, Russian exiles, and men lost on desert islands. His face was covered almost to his eyes with a curly brown beard that he kept trimmed short with a pocket-knife, and that had furnished him with his nom de route. Light blue eyes, full of sullenness, fear, cunning, impudence, and fawning, witnessed the stress that had been laid upon his soul.'[218]

For reasons Curly cannot fathom, Ranse, the boss of the cowpunchers and son of the elderly ranch owner, makes Curly go through the long and painful process of being washed, shaved and 'broken in' like a wild bronco until, protesting all the way, he is fit to work with the team in the cattle camp. Unbeknown to Curly, he is caught up in a saga of secret identities, thwarted love and ancient family feuds in which, in a final twist to the tale, he comes out on top – as O. Henry's underdogs always do.

An inveterate people-watcher, O. Henry would loiter in hotel foyers to observe the quirks of the upper classes. An amusement he allowed one of his characters in his story 'The Caliph and the Cab':

'Surely there is no pastime more diverting than that of mingling, incognito, with persons of wealth and station. Where else but in those circles can one see life in its primitive, crude state, unhampered by the conventions that bind the dwellers in a lower sphere?

There was a certain Caliph of Baghdad who was accustomed to go down among the poor and lowly for the solace obtained from the relation of their tales and histories.'

But O. Henry wants the poor to gaze upon the rich – and to realise that humble folk are in many ways superior to the upper set (or 'toffs' as the English would have said).

'There was one who saw the possibilities of thus turning the tables on Haroun al Raschid. His name was Corny Brannigan, and he was a truck driver for a Canal Street importing company. And if you read further you will learn how he turned upper Broadway into Baghdad and learned something about himself that he did not know before. [...] Every evening after Corny had put up his team and dined at a lunch-counter that made immediateness a speciality, he would clothe himself in evening raiment as correct as any you will see in the palm rooms. Then he would betake himself to that ravishing, radiant roadway devoted to Thespis, Thaïs, and Bacchus.

For a time he would stroll about the lobbies of the best hotels, his soul steeped in blissful content. Beautiful women cooing like doves, but feathered like bird of paradise, flicked him with their robes as they passed.'[219]

(Haroun al Raschid was an eighth-century caliph and the name of a character in 'The Story of the Sleeper Awakened' from *A Thousand and One Nights*.)

What Corny learned through an unexpected altercation with an upper class gent and his young lady was that, for all his modest means and background, Curly was a 'natural gentleman'.

Much of O. Henry's ironic humour depends on familiarity with contemporary events and political personalities which modern readers may lack, but his wide reading and knowledge of foreign news, which he clearly expected his readers to appreciate as well, are revealed in tales with passing references to King Arthur and his Round Table, wild Cossack horsemen, the Russo-Japanese war, Napoleon III, and Edgar Allan Poe. Many of his stories are set in the exotic environs of Central America, where Yankee speculators make dodgy deals with cunning creoles beside palm-fringed beaches. And this provides the clue to unravelling William Porter's secret.

Illustration to O. Henry's story 'Innocents of Broadway'.

Irregularities in accounts at the bank where Porter was a teller led to his being charged with embezzlement. Friends whisked him to safety in Honduras where he continued to write, setting his tales in a tropical atmosphere. But when news reached him of his wife's terminal illness, he returned home to be with her. A compassionate court did not put him on trial until after her death and handed down a lenient sentence: in 1898 Porter began a three-year stint in prison. Working the night-shift as a pharmacist in the prison hospital gave him time to write and sell stories to help support his little girl, Margaret. Among the pen-names he wrote under was 'O. Henry', the identity he chose to maintain after his release. He did not want his readers, or his daughter, to know he had 'done time'. And he succeeded: Margaret believed her father to have been away on business; only after his death in 1910 did she discover the truth.

With his writing, O. Henry fared much better financially than Poe had done. Editors paid him well, though not always enough to meet his expensive lifestyle. He strained to write fast enough under triple pressures of poor health, debt and popular demand for more and more of his home-grown tales. In the six years between 1904 and 1910, eight new collections were published, and it was during this period that he wrote also a story a week for the New York *World* and more stories for other magazines. He sought to relieve his stress (as his father had) with heavy drinking – a double-edged remedy that finally killed him. Further collections were published posthumously into the 1930s and his work has remained in print ever since. O. Henry was yet another prolific storyteller with an attenuated life.[220] At least he had the advantage over his predecessors of being able to produce his massive output on a typewriter rather than by laborious longhand. He probably used a Sholes and Glidden Type Writer, the most popular commercial machine which came onto the American market in 1874. O. Henry kept pace with his times: the narrator in 'The Adventures of Shamrock Jolnes' is a friend of the title character – 'the great New York detective' – and describes Jolnes as 'an expert in the use of the typewriter'. From now on, technology and invention play a major part in Story's future.

'Tell it how it is' has been a long journey with Story; she had a lot of reality to tell and there is more to come. Glancing back at her adventures in Russia, Europe and America – her artistic role in literary form, her political and social roles as she dodged censors, swayed public opinion, loosened chains – we see that a common element for her accomplices, the storytellers, was a 'shop window' to display their wares: the journals, magazines and newspapers which flourished in the nineteenth century and will continue to do so in the twentieth.

Poe had been well aware of a change in public taste towards magazine literature – 'to the curt, the terse, the well timed, and the readily diffused, in preference to the old forms of the verbose and ponderous…'[221] Inventive minds already explore ideas that would lead to new media of radio and film. They encourage the demand for immediacy and accessibility and expand the ways stories are told. But Story has yet to endure painful events, among them, the days of Empire and the 'Scramble for Africa' which, in practice, was part of a scramble for the world. Like some ghoulish global chess game, 'possessions' were taken, added to or swapped, in Africa, in Asia, the Pacific, the Middle East, even the Himalaya. South America had long been divided between Spain and Portugal; Russia expanded into Europe and Afghanistan; Britain took all of India; and the United States bought the Philippines from Spain. It will take two world wars and a pandemic to shake the chessboard into a different kriegspiel in which Story moves previously unheard voices into position to tell their own tales.

Chapter Thirteen

Hidden voices in a smaller world

Technology shrinks the world in which imperialism and Rudyard Kipling shout the loudest until Joseph Conrad shouts even louder. Story is fought over and sometimes bound and silenced, but she inspires some new voices as three decades of wars and affliction begin to change the world for ever.

Joseph Conrad and John Conrad.

13

Some kind of moral discovery
should be the object of every tale.

[Joseph Conrad]

In a semi-derelict building in one of London's disreputable slums, a ragbag of children jostled each other in the classroom of their 'Ragged School' – charitable establishments set up in an attempt to redeem society's 'dregs' – though the pupils were superior to their teacher in the cunning necessary to survive crushing poverty. And 'ragged' these children were: their tattered garments as ingrained with filth as the bodies they hung from. Suffused in a communal stench that vied with the open drain outside, every grubby little face was turned towards the opening door to catch a glimpse of unaccustomed visitors.

The first to appear retreated immediately, his handkerchief to his face. The second was met by derisive laughter because he was dressed in crisp white trousers and flashy boots. His name was Charles Dickens, a young journalist and successful novelist, keen to ask these unfortunates about their lives. With gentle encouragement he gained their confidence and they told him.[222] Not that he lacked some experience of his own: Dickens' father, a respectable clerk in the admiralty office, became embroiled in debt and spent fourteen months in debtors' prison, while twelve-year-old Charles, who had received scant education or regard up to that time, was sent to work in a boot-blacking factory in a dank, rat-infested building beside the Thames.

Though the family's finances later improved, they remained poor, struggling to maintain their gentility like so many other middle-class families clinging on to their hard-won status. The degrading shame that Dickens felt for his childhood experience never left him; he combined his humour, optimism and immense energy with a deep desire for reform. He made a habit of visiting the poorest enclaves of the city. When Dickens made the visit mentioned above, he had already published *Oliver Twist* (1839) in which the unscrupulous Fagin terrorises his hostages in his 'school' for young larcenists, and shortly after the visit he wrote *A Christmas Carol* (1843). Dickens' stories give voice to exploited young heroes and heroines of industrialisation, children drudging in factories, mills and mines while living in ignorant squalor where cholera and typhoid took a heavy toll. By the mid-nineteenth century, forty per cent of Britain's population worked in industry, average life-expectancy was about forty-three years – a figure weighted by infant mortality – and almost half the deaths in London were of children under ten years old.

Life for the poor was only marginally better in the countryside where old 'feudal' attitudes translated into the social gulf between farm labourers and the manor-house gentry – although the latter were sometimes generous in a *noblesse oblige* sort of way. While Dickens wrote urban settings, George Eliot (born Mary Ann Evans) wrote about rural realities from a more intellectual background, notably in her novel *Middlemarch*, although, like Dickens, most of her main characters occupy various rungs of the middle-class ladder. Eliot, too, was a reformer and she occasionally served on the same charitable committees as Dickens; both shared an interest in education.

The Elementary Education Act of 1880 opened the way for universal compulsory schooling up to ten years of age in England (universal education had been established in Scotland since1640), but Ragged Schools, as they were derisively called, had begun in the previous century as Sunday Schools to give moral training and, through Bible stories, to impart the basics of the three Rs: reading, writing and 'rithmatic. By chance, the initiative had been taken by a provincial magazine. Robert Raikes had inherited his father's publishing company, making him the owner of the *Gloucestershire Journal*. Raikes used the journal to fund early Sunday Schools and to advertise the movement – promotion taken up later by the more widely circulated *Gentleman's Magazine*. Perhaps an unusual crusade for a journal in the eighteenth century when most focused on essay-style articles, anecdotes, reviews and political and social satire, but a wider-reading public was in the long-term interests of the publishing industry, and by 1831 over a million children attended weekly Sunday Schools – the future new readers of the comics and penny editions of stories that were already circulating among industrial apprentices.

Periodicals had been around for a long time; the *Spectator*, one of the earliest, began in 1711. But from the early 1800s, new journals, sometime called 'miscellanies', blossomed like flowers after desert rain – and some faded as fast. Among the more successful were: *Cornhill Magazine*, *The Lady's Magazine*, *Fraser's Magazine for Town and Country*, *New Monthly Magazine*, *London Magazine,* the satirical *Punch* which started in 1841 and introduced 'cartoons', the Liverpool based *Kaleidoscope* (the first to publish Washington Irving's *Sketches),* and the Edinburgh based *Blackwood's Magazine*. Almost everyone wrote short fiction for them. Established authors as well as aspiring writers contributed pieces, normally under pseudonyms; Walter Scott wrote for several, including his publisher's magazine, *Constable's Miscellany*, and *Blackwood's* where his son-in-law, John Gibson Lockhart, was editor. Authors often worked as editors and some launched their own periodicals.

The content and political orientation of journals differed in line with successive editors, each aiming to meet the tastes of as many readers as they could attract. Competition was fierce, even deadly. *Blackwood's*, nicknamed 'the *Maga*', became the most notorious. Though an Edinburgh based publication, it was printed and distributed also in London to vie with its more staid rival, *London Magazine*. *Blackwood's* published many horror stories – extremely popular at the time – including those of Edgar Allan Poe, and perhaps the viciousness spread to its editors and contributors, because it was known for vitriolic reviews and criticism degenerating into personal abuse, especially against liberals and anyone connected to the *London Magazine.* Unfortunately, this 'murder' of reputations on paper became a reality in the flesh. After one particularly violent combat in print during 1821, John Scott, the editor of *London Magazine,* challenged *Blackwood's* with libel. A duel with pistols was arranged between John Scott and Jonathan Christie of *Blackwood's,* to be held at Chalk Farm, a traditional site for the 'defence of honour' and separated from London city by a mile or so of countryside. Duelling was not lawful, and there are suggestions that this occasion was not intended to be lethal, but the event was bungled by the seconds: John Scott was severely wounded and survived for only eleven days.[223]

Increasingly, magazines focused on the growing demand for stories, either short fiction or novels published in serial form: *New Monthly Magazine* had increased its story content from four in 1821, to thirty-three by 1839.[224] More importantly for writers, most magazines began to pay contributors and some paid well-known authors handsomely. In the mid-twenties, *London Magazine* paid twelve guineas a sheet to beginning writers, and *The Keepsake* paid Sir Walter Scott five-hundred pounds for two tales and a sketch in 1828. [225] Journal publication became the first career step for fiction writers, followed – if the writer proved popular – by story collections, then the debut novel published in weekly or monthly parts, and finally, the three-volume novel. Many did not progress that far, of course, while writers such as Maupassant, Poe and Kipling focused on short fiction as their preferred art-form, but periodicals were the major showcase and encouragement for writers of all kinds to create short stories. And after colour printing was developed, story magazines and chapbooks could carry lurid pictures on the covers to attract readers; the first coloured newspaper, *Illustrated London News* was published in 1844. Lifting the government paper tax in 1861 also helped make publishing cheaper. Cheap reading material for a penny or two widened access to stories, which were often read aloud in the tradition of oral storytelling; as an indication of purchasing power, in 1865 a labourer in a town earned about three-shillings and nine-pence for a sixty-hour week, carpenters and masons were paid around six-shillings and sixpence, and an engineer could take home seven-shillings and sixpence.

Charles Dickens' own magazine, *Household Words* began with mixed content of journalism, satire and anecdotes, but in 1859 he replaced it with *All Year Round*, a new two-penny weekly containing almost entirely stories and serialised novels by named authors – including George Eliot and his close friend Wilkie Collins – and circulation increased to a regular 100,000 copies. The initial number began with the first part of *A Tale of Two Cities* – Dickens was writing an episode of this historical novel of the French Revolution each week in time for the next edition. Uncannily, the opening paragraph resonates for us with our modern aspirations as we face the possibilities and threats of the twenty-first century:

> 'It was the best of times, it was the worst of times, it was the age of wisdom, it was the age of foolishness, it was the epoch of belief, it was the epoch of incredulity, it was the season of Light, it was the season of Darkness, it was the spring of hope, it was the winter of despair, we had everything before us, we had nothing before us, we were all going direct to Heaven, we were all going direct the other way –'

With readers' demands for tales of terror and a Victorian fascination with murder – crime stories often sold in separate cheap editions as 'sixpenny shockers' or the slightly upmarket 'shilling-shocker' – the middle and upper classes in particular were keen on scandal, as juicy as the Lord Chamberlain's moral censorship would allow. And the acknowledged mistress of this art was Mary Elizabeth Braddon (1837–1915) who brought a new sizzle to the 'sensational novel'. Crime among the working class was taken for granted and barely made the newspapers, but bigamy and murder in a middle-class home was a sensation that Braddon turned into her most successful novel, *Lady Audley's Secret,* first serialised in 1862 in *Sixpenny Magazine.* (And in case anyone is harbouring superior thoughts about the mentality of Victorian readers, the novel was made into a television series in 2000 and a radio serial in 2009 both followed by an avid audience of millions.) Braddon drew on elements of a recent murder case where a child of a respectable family was murdered and his body thrust down the outside privy. Britain's police force was still in its infancy, the skills of detection hardly known, and the unsolved case dragged on for nearly a year filling newspapers of every stripe – a broadsheet could sell over two-million copies on a bloody murder – and even after the child's teenaged sister 'confessed', it was hot gossip in and out of the press for years.[226] Fictionalising true crime, the gorier the better, was much favoured by writers and readers alike. Mary Braddon had written *Lady Audley's Secret* at the request of her publisher, John Maxwell, no doubt with this market in mind, and it was the most popular of her total output of seventy-five novels.

More serious readers were trying to digest Charles Darwin's *On the Origin of Species by Means of Natural Selection* published in 1859. A common response among the uncomprehending majority was to laugh his theories out of countenance, while others caught hold of 'survival of the fittest' and saw a rationalisation of the competition and conflict in the world as a natural 'law' that the strong overpower the weak. Adult unemployment in urban areas was high in Britain: as more industrial processes were mechanised, factory owners hired cheaper child labour for the less skilled tasks in preference to adults, leaving increasing numbers of people dependent on the workhouse– a social safety net that Dickens satirised in all its grim inhumanity. Life was an ongoing struggle according to each person's social level: to accumulate more wealth than your competitor; to hold on to enough income to maintain middle-class respectability; to progress up the social ladder or ensure your children did, or simply to find enough bread for today. People needed Story to lighten their lives.

Cartoon of Charles Darwin in London Sketchbook, 1874.

Darwin was too busy with beetles and bones to read many stories, but as a boy he could fall for a good yarn as well as anyone. On one occasion, a new school chum took him into a cake shop where he was given buns without having to pay for them. When Charles asked how this was possible, his friend told him: "'Why, do you not know that my uncle left a great sum of money to the town on condition that every tradesman should give whatever was wanted without payment to any one who wore his old hat and moved [it] in a particular manner.'" He demonstrated this at another baker's (where his family was also well known). Showing Charles how to move the hat, he handed it to him, encouraging him to try it for himself, which he did, in another cake shop. Inevitably, our young hero was chased from the premises by an angry proprietor, Charles dropping his ill-gotten cakes on the way, while his friend doubled up with laughter outside.[227]

The well-off were never short of pleasant diversions, but cheap theatres in London's burgeoning East End offered an additional source of fun for the working class that was healthier than gin. London's fast-developing docklands created an unprecedented concentration of working-class people (almost a million by 1880) and among the shops and taverns and boarding houses – and, indeed, bawdy houses – that emerged to serve them were a dozen or so theatres and music-halls, some accommodating over three-thousand punters.

Audiences wanted clearly recognisable villains and heroes, plenty of action and as much melodrama as the playwright could muster; even those unable to read could enjoy the oral storytelling of theatre. Performing arts drew on a rich heritage. Londoners' grandparents had revelled in the tumbling antics of Harlequin and other pantomime characters played by the famous clown, actor and dancer, Joseph Grimaldi (1778–1837), whose memoir, incidentally, was edited and partly written by Charles Dickens. For decades, Grimaldi had toured provincial theatres and played to full houses at Sadlers Wells and Covent Garden; at the age of fifty-eight, so incapacitated by then that he had to remain seated on stage, his farewell performance 'in the motley' at Drury Lane still drew appreciative laughter. And experience of both the music-hall stage and the workhouse later formed the unique talent of a young Charles Chaplin, avid reader of *Oliver Twist,* destined to become the first world celebrity of the silent screen.

From the mid-nineteenth century, new dramas, especially crime mysteries, were an attractive proposition for writers; Tom Taylor, an editor of *Punch* as well as a senior civil servant, wrote over a hundred plays and burlesques. Novels, too, were scripted for the stage; *Lady Audley's Secret* was quickly adapted for East End audiences, and it would be one of the earliest films as soon as talking pictures were invented – Thomas Edison and the Lumiere brothers were working on it.

Other technology was speeding up Story's range. Dickens crossed the Atlantic by steamer for his 1842 lecture tour in America, 'But what the agitation of a steam-vessel is, on a bad winter's night in the wild Atlantic, it is impossible for the most vivid imagination to conceive.'[228] Dickens chose to return under sail. But the speed of steamships had a huge advantage for mail runs, especially long hauls to the Far East. From 1850 onwards, steamships plied from Southampton to Calcutta and from Bombay to China and eventually to Australia. A tumultuous welcome greeted the P&O vessel *Chusan* when it reached Sydney harbour on 4 August 1852: it was the first mail steamer to arrive from England and had taken only eighty-four days (via the Cape of Good Hope – once the Suez Canal opened, it would halve the journey). Australia was agog with a gold rush and many had good news to send home. But it was a few years before the mail arrived again by steamer, because the company's fleet was requisitioned to carry troops and supplies to Britain's various wars of expansion.

The new screw-propeller steamships (as opposed to the original paddle steamers) were an expensive venture underwritten by government mail contracts, and as this was the era of 'Empire' writ large, two thirds of P&O's regular passengers were civil servants, soldiers and missionaries. Those who returned brought back tales of 'exotic lands' as travellers have done since before Herodotus. Later steamship passenger lists included some of Story's most industrious stewards: Rudyard Kipling bound for India and America; Henry Rider Haggard seeking his fortune in Africa; Somerset Maugham touring the empire is search of stories, and Robert Louis Stevenson retiring to Samoa in 1888. And a certain Józef Konrad Korzeniowski took to the sea as a professional sailor, but Story has him marked. We hear from them all in due time.

Though steam had put the 'revolution' into 'industrial' and transformed rail and sea travel, the invention of telegraphy did as much to shrink the world and speed the word. For ease of construction, initial telegraph lines followed Britain's rail routes and soon became a feature in the ubiquitous crime stories as communications could now race ahead of criminals – much as mobile phones complicate the plots of modern fiction. Public excitement grew to fever when the suspected murderer Dr Crippen and his accomplice Ethel Le Neve, both in disguise, were identified aboard the *Montrose* headed for Canada; the ship's captain telegraphed Scotland Yard which sent Inspector Drew on a faster steamer to arrive ahead of them, enabling their arrest on arrival.[229]

After the first fully successful laying of deep-sea cable under the Atlantic in 1866, the technology could be applied anywhere. Instant communication beyond the horizon to the other side of the world was a marvel of human ingenuity, seen as almost a mastery of time itself. Seemingly, there was nothing that technology and commerce in partnership could not achieve. Years later, Kipling saluted the feat in his poem 'The Deep Sea Cables':

'Hush! Men talk today o'er the waste of the ultimate slime,
And a new Word runs between: Whispering, 'Let us be one!'[230]

Preferably 'one' under the Union Jack, for telegraphic communication greatly advanced Britain's imperialist ambitions as cables careened across vast landscapes and ran along distant sea-beds. Of course it was not quite as easy as that: weather, terrain and security posed challenges and caused delays, but before the end of the century all but a sprinkling of remote islands among her 'possessions' were connected to government ministries and mercantile interests in London. Periodicals and newspapers could print fresher news from abroad, and a vested interest in what was happening in Britain's dominions was spread more widely among a population whose sons, brothers and lovers were among thousands of technicians and engineers sent around the world to extend and maintain telegraph and railway systems. Dickens had written largely domestic stories; an appetite was growing for tales from afar.

Stories about India were of special interest. But first, Story insists we make a brief diversion here for a narrative that was omitted from those tales from afar. Remember the East India Company, given a charter by Elizabeth I as an independent body of merchants? A new ambitious enterprise, initially it struggled to break into the competitive silk and spice trade in the East Indies; it had to out-sail Portuguese and Spanish ships and fight off rival Dutch and French trading companies. But once it achieved a toe-hold in India, the East India Company undermined the waning power of the Mughal Empire with political intrigue, bribery and force, until it clinched a deal that gave it massive economic advantages with no responsibilities – in effect, it became sole ruler of Bihar, Bengal and Orissa, backed by the company's private army and judiciary. Other states it simply annexed until the whole subcontinent was owned by a Board of Directors in London and controlled by a locally recruited force on the ground.

Without regulation the East India Company flourished, sending back to British stockholders massive wealth gleaned from trade tariffs and land-taxes as well as its own factories. The company pillaged rather than managed: it increased land taxes from ten to fifty per cent of the value of produce, and made farmers grow cash crops for trade, such as opium poppies and indigo, rather than food crops – policies which contributed to the Great Bengal Famine of 1770 in which some ten-million people died. The East India Company distributed no general relief during the famine, and in the aftermath, to recoup lost revenues, it increased land taxes by a further ten per cent, collecting them by brutal seizure of goods and assets. Bengal was left physically and socially devastated.

Eighteenth-century India, starved of its own resources, was in danger of disintegrating and so was the East India Company because of corruption within. Individual officials – the 'nabobs' – became immensely rich even as the company itself faced financial collapse. Political pressure ensured that British tax payers bailed the company out in 1773 with a million-pound loan (difficult to give an accurate modern value, but equivalent to bank bail-outs of recent memory).

Subsequently, despite resistance from the many parliamentarians who held company stocks, the power of the world's largest global private trading company was gradually curtailed and, from 1858, India was governed by a Viceroy appointed by the British government. Queen Victoria became Empress of India. Even more shiploads of civil servants, soldiers and missionaries arrived to implement the new administration – the Raj – with increasing, and often resented, intervention from the Crown which was hard to evade once telegraphy was installed. Matters did improve – if only for the Indian elite and growing middle class – as long as development benefited British interests.[231]

This is but a faint echo of India's ancient, illustrious and convoluted history, but it brings us to the India into which Rudyard Kipling was born in 1865, and exposes roots of the racial and cultural superiority assumed in Kipling's writing twenty-five years into Raj rule. And the sensibilities of the Victorian elite, who sought to repress the East India Company's excesses in a general amnesia, go some way to account for the extraordinary popularity of Kipling's more 'comfortable' tales and ballads. Though liberal voices spoke against imperialism and the abuses that went with it, they were not the loudest. It was the stories of the jingoists and drum-beating nationalists that caught public attention at the time, although other strands of Kipling's stories clearly resonate today, when new television adaptations of *Jungle Book* and collections of his work are still being produced. Even as attitudes changed after two world wars, George Orwell was able to write of Kipling:

'During five literary generations every enlightened person has despised him, and at the end of that time nine tenths of those enlightened persons are forgotten and Kipling is in some sense still there.'[232]

Kipling was born in Bombay (Mumbai) where his father, John Lockwood Kipling, was Dean of the Institute of Applied Art. Taken by his *ayah* through Bombay's streets and markets, young Kipling delighted in the sights, sounds and scents of this cosmopolitan city and became more fluent in Hindustani than in English. But as was usual for children of British residents in India, at the age of six, Kipling and his younger sister were sent to England for their education. They were fostered with a family in Southsea, in what he later described as 'a house of desolation'. A grim experience borne with a stiff upper lip until the beatings and bullying resulted in serious illness, when it was also discovered that his poor school performance was caused by defective eyesight. Kipling recovered on a holiday in company with his cousin, Stanley Baldwin (destined for three stints as British prime minister), before attending the United Services College, a new private boarding school in Devon for the sons of army officers. In his school-boy stories, *Stalky & Co*, Kipling draws on the college's manly approach to corporal punishment: boys were caned on their upper back, as sailors were flogged in the Navy, rather than on their buttocks as was usual in private schools. Kipling no doubt got into scrapes and took his punishment with fortitude. He had already found a talent for writing, applying it to the school magazine as contributing editor.

In his late teens Kipling returned to India, to Lahore where his parents then lived, and worked as assistant editor at the *Civil and Military Gazette* – a daily, English-language newspaper. Free once more to explore the Indian culture which had so charmed him, he began writing stories for the paper. The following year, he published his *Departmental Ditties* (1885) – cynically humorous verses on the rigours and snobberies of army life in India, and the misapplied power of 'the Little Tin Gods on the Mountain Side':

> 'By the Laws of the Family Circle 'tis written in letters of brass
> That only a Colonel from Chatham can manage the Railways of State,
> Because of the gold in his breeks, and the subjects wherein he must pass;
> Because in all matters that deal not with Railways his knowledge is great.'

After a stay in Simla – in the cool northern hill district where the Viceroy and anyone who was anyone avoided the broiling summer heat of the plains – Kipling wrote his series of amusing tales from the hills, published in the *Gazette* and in the *Pioneer* in Allahabad after he was transferred there. His tales follow the 'short-story' style of simple, tightly focused plots and two or three well defined characters: the redoubtable Mrs Hawksbee, wise and not above a little artifice for a good cause, a 'mother' to raw and lovelorn young subalterns; the manipulative vamp Mrs Reivers, whose sole cause is to trump Mrs Hawksbee; well-meaning missionaries who understand the gospel better than human nature; misguided English gentlemen 'gone native'; profiteering businessmen; unfaithful fiancés who squander their pay on amusements instead of a boat passage for the betrothed; and loyal but cunning Indian servants drawn with condescending affection. A collected edition, *Plain Tales from the Hills* was published in England in 1888; by the time Kipling returned to London in 1889, having spent almost a year touring parts of Asia and North America, he was hailed as a celebrity. British readers could identify with the human emotions and failings of his characters, while the 'exotic' settings were a bonus that confirmed for them the necessity and benevolence of Empire. Kipling was aware that his tales and ditties gave those at home only a partial view of life in India. In a Prelude to *Departmental Ditties* he writes:

> 'I have written the tale of our life
> For a sheltered people's mirth,
> In jesting guise – but ye are wise,
> And ye know what the jest is worth.'

And long after imperialist ambitions have faded, anyone who has worked in a previously colonised country alongside other expatriates will still recognise a few of Kipling's characters among their colleagues.

But significant contemporary narratives of which these 'sheltered people' were unaware flourished in India's indigenous literature, particularly in Bengal. Peary Chand Mitra (1814–1883), a journalist and curator of Calcutta Public Library, pioneered writing in the vernacular Bengali language rather than in Sanskrit or Persian which only the elite could understand. Though himself a scholar, he brought literature for the first time to a wider audience in Bengal as Chaucer had done in England, and Mitra wrote in prose, another departure from tradition. In response to ridicule by literary snobs, Mitra and a friend, Radhanath Sikdar, launched their own magazine, *Masik Patrika* in which they published sketches, stories and a serialised version of *Alaler Gharer Dulal*, the novel Mitra had written under the pseudonym Tek Chand Thakur. The magazine and the novel were an immediate success and forged the way for later Bengali writers such as Bankim Chandra Chatterji (aka Chattopadhyay, 1838–1894).

Chatterji graduated from the University of Calcutta in 1857 – one of its first students – and while working a day job as a senior civil servant in the Raj administration (and often in conflict with it) he produced religious commentaries, essays, comedies, and fourteen novels. Written in simple Bengali prose, his novels were serialised in his own monthly literary magazine, *Bangadarshan*. His first novel,

Rajmohan's Wife[233] is notable for its strong heroine, though cast in the traditional 'self-sacrificing' model – complex, sympathetic female characters also appear in his other romance, historical and political fiction. Chatterji published his last novel, *Sitarum*, as Kipling was writing his tales from the hills.

One might be forgiven for thinking so, but Kipling was not the only British resident in India – or 'Anglo-Indians' as they were called – writing distinguished works about the country, and the others were not all men. Flora Annie Steel (1847–1929) had married a British employee of the Indian Civil Service in 1867 and spent most of the following twenty-two years in the Punjab where she learned the language, befriended local women while she raised her own daughter, and became an Inspector of Government Schools. Deeply interested in indigenous culture, she helped Kipling's father promote Indian art and craft; he also illustrated her collection of traditional Punjabi folk-tales for children, *Tales of the Punjab* (1894), which contains many animal stories. Flora Steel's other works included novels, a history of India, over forty short stories, and contributions to a book of advice to other Anglo-Indian women on running their expatriate households.

Kipling's future wife would need no such advice because after his return to England he never again settled in India. In 1892, he married Carrie Balestier, the sister of his American writer friend, Wolcott Balestier, who had died suddenly of typhoid fever

A John Lockwood Kipling illustration for Tales of the Punjab.

(Henry James, a friend to so many, gave Carrie away at the wedding). They lived for a while on the Balestier family's estate in Vermont, and there Kipling published a story unlike anything else he ever wrote. *The Record of Badalier Herodsfoot* is a graphic depiction of the cruel lives of women in a London slum where beatings, drunkenness and disease are their daily reality. But Badalier, a costermonger or street-trader, is a strong, independent and fearlessly outspoken young woman:

'There is a legend in Gunnison Street that on her wedding-day she, a flare-lamp in either hand, danced dances on a discarded lover's winkle-barrow, till a policeman interfered, and then Badalier danced with the Law amid shoutings.'[234]

Kipling's story may owe a debt to Dickens, but he might also have been disappointed by what he saw when he returned to London. With journalistic realism, the story is full of insight into the lives of slum dwellers and of one spirited and wise young woman among them who was more effective in her short life than well-meaning dispensers of charity. One London critic claimed it was 'the best coster story ever written'; others considered it 'indecent'. Published in the collection *Many Inventions* (1893), it is mentioned here as a rare example for the period of a strong working-class heroine and as a tale that has largely slipped from notice.

Rudyard Kipling

While Kipling was still at college, Europe's attention had turned to Africa. After slavery was officially abolished, European trading nations continued to develop their ports and extend coastal holdings in Africa, importing indentured labourers from China and India – the so-called 'coolie trade', barely one step away from slavery. As settlements gradually encroached on their hinterlands, expanding along navigable rivers, explorers continued penetrating the interior where they found vast potential wealth in minerals, gold and ivory. Journals and articles published by explorers such as Mungo Park, David Livingston, Henry Morton Stanley and Richard Burton (of *Arabian Nights* fame) were eagerly read by a public avid for romance and adventure. Excitement was fuelled by accounts of 'a lost civilisation' evidenced by the standing ruins of Great Zimbabwe in central Africa.

The massive walls and tower built of friction-fitted granite blocks (i.e. built without mortar) are now known to be remnants of the capital city and King's palace of the Kingdom of Zimbabwe dating from the eleventh century and extending over 800 hectares; the grandest of some 300 earlier and later sites in the region built by the Bantu Shona peoples. That the city's estimated 10,000 inhabitants interacted with the wider medieval world is indicated by the presence of Chinese, Persian and Arabian trade-goods; trade probably involving the area's rich gold deposits.

To Victorian antiquarians, the identity of this 'lost civilisation' was a tantalising mystery – prevailing racial narratives of the eighteenth and nineteenth centuries ruled out its origins in indigenous African culture – but to colonial speculators, the ruins indicated only the potential riches to be gained. Young men ambitious for fame and fortune sailed to the African continent with high hopes. Among them was Henry Rider Haggard, sent by his father in 1875 as an unpaid assistant to the governor of Natal.

Haggard prospered, spending seven years in southern Africa and developing an imperialist fervour more rabid than Kipling's. He advocated annexing the Boer Republic, and stated in an article in *Macmillan's Magazine* that it was Britain's mission to conquer and hold the native population in subjugation, 'not from thirst of conquest but for the sake of law, justice, and order.'[235] Such views, generally current at the time, were given credence by 'science' when John Hunt, then president of the Anthropological Society of London, claimed that the Negro was less 'human' than Europeans. Similar views were current among scientists in the United States where a young man named Ota Benga, a member of the Mbuti tribe, had been kidnapped in the Belgian Congo and was 'exhibited' in 1904 as a 'pygmy' in an anthropological exposition at a trade fair in St. Louis, Missouri; two years later Ota Benga was transferred to the Monkey House enclosure at Bronx Zoo in New York.[236]

Darwin's misunderstood evolutionary theories had sparked anxieties about 'racial regression' (a sort of reverse evolution); many people in Britain either dismissed the idea of human descent from the Great Apes or adopted the delusion that Europeans – preferably the British rather than the French – were at the very top of the tree. Haggard returned to England during 1881/2 to pursue a career in law, though we hear from him again. Meanwhile, his ambitions for the white-man in Africa were furthered by two unconnected events in 1884 that would combine to wreak havoc on the 'dark continent' and provoke some of Story's most notable efforts.

In the first event, delegates from fourteen European nations and the United States gathered in Berlin to draw up the General Act that would carve up Africa: western powers already occupied about twenty per cent of the continent; they now set about dividing the remainder between them. The document was signed on 22 February 1885 and begins by citing the highest moral authority: 'In the name of God Almighty'. Arterial rivers, specifically the Niger and the Congo, were to remain neutral for trade and transport. One brief paragraph mentions an intended benefit to the 'moral and material wellbeing of the inhabitants' and that slavery is forbidden; the remainder of the long document concerns trade and tariffs. The 'Scramble for Africa' had begun. The map of the continent became criss-crossed by ruled lines eventually defining fifty colonies bearing no relation to reality on the ground. One of those colonies covered a vast area of the Congo River basin controlled by the king of Belgium, which he slyly named the 'Congo Free State'. This slab of Africa was seventy-five times larger than his Belgian kingdom – exceeding the combined extent of France, Germany and Spain – and encompassed some two-hundred disparate cultures each with their own social and political structures.

Belgium, a small insignificant nation historically hauled about between more powerful neighbours, lacked resources to acquire overseas dominions, but King Leopold II had pretensions to a personal empire. He had hired the explorer Henry Morton Stanley in 1879 as his agent. Stanley opened an access route from the mouth of the Congo to the furthest navigable point of the river at Stanley Falls (Kisangani) and set up a series of trading posts, setting in train events that formed one of the bloodiest colonial histories in which approximately half the local population died. Józef Konrad Korzeniowski worked in this 'heart of darkness' during 1890; when he becomes Joseph Conrad the writer, and can bear to recall those terrible days, Story will help him to tell us about them.

The second event was the brainchild of the American inventor and entrepreneur, Hiram Stevens Maxim. Maxim went to Europe to seek his fortune and found it with his invention of the first automatically reloading machine gun. In a demonstration for government officials and members of the British royal entourage, his bullets punched out the queen's initials 'VR' into a target with the ease of clipping a bus ticket. They were immensely impressed. In a bizarre reversal of 'swords to ploughshares', Maxim derived his fast-firing mechanism from a machine he had invented for drilling cotton seeds into the ground. Maxim travelled all over Europe including Russia, his order book soon full. The Maxim gun could kill more efficiently than any weapon then known. Eight years later in Rhodesia – one of those new African colonies – what Maxim had called a "little daisy of a gun" enabled fifty men with four Maxims to kill three-thousand attacking Zulus in less than ninety minutes. Had the inventor been present, he would have held a stop-watch. The Zulus, of course, were armed with hand-primed rifles and spears.

Those 'fifty men' were forces of the Rhodesia Charter Company, an offshoot of the British South Africa Company: apparently having learned nothing from recent history, the British government had issued a charter in 1889 enabling a private commercial company, headed by Cecil Rhodes, to pursue trade in and administer southern Africa. With the attraction of lands bearing gold and diamonds, the South Africa Company operated with similar brutality in Africa as the East India Company had in India. Kipling visited South Africa during the Boer War; he and Rhodes became friends, and Kipling mounted a fundraising effort with his poem 'The Absent-Minded Beggar' to improve conditions for the 'Tommies', the British soldiers fighting there. (Rhodes' statue still stands in the grounds of Oriel College at Oxford University.)

Hilaire Belloc (1870–1953), a liberal and a prolific writer (he wrote more than a hundred books and countless essays and verses), satirised the imperialist project: the mixed motives of explorers and 'civilisers'; the clamouring of investors at home; the co-option of missionaries; and the money to be made by publishing one's travels. In his long verse-story, *The Modern Traveller* (1898) the narrator joins the unscrupulous Commander Sin of dubious origins, and the buccaneering lover of gold, William Blood, on an expedition to find the 'mythical' city of Timbuktu. On the outward steamer, they complain of short measures of champagne – a beverage essential to tropical explorers:

> 'And stern indomitable men
> Have told me, time and time again,
> "The nuisance of the tropics is
> The sheer necessity of fizz."'

And lampooning the time-honoured exaggeration of intrepid travellers, he tells how a young shark climbed the ship's sides at night and ate the chaplain and the ship's mate. But once the party arrives from the coast into the African interior, they renege on the deal to pay their porters:

> 'A Mutiny resulted.
> I never shall forget the way
> That Blood upon this awful day
> Preserved us all from death.
> He stood upon a little mound,
> Cast his lethargic eyes around,

And said beneath his breath:
"Whatever happens we have got
The Maxim Gun, and they have not."'

The Maxim gun's death tattoo will be heard louder still in the Battle of the Somme, in the Great War yet to come, in which both sides were similarly armed. Hiram Maxim became a rich man, took up British citizenship and was knighted in 1901.

One reason why Story so often urges her protégé to write in fable, allegory and satire, is that their inner message can carry over centuries. Although Belloc's polemical style and strong religious and anti-capitalist[237] stance discredited him in the opinion of many contemporaries, reading *The Modern Traveller* today stirs significant questions about modern commercial imperialism: the amorality of supranational money markets, the power of global corporations, and the hypocrisies of *realpolitik* – not to mention Maxim's ghost in the arms industry.

Meanwhile, Rider Haggard had written a few mediocre novels. The story is told that his brother then challenged him to write a novel to match Robert Louis Stevenson's *Treasure Island* – a runaway success in 1883 when the combination of pirates, hidden treasure and a mysterious tropical island proved irresistible to readers. Whatever the spur, Haggard wrote *King Solomon's Mine* (1885), a fantasy adventure in a setting drawn from his African experience. The book was a bestseller. He followed it with *She*, a surreal adventure inspired by the ruins of Great Zimbabwe which Haggard had visited. That too was a bestseller, generating new editions for over a century, later film and television adaptations, and the still-current catch-phrase 'She who must be obeyed'. Haggard had created a new fiction genre – 'lost civilisations' – popular romances far from reality. Story longed to tell the true tale of Great Zimbabwe's founding by the ancestors of the Shona peoples, but she was bound and gagged. When archaeologists later confirmed that the site had been built by indigenous Africans, they were forbidden to make their findings public. Museum guides, schoolbooks, radio broadcasts and newspapers were all censored to deny the African origins of Great Zimbabwe. The Rhodesian colonial government controlled this narrative right up to the 1970s, because the real story of the site had strengthened indigenous identity and become a rallying cry for independence – finally achieved by the new Zimbabwe in 1980 after seventeen years of bloody civil war.

It required an outsider, Józef Konrad Korzeniowski – who took the name Joseph Conrad from 1894 when he began seriously as a writer – to reveal the realities of colonial Africa, initially in his short story 'An Outpost of Progress'. With buoyancy that belies the true impact of his Congo experience, Conrad described 'An Outpost of Progress' as 'the lightest part of the loot I carried off from Central Africa'.[238] Depicting the physical and psychological corrosion of two inexperienced white-men in an alien environment isolated from the props of society, the focus on individuals – inept agents of the Great Trading Company and their callously efficient African clerk – limits the scope for attacking an entire system. Conrad seems to have approached cautiously the 'Things I have tried to forget!' He was almost five years into a writing career – his 'new adventure of writing in print'– having begun with *Almayer's Folly* and other tales from his time in the south seas, before he plumbed those appalling memories to write *The Heart of Darkness,* completed in1899.

By then, nine years had elapsed since Conrad's eight-month stint in the Congo Free State. The intervening time provided a wider perspective to the immediate impressions recorded in the diary he kept for the first nine weeks: the dangerous toil of travelling hundreds of miles on foot and on small 'tin box' steamers; the recurrent bouts of fever and dysentery; the shock of finding dead Africans, shot, beside the track and the skeleton of a man tied to a post; the many villages burned or simply abandoned; the merciless climate and impenetrable jungle, and the ruthless avarice of white agents and businessmen oblivious to their cruelty in pursuit of quick profits. By the time Conrad could face these memories, he had gained an appreciation beyond the role of individuals to the full horror of the entire social enterprise cynically perpetrated in the name of 'progress and civilisation'; this is what he finally unleashes in *Heart of Darkness*.

But how did Conrad come to be in Central Africa? Although his three-year contract to command a river steamboat was an extension of his seamanship, the project was in the centre of a continent and part of a land-based venture: a far cry from the sea. Conrad – still using the name Józef Korzeniowski – was thirty-three years old, a naturalised British subject in the English Mercantile Marine since 1886, with a Master's Certificate and nineteen years experience. Among the vagaries of a sea career was that officers signed on for specific voyages, at the end of which they could hang about for weeks, months, before finding their next berth, especially if, like Conrad, they hoped for their own command. He had achieved that only once, on the small barque *Otago* in 1888/89 sailing between Bangkok and Australia and a voyage to Mauritius; other times he had been obliged to accept a position as chief mate. His time on the *Otago* was followed by a year ashore in London during which he began to write *Almayer's Folly* while seeking his next berth, battling with the bouts of illness and depression that punctuated his life, and expressing ambivalence towards a sailing life whose freedom he enjoyed but which isolated him from intellectual company. Casting his net wider for work, Conrad contacted friends in Europe and almost by accident was recommended to the director of the association set up for 'the exploration and civilisation of Africa'. While stating commerce as the means, the association's propaganda emphasised the 'humane and benevolent purposes of its civilising mission'. Though an offensive and inappropriate concept to us today, it was sufficiently accepted in nineteenth-century Europe to mask the truly rapacious nature of the Congo project. In his definitive biography, Zdzizlaw Najder argues that Conrad believed in the beneficial intentions of the enterprise, and if Conrad had read Henry Morton Stanley's glowing praise of the association's work in *The Congo and the Founding of its Free State*, he would have been further reassured. The depth of this deceit, the extent of betrayal and how close he came to being a part of it seem to heighten Conrad's loathing of colonisation.

Conrad's doubts began on the voyage out, hearing the cynical talk of speculators and old Congo hands among the other passengers, and his witnessing of a French warship firing blindly into dense jungle believed to be inhabited by Africans. In the event, the steamboat Conrad was to have commanded, the *Florida*, was damaged and unusable days before he was due to start work, and the only command he exercised was temporarily taking over the *Roi des Belges* while the captain was sick on the journey up river to Stanley Falls (Kisangani). Conrad despised the other whites' callous plundering of ivory, rubber and human labour for quick profits, and his relationship with the company manager, Camille Delcommune, was marked by mutual dislike and distrust – he was not 'one of them', they did not want him there as an unreliable witness to their activities. They might have guessed as much from the initial letter recommending Captain Korzeniowski to the association's deputy director in Brussels: 'This gentleman is very warmly recommended to me by friends in London. Besides being a past master of his profession and holding the highest certificates, his general education is superior to that of most seamen and he is a perfect gentleman.' [239] But there seems more to Conrad's initial credulity and the strength of his later reaction to the 'masquerading philanthropy' of the organisation he called a 'gigantic obscene beast'. His origins provide some clues.

Józef Korzeniowski was not a party to 'conquerors' mythologies': his heritage was of the governing class (*szlachta*) of the once-proud Kingdom of Poland, which lived according to a constitution long before its neighbours.[240] That Poland of his birth no longer existed as a political entity since being carved up in 1795 between the empires of Russia, Prussia and Austro-Hungary – Korzeniowski had been born in a city in Ukraine that once formed part of Poland and was now oppressed by Russia. An important motivation for him to gain British citizenship had been to release him from this subjugation and make him a free man in a free country. His father, Apollo

Korzeniowski, was a poet and political activist against serfdom and both parents had worked in the resistance to free Poland – until they were caught and punished. From infancy, little 'Konradzio' had shared their poverty and loneliness in exile in the harsh conditions of northern Russia. After his mother's death from tuberculosis, when the boy was only eight years old, he and his ailing father were alone. Together they recited Adam Mickiewicz' patriotic call to arms, *Konrad Wallenrod* (for whom the boy had been named), and in addition to the great Polish romanticists they read translations of Shakespeare, Dickens, Sir Walter Scott, the sea tales of Fenimore Cooper, and Victor Hugo's *Les Travailleurs de la Mer* – his father was translating this novel but the lad was already fluent in French. When his father died, twelve-year-old Konrad became the ward of his maternal uncle, Tadeuzs Bobrowski, the owner of a small estate in Ukraine. A staid and less politicised figure than his revolutionary bother-in-law, Bobrowski launched a life-long mission to bring commonsense, stability and a sense of responsibility to his nephew – the young dreamer and spendthrift who chaffed at authority and was already struggling with his health. Despite Uncle Tadeuzs' kindest efforts, from such an ambivalent and emotionally intense childhood, Joseph Conrad the writer evidently retained some of his father's passion for freedom and justice.

Rudyard Kipling, raised in the 'citadel' of the conqueror, nourished with his work a mythology of imperial benevolence, of the 'white man's burden' to bring civilisation and stability to a chaotic world. Kipling held such beliefs sincerely like most of his contemporaries, determinedly oblivious to practices that were far from the myth. Kipling declined the knighthood and laureate he was offered, but received a Nobel Prize for Literature in 1907 with the official citation: 'in consideration of the power of observation, originality of imagination, virility of ideas and remarkable talent for narration which characterises the creations of this world-famous author.'

Joseph Conrad's *Heart of Darkness* exploded the imperialist myth. Even so, the media averted its eyes from the fundamental issues in the story. The *Times Literary Supplement* focused its praise on narrative style; the *Manchester Guardian* forestalled its more perceptive readers by declaring, 'it must not be supposed that Mr Conrad makes attack upon colonisation, expansion, even upon Imperialism.'[241] Surprisingly, *Heart of Darkness* had been published by that most Tory organ *Blackwood's Magazine* (in three parts in *Maga's* special thousandth edition in 1899), and as a complete novella in the collection, *Youth*, in 1902. The novella was not particularly successful financially – Conrad was continually short of money. He declined a knighthood offered shortly before his death in 1924, but his work did increase awareness of Belgian atrocities in the Congo. An American journalist, Edmund Dene Morel, wrote pamphlets and books calling for enquiries into cruelty and slavery in the Congo Free State, drawing on Conrad's experience among other evidence. A review of Morel's *Leopold's Rule in Africa* included a statement by Conrad which began:

'It is an extraordinary thing that the conscience of Europe, which seventy years ago put down the slave trade on humanitarian grounds, tolerates the Congo State to-day. It is as if the moral clock had been put back many hours.'[242]

Edmund Morel and Roger Casement – the latter a British Consul whom Conrad had met and liked in the Congo – created the Congo Reform Association and, in 1903, Casement was asked by the British government to produce a report. The full history emerged of a scam which no modern corporate spin-doctor could have bettered: Leopold's 'front story' beginning with a sham conference in Brussels in 1876 to which scientists and philanthropists were invited to discuss, among other worthy issues, medical aid to Africa, and Leopold's setting up of the spurious *Association Internationale Africaine* for which he created obscure shell companies masking the trading entity, *Association Internationale du Congo* of which he was sole shareholder. In addition to Conrad's alternative narrative of the Congo, other writers added their weight, among them, Mark Twain with the pamphlet of political satire *King Leopold's Soliloquy*, and Arthur Conan Doyle's *The Crime of the*

Congo. Despite Leopold's manipulation of the press to discredit his critics, the Belgian government annexed his private empire in 1908, when it became the Belgian Congo. With such a history, it should probably not surprise us that some six-million people have since died in civil wars in the Democratic Republic of the Congo.

Understandably, nineteenth-century racial terms in Conrad's works offend some modern readers; Africans especially have been sensitive to the stereotyping of Africa and Africans as a 'dark continent' of undifferentiated needy people – an image that lingered into the present century and one which Story is fast correcting through a new diversity of voices. But in the Europe of his time, Conrad made an unequivocal stand against colonisation, which he described in one of his last essays as 'the vilest scramble for loot that ever disfigured the history of human conscience and geographical exploration.'[243]

In the cause of imperialism, the insidious creed of racial and cultural superiority allowed the near extermination of indigenous peoples in the Caribbean, in the Americas, in Australia, in Asia and in Africa; that 'white-men' did not invent the creed, that men of all shades and many cultures have slaughtered others in its name before, and since, is all the more reason to recognise our own truths full-face, in the hope that humanity may one day eliminate such a creed altogether. Above all, it reminds us to be vigilant in questioning the master narratives fed to us by those with power over Story.

As our tale glides into the twentieth century, public films are shown for the first time; they are silent and last only twelve exciting action-packed minutes, much of that excitement created by Charlie Chaplin's signature character 'the Little Fellow', the accident-prone but irrepressible Tramp whose bawdy humour and slapstick antics echo the Commedia dell'Arte and would have delighted Rabelais. In other fields, Mr Kellog has invented cornflakes; the first transatlantic radio transmission is sent; motor cars terrorise the streets at 8 miles per hour; in the spirit of discovery, H. G. Wells has already made his name with *The Time Machine* (1895) beginning the new genre of 'science fiction', and fame and fortune comes to another prolific writer of popular stories following the form perfected by Maupassant. But William Somerset Maugham was famous first for his drama.

Maugham had written three novels before he turned to writing stage plays as a more profitable means of earning a living. It was a good move. By 1908 four of Maugham's plays were running concurrently in London's West End theatres while others ran on Broadway, earning him thousands of pounds a week. From his mid-thirties, Maugham was an immensely rich celebrity with a life-style to match. In his late forties, he bought and renovated a house at Cap Ferrat on the French Riviera.[244] Villa Mauresque became a luxurious residence where Maugham could avoid paying British taxes, live freely as a homosexual without provoking the law, and entertain the rich and famous with skinny-dipping in the pool. Among his guests were Winston Churchill, H. G. Wells, and the Duke and Duchess of Windsor, catered for by more than a dozen staff. Maugham's success represented the aspirations of his time.

Pleasure travel was a necessity of life for those who could afford it and even for some who could not. The Orient Express had tooted its first departure from Paris in 1883, heading, via Vienna, Munich and Bucharest, for the banks of the Danube, where a ferry, train and steamer took passengers on to Constantinople (Istanbul) – a romantic option for the obligatory 'Grand Tour'. And new passenger liners became bigger and faster, though not always safer: 1912 saw the tragic sinking of the Titanic. But such freedom was about to end as events in Europe lead inexorably towards World War I. Among the millions who suffered personal tragedies was Rudyard Kipling. Kipling's only son, John, was intent on joining the Irish Guards but had been turned down, possibly due to weak eyesight. His father used his influence to obtain a commission for him and suffered the bitterness of remorse as well as grief when the eighteen-year-old was lost in action. Maugham joined the secret service, the source of his later 'Ashenden' espionage tales. And Conrad, now in his sixtieth year and struggling with rheumatism was 'painfully aware of being crippled, of being idle, of being useless'[245] as his eldest son, Borys, fought on the Somme.

As if the terrible carnage in the trenches and battle fields were not enough, in a further decade of annihilation more people died of the influenza pandemic – the 'Spanish 'Flu' – than had been killed during the war or had succumbed to the Black Death; a quarter of a million others perished in earthquakes in China and Japan; plague broke out in India, and six-million people died of starvation in the Russian famine of 1921. None would have believed that within the same generation, a second war would tear the world apart, and even if they had, it is unlikely to have dimmed the spirit of the 'Roaring Twenties' in Britain and North America celebrating freedom, survival, and a new prosperity.

War demand had boosted the incomes of manufacturers along with their share-holders and distributors, enabling an expanding middle class to buy into new mass-produced domestic technologies like washing machines and cars. Women who had been employed for the first time to relieve war-time labour shortages grew accustomed to more independence, while the younger generation exerted its freedom in 'shocking' permissiveness, experimenting with drink, dope and sex. 'Flappers' crowded the floors of night clubs, kicking up their heels to the Charleston wearing short skirts and long beads, replenishing their energy with cocktails – legally in Britain and illegally in the United States where prohibition had been in force since 1920. And with fresh perspectives after a war that everyone believed would 'end all wars', international travel again became a popular pursuit with the more adventurous able to do so by the latest novelty – the airplane.

From Villa Mauresque, Maugham toured the empire with his secretary-lover, Gerald Haxton. The loot he sought was the friction and scandal of European expatriates – planters, government administrators, commercial speculators and itinerant humbugs – stories he heard in the Malay islands sipping gin-slings on verandas and brandies in the club (he claimed to hate champagne). Expatriates found disparate ways of coping with the stress and isolation of exile and the unavoidable proximity of unappealing colleagues. Sexual licence, betrayal, breakdown and booze-driven dissipation of the professional middle classes let loose in the permissiveness of the tropics, written up into short stories with Maugham's distinctive touch of witty malice, made compelling reading – indeed, they were features in his own long, turbulent life.[246]

Although not everyone shared in the post-war prosperity – poverty remained in rural and urban areas – class divisions began to blur at the edges. P. G. Wodehouse could draw a large, enthusiastic audience for his farces, poking gentle fun at upper-class pretentions as the inept Bertie Wooster defers to his butler. 'The inimitable Jeeves' knew a solution to every trivial bourgeois dilemma. So entrenched has he become in our culture that if Google leaves you unimpressed, you can still go online to AskJeeves.

Rapid advance in technology allowed Story to tell her tales to the largest audiences ever: she flickered across silver screens in cinemas and spoke to millions gathered around the crackling family wireless. When the British Broadcasting Corporation (BBC) was chartered in 1922 and its first director-general, Scottish engineer John Reith, stated the corporation's mission 'to educate, inform and entertain', it became an institutional storyteller, for these are also key to Story's mission. One of the earliest 'soap operas', Mrs Dale's Diary, enabled millions to 'worry about Jim', and from 1951, an increasingly urban population could keep in touch with country life in Ambridge through Dan and Doris Archer. Both of these soap-opera wives were strong sensible women holding family and community together. Amazingly, the Archers still receive high ratings after more than fifty years. Whatever they appear to be on the surface, soap operas are essentially moral tales, modern gossip as oral storytelling revealing the causes and effects of social – and anti-social – behaviour and often challenging current mores.

Continuing demand for short stories took on a wider international dimension in the twenties. Spring Books published a thousand-page collection, *Great Short Stories of the World*, also *Great Sea Stories of all Nations* – as well as contemporary tales, the selections included ancient stories we have already met. Perhaps the most ambitious project was The Educational Book Company's issue of a ten double-volume set *Masterpiece Library of Short Stories: The World's Thousand Best Short Stories.* In all of these collections, many tales written in the vernacular had been especially translated into English allowing a multiplicity of storytellers to be heard outside their national borders for the first time (none however, were yet from Africa). Broadening appreciation of others' stories set in different cultures and times released Story from the corsets of literary form and the delusion that 'the short story' was an invention of nineteenth-century Europe:

'A short story may be a mere anecdote of three hundred words or a work of ten or fifteen thousand. In content it may be anything from a glimpse of character, an incident, to a highly finished picture of life.'[247]

Though the loudest voices of the nineteenth century had been predominantly 'white', from the early 1920s, Story nurtured a group of storytellers who spoke for themselves in their own 'black' voices in a literary movement in the United States that became known as the Harlem Renaissance. Prominent among these writers was a young doctor, musician and prize-winning orator, Rudolph Fisher (1897–1934) and his friend, Nella Larson (1891–1964), also known by her step-father's name, Walker, and her married name, Imes.

Rudolph Fisher was brought up in the north, in Rhode Island, later moving to New York and immersing himself in the rapidly expanding and increasingly prosperous black colony of Harlem. Though he wrote two novels, he is best known for his short stories, published in the *Atlantic Monthly* and other periodicals, and in the posthumously published collection *The City of Refuge* (1991). Perhaps Fisher's most significant gift to Story was portraying the true diversity of black lives as disparate as any other city community and doing so with humour and wit. His are not only 'black stories', but explorations of human relationships in stories whose characters are predominantly black and who speak their own argot. Fisher reveals how migrants from the Deep South, immigrants from the Caribbean, people born and raised in the north, or those from rural as opposed to city backgrounds all experienced the class and colour structures of Harlem in different ways. In 'High Yaller', Jay, who quips that he is as black as an Abyssinian prince, says to his friend Evelyn, who is fair enough to pass as white:

> "'Point is, there aren't any more dark girls. Skin bleach and rouge have wiped out the strain. The blacks have turned sealskin; the sealskins are high-brown, the high-browns are all yaller, and the yallers are pink.'" Evelyn says, later: "'Jay, can you imagine what it's like to be coloured and look white?'"[248]

There are unforgettable characters such as Miss Cynthie from the Deep South who, visiting New York for the first time to see her grandson, gives the porter her luggage but holds fast to her umbrella:

> "'Always like to have sump'm in my hand when I walk. Can't never tell when you'll run across a snake.'
> "There aren't any snakes in the city."
> "There's snakes everywhere, chile.'"[249]

Nella Larson's two novels, *Quicksand* (1928) and *Passing* (1929), give additional insights into gender and into the treacherous borderlands between black and white identities within a class divided society – both novels are partly autobiographical. Larson's mother was a working-class Danish immigrant, her father a mixed-race Afro-Caribbean from the Dutch West Indies. He died soon after Nella was born, and when her mother remarried to a Danish immigrant, Nella became a mixed-race child of a white family. She spent a few years with relatives in Denmark and a couple more working in Alabama: she belonged in neither place. Working as a nurse in New York, the doctors were white males, the nurses black females: the intersecting matrices of gender, colour and class appeared to exclude an acceptable space for a mixed-race woman who might 'pass' for white in the right environment. When Larson married an Afro-American, a highly qualified physicist comfortable with his professional middle-class status, they moved to Harlem where black origins were celebrated. During the next few years, Larson participated in the interracial art and literary scene in Harlem and wrote her novels. But after she and her husband divorced, she appears to have written no more and to have abandoned Harlem for a white community.

Both Fisher's and Larson's stories deny any meaning to the collective pronoun of racism: 'they'. One must ask which 'they' and who among them? There was never one 'black voice' as there has never been a single 'white voice'. Larson's position was less common then than now, but the issues she dealt with inspired a new generation of writers with a wide spectrum of stories and outcomes. Also clear, and affecting all colours and classes on both sides of the Atlantic, was that wealth became the dominant classifying factor in society.

However, the new prosperity was short-lived; recession was already gnawing at the economy when the Wall Street Crash tipped industrial nations into the Great Depression. Its effects were felt unevenly, but barely was recovery achieved before the world plunged into more carnage and the particular horrors of the Second World War. 'Empire' was buried in the rubble with all its untold stories, and unstoppable change drew societies into a new ambiguous global order. Albert Camus summed up the era: 'We must mend what has been torn apart, make justice imaginable again in a world so obviously unjust, give happiness a meaning once more to peoples poisoned by the misery of the century.'[250]

We took a step towards this ambition when the newly-formed United Nations proclaimed the Declaration of Human Rights; a beacon of intent often dimmed by fresh challenges and pre-occupations. Over the next fifty years, a man steps onto the moon, the human genome is deciphered, colonised countries gain independence, personal computers are invented and we are all snagged in the world-wide web. Aspirations towards equality of gender, race and culture expressed in words lurch uncertainly in practice, wars continue to erupt and multiple new voices strive to be heard. For Story, the digital age offers new freedoms ... or so it seemed.

Chapter Fourteen

Words caught in the global web

*N*ewly heard storytellers from many nations tell their tales of struggles endured, of independence gained and of new challenges to overcome. And Story adapts to a digital world which promises greater freedom and threatens greater oppression. Amidst the clamour of global voices Story stands at this fork in the path, waiting for us to choose.

A digital world which promises greater freedom and threatens new forms of oppression

14

They were nothing more than people, by themselves.
Even paired, any pairing, they would have been
nothing more than people by themselves. But all
together, they have become the heart and muscles and
mind of something perilous and new, something strange
and growing and great. Together, all together, they are
the instrument of change.

[Keri Hulme, *The Bone People*]

Computers whirred into our lives in 1952 with IBM, Apple issued its first portable model in 1976, a year later people could begin attaching themselves to cell phones, and by 1979 the internet was being commercialised, though Google would not goggle at us through our screens for another nineteen years. But Keri Hulme was not thinking of the Internet when she wrote of something 'perilous and new' in her only novel *The Bone People*: at her remote New Zealand home there was not even a telephone and only intermittent postal deliveries. More likely she thought of SPIRAL, the writers' collective who first produced her book after the manuscript had been turned down by three publishers – they must have felt regrets: *The Bone People* spiralled right out of the country in 1985 to win the Man Booker Prize.[251] For the time had come for many more voices to be heard.

By birth, Hulme is part Māori and part Pakeha (New Zealand European), an interwoven cultural heritage explored in her volume of short stories, *The Windeater,* as well as in her novel. Another, more prolific New Zealand author, Witi Ihimaera, with several story collections and fourteen novels to his name, published his first short-story collection *Pounami, Pounami* in 1972 followed by two novels, *Tangi* (1973) and *Whanau* (1974). Ihimaera centres his work on his Māori heritage; his stories probe the historical, political and community relationships that create Māori identity and the growing desire for its stronger recognition.

And across the Tasman Sea in Australia, the First National Conference of Aboriginal Writers held in Perth in 1983 gave rise to *Paperbark: a collection of Black Australian writings* (1990). Such an anthology had never been produced before, and in keeping with Aboriginal and Torres Strait Islander mores, the editorial process was communal and carried out in several locations, taking six years to accomplish. Nyoongah (Aboriginal Australian) oral culture had begun to be transcribed from the 1960s, frequently in collections of 'tales and legends' Anglicized and published by white Australians, and often without permission from or credit to the tribe or individual from whom they were collected. But oral tales were not the only Aboriginal literature: Oodgeroo Noonuccal published her first poetry collection in 1964, and poet, essayist and playwright, Mudrooroo Narogin (born Colin Johnson) published what was probably the first Aboriginal novel in 1965 – *Wild Cat Falling.*

Writers in *Paperbark* were not 'new' voices, but 'newly heard' voices speaking for themselves. The anthology includes a couple of traditional legends, but most of the stories, drama, novellas and polemical prose examine the shared history of black and white since the British invasion of the continent in 1788; a history of unspeakable atrocities by white settlers, of missionaries' misplaced 'kindness' that killed with disease, and of a generation of mixed-race children forcibly removed from their communities to be raised by white families or to labour on settlers' properties. Some of these early Aboriginal experiences are told for the first time, such as the massacre of an entire encampment in the early 1880s in the story 'Old Cobraboor': 'The true story was never written before because the shame of it prevented it from ever being disclosed.'[252] The writings in *Paperbark* are indivisible from the realities of ongoing Aboriginal struggle, not only within individual lives, but in wider issues of justice and equality of a people:

'If one accepts the proposition that all literatures are political expressions, then Aboriginal literature is one of those which has not yet succumbed to the rhetorical ploy of saying that: "politics gets in the way of literature". It asserts the contrary: literature is one of the ways of getting political things done.'[253]

While those in Silicon Valley chased technological dreams that would generate a digital revolution, others lived the dreams and nightmares of liberation, civil war, reconstruction and exile. During the second half of the twentieth century, Story kept extremely busy with voices rising to be heard beyond their national boundaries. Tremendous upheavals followed the Second World War: desolation left by the Holocaust, the destruction of Hiroshima, mass dislocations and migrations, armed resistance to wrench free from the colonial grip, and the violent aftermath that usually followed within country borders delineated by slide-rule regardless of cultural realities. All of these post-war and post-colonial traumas engendered streams of creativity out of devastation – Story helping us to understand and come to terms with new realities. But it took time, because the blinding rage of conflict tore communities and families apart leaving truth hard to face. After his country's seventeen-year struggle for independence with its brutal rivalry between revolutionary groups, Zimbabwean author and guerrilla fighter, Alexander Kanengoni, recognises this dilemma in his novel *Echoing Silences* (2002): 'It's shocking to see the reluctance we have to tell even the smallest truth. Ours shall soon become a nation of liars. […] And what is worst is that we have begun to believe our lies. What I fear most is that we will not leave anything to our children except lies and silence.'[254]

The lyrical voice of Yvonne Vera (1964–2005) broke into Zimbabwe's silence with her collection of short stories *Why Don't You Carve Other Animals* (1992) – stories which contrast the jubilation of independence with lingering grief and with the personal disillusionment of unmet hopes. Vera developed these themes in three of her subsequent novels set in the liberation movement – *Without a Name* (1994), *Under the Tongue* (1996) and *Butterfly Burning* (1998). And later, in *The Stone Virgins* (2002), a novel set in the ambiguity of political repression imposed by the heroes of liberation, she challenges contemporary African identity, moving closer to what Wole Soyinka has called a vision of 'self-apprehension' – an internally realised self-image neither deriving from European notions of 'Africa' nor from opposition to them. Vera's long-time editor, Irene Staunton, described her as '"An author who dared to voice the unspoken and hidden with a scrupulous sensitivity and courage."' In Vera's own words: '"I would love to be remembered as a writer who had no fear for words and who had an intense love for her nation."'[255]

Nigerian novelist, Chinua Achebe (1930–2013), was the first African writer to be recognised worldwide with his novel *Things Fall Apart* (1958), published two years before Nigeria's independence. Achebe wanted to record for succeeding generations the rich and diverse traditions in pre-colonial Africa; *Things Fall Apart* depicts the interlocking intricacies of social, political and religious systems in his native Igbo culture and the responses to colonisation expressed differently by the various characters. As in many parts of Africa at that time, the writing community in Nigeria was an active one, but almost entirely male. 'In a world where women were excluded from the educational and intellectual community that fostered creative work, it was near impossible for women to become writers.'[256]

Near impossible, but not entirely so for the right woman. Another Igbo story-writer, Flora Nwapa, dissatisfied with the shallow, stereotyped female characters portrayed by male African authors, wrote a novel herself at the age of twenty-seven. Doubting it was any good she sent the manuscript to Chinua Achebe. Not only did Achebe praise her work, he was so keen for her to submit the manuscript for publication in London that he sent her a guinea for the overseas postage. *Efuru* was published by Heinemann in

1966; the first novel published by a Nigerian woman. Nwapa's story is also centred on Igbo culture, but the protagonist, Efuru, is a strong, intelligent and beautiful young woman who chooses a poor farmer as her husband and helps him to pay her bride-price. Through subsequent challenges, betrayals and opposition, she holds her ground and wins the support of family and community members, although she cannot overcome her own fated loss.

Western critics often claim Nwapa as a 'feminist', though she did not accept a western feminism which places women as victims to be empowered by others. Efuru's choices are constrained by Igbo traditions, but she applies the influence she has to stretch the boundaries. What Nwapa pioneered as a storyteller, in addition to forging a path for other female writers in Africa, was the recognition of women's personal power in family and economic spheres and its expansion socially and politically. In *Efuru,* and in her subsequent novels, Nwapa's female characters possess initiative and energy to widen the cracks in social systems that seek to hold them down. And she was an enterprising exemplar, setting up Tana Press in the later 1970s as the first African publishing house run by a woman well before African women were expected to form a significant market of readers let alone writers. Her message is echoed by the American comedian, Roseanne Barr: 'The thing women have yet to learn, is nobody gives you power. You just take it.'

Many women authors followed Nwapa's precedent and gained world renown: for example, Igbo writer Chimamanda Ngozi Adichie, whose third novel *Americanah* (2013) crosses cultural borders to depict the tensions of moving in and out of exile; Petina Gappah's collection, *An Elegy for Easterly* (2009), which shows the perspective of disillusioned Zimbabweans coping with broken hopes; and NoViolet Bulawayo's *We need New Names* (2013), which delves into issues of identity, particularly for women defining new gender relationships within the complexities of ethnic identity in a foreign country. (*We need New Names* was short-listed for the Man Booker Prize in 2013; *An Elegy for Easterly* won the Guardian's First Book Award in 2009.)

Story has always nurtured her daughters, the keepers of knowledge and tales necessary for survival; women were prominent among traditional oral storytellers and remain primary narrators at the cradle. And behind many celebrated male writers are inspiring mothers and supportive wives, sisters and daughters – the unseen fixers, sounding boards and sometimes editors of literary works. That we have seen few 'famous' female authors in Story's biography up to now is because past societies have hidden her daughters, withheld their education, or denied them recognition. Some still do. Exceptions suggest what we might have lost: the eleventh-century Japanese novel, *The Tale of Genji,* exists only because Murasaki Shikibu's father allowed his exceptionally bright daughter to share her brother's education. When her talents were recognised and she was invited to the imperial capital at Heian (Kyoto) to be lady-in-waiting to Empress Akiko, inspiration and opportunity let her aptitude flourish; even so, Shikibu wisely concealed her familiarity with classical Chinese – knowledge considered inappropriate for women. At the other extreme, neither lack of education nor anything else could suppress the reputation of the redoubtable spinner of yarns, Mother Bunch, who sold strong ale on her London premises in the sixteenth century and was immortalised in several 'Jest Books' of the period:

'Mother Bunch, The onely dainty, wel favoured, sweet complexioned, and most delightful Hostesse of England […] she spent most of her time in telling of tales, and when she laughed, she was heard from Aldgate to the Monuments at Westminster, and all Southwarke stood in amazement, the Lyons in the Tower, and the Bulls and Beares of Parish-Garden roar'd (with terror of her laughter) lowder than the great roaring Megge […] But she died, and left behind her these pleasant tales following, which she used to tell those nimble spirits, which drank deepe of her Ale.'[257]

Mother Bunch's name on the cover of any collection of funny stories was sure to increase sales and she enlivened pantomime well into the nineteenth century, but we are left to wonder whether celebrity owed more to her ales than her tales.

But our own less bibulous tale moves on to India. Despite India's huge contribution in the First World War and Indians' subsequent expectation of independence, Britain clung to her 'jewel' for another thirty years; the story of India's and Pakistan's dramatic births as independent nations was related metaphorically by Salman Rushdie in the traumatic birth and life of the character Saleem Sinai in *Midnight's Children* (1981). The novel won the Booker Prize that year and was voted Best of the Booker in 2008. More recently, Indian women authors writing in English have also gained international recognition: Arundhati Roy's *The God of Small Things* won the Booker Prize in 1997; Anita Desai's *Fasting, Feasting* was short-listed in 1999; and Kiran Desai's *The Inheritance of Loss* won the prize in 2006. But of course, other talented female authors writing in the vernacular – Bengali, Hindi, Urdu, Punjabi, Malayalam – are read only by those familiar with these languages unless the effort is made to publish translations, an effort avoided wherever stories by or about women are considered less literary or important than those about men. As the capacity to write in English reflects an elite status – women from influential families began graduating from Indian universities as early as the 1880s – there is a danger that stories of the less privileged are misrepresented, and writers living outside the country may portray images of Indian life more sentimental than realistic. But some storytellers manage the best of both worlds. Though Saloni Narang frequently sips water from green bottles in the United States, she dipped her pen in the village wells of the Punjab for her tragic true story 'Close to the Earth':

'It is a beautiful country, my country. Never has nature manifested herself with such abandoned pride, never has the earth borne the traces of passionate love with such splendour.'[258]

Sawan Singh, a farmer proud and passionate to excess, loved his wife beyond her untimely death and raised his two sons with devotion and impatience in equal measures; the younger brother as hot-bloodied as his father, the elder, the peacemaker who bound the family in love. The clash between modernity and tradition is reflected in the challenge of the younger son to his father's authority. In the heat of his pride, Sawan Singh banished his younger son. But the elder brother could not abandon his sibling. For this disloyalty, in 'blind insane rage' the father kills his beloved elder son.

'It is a hot-bloodied land, the land of the Punjab, where anguished remorse stalks silently behind pride, and where a father died that day with his son, leaving an empty shell to walk, talk, and tend the silent fields; an empty shell to live among men, and gaze with unseeing eyes at the beautiful land he had once loved so well.'[259]

An increased awareness of Indian women writers was reflected in the many anthologies of short stories published in the 1980s and 90s, for example, *Truth Tales* (1986), *Other Words: New Writing by Indian Women* (1992), and *The Inner Courtyard* (1990).

Listening to these new voices dissolves away stereotypes of the 'other' and removes the expectation that people remain fixed in their cultural 'type' – a feature humorously depicted by writer LeAnne Howe, a Native American of the Choctaw tribe, who speaks as the narrator of her short story 'An American in New York' (1987). The narrator was working as a waitress at Oklahoma Airport coffee shop when a newly-arrived New Yorker asked her where all the Indians and tepees were:

'I stood there proudly pouring him a cup of coffee and said, "Right here, sir. I'm an Indian."

As I stood there in my stiffly starched yellow and white SkyChef's uniform, the New Yorker looked me up and down and asked, "You're it? I've come all this way to see Indians and you're telling me you're it? My God, darling, you mean you live in houses just like the rest of us?"

I said, "Well … I live in an apartment."'[260]

This brief episode is actually a flash-back in a story whose main theme is the narrator's visit to New York (to persuade new punters to buy her employer's bonds) and her impressions of Manhattan which her people, the *first* Americans, sold to the colonisers for 'twenty-six bucks and some beads'. What she finds is layer upon layer of new immigrants, each trying to adjust their own story to what it is to be 'American' – as she is also – and to buy their foot-hold in Manhattan for many more bucks. The story makes an intriguing mix of motifs in 'identity'.

In a world full of conflict, identity and being recognised to be 'on the right side' is as important to women's survival as it is to men's; both civil strife and indiscriminate modern warfare increasingly penetrate the home – though we invent words like 'collateral damage' to hide the fact. And women may be combatants, especially in guerrilla movements. It is misleading, though, to make assumptions about people's actions according to perceived ethnic or gender identities. In his story 'Girls at War' (1972), Chinua Achebe reveals not only the corrosive effects of the civil war, but also the persistence of fundamental *human* values shown in the final self-sacrifice of a young woman. Achebe was particularly sensitive to non-African fiction writers oversimplifying the complexities of African experience and he criticised the literary 'lionising' of Conrad's *Heart of Darkness* as perpetuating a dehumanising image of Africans.

Chinua Achebe speaking at Asbury Hall, Buffalo in 2008.

The endurance of a 'single story' of Africa was challenged more recently by novelist Chimamanda Ngozi Adichie, whose upbringing in a Nigerian middle-class family of professionals left her ill-prepared for the reception she experienced at university in the USA in her late teens. Her American room-mate was surprised that Adichie spoke fluent English, enjoyed western music and knew how to use modern appliances.

'She had felt sorry for me even before she saw me. Her default position toward me, as an African, was a kind of patronizing, well-meaning pity. My roommate had a single story of Africa: a single story of catastrophe. In this single story, there was no possibility of Africans being similar to her in any way, no possibility of feelings more complex than pity, no possibility of a connection as human equals.'[261]

While not denying catastrophes in Africa and wrongs to be righted, Adichie calls for the diversity of truth which gives each people dignity and enables us to recognise our equal humanity. We have already seen the many ways in which Story's mission to create identities, preserve knowledge and give meaning can be manipulated by the powerful to prop up rulers, legitimise inequalities and deny others' histories in creating a 'master narrative', whether in Mao's little Red Book, Mein Kampf, state-controlled and corporate-owned media or in any number of other places. As Adichie points out, how and when stories are told, who tells them, and how many of them are told, all depend on power.

Independence changed relations between nations, but Story saw deeper how change can twist old relationships into unpredictable expressions of power at a personal level. Kenyan storyteller, Leonard Kibera, grew up during the violent years of the Mau-Mau rebellion in the 1950s, and set his story 'The Spider's Web'[262] in the cultural chaos that marked the period through to independence in 1963. Kibera captures the emotional, mental, even surreal confusion of the times through the thoughts and dreams of his protagonist, the wrinkled and white-haired Ngotho, who had been a house-boy and cook to an English couple – no worse employers than might be expected. Indeed, they left him a generous tip when they fled the 'new' country along with many other expatriates. Ngotho stayed on to work for the next occupants of the house. His new memsahib was a young Kenyan woman whom he had known to be a fiery, outspoken teacher. Ngotho was pleased to work for this vociferous herald of a self-governing generation. Until, that is, his new boss turned out to be more oppressive than the old colonisers. 'Ngotho scratched at his gray hair and knew that respect for age had completely bereft his people. Was this the girl he once knew as Lois back in his home village? She had even been friends with his own daughter.'[263]

After paying a heavy price to regain control of their nation and return to their own ways of life, the prize had become distorted; what had been known and understood no longer prevailed. The stories had changed and there was no turning back.

But these are not issues only for India or Africa. Although nations in South and Central America had gained independence much earlier – by 1826 only Cuba and Puerto Rico remained European colonies – they, too, experienced decades of armed resistance, competing guerrilla movements, liberation often followed by autocratic tyranny, and disorienting change. In a similar trajectory to elsewhere in the world, existing inequalities – between peasants and landowners, slaves and masters, rural and urban dwellers, poor and rich – were exacerbated; some occupants of these categories may swerve and switch during the liberation process but the divisions remain the same. And they were transferred to the growing cities where elaborate racial colour coding to the nth degree classified social status. Story has not yet managed to bring us each of their voices, but some have been heard.

As early as 1609, Garcilaso de la Vega, known as El Inca, corrected the Spanish 'victor's narrative' by writing his own definitive history of the Incas, *Los comentarios reales de los Incas* ('Royal Commentaries of the Incas'). Vega was in a unique position to do so, born in Peru of a Spanish conquistador father and a mother of noble Inca lineage. Later in the same century, a woman of humble birth who became a nun, Sor Juana Inés de la Cruz, wrote poetry, prose and plays of such quality that scholars today place her work at the pinnacle of Spanish literature of the period. In particular, she advocated way ahead of her time that women should be allowed intellectual pursuits.

Of the host of gifted Latin American poets and prose writers who later emerged, a few must suffice here to honour Story's protégé. In Cuba, Cirilo Villaverde's novel *Cecilia Valdes* (1882) provides a vivid portrayal of life under Spanish rule and a strident condemnation of slavery. Fellow Cuban, José Marti, journalist and editor of his own newspaper as well as a poet, was a political activist for Cuban independence and died a guerrilla's death in battle. Marti's legacy is worldwide: who has not tapped their feet to the rhythm of 'Guantenamera'? – The song sprang from stanzas in his 1891 collection *Versos sencillos* ('Simple Verses').

Seeking national and regional identity, Latin American novelists in the first half of the twentieth century wove into their stories traditional myths and legends from Maya and other indigenous cultures as well as those brought by recent generations from Africa and India. Prominent among these writers were Miguel Asturias of Guatemala, Lydia Cabrera in Cuba, and in Ecuador, Jorge Icaza, whose 1934 novel *Huasipungo* ('The Villagers') was one of the earliest to expose persecution and exploitation of indigenous Indians.

In the second half of the century, Mexican author Juan Rulfo focused on rural life after the Mexican Revolution in his 1953 story collection *El Llano en Llamas* ('The Plain in Flames'). By this time, Carlos Fuentes in Mexico and Chilean poet Pablo Neruda were gaining international attention. And Guatemala's Miguel Asturias, Columbia's Gabriel Garcia Márquez and Peru's Mario Vargas Llosa were creating what became a new genre: 'magical realism'. Though varied in form and content, 'magical realism' intensifies reality through characters' beliefs in supernatural forces whether derived from indigenous religions or Christian doctrine. Allusions to indigenous and African traditions are found in these stories, too. In *A Hundred Years of Solitude* Márquez writes: 'in the southern extremes of Africa there are men so intelligent and peaceful that their only pastime was to sit and think.' Asturias, Neruda, Márquez, and Llosa each gained a Nobel Prize for literature, in 1967, 1971, 1982 and 2010 respectively.[264]

But sometimes it is the short, seemingly simple story than can encapsulate the experience of a generation. Guatemalan writer Arturo Arias was four years old when, in 1954, a military coup backed by the United States began a civil war to stop the land reform that had begun ten years earlier under President Juan Jose Arevalo. It was a war of wealthy landowners and American investors against the Guatemalan people which lasted for thirty-six years and took almost a quarter of a million lives – the majority of them Mayan villagers. Arias captures this period through the eyes of a four-year-old boy in his story, 'Guatemala 1954 – Funeral for a Bird', a deeply symbolic tale with layers of meaning, but on one level it is an extraordinary blending of loss and hope.

> 'Maximo Sanchez crawled into the light. He had been hiding with his mother under the big old desk. Now that the bombs had stopped, he could see the world.'
>
> Disregarding broken bodies littering the streets, the boy runs to play through the shattered town, enjoying his freedom. After a sudden fall of hail, a bird drops from the sky and lies dead almost at his feet. He has never seen a bird in reality before. It is beautiful, soft, precious. Other children gather round in reverent admiration. They decide to make a funeral for the bird and scrabble excitedly among the rubble gathering pretty things – a strip of coloured cloth, a picture of a rose, a gold ring around a finger, a candle – with which to give the bird a ceremonial burial.[265]

As a writer, Arturo Arias inherited a Mayan literary tradition that extended back for centuries. Though better known for the later oral transcript the *Popol Vuh,* which contains creation myths, by the early sixteenth century the Maya had produced hundreds of folded screen books written in a sophisticated hieroglyphic script; a literary output far exceeding anything found elsewhere in the Americas. Sadly, most of these books were burned by Christian missionaries after the Spanish conquest, and when Allen Christenson visited Guatemala in the early 1970s to pursue his translation of the *Popol Vuh*, the Mayan elders he met with had been unaware that their K'iche' language had ever been written. In such a way does the silencing of others' stories deny identity and weaken the power of cultural knowledge.

Lethal turbulence continues in various parts of Central and

South America as it does somewhere on every continent of our world. It would fill the next dozen pages simply to list all the places where lives are destroyed by violence each day – there is not space enough for them all in our newscasts. And if there were, it is doubtful that we could cope with such an onslaught on our senses and remain sane. Perhaps it is a sign of 'misery overload' that adults' colouring books and self-help manuals on de-cluttering and folding our underwear neatly are so popular in the West. Actions have consequences – that is the nature of all life that Story taught us from the beginning – so it is futile for nations to build walls and fences against the consequences of their histories, the dénouement of their own stories. History is not *in* the past, it comes *from* the past; it walks in our present and waits ahead of us with our future. Story has witnessed the oppression of one people by another for millennia. It is tempting to conclude that the drive to subjugate others is an inherent trait of humanity. Perhaps we need to ask different questions that focus more on the oppressed as suggested by South African storyteller, Njabulo Ndebele: 'Our literature ought to seek to move away from an easy preoccupation with demonstrating the obvious existence of oppression. It exists. The task is to explore how and why people can survive under such harsh conditions.'[266]

We saw that one of Story's earliest endeavours was helping us to live with others, to balance the needs of one with those of the many, and to relate as one group to another. From that pivotal moment in pre-history when we humans acquired conscious awareness, perceptions of 'otherness' began within each person, augmented by the accumulation of stories heard and internalised; stories that, among much other wisdom, helped us to differentiate future mates and allies from enemies and, perhaps, to identify potential human prey. Knowing others is as difficult a task as it has always been, not least because people are complex and constantly changing with mood and circumstance; we are all 'moving targets' and each one unique – the human sciences have not yet taken us beyond that simple, perplexing fact. 'It is only the story [...] that saves our progeny from blundering like blind beggars into the spikes of the cactus fence.'[267]

How we 'see' the 'other' and what we mean by 'love' are complex themes in a satirical tale by the Brazilian writer Clarice Lispector (1925–1977). The title story of *The Smallest Woman in the World* (1960) is set deep in the Eastern Congo, echoing the African heritage of so many Brazilians (though not Lispector's who was born in Ukraine) and an Africa symbolic of all that is dark, hidden and strange:

> A French explorer discovers a hidden tribe of pygmies who live in the tree tops to avoid their enemies, the savage Bahundes, who catch them in nets and eat them. The tiny Likoualas come down from the trees only to hunt and to cook their food. The explorer's exaltation knows no bounds when he finds the smallest of this tribe, a young pregnant woman. He measures her; she is seventeen-and-three-quarter-inches tall and he notes down as many details as he can the better to categorise this rarest specimen that no one else in the world but himself has ever seen. He names her, '"You are Little Flower"', and her picture is blazoned across the Sunday supplements – 'black as a monkey … she looks like a dog'. Readers respond with varieties of romanticism tempered by predation. One woman quickly turns the page because the picture gives her 'the creeps', another is consumed with terrible tenderness and pity. A small boy wants Little Flower as a playmate to frighten his younger brother; a teenage girl considers how tiny Little Flower's baby will be. And her mother contemplates the pleasure and prestige in possessing such a cute rarity. '"Imagine her serving our table, with her big little belly!"' Meanwhile, deep in the jungle, Little Flower is laughing with joy because she has not been eaten yet: 'Not to be devoured is the secret goal of a whole life.' She laughs because she loves this strange-coloured explorer as she

loves his boots and his ring. And she laughs because she has her own tree to live in with her husband – none of which the explorer would have understood had he known. Completely baffled by her soft, gleeful, primordial laughter, the explorer keeps making notes.[268]

The story still resonates. Meeting another opens up multiple possible paths our relationship could follow, even with Story as our guide we may become lost in the maze and prick ourselves on Achebe's 'cactus fence' of misunderstanding and miscalculation. On another level it speaks to our modern obsession with travel, with seeking ever more remote places and communities in search of 'unique' stories and rare artefacts to paw over and appropriate – 'hidden', 'lost' or 'secret' objects or persons remain highly marketable. There is nothing the avid traveller hates more than to find the footprint of a predecessor or the cultural litter of a package of tourists. We generate 'likes' to our Facebook and Instagram pages with selfies of our presence among the 'other'. And our postings open up the remotest communities to the vast labyrinth of fact, fiction and fancy we know as the world-wide web – a phenomenon strangely foreshadowed by the Argentinean storyteller Jorge Luis Borges (1899–1986). Borges' short stories, 'The Garden of Forking Paths' (1941) and 'The Library of Babel' (1942), are not so much 'tales' as explorations into multiple consequences in an ever expanding horizon of possibilities where destinations and understanding remain eternally elusive. In many ways they model our times.

Over the fifteen years since the digital revolution gained full steam, those 'forking paths' offer more ways of reading, from e-books on a Smartphone to the recent revival of the hardback book as an object of beauty to own and to hold. Our story-making has become increasingly visual, graphic novels and comic books fit well with image-led web content, giving fresh impetus, for example, to Japanese Manga comics which have been around since the nineteenth century. YouTube, Vlogs and other social media all tell stories in pictures – nobody bothers to read Tweets without images any more. The speed and compaction of digitised narrative has condensed stories, too. Some hefty novels are still published and the three-decker novel is replaced by the ubiquitous trilogy, but the novella, the 'short story' and particularly the briefest of 'flash fiction' suits our rapid scroll-down multi-distraction lives, our fingers if not our bodies in constant motion. Our opposing thumb, so vital to prehistoric tool-making, is now the digit of choice for scrolling through our mobile screens. Even language has been attenuated in text-speak: if Story looked over the shoulder of a modern teen pecking at his mobile, she might feel a certain *déjà vu* recalling cave paintings and proto-language of *Homo erectus*. We are in danger of seeing life only through the narrow window of a Smartphone, the stories we read reduced to speeding headlines. We seem to be driven by technology rather than the other way round, constantly urged to consume more, pressed to adopt new narratives, and increasingly forced to put more of our personal selves online to access basic services – at times it feels like a new 'scramble for the world'.

Our choices, though, have increased as never before. Though fashions and fads come and go with stories as with everything else, we wander in a literary labyrinth which embraces every genre and almost every possible mix of genres. Running through them are threads and echoes of all the epics, fables, myths, legends, fairy stories and folk-tales that have accompanied our human journey. Stories are like deep-rooted trees that survive through flood, drought, heat and cold to provide fruits that nourish each generation gathered within the shade of their branches. And we are still creating new myths and legends. In Papua New Guinea – 'the land of the unexpected' where anything can happen – Raymond Sigimet relates an urban legend in the making:

Sir Iambakey Okuk (1945–1986), a former deputy prime minister of Papua New Guinea, was a greatly respected and loved statesman, the first, in fact, to be given a state funeral after his death from liver cancer in 1986. 'His body was flown to major towns for viewing before being buried in Kundiawa. Sorcery was suspected and riots erupted as people mourned his premature death. The sense of loss demonstrated has not been experienced in PNG since.' Today, he is recalled in oral narratives that claim Okuk is still alive, incarcerated in Rome for secret nefarious purposes of his kidnappers involving international governments, brainwashing and shape-shifting. The body that was buried, people say, was a wax effigy; the coffin so closely protected by police and military that no one could approach close enough to see.[269]

The mixing of conspiracy theory and fantasy expressing communal loss, national pride and a tribute to good leadership is the same process that transformed tales of a local hero into the imaginative legends of King Arthur and his immortality in Avalon. In the way that such tales develop over the years, other especially talented Papua New Guineans who have died young are now woven into the main legend of Okuk as fellow captives in Rome. And as with all legends, belief is not required for enjoyment.

Our revolution in communication is increasingly accessible to everyone wherever they are in the world; storytellers have multiplied, their audiences potentially global. We are all storytellers, and now social media and cheaper, easier self-publishing allow us all to be publishers, too, opening a flood of memoirs and novels retrieved from desk-drawers and exposed to public gaze. Change is too fast and the twenty-first century too young to know which storytellers will engage decisively with history or still be known in fifty or a hundred years. Ray Bradbury (1910–2012), versatile and prolific author of some six-hundred short stories as well as novels and scripts, decided to become a writer from the age of twelve so that he would 'live forever' like the authors jostling on the bookshelves of his beloved public library. Another prolific modern storyteller, Neil Gaiman, pays tribute to Bradbury and his wish for immortality in his story, 'The Man Who Forgot Ray Bradbury', in which the protagonist is losing his memory – 'There are things missing from my mind and it scares me' – but he remembers the importance of words:

'And as long as your words which are people which are days which are my life, as long as your words survive, then you lived and you mattered and you changed the world and I cannot remember your name.'[270]

Digital technology enables all our uploaded words – even those we regret – to be preserved in the 'cloud' forever. However long 'forever' turns out to be. And Google, along with various 'free-knowledge' sites, proceed rapidly on their mission to digitise every text they can reach, aiming at an unprecedented continuity of the written word from past to present for anyone with the time and patience to follow all its pathways and byways. A feat not attempted since the Qing dynasty in eighteenth-century China tried to collect their entire literary and artistic heritage in the 800,000-page *Gujin Tushu Jicheng*. Google's digital library may be a modern expression of our ancient quest for immortality, perhaps still searching for the 'lost wisdom' that the gods withdrew from us in creation myths, but eternity remains elusive: the next 'cultural revolution' could be achieved by a simple 'click', a cyber wipe-out. We should hang on to our paperbacks and hardbound books to read by fire-light 'when the lights go out'.

Like all power, digital power is double-edged. It provides us with enormous advantages while also making us vulnerable. Since the earliest days when medicine-women, elders, and champion hunters told the tales that ensured a clan's survival, Story's freedom has waxed and waned with events of history: the technology of 'writing' – the magic of written words – was first guarded by priests and kings, and oral stories were often the esoteric preserve of religious celebrants as they were for the Druids. Later, while Story roamed freely among the lowly, education confined other narratives to elite classes, and printing fixed stories to the page stirring new issues of ownership. Over the centuries we saw Story gain freedom through vernacular languages to engage in social and political change, and struggle with censorship. And now digital technology has detached stories from their cultural firesides to a global arena. We can hear the multiple voices of our most distant human neighbours across the planet, but the digital net is woven by powerful forces: modern 'priests and kings' vie for control of our narratives. Fear of Story drives such forces to censor spoken and written words, burn books, close down websites, and imprison their poets and journalists; others use more subtle means in this perpetual battle between different values and alternative truths.

Remember the framed stories within stories within stories? Where the outer frame established the theme and setting and sometimes the main characters? The framing of meta-narratives told by spin-doctors – the story-spinners of governments, powerful supranational corporations and would-be dictators – determines the identity of heroes and villains, the causes and effects of action, and the conclusions they would have us believe. With the power of naming to change identities, 'resistance to oppression' becomes 'terrorism'; defence against 'climate change' becomes an 'anti-capitalist conspiracy'; 'inequality' becomes a 'law of economics'; 'displaced people' fleeing for their lives as humans have migrated throughout our history, enriching cultures in the process, become a 'threat', and 'surveillance and personal data-gathering' become a 'routine necessity'– already your television set can spy on you. Underlying these stories is a new survival narrative in which we must submit to the protection of those in power. It offers a narrative of fear sustained by hate – George Orwell trod this fork in the path before us.

A grim example of determining 'heroes and villains' by framing a story to subvert the truth began at Hillsborough football ground in Sheffield, England, on 15 April 1989, when ninety-six spectators were crushed to death in the stadium. To exonerate themselves from responsibility in this tragedy, members of the local police force carefully spread the story that drunkenness and lack of cooperation among the fans, and their breaking through a closed gate leading to the terraces, had created the crowding that caused the fatalities. Kindling the stereotype of the 'football hooligan', the police elaborated and stuck to this narrative, influencing the outcome of the initial formal enquiry in 1989, the verdict of the first inquest in 1991/2, and that of the private prosecution brought in 2000 by the families of the dead and injured. Only during the second, two-year-long inquest concluded on 26 April 2016 was the fabrication finally exposed and the truth told: that police inexperience and negligence in marshalling the crowd had directly caused the deaths of spectators who, neither drunk nor uncooperative, had been allowed by the police to enter the terraces through the gate, opened for that purpose. It took twenty-seven years of concerted opposition to powerful authorities to achieve justice for the families and vindication of the innocent dead. A prolonged and heartrending struggle as it was, in many parts of the world people do not have the freedom to pursue the truth of their own stories.

More widely, stories have become a powerful tool wielded by those who may not have our best interests in mind. The new academic discipline of the psychology of fiction continues to confirm the influence upon our attitudes and behaviour of stories both fictional and factual, while governments and commercial interests now use the results of these studies and hire professional narrators to create the most effective stories to achieve their goals or sell their brands. Attempting to control narrative is nothing new, but the immense potential of global digital communication to do so is unprecedented. All stories are underpinned by values, overtly or covertly; it is a wise listener who seeks them out. Chinua Achebe urged a duty on writers to work for better lives. In *Anthills of the Savannah* he wrote:

'Storytellers are a threat. They threaten all champions of control, they frighten usurpers of the right-to-freedom of the human spirit – in state, in church or mosque, in party congress, in the university or whatever.'

If silence is the sound of fear and oppression, the other path of digital technology is the possibility of breaking the silence, allowing others to be heard. The loudest voices may be those with the benefit of wealth and education, the elite, but a glorious clamour of tongues is emerging from power relations far more complex than black versus white, or coloniser versus colonised. Story now engages the digital revolution to seek freedom of ethnicity, location, language, gender, worship, expression, age and individuality, all of which depend on freedom from the two conditions that have stalked most of our human existence: poverty and tyranny. Humans run on stories as water flows with gravity, and although that makes us vulnerable we still have the gift to create our own narratives and imagine our own futures: that is our greatest source of optimism and hope. Since our species crossed vast savannahs, followed winding valleys, penetrated forests and braved the seas, our various stories have mingled, often competing or conflicting, but if we face our global challenges together, our stories have the chance to merge and blossom into 'something strange and growing and great … the instrument of change.'

After living through so many millennia and surviving a multitude of dangerous adventures, when Story glimpses her reflection on the screen does she still recognise herself? Of course. Some of our tools of storytelling are transformed beyond recognition, change is faster, perhaps our challenges seem more intense to us, the stakes are certainly higher and there are many more of us, but ageless and omniscient as she is, Story still serves us and sorrows for our follies. She continues to nurture her daughters, sons, lovers and protégé because we need the same stories. Her mission has not changed. Story will stay with us for as long as a human brain sparks.

We know that the pace of our scientific and technological change is without precedent. What we do not know is where it is leading us. Will Story be finally overpowered and captured? Could genetic engineering change the stories in our heads? Whose values will be programmed into artificial intelligence and could it snuff out our spark? These are challenging questions we can tackle only while Story is free. Like Scheherazade, we must believe in our own story-power and tell another tale before the dawn.

'There was once a…

Last Thoughts

Each of us … constructs and lives a 'narrative'
and is defined by this narrative.
Oliver Sacks
On the Move: A Life

The story is our escort; without it, we are blind.
Chinua Achebe
Anthills of the Savannah

To survive, you must tell stories.
Umberto Eco
The Island of the Day Before

Illustration credits

Pages xxi, 2, 20: ©Graeme Neil Reid (commissioned). **Page 14**: ©David Moolooloo of Naiyarindji (1999) (author's collection). **Pages 28, 34**: illustrations from *Ancient History*, P.V.N. Myers (1904). **Page 37**: terracotta relief in Royal Museums of Art and History, Brussels. Photo: U0045269 [CC BY-SA 4.0 via Wikimedia]. **Page 56**: Jan Luyken drawing (17th century) [CC PD via Wikimedia]. **Page 58**: Wenzel Hollar (1687) illustration of *Aesop fables with his life* [licensed by Getty Images]. **Pages 70, 73**: J. Kirk etchings after F. Barlow (18th century) [CC 4.0 via Wellcome Images]. **Page 82**: illustration from *Pictures of English History*, Joseph Martin Kronheim (1868) [CC 1.0 via Wikimedia]. **Pages 98, 101**: illustrations from *Myths and legends*, T. W. Rolleston (1910) [Internet Archive book images]. **Page 112**: R. H. Brock (1871-1943) illustrations from *Reading and Learning – Book IV*, Richard Wilson (ed.) (Nelson, c.1920). **Page 127**: Christian Krohg painting *Leiv Eiriksson discovers North America* (1893), National Gallery, Norway [CC 1.0 PD via Wikimedia]. **Page 141**: Olaus Magnus illustration from *Coureurs des mers* (1555) [CC 1.0 PD via Wikimedia]. **Page 146**: Sophie Gengembre Anderson (1850-1900) painting *Sheherazade* [The New Art Gallery, Walsall via CC Wikimedia]. **Page 166**: T. Greenup, illustration from *Reading and Learning – Book IV*, Richard Wilson (ed.) (Nelson, c.1920). **Page 172**: detail from an illustration in a 19th century Chinese edition of tales of Pu Songling (1640-1715). **Page 175**: J. Larwood (1827-1918) illustration from *The History of Sign Boards from the Earliest Times to the Present Day*, Jacob Larwood & John Camden Hotten (Chatto & Windus, 1908). **Page 182**: frontispiece to William Caxton's *Canterbury Tales* (c.1478), British Museum [PD CC0 via Wikimedia]. **Page 190**: Francesco Allegrini (1760–1786) engraving, from Alfred Gudeman *Imagines philologorum* (Teubner 1911). **Page 197**: John Cassell illustration from *Cassell's Illustrated History of England, Volume 1* (1865) [Internet Archive Book Images]. **Page 199**: illustration based on the Ellesmere MS. of Chaucer's *Canterbury Tales* in *The pageant of Medieval England,* Nicholas Guildford (G. Bell & Sons, 1923). **Page 206**: unknown artist's portrait of William Caxton [licensed by Getty Images]. **Page 214**: illustration from *Die Gartenlaube* (Ernst Keil's Nachfolger 1857). **Page**

217: Christine de Pisan (c.1364–c.1431) woodcut in *Faits d'armes et de Chevalerie* (William Caxton, 1489), published in *The Tradition of Technology*, Leonard C. Bruno [Library of Congress]. **Page 224**: Daniel Maclise (1811-1870) painting published in *Cassell's History of England* (1909). **Page 242**: John James Hinchliff (1805-1875) engraving for *The Heptameron of Margaret, Queen of Navarre* (1864) [CC PD via Wikimedia]. **Page 256**: unknown artist's early engraving of François Rabelais [licensed by Getty Images]. **Page 262**: Alfred Albert illustration *Maquette de costume pour an opéra bouffe* (c.1856) held in Bibliothèque Nationale de France [CC PD via Wikimedia]. **Page 268**: George Henry Hall (1825-1913) study sketch for an ideal portrait [Folger Shakespeare Library]. **Page 272**: detail from photograph by Carole Raddato of Dionysus Mosaic (220/230 AD) in Romisch-Germanisches Museum, Frankfurt [CC via flickr]. **Page 285**: unknown artist's 19th century etching [Folger Shakespeare Library]. **Page 292**: Charles Chabot (1790-1866) lithograph (c.1815) [CC PD via Wikimedia]. **Page 296**: H. S. Sadd (1835-1884) engraving from a painting by W. Allan (1872-1850) [Library of Congress]. **Page 305**: Mathew Brady (1822-1896) photograph (c.1865) [National Archives and Records Administration]. **Page 311**: Gustave Doré (1832-1883) detail from an illustration for a 19th century edition of Charles Perrault's fairytales. **Page 319**: Thomas H. Shepherd (1792-1864) illustration for *Edinburgh in the nineteenth century,* John Britton (1829) [British Library via Flickr Commons]. **Page 328**: unknown photographer's postcard print of Anton Chekhov (1905), [Winokur-Munblit Collection of Russian Empire Postcards via Library of Congress]. **Page 348**: book cover illustration, Courier-Litho Co. (c.1899) [Library of Congress]. **Page 349**: artist Alonzo Chappel (1828-1887) portrait (c.1872) [Library of Congress]. **Page 357**: H. C. Greening (1876-1946) illustration for 'Innocents of Broadway' in *The Gentle Grafter*, O. Henry (Doubleday Doran & Co., 1929). **Page 360**: unknown photographer, bromide postcard print mid-1910 [licensed by National Portrait Gallery]. **Page 367**: cartoon 'Darwin Satirised' in *London Sketchbook* (1874). **Page 375**: John Lockwood Kipling (1837-1911) illustration for *Tales of the Punjab*, Flora Annie Steel (Macmillan, 1917) [PD via Internet Archive Book Images]. **Page 376**: unknown photographer, portrait from *Rudyard Kipling*, John Palmer (Henry Holt & Co., 1915) [CC via Wikimedia]. **Page 396**: photograph by the author. **Page 405**: photograph by Stuart G. Shapiro (2008) [GFDL http://www.gnu.org/copyleft]. **Page 418**: woodcut from an 18th century chapbook *The World Turned Upside Down*, in *Chapbooks of the Eighteenth Century* (1882) John Ashton (ed.) [PD Public Domain Review via Internet Archive].

End Notes

1   Summary of 'Baiame's Gift of Manna' in *Aboriginal Tales*, A. W. Reed (Reed Books, 1965). During the early and mid-twentieth century, a number of collections of Aboriginal stories were published by Europeans, often without permission from or credit to the tribe or individual who originated them. Sometimes this was because stories were part of ancient oral tradition which collectors simply appropriated. The moral and intellectual rights of Aboriginal ancestors to whom Baiame's tale rightly belongs are acknowledged with gratitude.

2   Ibid.

3   Summary of 'Ko-ishin-mit and Paw-qwin-mit', in *Son of Raven Son of Deer*, George Clutesi (Gray's Publishing, 1967).

4   For a fuller account of the *Jukurrpa*, see *Daughters of the Dreaming* by anthropologist, Diane Bell (McPhee Gribble, 1983).

5   Details of this and the following paragraph are drawn from *The Last Sea Nomads: Inside the Disappearing World of the Moken*, Susan Smillie (Guardian Shorts, 2014).

6   R. Shahack-Gross, et al, *Journal of Archaeological Science*, vol.44 April 2014 pp.12-21.

7   Summarised from a story translated by Russell Maddicks and posted at http://www.venezuelanindian.blogspot.co.nz/2006/03/yanomami-sanema-origin-of-the-fire.html The original source was a report by Daniel de Barandiaran published in the Venezuelan journal *Antropologica* in January 1968.

8   Summary of 'How the Human People Got the First Fire', in *Son of Raven Son of Deer,* George Clutesi (Gray's Publishing, 1967).

9   Material in this summary of Maori myth was drawn from several online sources: maaori.com/whakapapa/creation.htm; Te Ahukaramu, Charles Royal, 'Maori creation traditions – Creation and the Maori

world view'; Te Ara – the Encyclopaedia of New Zealand; and from Hōne Sadler, *Ko Tautoro Te Pito O Tōku Ao: A Ngāpuhi Narrative* (Auckland University Press, 2014).

10 Summary based on Allen J. Christenson's translation of the Popol Vuh, *The Sacred Book of the Maya* (University of Oklahoma Press, 2007).

11 Summary of 'Setna and the Magic Book', in *Great Short Stories of the World*, Barrett H. Clark, Maxim Lieber (eds.) (Spring Books, 1925).

12 The story is quoted in *Voices in Stone*, Ernst Doblhofer (Paladin, 1961).

13 Alberto Manguel, *A History of Reading* (Flamingo, 1997), quoting William W. Hallo & J. J. A. Van Dijk, *The Exaltation of Inanna* (Newhaven, 1986).

14 Prose summary (quoting some original dialogue) of R. Campbell Thompson (trans.) *The Epic of Gilgamish* (BiblioBazaar, 2007, original copyright 1928).

15 Vybarr Cregan-Reid, *Discovering Gilgamesh* (Manchester University Press, 2013).

16 Quoted in *Great Short Stories of the World,* Barrett H. Clark, Maxim Lieber (eds.) (Spring Books, 1925).

17 The discussion is given in Plato's *Dialogues*, 'Phaedrus', Jowett 1892 which can be found online at http://www.oll.libertyfund.org/titles/111

18 Homer, *Odyssey*, Book 21, Ian Johnson (trans.) (Vancouver Island University, Canada). Accessed online at https://records.viu.ca/~johnstoi/homer/odyssey21.htm Lines 1-5, Lines 1-5, 81-86.

19 Summary of Eumaeus' story, *Homer: The Odyssey*, T. E. Lawrence (trans.) (Wordsworth Classics, 1992).

20 Outline of, *The Ramayana*, R. K. Narayan (trans.) (Chatto and Windus, 1973).

21 From, *The Story of Kalilah and Dimnah (Fables of Bidpai)*, I. G. N. Keith-Ferguson (trans.) (Cambridge University Press, 1885). Translation of a Syriac version accessed online at Project Gutenberg.

22 Ibid. (Summarised.)

23 Ibid. (This source includes an extensive and scholarly criticism of the history and authenticity of various translations of *The Story of Kalilah and Dimnah)*.

24 Quotations from, *Kalila and Dimna – Selected Fables of Bidpai*, Ramsay Wood (Inner Traditions International, 1986).

25 Hesiod, *Works and Days*, ll. Lines 202-211 (Project Gutenberg).

26 'A Bird in the Hand', *Fables of Aesop*, S. A. Handford (trans.) (Penguin, 1964).

27 *The History of Herodotus*, G. C. Macaulay (trans.), Vol.1, Book II: 134 (Project Gutenberg.).

28 'The Abaluyia of Kaviron', in *African Worlds*, Gunter Wagner (Oxford University Press, 1954).

29 'A Respecter of Persons', in *Fables of Aesop*, S. A. Handford (trans.) (Penguin, 1964).

30 These and other stories, along with a complete list of all fable collections in Latin, can be read online at aesopus.pbworks.com, and at Aesopica.net, a site for Latin education edited by Laura Gibbs.

31 Diodorus Siculus, *Celtic Ethnography*, written around 70-21 BCE, translated by Oldfather, C. H. Loeb Classical Library (Harvard University Press, 1935).

32 *Cormac's Glossary* (Codex A), in *Three Irish Glossaries*, Whitley Stokes (ed.) 1862. Online at http://archive.org

33 From the Preface to the *Amra of St Columba,* translated into English at www.maryjones.US/ctexts/amra-columcille.html

34 Paraphrased from the account in 'Courts and Coteries' (based on a 1914 translation from German by Rudolph Thurneyen), in *The Field Day Anthology of Irish Writing: Irish Women Writers* Vol. IV, pp.303-30, Angela Bourke et al. (eds.) (Cork University Press, 2002).

35 *Cormac's Glossary* (Codex A), in *Three Irish Glossaries*, Whitley Stokes (ed.) 1862. Online at http://archive.org.

36 *Cormac's Glossary* is quoted in the *Book of Leinster*, the *Annals of the Four Masters*, and the *Book of Lecan*, among others, being a standard reference for scribes well into the sixteenth century, and continues as a source for modern scholars.

37 Summarised from *Cormac's Glossary* (Codex A), in *Three Irish Glossaries*, Whitley Stokes (ed.) 1862.

38 From *Three Fragments* in the Burghundian Library translated by Dr O'Donovan and quoted in *Three Irish Glossaries*.

39 *The Roman History of Ammianus Marcellinus*, Book XV: Ch.XII Para 1, C. D. Yonge (trans.) (G. Bell and Sons, London, 1911).

40 *Lebor na hUidre, Book of the Dun Cow*, Section X Intro. II. R. I. Best and Osborn Bergin (eds.) (Royal Irish Academy, 1929). Online at Internet Archive.

41 Details of the story in this chapter have been drawn from *The Tain*, Thomas Kinsella (trans.) (Oxford University Press, 1970), and the *Táin Bó Cuailnge Recension 1,* Cecile O'Rahilley (ed.) (Corpus of Electronic Texts), also from Joseph Dunn's translation (David Nutt, 1914).

42 In *A Dictionary of Irish Mythology* (Oxford University Press, 1991), Peter Beresford Ellis cites the medical school at Tuaim Brecain (County Cavan), founded in the fifth century AD by physician Bracan Mac Findloga, as being regarded the premier medical school in Europe during the Dark Ages.

43 *The Tain*, Thomas Kinsella (trans.) (Oxford University Press, 1970). p. 208.

44 Ibid. (Summarised with some original dialogue.)

45 Ibid.

46 Dates are based on those cited in, *In Search of Ancient Ireland*, Carmel McCaffrey and Leo Eaton (New Amsterdam Books, 2003) and in *Ancient British Rock Art*, Chris Mansell (Wooden Books, 2007).

47 Lara M. Cassidy et al. 'Neolithic and Bronze Age migration to Ireland and establishment of the insular Atlantic genome', in the *Proceedings of the National Academy of Sciences,* Published online 28 December 2015; doi:10.1073/pnas.1518445113.

48 *Egil's Saga*, translated by W. C. Green, from the original 'Egils saga Skallagrímssonar', 1893, Icelandic Saga Database, accessed via Internet Archive at http://sagadb.org/egilssaga.en

49 Quoted by Nick Attwood in *The Vikings are Coming*! https://www.lindisfarne.org.uk/793/

50 Quotations and references in this section are from *The Prose Edda* Arthur Gilchrist Brodeur's (trans.) (Dover Publications, 2006), a republication of the original of 1916.

51 Ibid.

52 Icelandic Saga Database, http://sagadb.org/egilssaga.en

53 Ibid.

54 *The Saga of the Volsungs*, Jesse L. Byock (trans.) (Penguin Classics, 1999).

55 See, for example, Adam Nicolson's study in rural Romania, *The Hand's Breadth Murders*, *Granta* December 2015.

56 Introduction to *Beowulf*, Seamus Heaney (Faber and Faber, 1999).

57 *An Orkney Tapestry*, George Mackay Brown (Quarter Books, 1973).

58 Ibn Fadlan quoted in *The Vikings*, Johannes Brøndsted, (trans.) Kalle Skov (Pelican Books, 1965).

59 *Hrafnkel's Saga and Other Stories*, Herman Palsson (trans.) (Penguin Classics, 1971).

60 Ibid. (Summarised, quoting some original dialogue.)

61 Ibid. (Summarised, quoting some original dialogue.)

62 As it happened, twenty years after Snorri's death, Norway took over sovereignty of Iceland until 1814.

63 *The Prose Edda,* Arthur Gilchrist Brodeur's (trans.) (Dover Publications, 2006) originally published 1916.

64 *The Arabian Nights' Entertainments*, translated from the Arabic (James Blackwood, undated c.1900).

65 Ibid. (Summary drawn from pages 1-12.)

66 A *jinni* (plural *'jinn'*) is a spirit being, the sort that pops out of a magic lamp and can do both good and bad deeds.

67 A story quoted by Joshua J. Mark in *Silk Road*, posted online 28 March 2014 at www.ancient.eu/Silk_Road/

68 An alternative explanation frequently quoted is that these poems were 'hung' on the walls of the Ka'abah and later incorporated in the Great Mosque complex in Mecca, but there is no evidence of poems being found or preserved when the Ka'abah was later stripped of its pre-Islamic pagan statues and artefacts.

69 Summarised from the 1820 English translation of *Antar of Antarah* by Terrick Hamilton, available online at http://elfinspell.com/Masterpieces1Antar.html

70 Summarised, with some original dialogue, from Terrick Hamilton's translation in *A Bedouin Romance,* (London 1820), quoted in *Great*

Short Stories of the World, Barrett H. Clark, Maxim Lieber (eds.) (Spring Books, 1925).

71 The full story of Miqdad and Mayasa is in *Tales of the Marvellous and News of the Strange*, Malcolm c. Lyons (trans.) (Penguin Classics, 2014).

72 For this and further detailed information on the history of *The Arabian Nights* see online source: www.iranicaonline.org/articles/alf-layla-wa-layla

73 For further details on Al Nadim and especially the *Fihrist al-'Ulum*, see *The First Arab Bibliography: Fihrist al-'Ulum,* Hans H. Wellisch (University of Illinois Occasional Papers Number 175, December 1986) accessible online at: http://www.ideals.illinois.edu

74 *Rubâiyât of Omar Khayyâm*, Edward Fitzgerald (trans.), Reynold Alleyne Nicholson (ed.) (Adam and Charles Black, 1909).

75 For more, refer to *The Arabian Nights: A Companion*, Robert Irwin (Penguin, 1995).

76 Quoted in the Glossary of *More Stories from the Arabian Nights, An unexpurgated selection*, Sir Richard Burton,. Julian Franklyn (ed.) (Panther, 1961).

77 For detailed literary analysis of *maqama* and *risala* refer to: 'Prosimetrical Genre in Classical Arabic Literature', Wolfhart Heinrichs, in *Prosimetrum: Crosscultural Perspectives on Narrative and Verse*, Joseph Harris and Karl Reichl (eds.) (D. S. Brewer, 1997). Also, *Maqama: A History of a Genre*, Jaakko Hameen-Antilla (Otto Harrassovitz, Wiesbadan, 2002).

78 Quoted in Gene Z. Hanrahan's introduction to *50 Great Oriental Stories* (Bantam, 1965).

79 For a discussion on whether *hua-pen* originated primarily from oral or from written texts, see *Chinese Vernacular Fiction: the Formative Period*, W. L. Idema (Brill Academic Publishers, 1997).

80 A scholarly analysis and assessment of the literature is given by Peter Raedts in 'The Children's Crusade of 1212', *Journal of Medieval History* 3, 1977, and an irreverent account of why it probably never happened may be found in the *History House Magazine* online at www.historyhouse.com/in_history/childrens_crusade/

81 Quoted in *Godefroi de Buillon, Volume X of the Old French Crusade Cycle*, Jan Boyd Roberts (ed.) (University of Alabama Press, 1996). See also *An Introduction to the Chanson de Geste*, Catherine M. Jones, (University Press of Florida, 1914).

82 'Horses, no matter how well-trained, will not charge head-long into an unmoving wall of men, especially when this monolith is bristling with sharpened steel.' Quoted from *The Myth of the Mounted Knight*, James G. Patterson, in *The ORB* (On-line Reference Book for Medieval Studies) at www.the-orb-net

83 Since 2011, the wreckage of three Mongolian warships has been discovered around the coast of Japan by archaeologists from the University of Ryukyus. The latest was discovered in July 2015.

84 This is not to suggest a simple environmental determinism: it reflects my own experience of the Mongolian plains and, to a lesser extent, in the Himalaya. John Man alludes to this effect in his comprehensive study *Genghis Khan: Life, Death and Resurrection* (Bantam, 2004).

85 The first English translation of *The Secret History of Mongols* by Francis Woodman Cleaves (Harvard University, 1982) can be read online at http://altaica.ru/shengl.html Seven other language translations are also available on the site.

86 From Chaucer's poem 'Truth' lines 5-7, in *The Riverside Chaucer*, Larry D. Benson and F. N. Robinson (eds.) (Oxford University Press, third edition 2008).

87 John Larner suggests that part of Boccaccio's description of the plague was based on Paul the Deacon's account in *Historia Romana*. See page 260 in Larner's *Italy in the Age of Dante and Petrarch* (Longman, 1983).

88 Stories from *The Decameron of Boccaccio*, Colin Bennett (ed.) (Methuen Australia, 1981).

89 Ibid.

90 Ibid.

91 Summarised from *Decameron of Boccaccio (unexpurgated)*, J. M. Rigg (trans.) Volume 2 (Privately Printed for the Navarre Society, undated c. 1921). You can also read the stories online in Italian and with the English translation at : http://digilander.libero.it/il_boccaccio/translate_english/index.html

92 A version of 'Novelle Antiche' from *The Italian Novelists*, Thomas Roscoe (trans.) (undated c. 1900) can be read online at: http://elfinspell.com/RoscoeNovelle.html

93 Ibid. Novella No: 72, re-written by Boccaccio as the Third Story on the First day: *Decameron of Boccaccio (unexpurgated)*, J. M. Rigg (trans.) Volume 1 (Navarre Society, undated c.1921).

94 Ibid. Volume 2.

95 *Geoffrey Chaucer: The Canterbury Tales – a prose version in modern English*, David Wright (Vintage, 1964).

96 'General Prologue' from *The Canterbury Tales*, original Middle English text on line, http://www.librarius.com/cantales/genpro.htm lines 209-214

97 *Geoffrey Chaucer: The Canterbury Tales – a prose version in modern English*, David Wright, (Vintage, 1964).

98 Ibid.

99 Ibid.

100 'Caxton's Prologues and Epilogues', in *Prefaces and Prologues to Famous Books*, Charles W. Eliot (Harvard Classics, Little Brown & Company, 1909) online at Project Gutenberg

101 Much has been published about the Phaistos Disk, and a few scholars even doubt it is genuine. A list of sources to competing interpretations can be found online http://en.wikipedia.org/wiki/Phaistos_Disc_decipherment_claims

102 Pu Songling, *Strange Tales from a Chinese Studio*, John Minford (trans. & ed.) (Penguin, 2006).

103 Details in this section are drawn principally from the full biography and sources in Diana Childress, *Johannes Gutenberg and the Printing Press* (Twenty-first Century Books, 2008) and from the Gutenberg Homepage online http://www.mainz.de/Gutenberg/English/index.htm

104 Diana Childress, *Johannes Gutenberg and the Printing Press.*

105 Ibid.

106 'Caxton's Prologues and Epilogues', in *Prefaces and Prologues to Famous Books*, Charles W. Eliot (trans. & ed.) (Harvard Classics, Little Brown & Company, 1909). Online at Project Gutenberg.

107 Ibid.

108 Sotheby's catalogue entry for *The Recuyell of the Historyes of Troye* is available online: http://www.sothebys.com/en/auctions/ ecatalogue/2014/english-literature-history-childrens-books-illustrations-l14404/lot.502.html

109 *The Life and Typography of William Caxton, England's First Printer*, William Blade (himself a printer) Vol. 2 (Cambridge Library Collection, 1861-3).

110 A full annotated list is given by Sidney Lee in, *Dictionary of National Biography* 1885-1900 Vol. 9.

111 From the Prologue to *The Recuyell of the Historyes of Troye*

112 Summarised from Jacobus de Voragine, *The Golden Legend (Legenda Aurea)* translated by William Caxton, Volume 3, Fordham University's Medieval Sourcebook site: http://www.legacy.fordham.edu/halsall/ basis/goldenlegend/

113 *The Riverside Chaucer,* Larry D. Benson (ed.) (Oxford University Press, 2008).

114 Summarised from *Decameron of Boccaccio (unexpurgated),* J. M. Rigg (trans.) Volume 1, Novel II (Navarre Society, undated c.1921)..

115 Ibid.

116 Quoted in Marianne E. Kalinke, *The Book of Reykjahólar, The Last of the Great Medieval Legendaries* (University of Toronto Press, 1996). Kalinke's book gives a detailed analysis of legendaries in the Germanic and Norse language groups.

117 'Caxton's Prologues and Epilogues', in *Prefaces and Prologues to Famous Books*, Charles W. Eliot (Harvard Classics, Little Brown & Company, 1909) online at Project Gutenberg

118 Ibid.

119 Ibid.

120 Sources and references discussing the development of the King Author legend are too numerous to list, but a good start is provided by the dedicated website, *Caerleon Net* which cites many useful references.

121 *Early Prose Romances*, The Carisbrooke Library, volume IV, Henry Morley (ed.) (George Routledge and Sons, 1889).

122 Summary and quote from 'Rukenaw's counsel to Reynard', in *The History of Reynard the Fox*, translated and printed by William Caxton 1481, Edward Arber (ed.) (Archibald Constable and Co, 1899). Online at Internet Archive, openlibrary.org. This edition is a faithful rendering of Caxton's original publication.

123 Ibid.

124 Ibid.

125 Diana Childress, *Johannes Gutenberg and the Printing Press* (Twenty-first Century Books, 2008).

126 Letter to Wolfgang Capito, 26 February 1517, quoted by Myron Gilmore in *The World of Humanism* (Harper & Brothers, 1952), p.261.

127 Quoted in George Saintsbury's introduction to *Tales of the Heptameron, Vol.1*, Margaret, Queen of Navarre (Printed for the Society of English Bibliophilists, 1894). (Translated by George Saintsbury 'from the true text of M. Le Roux de Lincy') online at Project Gutenberg.

128 Ibid. Summarised from the prologue.

129 Ibid. Tale V.

130 Ibid. Pierre Brantôme is quoted by Saintsbury in his Note 3 to Tale IV.

131 Ibid. Note 7.

132 Quoted from 'Author's Advice to Readers', in François Rebelais, *The Histories of Gargantua and Pantagruel*, J. M. Cohen (trans.) (Penguin Books, 1955).

133 Ibid. Note that *Pantagruel* was Rabelais' 'first book', *Gargantua* was his second, but modern versions, including the one referred to above, generally reverse this order to provide a better chronology to the story. In my main text, when referring to each of Rabelais' books, I refer to the order in which he originally wrote them.

134 Jean Markale's *King of the Celts: Arthurian Legends and Celtic Tradition* (Bear and Co., 1993). Markale mentions that some commentators attribute the *Chronicles* to Rabelais, but it is contentious and she considers his authorship unlikely.

135 These and other fascinating details about mythological and real giants are given in J. C. Cooper (ed.) *Brewer's Book of Myth and Legend* (Helicon, 1993).

136 *The Histories of Gargantua and Pantagruel* (Penguin Books, 1955).

137 Ibid.

138 Ibid. Mentioned by the translator J. M. Cohen.

139 Ibid.

140 Ibid.

141 The child in Montpellier died, but Pope Julius III legitimated the two surviving children in 1553, probably at Rabelais' request.

142 Quote of Pantagruel and summary of the story from, *The Histories of Gargantua and Pantagruel.* (Penguin Books, 1955).

143 This little book, which Elizabeth made in 1544, is preserved in the Bodleian Library in Oxford.

144 *Midsummer-Night's Dream*, Act II, Scene I, lines 166-167.

145 This is probably where they performed as it is doubtful if the Theatre of Dionysus had yet been built on the south side of the Acropolis only eight years after the Persians destroyed several buildings.

146 In later Roman mythology, Dionysus was identified as Bacchus; we use 'Bacchanalian' to describe intoxicated pleasures having lost the deeper meanings attached to Dionysus.

147 John Gassner (ed.), *Medieval and Tudor Drama* (Bantam Books, 1971).

148 Ibid.

149 By the Act of Supremacy, 1534.

150 Tacitus: Annals, Book 15, Alfred John Church and William Jackson Brodribb (trans.). Full text online at http://classics.mit.edu/Tacitus/annals.html

151 Details for this section are drawn from John Gassner (ed.) *Medieval and Tudor Drama* (Bantam, 1971) which contains the play's full script.

152 Ibid. The play was written by Thomas Hughes and fellow law students at Gray's Inn, and was performed before Queen Elizabeth.

153 Shakespeare, *Winter's Tale*, Act IV, Scene III.

154 *Old London Cries, with Heaps of Quaint Cuts* (Leadenhall Press, 1885). The little hard-bound book with ribbon ties sold for a shilling.

155 Robert Greene, *Greene's Groats-worth of witte, bought with a million of repentance,* autobiographical pamphlet printed in 1592.

156 Ben Jonson, 'Eulogy to Shakespeare' printed in the First Folio, accessed online at www.shakespeare-online.com

157 Spoken by Oberon, Act II, Scene 1.

158 James Shapiro, *Shakespeare: the Year of King Lear* (Simon and Schuster, 2015).

159 For those who like to follow fine detail: Elizabeth was succeeded by James I (King James VI in Scotland for the previous 29 years); he was succeeded by his son Charles 1, who was executed in 1649 in the run-up to the Civil War which resulted in Oliver Cromwell's Republic. The monarchy was restored with Charles II in 1660. Charles II was followed in 1685 by his younger brother, James II, who was forced into exile in the Bloodless Revolution of 1688. James II was the grandfather of Prince Charles Edward Stuart, The Young Pretender, aka Bonnie Prince Charlie.

160 Scott's own description quoted by Washington Irving in 'Abbotsford and Newstead Abbey', *Tales of a Traveller* (Project Gutenberg). Irving spent several days with Scott at Abbottsford in 1817.

161 By Act of the Scottish Parliament (reinforced in 1696 when every parish was required to provide an elementary school), see Arthur Herman, *How the Scots Invented the Modern World* (Crown Publishers, NY, 2001).

162 John Buchan, *Sir Walter Scott* (Cassell and Company, 1931).

163 Thomas R. Lounsbury, *James Fenimore Cooper* (Kegan Paul, Trench & Co., London, 1884).

164 Fenimore Cooper had left instructions that there should be no official biography, so his personal papers were not available to early biographers.

165 'Fenimore' (his mother's family name) was officially added to his name in adult life at the behest of his maternal grandmother when there were no male heirs to continue the name.

166 A quip attributed to Sir Walter Scott. In his Journal, Scott recognises Byron's genius, but describes him as unreliable and a mischief-maker among his contemporaries.

167 Thomas R. Lounsbury, *James Fenimore Cooper* (Kegan Paul, Trench & Co., London, 1884).

168 For the full story, see Italo Calvino, 'Animal Speech' in *Italian Folktales*, George Martin (trans.) (Penguin Classics, 2000).

169 Comparative phylogenetic analysis by Dr Jamie Tehrani (Durham University) and Sara Graça da Silva (New University of Lisbon) published in the *Royal Society Open Science* journal: 3(1) January 2016.

170 Charles Perrault, *The Complete Fairy Tales*, Christopher Betts (trans.) (Oxford University Press, 2009), p. 52.

171 Ibid. p.53.

172 Another example of Perrault's inventiveness: although Cinderella was already a well known story, when he rewrote it for his collection, he created the glass slipper which has since become the definitive version of the tale.

173 Footnote on page 401 of *Ossian* (Patrick Geddes & Colleagues, Edinburgh, 1896).

174 Scott praises Maria Edgeworth's Irish novels in the postscript to an early edition of *Waverley* (Thomas Nelson & Sons, 1905) and mentions two other female authors writing non-fiction accounts of Scottish culture: Mrs Hamilton, and Mrs Grant of Laggan.

175 Such 'anonymity' was a common practice. It was soon widely known who the author of *Waverley* was, but it became official when a second edition was brought out in 1820 under Scott's name.

176 John Buchan, *Sir Walter Scott* (Cassell and Company, 1931).

177 James Fenimore Cooper, *The Pioneers*, chapter 1.

178 Washington Irving, 'Abbotsford and Newstead Abbey', in *Tales of a Traveller* (Project Gutenberg).

179 Suggesting a modern figure for comparison is fraught with difficulties, but it was equivalent to the entire profit on a new edition of Scott's Waverley novels – Constable had earlier estimated this to be £10-15,000.

180 For an excellent summary of this crisis and its effects on literature, see: Alexander J. Dick, 'On the Financial Crisis, 1825-26', in *Britain, Representation and Nineteenth Century History,* Dino Franco Felluga (ed.) on the website of BRANCH: www.branchcollective_org

181 *The Journal of Sir Walter Scott*, entry on 24 April 1826.

182 Ibid. 22 January 1826.

183 Ibid. 24 August 1826.

184 Ibid. 30 April 1826.

185 The remaining debt was cleared after Scott's death by the sale of his copyrights. His beloved Abbotsford remained intact.

186 John Buchan, *Sir Walter Scott* (Cassell and Company, 1931).

187 Lockhart, though trained as an advocate, was a writer and editor of the *Quarterly Review*. He became also Scott's son-in-law, having married Scott's eldest daughter, Sophia.

188 Some literary critics give this accolade to Scott's story from *Chronicles of Canongate*, 'The Two Drovers' – a tale of a fatally failed friendship between an English drover and a Highland drover.

189 Leo Tolstoy, *What Then Must We Do?* Ch.16. Maude (trans.) *Chamber's Dictionary of Quotations*.

190 Extract from Ivan Krylov, *Russian Fables of Ivan Krylov*, Bernard Pares (trans.) (Penguin Books, 1942).

191 Ibid. Introductory comments by Bernard Pares.

192 Modern visitors following this route should be careful not to be diverted by the Chocolate Museum (Muze Shokolada) shortly before the library on the right-hand side of Nevsky Prospekt.

193 Extract from a letter quoted by Richard Pevear in the preface to *The Collected Tales of Nikolai Gogol*, Richard Pevear and Larissa Volokhinsky (trans.) (Granta, 2003).

194 *The Government Inspector*, Act 5 Scene viii, Arthur A. Sykes (trans.) 1892. Project Gutenberg.

195 John Cournos in the Introduction to Gogol's *Dead Souls*, D. J. Hogarth (trans.) (1916). Project Gutenberg.

196 Leonard Shapiro, *Turgenev, His Life and Times* (Harvard University Press, 1982).

197 John Cournos, in the Introduction to Gogol's *Dead Souls*. D. J. Hogarth (trans.) (1916).

198 Extract from obituary quoted by Leonard Shapiro, *Turgenev, His Life and Times*.

199 It is worth noting that it was another four years before the Thirteenth Amendment was passed in the USA to abolish slavery.

200 *Chekhov's Diary 1897*, online at Project Gutenberg.

201 Chekhov's letter to Grigorovich, 28 March 1886, in *Anton Chekhov – A Life in Letters*, Rosamund Bartlett and Anthony Phillips (trans.) (Penguin, 2004).

202 Chekhov's letter to a friend in *Letters of Anton Chekhov*, M. H. Heim and Simon Karlinsky (trans.) (Bodley Head, London 1973).

203 Anton Chekhov, *The Island: a Journey to Sakhalin*, Luba and Michael Terpak (trans.) (Century, 1987).

204 In Chekhov's letter to Anatoly Koni, 26 January 1891 in *Anton Chekhov – A Life in Letters.*

205 Anton Chekhov, *The Island.*

206 Maupassant was diagnosed with syphilis in his early twenties (as was his younger brother) contracted either congenitally or through his life style. He refused treatment and his symptoms accumulated during his life, ending with a brief period of insanity before his death a few days before his forty-third birthday.

207 Philip Callow, *Lost Earth: A Life of Cezanne* (Ivan R. Dee, 2003).

208 In the preface to Maupassant's 1877 novel, *Pierre et Jean.*

209 Joseph Conrad, *Notes on Life and Letters*, 1904. Online at Project Gutenberg.

210 For an insightful and compassionate account of Poe's life read Peter Ackroyd, *Poe: a life cut short* (Vintage, 2009).

211 However, Peter Ackroyd states that 'Poe always defended the institution of slavery.' Ibid.

212 Charles Dickens, *American Notes* (Chapman and Hall, undated c. 1920), chapter XVIII.

213 Dr Claire Parfait, *The Publishing History of Uncle Tom's Cabin 1852-2002* (Ashgate, 2007).

214 Charlotte Hodgman, 'The abolition of the British slave trade', in *Historyextra*, BBC History online magazine, posted 23 August (Slavery Remembrance Day) 2012, www.historyextra.com/slavery. Further information on slavery can be found in James Walvin, *The Slave Trade* (Thames and Hudson, 2011).

215 Lines 5-8 of 'The Negro's Complaint', in *The Works of William Cowper. His life, letters and poems*, T.S. Grimshawe (ed.) (William Tigg & Co. 1849). Online at Project Gutenberg.

216 Charlotte Hodgman, 'The abolition of the British slave trade', in *Historyextra* online. Figures for this illegal trading can be only estimates because of the nature of the trade and the secrecy involved. And it is worth noting that other forms of slavery continue.

217 *More O. Henry: one hundred more of the master's stories* (Hodder and Stoughton, 1933). Most of O. Henry's stories are also available online at Project Gutenberg.

218 Ibid.

219 Ibid.

220 Further information on O. Henry's life may be found in the seventy-two page collection: *O. Henry Papers: Some Sketches of His Life Together with an Alphabetical Index of His Complete Works* (University Press of the Pacific, 2003).

221 Quoted from one of Poe's letters in Peter Ackroyd, *Poe: a life cut short* (Vintage, 2009).

222 Based on Charles Dicken's visit to Field Lane School in Saffron Hill, described by Peter Ackroyd in *Dickens* (Vintage, 2002).

223 For more on this event see Mark Parker, *Literary Magazines and British Romanticism* (Cambridge University Press, 2000).

224 Carol Polsgrove, 'They Made it Pay: British Short-Fiction Writers, 1820-1840', *Studies in Short Fiction*, 11:4 p.420 (1974: Fall).

225 Ibid.

226 The murder of Francis Kent in 1860, see Judith Flanders, *The Invention of Murder* (Harper Press, 2011).

227 Darwin's reminiscences in *The Life and Letters of Charles Darwin*, Project Gutenberg.

228 Charles Dickens, *American Notes* (Chapman and Hall, undated c. 1920), chapter II, p.27.

229 DNA tests carried out in 2007 now suggest that Dr Crippen was innocent, as he claimed.

230 The last two lines of the poem 'The Deep Sea Cables', Rudyard Kipling, in *The Works of Rudyard Kipling* (Wordsworth Poetry Library, 1994).

231 Useful modern sources on the East India Company, the Bengal Famine, and British rule in India: Kumkum Chatterjee, *Merchants, Politics and Society in Early Modern India* (Brill Academic Publishers, 1996); Sushil Chaudhury, *From Prosperity to Decline: Eighteenth Century Bengal* (Manohar Publishers, 1999); William Dalrymple, 'The East India Company: The original corporate raiders' (*The Guardian* 4

March 2015) an article foreshadowing his upcoming book in 2016 published by Bloomsbury. See also the website: www.britishempire. co.uk/india.

232 George Orwell, in an essay originally published in February 1942 in the journal *Horizon* as a review of T. S. Eliot's, *A choice of Kipling's Verse*, and reprinted as the Introduction to *The Works of Rudyard Kipling* (Wordsworth Poetry Library, 1994).

233 An English edition of *Rajmohan's Wife* was published by Penguin Books India in 2009, and a collection of three of Chatterji's novellas, *The poison Tree*, is available in English translation online at Project Gutenberg.

234 Rudyard Kipling, 'The Record of Badalia Herodsfoot', first published in *Harper's Weekly* (November 1890), and later in the collection *Many Inventions* (1893), Project Gutenberg.

235 Henry Rider Haggard, 'The Transvaal,' *Macmillans Magazine* (May 1877).

236 'The Man Who Was Caged in a Zoo', (*The Guardian*, 3 June 2015) an article based on the book *Spectacle: The Astonishing Life of Ota Benga*, Pamela Newkirk (Harper Collins, 2015).

237 Hilaire Belloc had little time for contemporary socialists either. He outlined his own ideas of 'Distributionism' (based on small land-holdings) in his article 'The Servile State' in *Everyman: his life, work and books*, No.1, Vol.1, pp. 203-4 (J. M. Dent, 1912). *Everyman* is a compendium of periodical articles, stories and letters concerning topics of the time, including a story by Chekhov, amounting to over 800 pages – a fascinating read, including the advertisements. It can be downloaded from Internet Archive: https://archive.org/stream/ everymanhislifew01sarouoft#page/326/mode/2up

238 Joseph Conrad, 'Author's Note' in *Tales of Unrest* (Penguin, 1977).

239 Conrad's enquiries to a shipping company about employment had been passed on; a ship-broker in Ghent, de Baerdemaecker, wrote this recommendation to Albert Thys, Deputy Director of the association. Quoted in *Joseph Conrad: A Life*, Zdzislaw Najder, Halina Carroll-Najder (trans.) (Camden House, revised 2007 edition).

240 Ibid.

241 Ibid.

242 The statement appeared in the London *Morning Post* in 1903, sourced from the website of the Joseph Conrad Society, www.josepgconradsociety.org

243 From Conrad's, *Last Essays*, quoted by Zdzislaw Najder, *Joseph Conrad: A Life*.

244 By one of the strange coincidences of history, King Leopold II of Belgium had owned most of Cap Ferrat since the beginning of the century and built himself a palace there. Maugham's house had originally been built by Leopold for the retirement of his elderly confessor, Monseigneur Charmeton, mentioned in, Selina Hastings, *The Secret Lives of Somerset Maugham* (John Murray, 2009).

245 Zdzislaw Najder, *Joseph Conrad: A Life*, Halina Carroll-Najder (trans.) (Camden House, revised 2007 edition).

246 Born in 1874 (only four years after Dicken's death), Maugham was three weeks from his ninety-second birthday when he died in 1965. For full details of Maugham's life see, Selina Hastings, *The Secret Lives of Somerset Maugham* (John Murray, 2009).

247 J. A. Hammerton, 'Editorial Note' to *Masterpiece Library of Short Stories* (The Educational Book Company, undated c.1925).

248 'High Yaller', in *The City of Refuge: The Collected Stories of Rudolph Fisher* (University of Missouri Press, 2008).

249 'Miss Cynthie', ibid.

250 Albert Camus, 'The Almond Tree', in *Lyrical and Critical Essays*, 1940.

251 Keri Hulme, *The Bone People* (SPIRAL in association with Hodder and Stoughton, 1985).

252 Ellen Draper, introduction to 'Old Cobraboor', in *Paperbark,* Jack Davis, Stephen Mueke, Mudrooroo Narogin, Adam Shoemaker (eds.) (University of Queensland Press, 1990).

253 Ibid. 'Introduction'.

254 Alexander Kanengoni, *Echoing Silences* (Baobab Books, 2002).

255 Both quotations from Helen Habila, 'Obituary: Yvonne Vera', (*The Guardian* 27 April 2005).

256 From the website of Nigerian literary magazine *Brittle Paper*, posted 3 February 2016 on brittlepaper.com

257 *Pasquil's Jests: mixed with Mother Bunches Merriments* (1604) editcd and reprinted by W. Carew Hazlitt, 1866 (available through Nabu Public Domain Reprints). The escapades of an earlier famous ale-wife, *The Life of Long Meg of Westminster*, can be found online at http://internetarchive.com

258 Saloni Narang, 'Close to the Earth', in *Global Cultures: A Transnational Short Fiction Reader*, Elisabeth Young-Bruehl (ed.) (Wesleyan University Press, 1994). See also Saloni Narang's collection of short stories, *The Colored Bangles* (Three Continents Press, 1983).

259 *Global Cultures: A Transnational Short Fiction Reader*, Elisabeth Young-Bruehl (ed.) (Wesleyan University Press, 1994).

260 LeAnne Howe, 'An American in New York', in the anthology *Spider Woman's Granddaughters: Traditional Tales and Contemporary Writing by Native American Women*, Paula Gunn Allen (ed.) (Fawcett Columbine, 1989).

261 Chimamanda Ngozi Adichie, 'The Danger of a Single Story', a TED talk delivered in October 2009, available as a video and transcript from the TED website.

262 Leonard Kibera, 'The Spider's Web', in *Looking for a Rain God: An Anthology of African Short Stories*, Nadezda Obradovic (ed.) (Fireside/Simon and Schuster, 1990).

263 Ibid.

264 Much of this section on South and Central American writers owes a debt to the work of Roberto González Echevarría, particularly *The Cambridge History of Latin American Literature* (1996) which he co-edited.

265 An outline of the story given in full in *Global Cultures: A Transnational Short Fiction Reader*, Elisabeth Young-Bruehl (ed.) (Wesleyan University Press, 1994).

266 Ibid.

267 Chinua Achebe, *Anthills of the Savannah*.

268 An outline of Clarice Lispector's 'The Smallest Woman in the World' given in full in *Global Cultures: A Transnational Short Fiction Reader* Elisabeth Young-Bruehl (ed.) (Wesleyan University Press, 1994).

269 Raymond Sigmit, 'Sir Iambakey Okuk lives in Rome, or so the legend says', on the blog *PNG Attitude* run by Keith Jackson. The website contains much Papua New Guinean literature worth reading

270 Neil Gaiman, 'The Man Who Forgot Ray Bradbury', in the short-story collection *Trigger Warning* (William Morrow/Harper Collins, 2015).

Acknowledgements

What better way to thank all the people who have led me to Story over and over again than by writing this book? It may have taken six years to put on to paper, but it took a lifetime to write. A lifetime of listening, reading, travelling and watching; of reaping the seeds planted in childhood by those who encouraged me to seek out the wisdom and delights of stories. I acknowledge my debt to them and to all the story-makers who have made me who I am. Many of these storytellers, though by no means all, join us in these pages. Special thanks are due to Graeme Neil Reid for his inspired artwork; to Lorraine Mace for her usual insight and sound advice; to my careful editor, Christine O'Reilly; to Kenneth Glazier who read the entire manuscript with an eagle's eye and an owl's wisdom, and to Adam Green for his kind help in sourcing some of the illustrations. I am grateful also to those who read parts of early drafts and were generous with their encouragement, corrections or suggestions: Sue and Tim Uden, Joe Stein, Earnest Swain, Anne Coates, Mary Pery, Bonita Cron, Karen Phillips, Christine Cotman, Leena Taylor, and Stephen Yuretich, and I thank my support team at Troubador for their expertise and professionalism. All errors are entirely my own – in a work of this scope no doubt some fleas will have escaped the curry-comb – I hope not too many. After careful research, all extracts of original material quoted in this book are understood to be in the public domain or to come within the definition of 'fair use' for educational purposes. If any copyright has been inadvertently overlooked, the author and publisher will be happy to make necessary arrangements at the earliest opportunity.

Index